LEGAL AID HANDBOOK
1990

AUSTRALIA AND NEW ZEALAND
The Law Book Company Ltd.
Sydney : Melbourne : Perth

CANADA AND U.S.A.
The Carswell Company Ltd.
Agincourt, Ontario

INDIA
N. M. Tripathi Private Ltd.
Bombay
and
Eastern Law House Private Ltd.
Calcutta and Delhi
M.P.P. House
Bangalore

ISRAEL
Steimatzky's Agency Ltd.
Jerusalem : Tel Aviv : Haifa

PAKISTAN
Pakistan Law House
Karachi

LEGAL AID HANDBOOK 1990

Prepared by

The Legal Aid Board

LONDON   SWEET & MAXWELL   1990

Published in 1990 by
Sweet & Maxwell Limited of
South Quay Plaza, 183 Marsh Wall,
London E14 9FT.
Computerset by MFK Typesetting Ltd., Hitchin, Herts.
Printed in Great Britain by
Butler and Tanner Limited, Frome, Somerset.

British Library Cataloguing in Publication Data.
Legal aid handbook.
1990 —
1. England. Legal aid. Law
I. Legal Aid Board
344. 20717

ISBN 0-421-42250-7

Preface

Legal aid is a system of Government funding for those who cannot afford to pay for legal advice, assistance and representation. It is a statutory system administered by the Legal Aid Board on behalf of the Lord Chancellor. One of the aims of the Legal Aid Board is to produce a consistent quality of decision-making throughout the legal aid offices. The Act and Regulations contain many cases where the decision of the Area Director or the area committee is discretionary. It is in these areas particularly that variations creep in. While the exercise of discretion is always a judgmental matter for the person concerned, so that there is always likely to be a variation between individuals, the Board takes the view that guidance on the factors to be taken into account when exercising a discretion may help to minimise variations.

It is particularly important in legal aid that discretionary decisions are justifiable. Legal aid serves a number of stakeholders who may have conflicting interests, but each one has to be borne in mind when a decision is made. The stakeholders are the applicant (or assisted person), the legal adviser, the court and the Government (the taxpayer). What is the right decision for the applicant may not be right for the court or the taxpayer if legal aid is granted when it is unreasonable; what may be the right decision for the taxpayer may not be right for the applicant if legal aid is refused when it should be granted. The decision must be capable of being justified to the unsuccessful stakeholder in any particular case.

The Legal Aid Board is convinced that the more is known about the grounds on which a decision is reached, the greater the chance that the decision will be justifiable to, and understood by, the various stakeholders. In addition, there will be greater understanding of the information required by area offices in order to reach correct decisions.

The general principles are set out in the Legal Aid Act 1988. Detailed procedures are contained in various sets of regulations made by the Lord Chancellor. Each type of legal aid has different sets of regulations: advice and assistance, assistance by way of representation (ABWOR), civil legal aid and criminal legal aid. There are also different regulations governing financial eligibility for each type of legal aid.

The aim of the Notes for Guidance is to highlight the most common points of decision-making as they affect the profession and the public and to indicate what matters are taken into account when decisions are made. Notes for Guidance 1 to 6 have been redrafted and the remaining Notes for Guidance, which were prepared by the Council of the Law Society, have been updated.

JOHN PITTS
CHAIRMAN
LEGAL AID BOARD

Contents

NOTE.

All financial limits are those in force on April 1, 1990.

The law is stated as at July 1, 1990.

Introductory Guide to Legal Aid

1.1 The different kinds of Legal Aid

(a) Legal Advice and Assistance (also known as the green form scheme). This covers advice and help with any legal problems (see section 2); and in some cases, under Assistance by Way of Representation (ABWOR), it also covers going to court (see section 3).

(b) Civil Legal Aid. This covers representation in court proceedings including assistance in the steps preliminary or incidental to proceedings (see section 4).

(c) Criminal Legal Aid for criminal offences (see section 5).

1.2 Duty solicitor schemes

Duty solicitors are available at most magistrates' courts and police stations and offer free legal advice (see 5.2).

1.3 How Legal Aid is administered

The Legal Aid Board administers legal advice and assistance (including ABWOR) and legal aid for civil proceedings under the general guidance of the Lord Chancellor. The Board is based in London and a list of Board members appears on page 357. The Legal Aid Head Office, which is also based in London, consists of the Chief Executive's Section, the Secretariat which services the Board and the Legal Department. The Accounts and Computer Departments are also based in London. For administrative purposes, England and Wales are divided into a number of areas. Each area has a legal aid area office, run by a Group or Area Manager, and an area committee made up of practising solicitors and barristers.

The area office decides whether an application for civil legal aid is reasonable (see 4.4). The area office can either grant or refuse legal aid. The area committee deals with appeals against refusals of legal aid by the area office.

Area offices are also responsible for legal advice and assistance (see section 2, below).

The administration of criminal legal aid is the responsibility of the Lord Chancellor (see section 5, below).

1.4 Legal Aid in Scotland and Northern Ireland

There are similar legal aid schemes in Scotland and Northern Ireland. For information about Legal Aid in Scotland, write to The Scottish Legal Aid Board, 44 Drumsheugh Gardens, Edinburgh EH3 7SW. Tel: 031–226–7061.

For Northern Ireland, write to the Incorporated Law Society of Northern Ireland, Legal Aid Board, Bedford House, 16–22 Bedford Street, Belfast BT2 7FL. Tel: 0232–246441.

1.5 Legal Aid abroad

Many foreign countries have legal aid schemes but some are not as comprehensive as the system in England and Wales. For information about legal aid abroad write to the Legal Aid Board, Newspaper House, 8–16 Great New Street, London EC4A 3BN. Tel: 071–353–7411. (See also p. 81).

1.6 Statutory provisions

The provisions relating to legal advice and assistance (including ABWOR) and civil legal aid are set out mainly in Parts III and IV of the Legal Aid Act 1988 and in regulations made by the Lord Chancellor.

The provisions relating to Criminal Legal Aid are set out mainly in Part V of the Legal Aid Act 1988, Legal Aid Act 1982, and in regulations.

1.7 Other information about Legal Aid

A series of leaflets is produced about legal aid. *Getting Legal Help* gives very general information about legal aid including financial eligibility. The *Legal Aid Guide* contains a fairly comprehensive explanation of legal aid in similar terms to this introduction. There is also *Legal Aid—Getting Legal Help* which should be handed to all clients who complete an application for civil legal aid, a leaflet on criminal legal aid called *Legal Aid for Criminal Offences* and *Your Right to Free Legal Advice* which is available at police stations.

The Legal Aid Board also publishes each year an Annual Report which contains statistical information about legal aid for the previous year.

1.8 The Law Society's "Solicitors' Regional Directory"

This lists most local solicitors' firms and gives details of the categories of work they do. It also lists solicitors who are prepared to give a Fixed Fee Interview (up to half an hour's legal advice for £5 or less, payable by the client). Copies of the Directory, which is published each Spring, are available in libraries, town halls and most advice centres.

LEGAL ADVICE AND ASSISTANCE

2.1 What does Legal Advice and Assistance cover?

Giving general advice, writing letters, negotiating, getting counsel's opinion and preparing a written case to go before a tribunal. This can cover most legal problems such as divorce or maintenance, and in certain circumstances, the making of a will.

It enables people of small or moderate means to get help from a solicitor free, or for a contribution, until the solicitor's charges reach a total of two hours' worth of work, or three hours' worth of work in matrimonial cases involving the preparation of a petition. Solicitors cannot claim more without the authority of the legal aid area office.

If a client needs to go to court in civil proceedings it may be necessary to apply for civil legal aid (see section 4, below); or, if the civil proceedings are in a magistrates' court, ABWOR (see section 3, below). If the client has to go to court in a criminal case, it may be necessary to apply for criminal legal aid (see section 5, below).

Legal advice and assistance is available in England and Wales and applies only to questions of English law. It does not cover the law of Scotland or Northern Ireland, nor that of any other country.

2.2 How to apply for Legal Advice and Assistance

Generally clients should call at a solicitor's office. If they are ill or live too far away or cannot travel, they should ask a friend to call at the solicitor's office for them—or the solicitor may be able to visit them. The solicitor should ask about their savings and income. He/she should then fill in an application form (the green form). Using the green form key card (which is issued in April of each year) the solicitor will be able to tell clients whether they qualify on financial grounds and whether they will have to pay any contribution. If the client wants the solicitor to advise and is content to pay the contribution (if any) the client should sign the application form. A solicitor can refuse to give legal advice and assistance. He/she need not give the client a reason but may be asked to explain the reasons for refusal by the area office.

2.3 Children

Children are eligible for legal advice and assistance. In most cases where a child under school-leaving age (at present 16) requires the help of a solicitor, a parent or guardian should apply on his/her behalf. A solicitor can, however, ask the legal aid area office for permission to advise a child in special circumstances. (See p. 26).

2.4 Does the client qualify financially?

A client must be able to show that his/her savings and income are within the current financial limits (see Eligibility Tables, pp. 9–12).

If the client is receiving income support or family credit, he/she will be eligible for free legal advice and assistance unless his/her disposable capital exceeds £935.

The client should not be asked to pay any contribution out of savings. Neither will he/she have to pay anything if the disposable income is £64 or less.

2.5 Contributions

The solicitor will normally ask the client to pay the contribution at once but if this is inconvenient he/she may accept payment by instalments. The solicitor should discuss this with the client before the interview starts.

In cases where legal advice and assistance is initially limited to two hours' worth of work, the contribution will also be limited to that amount unless the solicitor gets permission to exceed that amount because there is additional work to be done. The client may be liable to contribute more, but only up to the maximum contribution.

If the contribution is more than the solicitor's bill, he/she should refund the balance to the client. If the client is eligible for legal advice and assistance and pays the contribution (if any), the solicitor can start acting at once.

2.6 What happens if money or property is recovered or preserved?

Where money or property is recovered or preserved under legal advice and assistance, the solicitor must use this to pay his/her bill if the bill is more than the client's contribution (if any). (See p. 32).

2.7 How does the solicitor get paid?

The solicitor's bill, less any contribution from the client and the value of any property which is recovered or preserved, will be paid by the area office.

ASSISTANCE BY WAY OF REPRESENTATION

3.1 What does ABWOR cover?

ABWOR covers the cost of a solicitor preparing the client's case and representing him/her in most civil cases in magistrates' courts. These cases include separation, maintenance, custody, affiliation and defended adoption proceedings. It is also available to patients before Mental Health Review Tribunals, parents and some children in care proceedings and prisoners facing disciplinary charges before boards of visitors.

3.2 How does a client apply for ABWOR?

The solicitor should fill in the green form (see section 2.2, above) and form ABWOR 1 which should be sent to the area office. The area office will then decide whether it is reasonable for the client to receive ABWOR. The area office can either grant or refuse ABWOR but, if the application is refused, the client can appeal to the area committee.

3.3 Does the client qualify financially?

The same income conditions apply as for legal advice and assistance (see Eligibility Tables, pp. 9–12). A client who does not qualify for legal advice and assistance may still qualify for ABWOR if he/she has savings of up to £3,000, or is in receipt of income support.

3.4 Contribution

The same rules apply as for legal advice and assistance (see section 2.5, above). If the client has already paid a contribution under legal advice and assistance concerning the same problem but now needs representation, it will count towards the maximum contribution under ABWOR.

3.5 What happens if money or property is recovered or preserved?

The same rules apply as for legal advice and assistance (see section 2.6, above).

3.6 How does the solicitor get paid?

The solicitor's bill, less any contribution from the client and the value of any property which is recovered or preserved, will be paid by the area office.

CIVIL LEGAL AID

4.1 What kinds of courts and cases are covered?

Civil legal aid is available for cases in:

(a) The House of Lords

(b) The High Court and Court of Appeal

(c) County courts (but not judgment summonses nor, usually, the decree proceedings for undefended divorce and judicial separation)

(d) Magistrates' courts for cases about marriage and the family, including separation, maintenance, custody, affiliation and defended adoption proceedings—although these are normally covered by ABWOR (see Section 3)

(e) The Crown Court (for appeals about affiliation orders)

(f) The Employment Appeal Tribunal

(g) The Lands Tribunal

(h) The Commons Commissioners

(i) The Restrictive Practices Court (for some cases)

(j) Appeals to the Court of Appeal on points of law from Social Security Commissioners

Civil legal aid is not available for proceedings before a coroner's court and most tribunals (except those listed above), nor normally for proceedings involving libel and slander. However, advice may be given about these proceedings under legal advice and assistance (see section 2.1, above). Civil legal aid is not available for court cases outside England and Wales.

4.2 Applications for Civil Legal Aid

The solicitor or applicant should complete form CLA1 (for non-matrimonial cases) or form CLA2 (for matrimonial cases) together with form CLA4 (statement of applicant's circumstances). The forms should then be sent to the area office. (For a list of addresses of area offices, see page 359).

It is important that the form is completed correctly. A badly completed form containing insufficient information may result in the application being refused. A solicitor can be paid for filling in the form under legal advice and assistance if the applicant qualifies for it.

The assessment officer will then work out whether the client qualifies financially. In the meantime the area office will decide whether it is reasonable for the applicant to receive civil legal aid (see section 4.4, below).

A certificate does not cover a solicitor for any work done before it is issued and a certificate cannot be backdated (but see regulation 103(6) of the Civil Legal Aid (General) Regulations 1989 (page 211).

4.3 Emergency certificates

If the case is urgent, an applicant can apply for emergency legal aid. This can be granted at once. Emergency legal aid lasts only until a decision has been taken on the full application for civil legal aid.

When an applicant applies for emergency legal aid, he/she must agree to co-operate with the assessment officer in the enquiry into the applicant's financial position and must also agree to pay any contribution that is assessed. The applicant will also have to agree to pay the full cost of any steps taken under the emergency certificate if it is found that he/she does not qualify for civil legal aid or if an offer of a full certificate is refused.

4.4 Consideration of applications for Civil Legal Aid
The applicant must:

(a) qualify financially (see Eligibility Tables—pp. 9–12);

(b) show that he/she has reasonable grounds for taking or defending a court action and that it is reasonable to grant legal aid in the circumstances of the case.

The application will be considered by the area office who will consider all questions of fact and law arising out of the application. They may decide to grant a limited certificate, for example, for the purpose of obtaining counsel's opinion. They may also refuse legal aid, in which case there is a right to appeal to the area committee in most cases.

4.5 Assessment of an applicant's means
Assessment officers of the DSS who specialise in civil legal aid cases carry out the assessment of means. The assessment officer will assess the applicant's disposable income and capital and the maximum contribution, if any (see Eligibility Tables pp. 9–12).

4.6 The financial limits
Children are now assessed in their own right and not under their parents' financial position. The current financial limits apply to children and adults alike. If a person is granted civil legal aid and his/her finances, liabilities or dependants change, he/she must inform the area office.

4.7 Acceptance of offers
If the client qualifies financially, the area office decides if it is reasonable to grant the applicant civil legal aid (see section 4.4, above). The area office will either issue a certificate, if the applicant does not have to pay a contribution, or send an offer of a certificate if a contribution is payable.

Once the offer has been accepted, a contribution from savings is normally paid immediately. Contributions from income are normally paid by 12 monthly instalments, of which the first is paid on acceptance of the offer. A certificate will then be issued and only then can the solicitor start to deal with the case under civil legal aid.

Normally the applicant will not be asked to pay more than the maximum contribution towards the cost of the case (but see section 4.9, below). However, if the applicant's income increases within 12 months of the application, he/she must notify the area office and his/her means may be reassessed. If the applicant's income decreases during the 12 months period he/she may apply for a reassessment of means and the maximum contribution may be reduced. If the applicant comes into money, for example on selling his/her house or winning the pools, while a legal aid certificate is in force, the disposable capital may be reassessed.

If the case costs less than the applicant's actual contribution, he/she will get a refund. If the applicant has a contribution to pay by instalments, it is very important that the payments are kept up. If they are not, the legal aid certificate may be withdrawn.

4.8 What costs are payable by a successful assisted person?
The amount the applicant will have to pay will depend on whether:

(a) the other side is ordered to pay costs and in fact does so;

(b) the applicant is awarded any money by the court or recovers or preserves any property as a result of the proceedings.

If the other side does pay the costs in full, the applicant will receive a refund of any contribution.

5

If the other side does *not* pay the costs in full, the area office may deduct from any moneys ordered by the court to be paid to the assisted person (and actually paid) sufficient to cover those costs. This deduction is known as the *statutory charge* and it will also apply to any property recovered or preserved in the case. Maintenance and the first £2,500 of any money or property recovered or preserved in matrimonial proceedings are exempt from the statutory charge—and so are many state benefits. (See p. 204).

4.9 What costs are payable by an unsuccessful assisted person?
The most the applicant will normally have to pay towards the solicitor's costs and counsel's fees will be the maximum contribution, if any.

The court may also order the applicant to pay part or all of the opponent's costs. The court decides how much should be paid towards those costs and this will depend on the applicant's means and conduct in connection with the dispute (the amount is often equal to the applicant's contribution).

4.10 Legal Aid for appeals to a higher court
If the assisted person is unsuccessful, he/she can apply for legal aid to appeal to a higher court. The rules in section 4.4 still apply to such appeals. The applicant will be liable to pay the balance of the maximum contribution if this has not been used up in the proceedings at first instance (see section 4.7, above).

CRIMINAL LEGAL AID

5.1 Criminal Legal Aid
If a person has been charged with a criminal offence, he/she can apply for criminal legal aid.

5.2 Duty solicitor schemes
A person who is questioned by the police about an offence—whether or not he/she has been arrested—has a right to free legal advice. There is no means test for such advice. (The questioning may be at the police station or elsewhere). The person may ask for a solicitor he/she knows, the 24-hour duty solicitor, or may choose a solicitor from the list kept by the police.

If a person has to go to the magistrates' court on a criminal case there will often be a duty solicitor available either at the court or on call to give free advice and representation on the first appearance. Again, there is no means test.

5.3 Advice
If a person needs legal advice about a criminal matter, he/she can see a solicitor under the legal advice and assistance scheme (see section 2, above). The solicitor can also give the client advice and prepare the case for court under that scheme.

5.4 What does Criminal Legal Aid cover?
Criminal legal aid covers the cost of a solicitor to prepare the client's defence before he/she goes to court and to represent the client there. If the case requires counsel, particularly if it is to be heard in the Crown Court, that may also be covered. Criminal legal aid can also cover advice on appeal against a verdict or sentence of the magistrates' court, the Crown Court or the Court of Appeal, and preparing the appeal itself. Criminal or civil legal aid may also be available for an application for bail. Legal aid is not available to bring a private prosecution.

5.5 Application for Criminal Legal Aid
An application should be made as soon as possible after the applicant has been charged with a criminal offence to the court that is dealing with the case. The court will supply the necessary forms. The applicant will be asked to give details of income and savings.

If he/she is under 17, the parents or guardian can apply for him/her. If the court refuses criminal legal aid, he/she can apply again. There is no limit to the number of applications which can be made to the court, and these can be made at any time up to the trial itself.

5.6 Criteria for the grant of Criminal Legal Aid

The court will grant criminal legal aid if it decides that it is in the "interests of justice" that the defendant should have legal representation, and that he/she needs help to pay the costs of the case. The court's decision will be based on the information given in the criminal legal aid application form and statement of means form.

The court may decide that it is in the "interests of justice" to grant criminal legal aid where, for example, the defendant, if found guilty, is likely to go to prison or lose his/her job, or where there are substantial questions of law to be argued, or where the defendant is unable to follow the proceedings and explain his/her case because he/she does not speak English well enough or is mentally ill.

5.7 Application for review of refusal

If legal aid is refused, the court will write to the applicant giving the reason for refusing criminal legal aid. In some more serious cases, if the court has decided that criminal legal aid is not in the interests of justice, the defendant may be able to make another application.

For less serious offences or where the court has refused criminal legal aid on financial grounds, the defendant can also apply again but only to the court. If he/she is refused criminal legal aid by the magistrates' court and has to go to the Crown Court, an application can be made to that court for criminal legal aid. A solicitor may be able to give help under legal advice and assistance to assist a defendant in preparing a case for court.

5.8 Payment of contributions

A defendant may be asked to pay towards his/her costs as a condition of criminal legal aid. If a contribution has already been paid under legal aid advice and assistance in the same matter, it will count towards any further contribution which may be required. A defendant who is in receipt of income support or family credit cannot be asked for a contribution from income or if his/her disposable income (which is the amount left after allowances for tax, National Insurance contributions, housing, travel to and from work, dependants such as children, and any other reasonable living expenses) is £55 per week or less.

If his/her weekly disposable income is more than £55, the defendant will be asked to make a weekly contribution over six months of a quarter of the amount over £55. For example, if the weekly disposable income is £63 the contribution will be £2 per week for six months. If the defendant's capital, which includes savings and the value of any luxury goods such as expensive jewellery or a yacht, is £3,000 or less, no contribution will be required from capital. If it is above £3,000 he/she will be asked to pay the excess over £3,000 toward the cost of the case. A defendant who is in receipt of income support cannot be asked to pay a contribution from capital.

The court will send the defendant a notice indicating how much he/she will have to pay. The defendant can ask for criminal legal aid to be withdrawn because he/she does not want to pay the contributions, but must tell the court and the solicitor immediately.

5.9 Change of financial circumstances

The defendant must tell the court if his/her income or savings change during the six months he/she is making a contribution.

5.10 Refund of contributions

At the end of the case, the court will decide what should happen to any contributions which have not yet fallen due. The court may ask the defendant to pay off any outstanding contributions or it may cancel them. If, at the end, the contributions paid are more than the actual costs of the case, the court will refund the difference to the defendant. If he/she is acquitted it is likely that all the contributions will be returned, unless the court decides that the defendant brought the prosecution on himself/herself.

5.11 Choice of solicitor

In general a defendant has the right to choose any solicitor who is willing to act. If he/she has been granted criminal legal aid and has not chosen a solicitor, the court can assign one to act. If he/she is being tried with others, the court may make one criminal legal aid order to cover representation of all the defendants unless there is a conflict of interest.

If the defendant wants to change solicitors, he/she will have to give the court a good reason. If the court does not think the request is reasonable it will refer the application to one of the criminal legal aid committees of the Legal Aid Board.

Eligibility Tables for Advice and Assistance, ABWOR and Civil Legal Aid

(1) Advice and Assistance

(a) Disposable Income
If the client is receiving income support or family credit, or has a weekly disposable income of less than £64 he will be eligible for free legal advice and assistance.

His maximum contribution, if his weekly disposable income is between £64 and £135, will be on the following scale:

Disposable income	*Maximum contribution*
Between £64 and £72 a week	£5
£73 and £78 a week	£12
£79 and £84 a week	£19
£85 and £90 a week	£25
£91 and £96 a week	£32
£97 and £102 a week	£38
£103 and £108 a week	£45
£109 and £114 a week	£51
£115 and £120 a week	£58
£121 and £125 a week	£64
£125 and £130 a week	£70
£131 and £135 a week	£75

He will not be eligible for advice and assistance if his weekly disposable income exceeds £135.

(b) Disposable Capital
An allowance is made for dependants at the rate of £335 for the first, £200 for the second and £100 for every other dependant. If the disposable capital, after taking into account allowances, is more than £935 the client will not be eligible.

(2) Civil Legal Aid

(a) Disposable Income
No contribution is payable out of income if the disposable income (*i.e.* estimated gross income over the 12 months following the application less rent, rates, income tax and other necessary allowances) is £2,515 a year or less. Between £2,515 and £6,350 a year a contribution is payable up to a maximum of one quarter of the amount by which the disposable income exceeds £2,515 a year. Over £6,350 a year, legal aid cannot be

granted (in cases including a claim in respect of personal injuries the upper income limit is £7,000 a year).

Table illustrating the Gross Income of Persons Entitled to Legal Aid, either Free or on Payment of Contributions, taking into account the change in Income Tax rates from April 6, 1990 and the Social Security uprating from April 9, 1990

Type of Applicant	Income from all sources before deduction of Income Tax, NI Contribution and housing costs	
	Maximum permitting free legal aid (DI £2,515)	*Minimum which makes applicant ineligible for legal aid* (DI £6,350)
	Gross income incl. child benefit	*Gross income incl. child benefit*
	£	£
1. Single non-householder	4,992 (96 pw)	10,608 (204 pw)
2. Single non-householder with 2 children aged 4 and 12	6,812 (131 pw)	12,428 (239 pw)
3. Couple non-householders	7,696 (148 pw)	13,312 (256 pw)
4. Couple non-householders with 2 children aged 4 and 12	10,296 (198 pw)	15,912 (306 pw)
5. Single householder	10,192 (196 pw)	15,808 (304 pw)
6. Single householder with 2 children aged 4 and 12	12,012 (231 pw)	17,628 (339 pw)
7. Couple householders	12,896 (248 pw)	18,460 (355 pw)
8. Couple householders with 2 children aged 4 and 12	15,236 (293 pw)	20,852 (401 pw)

Notes: The examples in the above tables are intended to be illustrative only and are based upon the following assumptions:

(1) The national average for rented accommodation (including water rates of £1,212.12 per anum (£23.31 per week) has been given in examples 1 to 4 inclusive. In addition an allowance of £7.12 per person per week is allowed in respect of the Community Charge.

(2) The national average for owner-occupied accommodation, subject to an endowment mortgage, (including water rates) of £4,439.24 per annum [£85.37 per week] has been given in examples 5 to 8 inclusive. In addition, an allowance of £7.12 per person per week is allowed in respect of the Community Charge.

(b) *Disposable Capital*
If disposable capital is less than £3,000 no contribution is payable. If more than £3,000 but less than £6,310 a contribution of the excess over £3,000 will be payable. If disposable capital is £6,310 or more legal aid will only be granted in exceptional circumstances where the costs of the case are likely to be very high.

(3) Assistance by way of Representation
From April 9, 1990 the eligibility limit for capital in respect of assistance by way of

representation is £3,000. The green form capital limit is £935.

This means that some clients may be eligible for assistance by way of representation but not for green form advice and assistance. The table set out below shows how the new financial eligibility limits will affect clients.

Where a client is eligible for both green form advice and assistance and assistance by way of representation the solicitor should complete pages 1 and 2 of the green form. The form ABWOR 1 should be used when applying for assistance by way of representation. This indicates that the solicitor is acting for the client under a green form and contains details of the client's contribution.

Where the client is not financially eligible for advice and assistance but is within the limits for assistance by way of representation, the solicitor will need to complete only page 1 of the green form showing the assessment of means. Form ABWOR 1 should be used to apply for assistance by way of representation. This will indicate that the client is not eligible for green form advice and assistance and will contain details of the contribution required in connection with any assistance by way of representation.

Table Showing Financial Eligibility for Advice and Assistance (Green Form) and Assistance by Way of Representation (ABWOR) as from April 9, 1990.

Means of Client (See Keycard 22 for details)		Whether eligible for advice and assistance (Green Form)			Whether eligible for assistance by way of representation (ABWOR)			Action to be taken by Solicitor
Net income after deductions	Capital plus dependants' allowance	Yes/No	Free	Contri-bution	Yes/No	Free	Contri-bution	
£64 per week or below	Below £935	Yes	Yes	No	Yes	Yes	No	Assess green form means with use of keycard 22. Advise and assist client as necessary under green form. Apply for ABWOR if necessary on form ABWOR 1
Between £64 per week and £135 per week	Below £935	Yes	No	Yes	Yes	No	Yes	Assess green form means with use of keycard 22. Collect contribution. Advise and assist client as necessary under green form. Apply for ABWOR if necessary on form ABWOR 1.
Above £135 per week	Below £935	No	No	No	No	No	No	Assess green form means with use of keycard 22. Client not eligible so must instruct solicitor privately.
£64 per week or below	Between £935 and £3,000	No	No	No	Yes	Yes	No	Assess green form means with use of keycard 22. Client must instruct solicitor privately for advice and assistance. Apply for ABWOR if necessary on form ABWOR 1.

Means of Client (See Keycard 22 for details)		Whether eligible for advice and assistance (Green Form)			Whether eligible for assistance by way of representation (ABWOR)			Action to be taken by Solicitor
Net income after deductions	Capital plus dependants' allowance	Yes/No	Free	Contri-bution	Yes/No	Free	Contri-bution	
Between £64 per week and £135 per week	Between £935 and £3,000	No	No	No	Yes	No	Yes	Assess green form means with use of keycard 22. Client must instruct solicitor privately for advice and assistance. If ABWOR needed collect contribution. Apply for ABWOR on form ABWOR 1.
Above £135 per week	Between £935 and £3,000	No	No	No	No	No	No	Assess green form means with use of keycard 22. Client must instruct solicitor privately for advice and assistance or representation. Consider whether full legal aid available.
Above £135 per week	Above £3,000	No	No	No	No	No	No	Assess green form means with use of keycard 22. Client must instruct solicitor privately for advice and assistance or representation unless considering whether full legal aid available.

Table of Remuneration Rates

REMUNERATION IN RESPECT OF WORK DONE ON OR AFTER APRIL 1, 1990

Criminal Legal Aid in the magistrates' court

The Legal Aid in Criminal and Care Proceedings (Costs) (Amendment) Regulations 1990 came into operation on April 1, 1990, amending the Legal Aid in Criminal and Care Proceedings (Costs) Regulations 1989. Regulation 3(3) prescribes new standard hourly rates for work done on or after April 1, 1990. The new standard hourly rates for legally aided criminal work in the magistrates' court are as follows:

	Standard Rate	*London Rate*
Preparation	£39.25 per hour	£41.75 per hour
Advocacy	£49.50 per hour	—
Attendance at Court where Counsel assigned	£26.25 per hour	—
Travelling and Waiting	£22.00 per hour	—
Letters Written and Telephone Calls (Routine)	£3.05 per item	£3.15 per item

The London rate applies to work done by a fee earner whose office is situated within what is now legal aid area 1.

Care Proceedings

Regulation 3(3) of The Legal Aid in Criminal and Care Proceedings (Costs) (Amendment) Regulations 1990 also increases the rates of remuneration in care proceedings. The rates for work done on or after April 1, 1990 are as follows:

	Standard Rate	*London Rate*
Preparation	£47.25 per hour	£50.50 per hour
Advocacy	£57.00 per hour	—
Attendance at Court where Counsel assigned	£30.00 per hour	—
Travelling and Waiting	£26.50 per hour	—
Letters Written and Telephone Calls (Routine)	£3.40 per item	—

The London rate applies to work done by a fee earner whose office is situated within what is now legal aid area 1.

ABWOR

The hourly rates for work done on or after April 1, 1990 for ABWOR will be as follows:

	Standard Rate	*London Rate*
Preparation	£39.25 per hour	£41.75 per hour
Advocacy	£49.50 per hour	—
Attendance at Court where Counsel assigned	£26.25 per hour	—
Travelling and Waiting	£22.00 per hour	—
Letters Written and Telephone Calls (Routine)	£3.05 per item	£3.15 per item

The London rate applies to work done by a fee earner whose office is situated within what is now legal aid area 1.

Green Form

The hourly rate for work done on or after April 1, 1990 under the green form is £39.25 per hour (£41.75 per hour in respect of work done by a fee earner whose office is situated within what is now legal aid area 1). The rate for routine letters written and telephone calls is £3.05 per item (£3.15 per item in respect of work done by a fee earner whose office is situated within legal aid area 1).

Court Duty Solicitors

Remuneration for duty solicitors for time spent at court is fixed by reference to the rate payable for advocacy and travelling and waiting contained in Schedule 1 of The Legal Aid in Criminal and Care Proceedings (Costs) Regulations 1989 as amended by The Legal Aid in Criminal and Care Proceedings (Costs) (Amendment) Regulations 1990. By reference to that rate, the new hourly rate for work done by court duty solicitors on or after April 1, 1990 is £35.75 per hour. The rate for travelling to and from court is £22.00 per hour.

Where time is spent at court on a bank holiday, a Saturday or Sunday a premium payment is payable. This is by way of a 25 per cent. enhancement to the standard rate. Therefore, the rate recoverable for such work is £44.69 per hour. The rate for travelling to and from court on a bank holiday, a Saturday or Sunday is £22.00 per hour.

Advice and assistance at police stations

The Legal Advice and Assistance at Police Stations (Remuneration) (Amendment) Regulations 1990 came into operation on April 1, 1990 amending the Legal Advice and Assistance at Police Stations (Remuneration) Regulations 1989. Regulation 2 of The Amendment Regulations inserts a new Schedule at paragraph 1(1) of the Remuneration Regulations and provides for the following rates:

Class of Work	*Rate*
(a) Availability during duty period (standby payment)	£3.15 per hour served, to a maximum of £75.60 (£3.20 per hour served, to a maximum of £76.80 in respect of a solicitor whose office is situated within what is now legal aid area 1)
(b) Advising and assisting a person arrested and held in custody, or being interviewed in connection with a serious service offence or to a volunteer:	
(i) by a duty solicitor in unsocial hours	£52.25 per hour
(ii) by a duty solicitor in all other hours	£39.25 per hour (£41.75 per hour in respect of a solicitor whose office is situated within what is now legal aid area 1)
(iii) by an own solicitor	£39.25 per hour (£41.75 per hour in respect of a solicitor whose office is situated within what is now legal aid area 1)
(c) Travelling and waiting	
(i) by a duty solicitor in unsocial hours	£52.25 per hour
(ii) by a duty solicitor in all other hours	£39.25 per hour (£41.75 per hour in respect of a solicitor whose office is situated within what is now legal aid area 1).
(iii) by an own solicitor	£22.00 per hour

(d)	Advising and assisting over the telephone	£17.75 per item (£18.25 per item in respect of a solicitor whose office is situated within what is now legal aid area 1)
(e)	Routine telephone calls	£1.90 per item (£2.00 per item in respect of a solicitor whose office is situated within what is now legal aid area 1)

ABWOR—Warrants of Further Detention

The hourly rates for work done on or after April 1, 1990, where a solicitor has provided ABWOR on an application by the police for a warrant of further detention or the extension of such a warrant, are as follows:

	Standard Rate	*London Rate*
ADVOCACY		
(i) by a duty solicitor in unsocial hours	£66.00 per hour	—
(ii) by a duty solicitor in all other hours	£49.50 per hour	—
(iii) by an own solicitor	£49.50 per hour	—
PREPARATION		
(i) by a duty solicitor in unsocial hours	£52.33 per hour	£55.66 per hour
(ii) by a duty solicitor in all other hours	£39.25 per hour	£41.75 per hour
(iii) by an own solicitor	£39.25 per hour	£41.75 per hour
TRAVELLING AND WAITING		
(i) by a duty solicitor in unsocial hours	£29.33 per hour	—
(ii) by a duty solicitor in all other hours	£22.00 per hour	—
(iii) by an own solicitor	£22.00 per hour	—
LETTERS WRITTEN AND TELEPHONE CALLS		
(i) by a duty solicitor in unsocial hours	£4.06 per item	£4.20 per item
(ii) by a duty solicitor	£3.05 per item	£3.15 per item
(iii) by an own solicitor	£3.05 per item	£3.15 per item

The London rate applies to work done by a fee earner whose office is situated within what is now legal aid area 1.

Civil Legal Aid in Matrimonial Proceedings in the High Court and County Court

The Matrimonial Causes (Costs) (Amendment) Rules 1990 came into operation on April 1, 1990, amending The Matrimonial Causes (Costs) Rules 1988. Rule 2 inserts a substituted Schedule 2 prescribing new standard rates payable in respect of matrimonial proceedings in the High Court and County Court. These are as follows:

PREPARATION

	Item	*High Court*	*County Court*
(1)	Writing routine letters	£3.75 per item	£3.25 per item
(2)	Receiving routine letters	£1.85 per item	£1.60 per item
(3)	Routine telephone calls	£3.75 per item	£3.25 per item

15

Item	High Court	County Court
(4) All other preparation work including any work which was reasonably done arising out of or incidental to the proceedings, interviews with client, witnesses and other parties; obtaining evidence; preparation and consideration of, and dealing with, documents; negotiations and notices; dealing with letters written and received and telephone calls which are not routine	Where the proceedings were conducted in the divorce registry or in another court on the South-Eastern Circuit at the time when the relevant work was done: £41.50 per hour All other circuits; £39.00 per hour	£36.50 per hour £34.50 per hour
(5) In addition to items 1–4 above, to cover the general care and conduct of the proceedings	+50%	+50%
(6) Travelling and waiting time in connection with the above matters	£28.50 per hour	£26.25 per hour

CONFERENCES WITH COUNSEL

Item	High Court	County Court
(7) Attending counsel in conference	£33.00 per hour	£29.00 per hour
(8) Travelling and waiting	£28.50 per hour	£26.25 per hour

ATTENDANCES

Item	High Court	County Court
(9) Attending with counsel at the trial or hearing of any summons or other application at court, or other appointment	£33.00 per hour	£29.00 per hour
(10) Attending without counsel at the trial or hearing of any cause or the hearing of any summons or other application at court, or other appointment	£50.00 per hour	£47.00 per hour
(11) Travelling and waiting	£28.50 per hour	£26.25 per hour

FEES FOR JUNIOR COUNSEL (S) = Standard (M) = Maximum

Item	High Court	County Court
(12) With a brief on an unopposed application for an injunction, or procedural issue	£79.00 (S) £131.00 (M)	£68.00 (S) £113.00 (M)
(13) With a brief on the trial of a cause or matter or on the hearing of an ancillary application or on a children appointment where the hearing lasts for:		
(a) One hour	£119.00 (S) £239.00 (M)	£102.00 (S) £204.00 (M)
(b) A half day	£165.00 (S) £272.00 (M)	£142.00 (S) £239.00 (M)

Item	*High Court*	*County Court*
(c) A full day	£329.00 (S) £522.00 (M)	£284.00 (S) £454.00 (M)
(d) More than a full day	Discretionary	Discretionary
(14) For each day or part of a day on which the trial of a cause or matter, or the hearing of any ancillary application, or a children appointment, is continued after the first day	Discretionary	Discretionary
(15) Conference (including time reasonably spent in preparation and conference, but not otherwise remunerated)	£18.00 per ½ hour (S)	£16.00 per ½ hour (S)
(16) (a) Complex items of written work (such as advices on evidence, opinions and affidavits of a substantial nature, requests for particulars or answers)	£86.00 per item (S)	£74.00 per item (S)
(b) All other written work	£51.00 per item (S)	£45.00 per item (S)
(17) Except where the court is within 25 miles of Charing Cross or where there is no local Bar in the court town, or within 25 miles thereof, for travelling time	£16.50 per hour (S) + expenses	£14.20 per hour (S) + expenses

TAXATION AND REVIEW OF TAXATION

(18) Preparing the bill (where allowable) and completing the taxation (excluding preparing for and attending the taxation)	£28.50–£80.00	£28.50–£45.50
(19) Preparing for and attending the taxation (including travelling and waiting)	Discretionary	Discretionary
(20) Review by registrar or judge (including preparation)	Discretionary	Discretionary

Independent Social Workers

From April 1, 1990 the fees payable to independent social workers have been increased by the Board as follows:

Preparation	£15.00 per hour
Travel	£10.00 per hour

Legal Aid Forms

Reference No.	Description	Obtainable from: Legal Aid Court Office
CLA 1	Application for Legal Aid—Non-matrimonial	*
CLA 2	Application for Legal Aid—Matrimonial	*
CLA 3	Application for Emergency Legal Aid	*
CLA 4	Statement of Applicant's Circumstances	*
GF 1	Green form	*
GF 2	Consolidated claim for fees	*
GF 3	Application for green form extension	*
GF 4	Advice and Assistance for wills	*
ABWOR 1	Application for Assistance by way of Representation	*
ABWOR 3	Assistance by way of Representation report on case form	*
SJ 1	Application for Legal Aid (Summary Jurisdiction cases)	*
SJ 6	Summary Jurisdiction Report on case form	*
CLA 16	Report of case and claim for costs	*
CLA 17	Proforma Bill of Costs used for civil assessment	*
CLA 28	Application for Payment on account of profit costs, disbursements and/or counsel's fees	*
CLA 29	Undertaking as to costs	*
CRIM 5	Report on case for criminal and care work in the magistrates' court	*
CRIM 6	Combined case memorandum and fee note (counsel's fees)	*
DSC	Report by Court Duty Solicitor	*
DSPS 1	Advice at Police Stations Report	*
DSPS 2	Advice at Police Stations Standby Claim	*

Reference No.	Description	Obtainable from: Legal Aid Court Office
FORM L1(A)	Statement of financial circumstances of an applicant for Legal Aid when resident outside England or Wales	*
FORM L20/L21 HMF	Statement of financial circumstances of an applicant for Legal Aid who is a member of HM Forces	*
FORM L17 HMF	Statement of emoluments of a member of HM Forces	*
FORM 1	Application for Legal Aid in Criminal proceedings—Magistrates' or Crown Court	*
FORM 2	Notification of Refusal to grant Legal Aid and determination of contribution	*
FORM 3	Application for review of refusal to grant Legal Aid	*
FORM 4	Notification of decision of area committee on review of refusal to grant Legal Aid	*
FORM 5	Statement of means by applicant or appropriate contributor for Legal Aid purposes	*
FORM 16	Application for Legal Aid in care proceedings in the Juvenile Court or Crown Court	*

Notes for Guidance

CONTENTS

Notes for guidance prepared by the Legal Aid Board.

2.8   *Does the proper conduct of the proceedings require counsel?*
2.9   *Should ABWOR be withdrawn?*

3. EMERGENCY CIVIL LEGAL AID APPLICATIONS
3.1   *Will an applicant as a matter of urgency be granted civil legal aid?*
3.2   *What does an applicant have to know about emergency legal aid?*
3.3   *Some examples of decisions in emergency cases*

4. CIVIL LEGAL AID
4.1   *Statutory framework and conditions—general guide*
4.2   *Matters for consideration by area offices on receipt of applications for legal aid*

   (*a*) Is civil legal aid available for the proceedings?

   (*b*) Is the applicant a person to whom legal aid can be granted?

4.3   *Is the applicant within the financial eligibility limits?*
4.4   *Has the applicant reasonable grounds for taking, defending or being a party to the proceedings (the legal merits test)?*
4.5   *Is it reasonable in the particular circumstances of the case for the applicant to be granted civil legal aid (the reasonableness test)?*
4.6   *Do persons other than the applicant have an interest?*

5. THE STATUTORY CHARGE
5.1   *Statutory authority and framework*
5.2   *Has the assisted person been successful wholly or in part in the proceedings or obtained an out of court settlement with the benefit of legal aid?*
5.3   *Is there a net liability of the Legal Aid Board on the assisted person's account in respect of any proceedings?*
5.4   *Has money or property been "recovered" or "preserved" out of which the net liability can be met in whole or in part?*
5.5   *Does the case come within any of the exemptions?*
5.6   *Enforcement*
5.7   *Does the Board have power to refuse to pay solicitors' costs?*

Notes for guidance prepared by the Law Society and adopted by the Legal Aid Board.

6. APPLICATIONS FOR LEGAL AID FOR APPEALS

7. APPEALS TO THE DIVISIONAL COURT OF THE FAMILY DIVISION

8. APPEALS TO THE COURT OF APPEAL AND APPLICATIONS FOR EXTENSION OF TIME

9. APPEALS FROM PENSIONS APPEAL TRIBUNAL

10. APPEALS FROM EMPLOYMENT APPEAL TRIBUNAL

11. CHOICE OF FORUM IN MATRIMONIAL PROCEEDINGS

1 ADVICE AND ASSISTANCE—(THE GREEN FORM SCHEME)

1.1 Statutory framework and conditions—general guide

The statutory framework for advice and assistance is contained in Parts I and III, sections 1, 2 and 8–13 of the Legal Aid Act 1988 (see p. 85).

Details of the system are set out in the Legal Advice and Assistance (Scope) Regulations 1989 (p. 139), the Legal Advice and Assistance Regulations 1989 (p. 145); the Legal Advice and Assistance (Duty Solicitor) Remuneration Regulations 1989 (p. 319); and the Legal Advice and Assistance at Police Stations (Remuneration) Regulations 1989 (p. 323).

The general principle of Part III of the Legal Aid Act 1988 is that advice and assistance is available to any person whose financial resources make him/her eligible, subject to exclusions and conditions contained in regulations.

NOTE: The regulations use the phrase "application for advice and assistance." This "application" is made by the client to the solicitor by signing the green form, which form also includes the client's assessment of means and the solicitor's claim for costs.

1.2 Decisions which have to be made by solicitors

(a) Is advice and assistance available?

The rule is that where a solicitor has carried out work under the green form which does not require any additional authority from the Area Director, payment can be refused if the advice and assistance does not come within the basic requirements of the Legal Aid Act 1988 and the regulations. Before agreeing to give a client advice and assistance therefore the solicitor must ensure:

(i) *The matter is one of English law* Advice or assistance must be given on matters relating to the application of English law, which are not excluded by regulation. Advice cannot be given on matters of foreign law but advice is available on the transmission of applications for legal aid to some other countries under the European Agreement on the Transmission of Applications for Legal Aid, Strasbourg, January 27, 1977.

(ii) *The matter is not excluded from the scheme* Matters excluded by the Legal Advice and Assistance (Scope) Regulations 1989 are:

(a) conveyancing services, except rental purchase agreements or conditional sale agreements for the sale of land and any conveyancing necessary to give effect to an order of court or the terms of a matrimonial agreement;

(b) wills, except where the client is aged 70 or over, or is mentally or physically disabled, or is a parent or guardian wanting to provide for a child in care, or as a one-parent family wishes to appoint a guardian for a minor living with the client.

(iii) *The matter does not involve steps in proceedings* Advice and assistance is not available for the taking of any step in the institution or conduct of proceedings (except to a limited degree in undefended divorce, see NFG 13). Therefore it is not available for obtaining a grant of representation to an estate, since a grant is an order of court for which application must be made to the court.

NOTE: If advice and assistance relates to excluded matters or matters not affecting the application of English law, payment will not be made out of the legal aid fund for the work done, even if the cost is within the prospective cost limit.

(b) Is the client financially eligible? How are the means assessed?

The financial limits for eligibility for advice and assistance are prescribed in April each year in regulations produced by the Lord Chancellor's Department. There are both income and capital limits which are different from assistance by way of representation and legal aid. The assessment of means for advice and assistance and assistance by way of representation is the responsibility of the solicitor who also collects any contribution due. A key card for use with the advice and assistance green form is issued by the Legal Aid Board each year to each legal aid practitioner giving the up to date figures for allowances, etc.

Some cases are exempt from the requirement to assess the client's means:

    (i) advice and assistance at police stations;

    (ii) advice and assistance in some criminal proceedings in the magistrates' court for which ABWOR is available; and

    (iii) ABWOR for applications for warrants of further detention.

In all other cases, however, the solicitor has, as a first step, to determine the client's financial eligibility on information provided by the client. Except where a postal application is possible or the client is represented by another person authorised by the client, the client has to make the application for advice and assistance in person, at which time the solicitor must carry out the assessment of means, before giving advice and assistance. He will also need to collect any contribution at this stage. If he decides not to collect the contribution, the amount will still be deducted from his costs when payment is made out of the legal aid fund (see NFG 1.6, p. 35).

1.3 Decisions which have to be made by area offices

(a) Is it reasonable for the solicitor to accept an application personally from a child?
(Legal Advice and Assistance Regulations 1989, reg. 14)

The rule is that (except where the child is at a police station) a solicitor can only accept an application for advice and assistance direct from a child (*i.e.* a person under the age of 16) where he has been authorised to do so by the Area Director. (He can accept an application on behalf of a child by the persons specified in reg. 14(3)(a) and (c) Legal Advice and Assistance Regulations 1989 but see the following note for reg. 14(3)(d)).

Will such authority be given?
YES

    (i) if there is good reason why the parent or guardian is not applying (*e.g.* conflict of interest, or the child is in care and needs separate representation); and

    (ii) the child is old enough to give instructions and understand the nature of the advice and assistance.

In such cases the solicitor may well consider it just and equitable not to aggregate the child's means with those of the person liable to maintain him (see Legal Advice and Assistance Regulations, 1989, Sched. 2, para. 5, p. 159).

(b) Is it reasonable for the solicitor to accept an application from "any other person" acting on behalf of a child or patient? (Legal Advice and Assistance Regulations 1989, reg. 14(3)(d))

The rule is that a solicitor can accept an application for advice and assistance on behalf of a child, (*i.e.* a person under the age of 16) by a parent or guardian, and on behalf of a patient (*i.e.* under the Mental Health Act 1983) by either a receiver or the nearest relative or guardian.

A solicitor can only accept an application for advice and assistance to "any other person" where he has received prior authority from the Area Director.

Will such authority be given?
YES

 (i) if there is good reason why the patient or guardian cannot make the application (*e.g.* conflict of interest); and

 (ii) there is sufficient connection between the child or patient and the other person to ensure that the other person is likely to act responsibly in the interests of the child/patient; and

 (iii) the other person has sufficient knowledge of the child or patient, the problem and the final circumstances, to give proper instructions to the solicitor.

(c) Is it reasonable for the solicitor to accept a postal application from a person residing outside England and Wales? (Legal Advice and Assistance Regulations 1989, reg. 15)
The rule is that where a client resides outside England and Wales, a solicitor can, with the prior authority of the Area Director, accept a postal application for advice and assistance.

Will such authority be given?

YES where there is good reason why the client cannot attend personally or authorise another person to attend the solicitor on his behalf.

NO where the client's residence is purely temporary and the solicitor can, without disadvantage to the client, postpone giving advice and assistance until the client returns to England and Wales.

NOTE: The solicitor should not start work until he has received from the client the completed green form, to ensure that the client is financially eligible.

(d) Is it reasonable for advice and assistance for the same matter to be given by more than one solicitor? (Legal Advice and Assistance Regulations 1989, reg. 16)
The rule is that (except where advice and assistance is given at police stations or by a duty solicitor at a magistrates' court) advice and assistance cannot be given for the same matter by more than one solicitor without authority from the Area Director.

NOTE:

 1. The "same" matter means the same proceedings or the same problem on which advice and assistance has previously been sought.

 2. "One" solicitor is for practical purposes treated as one firm of solicitors because legal aid pays firms of solicitors rather than individuals. If a client changes solicitors within the same firm no authority is needed for the new solicitor to carry on with the advice and assistance under the same green form. If the solicitor changes firms and wishes to take the client with him authority is needed.

 3. Once authority has been given, the new solicitor should start on a fresh green form and not act as if an extension had been granted for the first green form. This means a new assessment of means and contribution if appropriate.

Will such authority be given?
YES

 (i) if there is a substantial gap of time between the first and second occasion when advice and assistance has been sought;

 (ii) if circumstances have changed materially between the first and second occasions, *e.g.* a reconciliation which has failed;

(iii) if the client is dissatisfied with the service provided by the first solicitor (see (i) below);

(iv) if the client has moved a distance away from the first solicitor and communication is difficult;

(v) if the client wants to follow an individual solicitor who has changed firms and is prepared to continue advice and assistance;

NO

(i) if the client merely finds the first advice unpalatable and wants a second opinion;

(ii) if there is only a short time between the first and second occasion when advice and assistance is sought and no material change of circumstances has occurred.

(iii) if there has already been one authority granted, *i.e.* the change requested is from a second to a third solicitor;

(iv) if there is no reasonable explanation for the client seeking advice and assistance from a new solicitor.

(e) Is it reasonable to treat an application for advice and assistance as a separate matter from a previous application? (Legal Advice and Assistance Regulations 1989, reg. 17)

The rule is that where two or more separate matters are involved each matter must be the subject of a separate application for advice and assistance except for matters arising from or in connection with divorce or judicial separation.

NOTE: This is not a matter for which the Area Director can give an authority. The decision is one of fact for the area office to make on (*a*) an enquiry from a solicitor; (*b*) an application for extension of a green form; or (*c*) claim for payment under a green form. If there are separate matters included in one green form where they should not be or there are a number of green forms submitted for matters which are not separate, the solicitor runs the risk of an extension being refused or payment being withheld or reduced. The solicitor therefore has to make the decision which sooner or later he will have to justify. The following examples may be helpful in reaching that decision, bearing in mind that divorce and judicial separation have different rules from non-matrimonial proceedings.

NON-MATRIMONIAL CASES—GENERAL

(i) Are the two matters genuinely different problems requiring separate advice and assistance, albeit at the same time?
   If **YES**: these are probably separate matters justifying separate green forms.

(ii) Do the two matters arise from the same set of circumstances?
   If **YES**: the chances of their being genuinely separate matters diminish.

(iii) Will the two matters lead to one single action cause or matter?
   If **YES**: it is unlikely that they can be treated as separate matters.

NON-MATRIMONIAL—COMMON CASES

(i) *Debt* As a general rule each individual debt would not justify the use of a separate green form *but* where separate proceedings have been issued in respect of different debts, separate green forms in respect of each set of proceedings could be justified.

(ii) *Welfare benefits* Advice and assistance in relation to various or separate state benefits would not normally justify the use of separate green forms (but see the *Law Society's Gazette*, January 21, 1987, p. 162).

(iii) *Housing problems* Varying problems or remedies arising out of housing difficulties (possession/repairs, etc.) would not normally justify the use of separate green forms.

MATRIMONIAL (DIVORCE AND JUDICIAL SEPARATION)

(i) One green form relates to the whole proceedings, *i.e.* decree proceedings and all ancillaries are treated as one matter.

(ii) Even when there are two sets of proceedings, *e.g.* judicial separation followed by divorce proceedings or two sets of divorce proceedings, provided that they relate to the same marriage they are still to be treated as one matter for green form purposes.

(iii) Magistrates' court proceedings relating to the marriage do not come within (ii) above and can therefore be treated as separate matters for green form purposes.

(iv) Even if a solicitor has been paid for advice and assistance in respect of divorce or judicial separation proceedings and he is subsequently requested to give further advice and assistance in connection with the divorce or judicial separation proceedings, he will need to apply to the area office for an extension in respect of that further advice and assistance, since the regulations are mandatory.

(f) Is it reasonable to grant an authority to exceed the prescribed limit (i.e. grant an extension)? (Legal Advice and Assistance Regulations 1989, reg. 21)
The rule is that (except where advice and assistance at police stations or in criminal proceedings in magistrates' courts are concerned) a solicitor cannot exceed the initial green form costs limit without obtaining from the Area Director an extension.

The Area Director has to be satisfied that it is reasonable for the advice and assistance to be given *and* that the estimate of costs to be incurred in giving it is reasonable.

NOTE: The area office will not have seen the matter before. The solicitor must therefore submit with the application for an extension sufficient information to enable the Area Director to make his decision about what the problem is, what work has already been done, what needs to be done and why, and the estimated cost of the work needing to be done.

Will the extension be granted?
1. *The area office have to answer some basic questions before dealing with the reasonableness of the extension:*

Is the problem one of English law? (Legal Aid Act 1988, s.2; p.89)	If **NO,** the extension will not be granted, and the bill for the required advice and assistance will not be paid.
Is the problem one which is excluded from the advice and assistance provisions? (Legal Advice & Assistance (Scope) Regs. 1989; p.139)	If **YES** the extension will not be granted and the bill for the required advice and assistance will not be paid.
Is legal aid available for the matter?	If **NO** this is not a bar in itself to an extension being granted.
	If **YES** the questions below need to be answered.
Has legal aid (whether civil or criminal) or ABWOR already been granted?	If **YES** the extension will not be granted— but the bill for the required advice and assistance will be paid.

29

Has legal aid (whether civil or criminal) or ABWOR already been refused?

If **YES** the extension may still be granted. A limited extension may be granted to prepare an appeal against refusal to an area committee in the case of civil legal aid provided the appeal is not in connection with repeated applications for legal aid.

Has legal aid (whether civil or criminal) or ABWOR already been applied for?

If **YES** the extension may still be granted if there is likely to be delay before the application is determined and further work needs to be done.

Does the applicant have any alternative source of finance for the legal costs?

If **YES** it may well be unreasonable to grant an extension. The element of hardship will be an important consideration.

2. *Once the basic questions have been answered in the affirmative, the reasonableness of the extension in the particular case can be considered:*

Is the opponent worth pursuing?

If **NO** it may well be unreasonable to authorise further expenditure.

Does the money or benefit at stake justify the expenditure?

If **NO** it is unlikely that an extension will be granted.

Where proceedings are possible, should the matter be dealt with by way of an application for legal aid rather than an extension of advice and assistance?

Probably **YES** where proceedings are imminent or unavoidable in which case extension will be granted only for limited amounts to enable an application to be prepared if work cannot be done within the original limit.

Probably **NO** where solicitor can show real prospects of settling without having to issue proceedings.

Should an extension be granted to obtain an opinion of counsel?

Generally **NO** where the application relates to potential litigation. The matter should be dealt with by applying for legal aid (see above).

Possibly **YES** if no potential litigation and the matter appears to be beyond the capability of a reasonably competent solicitor.

In matrimonial cases does the upper limit apply? (Reg 4(1)(b) The Legal Advice & Assistance Regulations 1989 p.148). If so, why is that limit not sufficient?

The upper limit (3 hours work) only applies to a petitioner for divorce or judicial separtion who has had advice or assistance in the preparation of a petition. Unless an exceptional need is shown it will probably not be reasonable to grant an extension.

3. *The following are examples of the work that a solicitor may be expected to carry out under a green form and within the limit of expenditure authorised by the general matrimonial authority:*

(i) preliminary advice on the grounds for divorce or judicial separation, the effects of a decree on status, the future arrangements for the children, the income and assets of the family and matters relating to housing and the matrimonial home;

(ii) drafting the petition and the statement of the arrangements for the children and where necessary typing or writing the entries on the forms;

(iii) advising on filing the documents at court and the consequential procedure, including service if no acknowledgment of service is filed;

(iv) advising a client when the acknowledgment of service is received as to the procedure for applying for directions for trial, and typing or writing the entries on the form of affidavit of evidence;

(v) advising as to attendances before the judge to explain the arrangements for the children and as to what, if any, evidence will be required by the judge other than that of the petitioner, but not attending court;

(vi) advising on the decree absolute.

Examples of values attributable to certain steps in matrimonial cases are given as follows:

```
Bailiff service ........................................................ £10
Marriage certificate................................................... £8
Omit address from Petition ........................................... £15
Personal service (including enquiry agents' fee) ...................... £30
Deemed service.................................................... £20–£25
Substituted Service plus advert fees.................................. £30
Dispense with Service (including enquiries to trace Respondent)........ £45
Amend Petition.......................................... minor £15-£20
                                                 substantive £25–£30
Supplemental Petition ........................................... £30–£35
Dismiss Petition ..................................................... £20
Medical Report (if necessary for Section 41 appointment) ............. £25
Further Affidavit.......................................... £15 upwards
Settle ancillary relief (including legal aid application if no agreement reached)£50
Settle custody/access (including legal aid application if no agreement reached)£50
Transfer of matrimonial home ..................... £75 plus disbursements
Sever joint tenancy................................................... £15
Caution or Class F charge............................................ £15
```

(g) Special cases

1. MCKENZIE ADVISERS

Following the principles laid down by the case of *McKenzie* v. *McKenzie* [1971] P. 33, counsel has advised that the definition of advice and assistance in the Legal Aid Act 1988 includes a solicitor acting as a "McKenzie Adviser," *i.e.* advising a client informally without actually representing that client in any proceedings. There is accordingly jurisdiction to grant an extension under the green form scheme for this purpose and to pay appropriate costs out of the legal aid fund.

An application for an extension to the green form limit to enable a solicitor to act as a McKenzie Adviser falls within the general principles laid down by regulation 21 of the Legal Advice and Assistance Regulations 1989.

When considering whether it is reasonable for advice and assistance to be given in these circumstances, the area office will bear in mind the following criteria:

(i) it will normally be unreasonable to grant an extension where full legal aid is available for the proceedings and the client will be better served by being fully represented in such proceedings;

(ii) it will normally be unreasonable to grant such an extension unless the solicitor can satisfy the area office that, by reason of either the difficulty of the case or the importance to the client or the inability of the client to act on his or her own without legal help, it is necessary for the client to have the services of a solicitor acting as a McKenzie Adviser.

When a green form bill which includes a claim for costs for a solicitor acting as a McKenzie Adviser is submitted, the area office will call for the solicitor's file. This will enable the area office to be satisfied, before payment is authorised, that there is no element of representation in the claim.

2. CONVEYANCING

The Legal Aid Act 1988 excludes advice and assistance for conveyancing services except for (*a*) advice or assistance relating to a rental purchase agreement or a conditional sale agreement for the sale of land and (*b*) such conveyancing services as are necessary in order to give effect to an order of the court or agreement (reg. 3 of the Legal Advice and Assistance (Scope) Regulations 1989, p. 141).

Extension will therefore only be available for the cases which are not excluded and ordinary green form bills will not be paid where they relate to excluded work.

3. WILLS

Advice and assistance in the making of a will are excluded from being given under the Legal Aid Act 1988 except where the client is aged 70 or over, or suffers from a physical or mental handicap (or is the parent or guardian of the person suffering from such handicap for whom the client wishes to provide in the will), or is the mother or father of a minor who is living with the client, where the client is not living with the minor's other parent and the client wishes to appoint a guardian for that minor (reg. 4 of the Legal Advice & Assistance (Scope) Regulations, p. 142).

Extensions will therefore only be available for the cases which are not excluded and ordinary green form bills will not be paid where they relate to excluded work.

4. WELFARE LAW

Advice and assistance can be given about assessment of a client's entitlement to social security and other welfare benefits and for verifying an assessment by the DSS or other benefit-granting bodies such as local authorities.

5. GRANT OF REPRESENTATION TO AN ESTATE

A solicitor may give advice and assistance to a client to enable that client to make a personal application for a grant of representation but the client will be responsible for payment of the court fees.

(h) Is it reasonable to grant a solicitor authority not to enforce the green form charge?
(Legal Advice and Assistance Regulations 1989, reg. 33)
The rule is that in paying for advice and assistance the legal aid fund is only responsible for the deficiency after taking into account the client's contribution, costs paid by the other side and the charge on property recovered or preserved for the legally assisted person in connection with that matter (Legal Aid Act 1988, s.11, p. 95).

NOTE: The green form statutory charge is different from the legal aid statutory charge (see NFG 5) because:

1. There are different exemptions (see Legal Advice and Assistance Regulations 1989, Sched. 4, p. 161, compared to the Civil Legal Aid (General) Regulations, reg. 94, p. 204).

2. The green form charge is wholly handled by the solicitor who receives money or property recovered or preserved and sets it off against any deficiency he is claiming out of the legal aid fund whereas the legal aid charge involves payments in and out of the legal aid fund.

3. The Area Director has power to authorise the solicitor not to enforce the green form charge (whereas there is no power to waive the legal aid charge). The grounds are grave hardship or distress to the client or unreasonable difficulty in enforcement because of the nature of the property.

GRAVE HARDSHIP

(i) *What are the personal or financial circumstances of the client compared with the value of the money or property recovered or preserved?*

Since the hardship must be grave, the lower the value of the money or property recovered or preserved the less chance there is of grave hardship being suffered.

(ii) *What are the personal or financial circumstances of the client?*

If the client is on a low income, or even income support, authority will usually be given.

If the client is on a high income with a contribution any hardship may not be so grave as to justify authority.

(iii) *What is the value of the money or property recovered or preserved?*

If so low that enforcement would substantially diminish or wholly extinguish the benefit to the client authority might be justified. In such circumstances however the area office is also likely to take the line of disallowing the solicitor's costs on the grounds that he should have advised the client from the outset that the work would not be cost effective.

(iv) *What is the nature of any property recovered or preserved?*

If the property is an essential item such as a cooker, refrigerator, or furniture, authority will be granted.

If the property is a luxury item such as jewellery, a video or television, authority will usually be refused.

GRAVE DISTRESS

(i) *What are the circumstances in which the property has been recovered or preserved?*

If the circumstances have been distressing to the client, for example, following death, then authority will usually be granted on compassionate grounds.

(ii) *Does the property itself have any special meaning for the client?*

If the item is of genuine sentimental value, for example, a wedding ring, authority may be granted.

DIFFICULTY IN ENFORCEMENT DUE TO NATURE OF PROPERTY

(i) *What are the problems in enforcement?*

Authority will be given only where there is real difficulty as opposed to inconvenience or delay, for example where the property is outside the jurisdiction (but query should the advice and assistance have been given in the first place if difficulty in enforcement could be foreseen?).

Payment to client by mistake and the difficulty of recovering the money is not a matter for authority under regulation 33. It is a matter for the area office to consider when assessing the solicitor's costs.

1.4 Police Stations

(a) Is it reasonable to grant an extension to the costs limit in respect of a claim by a solicitor attending at a police station? (Legal Advice and Assistance Regulations 1989, reg. 4(2)(a))

OPTIONS: 1. Grant extension in whole or in part.
2. Refuse extension.

Check that the offence was arrestable (often the solicitor states it was when it was not) or a serious service offence, and that an adequate reason has been given that "the interests of justice required advice and assistance to be given as a matter of urgency," (*e.g.* age of client/physical or mental capacity/language difficulties).

Was the *extent* of advice given necessary, or excessive? (If necessary call for the solicitor's interview notes.)

NOTE: Distance between solicitor's office and police station—if it is an *own solicitor* case, should an agent or the duty solicitor have been used? (*i.e.* a common situation in some areas is that the claim for an extension to the upper limit has to be made only because of a large travelling costs claim).

1.5 Disbursements

GENERAL

Problems have arisen for practitioners, area committees, and area office staff in determining which disbursements can, subject to the appropriate limit on the costs to be incurred, be recovered under the green form scheme. Technically, the question of determining whether a disbursement is recoverable can be difficult, but it is in the interests of the public and practitioners that guidance be kept as simple as possible. Therefore, there follows a list of those disbursements which will normally be treated as recoverable under the green form scheme, provided:

(i) it is reasonable for the solicitor to incur the disbursement for the purpose of giving advice or assistance to the client; and

(ii) the amount of the disbursement is reasonable.

There also follows a list of those disbursements which are unlikely ever to be properly recoverable. In connection with disbursements which are in neither list practitioners are advised to seek advice and authority from the relevant area office.

Recoverable Disbursements	*Irrecoverable Disbursements*
Birth and other certificates	*Ad Valorem* stamp duties
Conciliation referral fees	Capital duty
Counsel's fees	Client's travelling and accommodation expenses
Enquiry agent's fees	
Experts' fees	Discharge of debts owed by the client, *e.g.* rent or mortgage arrears
Interpreters' fees	
Land Registry fees	Mortgagees' or lessors' solicitor's costs and disbursements
Newspaper advertisements	
Fees recoverable on oaths	Naturalisation fees
Photographers' accounts	Passport fees
Search fees	Fees payable on voluntary petitions in bankruptcy
Stamp duties of a nominal amount, *e.g.* the 50p paid on a power of attorney	
	Court fees
Travelling expenses of a solicitor	Probate fees

BLOOD TESTS—IMMIGRATION CASES

There are two principal classes of cases in which solicitors apply for an extension of the green form financial limit to cover the cost of blood tests to resolve an issue of paternity:

(1) *To avoid court proceedings* An extension may be granted, provided that the area office is satisfied that the parties have agreed to accept the result of the blood test as conclusive and that the costs are reasonable.

(2) *Immigration cases* In principle, the cost of blood tests is an expense which may be incurred in connection with the giving of advice and assistance to a sponsor here, whose alleged child or children abroad have applied for leave to enter the United Kingdom. The following points must be carefully noted:

(i) Entry Clearance Officers employ an extended interview procedure for dealing with difficult applications; for instance where acceptable marriage or birth certificates are not available. An extension should not normally be granted to cover the cost of obtaining blood tests at that stage, therefore, unless the solicitor certifies that, without blood tests, the available evidence is likely to be insufficient to satisfy the Entry Clearance Officer as to an alleged blood relationship upon which the application for entry hinges.

(ii) Where the blood tests are required for any appeal following the refusal of an application for entry clearance, the extension should be granted if the solicitor certifies that the blood tests are necessary to establish a blood relationship upon which the outcome of the appeal hinges, and that there are reasonable prospects that any other grounds for refusing entry can be overcome.

(iii) In the case of blood samples taken abroad, the Immigration Authorities will only accept blood tests where the samples are taken in accordance with a strict procedure. On the Indian sub-continent, facilities which comply with that procedure are only at present available in Islamabad in Pakistan and Dhaka in Bangladesh. Unless and until facilities become available in other places, applications must be refused as fruitless unless the person resident abroad can take advantage of the facilities at Islamabad or Dhaka.

(iv) Blood samples from a person who has gained entry to the United Kingdom, or who has been stopped at the port of entry, must be taken by a consultant haematologist, a medical practitioner in a Regional Blood Transfusion Centre, or an appointed blood tester. The Immigration Authorities have laid down a detailed procedure which the person taking the sample must follow.

MEDICAL REPORTS

In personal injury cases an extension for a medical report will only be granted where there is a reasonable case on liability *and* there is a real prospect of the solicitor being able to settle the case without having to issue proceedings (and hence the solicitor would not propose applying for legal aid). Where an application for legal aid has been made an extension will not be granted, unless the circumstances are exceptional, as a medical report is seldom required merely for the purpose of ascertaining whether the likely *quantum* of damages justifies the issue of proceedings.

PHOTOGRAPHS

Where a solicitor seeks an extension to take photographs in a personal injury case, in a normal "pavement trip" case it is reasonable to expect someone from the solicitor's office or the client or a friend or relative to take photographs. Such a case does not justify employing a professional photographer. A more complex case, *e.g.* a serious road or industrial accident might justify employing a professional, although this would almost invariably be done once a legal aid certificate has been issued. It would only be reasonable to justify a green form extension if, for example, the evidence to be photographed stood a real risk of disappearing. In such a case normally £50 to £60 would be reasonable for the site visit and £2 to £3 per print.

1.6 Assessment of Costs—General Principles

The solicitor is limited as to the amount of costs he can incur without obtaining an extension from the area office—£90 for advice and assistance in police stations, three hours' work at current rates of remuneration for petitioners for divorce or judicial separation, and two hours' work at current remuneration rates in other cases.

The costs of giving advice and assistance include disbursements as well as legal fees. Payment is made to the solicitor in the following order of priority: client's contribution (collected by solicitor), solicitor's charge on costs recovered from the other side and property recovered (collected by solicitor) and balance (paid out of legal aid fund).

If conditions as to availability of advice and assistance are not met (*e.g.* that the matter must be one of English law not specifically excluded by the regulations), costs out of the legal aid fund will be refused even if the amount of costs claimed is under the prospective cost limit.

Costs are assessed and paid by the Legal Aid Board.

The solicitor's charge can in certain circumstances be waived by the area office (see NFG 1.3, p. 32). If, however, the basis of the application for waiver is that enforcement would substantially diminish or wholly extinguish the benefit to the client of any property or money recovered or preserved, the area office, even if authorising the waiver, is likely to consider disallowing costs on the grounds that the solicitor should have advised the client from the outset that the work would not be cost effective.

What happens if the limit is exceeded?

A solicitor who exceeds the prescribed financial limit cannot obtain payment of the balance from the legal aid fund, nor can payment be obtained from the client on a private basis unless there has first been an application to the Area Director for an extension which has been refused, and the client, having been informed of such refusal, elects to instruct the solicitor on a private basis.

2. ASSISTANCE BY WAY OF REPRESENTATION

2.1 Statutory framework and conditions—general guide

The statutory framework for assistance by way of representation is contained in Parts I and III, sections 1, 2 and 8–13 of the Legal Aid Act 1988 (see p. 85 *et seq.*).

Details of the system are contained in the Legal Advice and Assistance (Scope) Regulations 1989 (see p. 139 *et seq.*); the Legal Advice and Assistance Regulations 1989 (p. 145 *et seq.*); the Legal Advice and Assistance (Duty Solicitor) Remuneration Regulations 1989 (p. 319 *et seq.*); and the Legal Advice and Assistance at Police Stations (Remuneration) Regulations 1989 (p. 323 *et seq.*). Assistance by way of representation is a half-way house between advice and assistance and civil legal aid.

The rules about financial eligibility and determination of eligibility are similar to advice and assistance in that the income limits are the same as advice and assistance, payment of contribution is by one payment to the solicitor who is responsible for assessing eligibility. The capital limit is, however, different, but this does not affect contribution.

ABWOR itself is akin to legal aid since it concerns representation in court and there are no predetermined limits on the amount of costs. It is however simpler than legal aid particularly when considering grant and withdrawal.

Payment is made to the solicitor in the same order of priority as in advice and assistance: client's contribution (collected by solicitor); solicitor's charge on costs recovered from the other side and property recovered (collected by solicitor) and balance (paid out of legal aid fund).

Costs are assessed and paid by the Legal Aid Board. There are powers to assess a global sum for division between solicitors and counsel where counsel has not been authorised.

2.2 Is ABWOR available for the proceedings?

YES   if the proceedings are specified in Part III of the Legal Advice and Assistance (Scope) Regulations 1989 (see p. 142). (Re-enactment of provisions specified in the Schedule are automatically effective in relation to this list by virtue of the Interpretation Act 1978.)

ABWOR is available for certain domestic and criminal proceedings in the magistrates' court; hearings in relation to application for warrants of further detention; hearings before Mental Health Review Tribunals and Boards of Prison Visitors; and hearings in the magistrates' court or county court where authority is given by the court.

NOTE:

1. There is no way to establish for what ABWOR is available other than to check the regulations.

2. The approval of ABWOR includes the cost of giving notice of appeal or applying for a case to be stated within the ordinary time for so doing and matters preliminary thereto.

2.3 Is the applicant within the financial eligibility limits?

Assistance by way of representation is part of the advice and assistance section of legal aid. The assessment of means is therefore carried out by the solicitor under the green form, preparatory to applying for ABWOR (as opposed to an assessment of means by the DSS).

The income eligibility limits for assistance by way of representation are the same as for advice and assistance (see NFG 1.2, p. 26 and the Legal Advice and Assistance Regulations 1989, p. 145 *et seq.*). Income can give rise to a contribution but the green form contribution will cover ABWOR also. The capital limit for ABWOR is however higher than for advice and assistance but not as high as for civil legal aid and it does not give rise to any contribution from capital.

If the capital assessed is above the ABWOR limit but within that of civil legal aid, an application for civil legal aid may be necessary (see NFG 4, p. 47). If that happens a fresh assessment will be needed from the DSS which may include a capital contribution element.

The procedure is that:

(i) the solicitor assesses means as if for advice and assistance;

(ii) if the client is within the advice and assistance limits, the solicitor collects any contribution and prepares and submits the application for ABWOR sending with it the green form;

(iii) if the client is outside the advice and assistance capital limit but within the ABWOR limit but his income is within the limits, the solicitor collects any contribution and submits the application for ABWOR sending with it the green form assessment;

(iv) if the client is outside the ABWOR capital limit but within the maximum civil legal aid limit, an application for civil legal aid has to be submitted to the area office with a civil legal aid means form. The matter will then be dealt with on a legal aid basis and not under ABWOR.

2.4 Is the approval of the Legal Aid Board required? (Legal Advice and Assistance Regulations 1989, reg. 22)

YES   *except for:*

(i) duty solicitor representation which is dealt with by the Legal Aid Board under general arrangements (see p. 329);

(ii) cases where either a magistrates' court or county court requests a solicitor within the precincts of the court to represent a client at a hearing that day (see the Legal Advice and Assistance (Scope) Regulations 1989, p. 139);

(iii) application for warrants of further detention or extensions of such warrants.

Otherwise an application has to be made to the appropriate Area Director for approval.

2.5 Where approval of the Area Director is required, has the applicant reasonable grounds for taking, defending or being a party to the proceedings? (Legal Advice and Assistance Regulations 1989, reg. 22(5))
YES

    (i) if the solicitor would advise the applicant to take or defend proceedings privately, *i.e.* if he had means which were adequate to meet the likely costs of the case or would make payment of the likely costs possible although something of a sacrifice;

    (ii) if the applicant shows that, as a matter of law, he has reasonable grounds for taking or defending proceedings, *i.e.* that there is a case or defence which is likely to succeed assuming the facts are proved;

    (iii) if there is an issue of fact or law which should be submitted to the court for decision.

An application must however not only satisfy this criterion on the legal merits but also the reasonableness test; see NFG 2.6.

2.6 Where approval of the Area Director is required is it reasonable in the particular circumstances of the case for approval to be granted? (Legal Advice and Assistance Regulations 1989, reg. 22(6))
Since the proceedings for which ABWOR can be granted are finite (unlike civil legal aid) comments on reasonableness have been categorised under particular proceedings following the order on page 1 of the form of application for approval of assistance by way of representation.

1 FINANCIAL PROVISION UNDER SECTION 2 OF THE DOMESTIC PROCEEDINGS AND MAGISTRATES' COURTS ACT 1978 INCLUDING CUSTODY AND ACCESS

If taking proceedings, will ABWOR be granted?
YES *unless*:

    (i) divorce proceedings are pending or are imminent, in which case it would be more appropriate for all matters to be dealt with ancillary to divorce proceedings; or

    (ii) there will be no personal benefit to the applicant or no worthwhile order is likely to be made, *e.g.* short childless marriage between relatively young people both with earning capacity or *both* parties are unemployed.

NOTE: *Personal benefit* does not necessarily have to be financial benefit, *e.g.* an applicant may need to obtain an order, albeit a nominal one, to help secure housing. ABWOR may be granted to an applicant although he/she is in receipt of benefits if the opponent is working, to allow the applicant to obtain a first-time order and to plan financially.

If defending proceedings, will ABWOR be granted?
YES *unless*:

    (i) there is no dispute between the parties on any issue. In that case representation is not necessary unless the applicant is suffering from a physical or mental disability.

2 AGREED PAYMENTS UNDER SECTION **6** OF THE DOMESTIC PROCEEDINGS AND MAGISTRATES' COURTS ACT **1978**

If taking or defending proceedings, will ABWOR be granted?
    NO   representation is unnecessary unless the ABWOR applicant needs representation because of a physical or mental disability.

3 CONFIRMATION OF VOLUNTARY PAYMENTS OR INTERIM ORDERS UNDER SECTIONS **7** AND **19** OF THE DOMESTIC PROCEEDINGS AND MAGISTRATES' COURTS ACT **1978**

If taking proceedings, will ABWOR be granted?
    YES *unless*   divorce proceedings are pending or are imminent in which case it would be more appropriate for all matters to be dealt with ancillary to divorce proceedings.

If defending proceedings, will ABWOR be granted?
    YES *unless*   there is no dispute between the parties on any issue. In that case representation is not necessary unless the ABWOR applicant is suffering from a physical or mental disability.

4 VARIATION/REVIVAL OR REVOCATION OF FINANCIAL ORDERS

If taking or defending variation proceedings, will ABWOR be granted?
    NO *unless*:

(i) the applicant is able to show that substantial personal benefit will result in the proceedings *and* the case involves more than a simple arithmetical exercise, *e.g.* one party is self-employed; or

(ii) he or she is under a physical or mental disability; or

(iii) the circumstances of the case are very exceptional in some other way.

NOTE: The fact that a court has adjourned a hearing to enable an applicant to seek ABWOR or to seek representation does not itself amount to "exceptional circumstances."

If taking or defending proceedings to revive or revoke an order, will ABWOR be granted?
    YES *unless*:

(i) divorce proceedings are pending or imminent and it is possible for the matter to be dealt with within those proceedings; or

(ii) no real personal benefit from the outcome can be shown.

5 CUSTODY/ACCESS PROCEEDINGS UNDER THE GUARDIANSHIP OF MINORS ACT **1971** AND **1973**

If taking proceedings, will ABWOR be granted?
    YES *unless*:

(i) divorce proceedings are pending or are imminent in which case it would be more appropriate for all matters to be dealt with ancillary to divorce proceedings; or

(ii) *All* matters, *i.e.* custody, access, maintenance and paternity are agreed in which case representation would not be necessary unless the applicant was suffering from a physical or mental disability.

If defending proceedings, will ABWOR be granted?
   YES *unless*:

> (i) *All* matters, *i.e.* custody, access, maintenance and paternity are agreed, in which case representation would not be necessary unless the applicant was suffering from a physical or mental disability; or

> (ii) On the issue of paternity, no reasonable grounds for defence have been shown.

6 VARIATION OF CUSTODY

If taking proceedings, will ABWOR be granted?
   YES *unless*:

> (i) divorce proceedings are pending or are imminent in which case it would be more appropriate for all matters to be dealt with ancillary to divorce proceedings; or

> (ii) *All* matters, *i.e.* custody, access and maintenance are agreed, in which case representation would not be necessary unless required because the applicant was suffering from a physical or mental disability.

If defending proceedings, will ABWOR be granted?
   YES *unless*   there is no dispute between the parties on any issue in which case representation is not necessary unless the applicant is suffering from a physical or mental disability.

7 PROTECTION/EXCLUSION ORDERS UNDER SECTION **16** OF THE DOMESTIC PROCEEDINGS AND MAGISTRATES' COURTS ACT **1978**

If taking proceedings, will ABWOR be granted?
   YES *unless*:

> (i) there have been no recent incidents or violence or serious threats of violence or no likelihood of repetition; or

> (ii) divorce proceedings are pending or are imminent in which case it *might* be more appropriate for all matters to be dealt with ancillary to divorce proceedings.

If defending proceedings, will ABWOR be granted?
   YES, *unless*:

> (i) a protection order only is being sought in which case representation is not necessary; or

> (ii) an exclusion order is sought but the respondent is already out of occupation and has no wish to return.

NOTE: In the above it may be appropriate to grant ABWOR if the applicant is suffering from a physical or mental disability.

8 GUARDIANSHIP

If taking proceedings, will ABWOR be granted?
   YES *unless*:

> (i) divorce proceedings are pending or are imminent in which case it *might* be more appropriate for the question to be determined by intervention in those proceedings; or

(ii) other relevant proceedings are or have been brought in a higher court in which case it would be more appropriate for all matters to be dealt with in those proceedings; or

(iii) there is no dispute between the parties on any issue. In such a case representation is not necessary.

If defending proceedings, will ABWOR be granted?
YES *unless*   there is no dispute between the parties on any issue. In such a case representation is not necessary unless warranted because of a physical or mental disability.

9 MENTAL HEALTH REVIEW TRIBUNAL

See NFG, para. 36, p. 78.

10 REPRESENTATION BEFORE BOARD OF PRISON VISITORS

If taking or defending proceedings, will ABWOR be granted?
YES *unless*   confirmation has not been given to the Area Director that the applicant has been permitted by the Board of Prison Visitors to be legally represented (Legal Advice and Assistance (Scope) Regulations 1989, reg. 9(b)) and/or unless it appears, for some reason, known to the Area Director, unreasonable that approval should be granted. The applicant for ABWOR does not have to show that he has reasonable grounds in the proceedings [see regulation 3(2) of the Legal Advice and Assistance (Amendment) Regulations 1990 which disapplies regulation 22(5) of the Legal Advice and Assistance Regulations 1989 to Board of Prison Visitors cases.]

11 ADOPTION

If taking proceedings, will ABWOR be granted?
YES *unless*:

(i) the matter should be dealt with in a higher court because there exists a relevant custody order made in that higher court; or

(ii) there is no dispute between the parties in which case ABWOR is not available.

If defending proceedings, will ABWOR be granted?
YES *unless*   there is no dispute between the parties, in which case ABWOR is not available.

12 CUSTODIANSHIP

If taking proceedings, will ABWOR be granted?
YES *unless*:

(i) there is in existence an order of a higher court in which case it *might* be more appropriate for the matter to be dealt with in that higher court or by way of intervention in existing proceedings; or

(ii) there is no dispute between the parties on any issue, in which case representation is not necessary.

If defending proceedings, will ABWOR be granted?
YES *unless*   there is no dispute between the parties on any issue. In such a case representation is not necessary unless it is felt necessary by virtue of a physical or mental incapacity.

13 ENFORCEMENT OF CUSTODY

ABWOR will usually be granted.

14 ENFORCEMENT OF MAINTENANCE

If taking proceedings, will ABWOR be granted?

NO   to enforce a maintenance order to recover arrears because it is the responsibility of the court to instigate such proceedings at the request of the
complainant.

If defending proceedings, will ABWOR be granted?

NO   to defend enforcement or recovery of arrears unless there are very exceptional circumstances, *e.g.* the applicant is facing a real likelihood of imprisonment or there is a substantial argument on remission of arrears.

NOTE: ABWOR is not available for representation on enforcement/arrears proceedings in respect of a registered order.

2.7 Is it reasonable to permit expenditure for experts on unusual matters? (Legal Advice and Assistance Regulations 1989, reg. 22(7))

The rule is that prior permission must be obtained from the Area Director before
expenditure is incurred on any of the following:

    (i) obtaining a report or opinion of an expert;

    (ii) tendering expert evidence;

    (iii) taking some action which is either unusual or involves unusually large
expenditure.

NOTE: 1. This provision is mandatory. Even if the court has ordered the work to
be done, *e.g.* taking a blood test, permission from the Area Director is
required.
    2. Permission cannot be granted retrospectively. It must be obtained in
advance of any work being done.
    3. If no prior permission has been obtained, payment will not be made
out of the legal aid fund.

Will such permission be given?

YES   if the expense is necessary and reasonable having regard to the nature of the
proceedings and the likely benefit to the applicant.

NO   if the client, as a privately funded client would be advised:

    (i) *NOT* to incur the expense; or

    (ii) to use a cheaper alternative, *e.g.* obtaining a report from a GP rather than a
consultant; making enquiries himself rather than employing an enquiry
agent.

NOTE: If such permission is given:

    1. An *upper limit* will be stated in the permission. For this the legal aid offices
use the guidance for taxing/determining officers issued annually by the Lord
Chancellor's Department for Crown Court cases.

    2. Sometimes area offices will, as well as stating the upper limit for obtaining a
report or opinion of an expert, indicate in a covering letter the daily or
half-daily rate which would be allowed for such an expert to tender evidence.
This is intended to help the solicitor to avoid a situation where he might
become committed to an expert whose fee for a report is reasonable but whose
fee for court attendance may turn out later to be unreasonable.

SPECIAL CASES

Enquiry Agents   Normally an enquiry agent's fees will not be permitted. He is not an expert, nor are his services unusual in their nature. The only category within which such fees could be permitted is unusually large expenditure if for example the where-abouts of a respondent need to be traced.

Blood Tests   See NFG 1.5, p. 34.

Mental Health Review Tribunal   Permission for an independent psychiatric report will usually be granted if the responsible medical officer's report contains recommendations which are not acceptable to the client.

2.8 Does the proper conduct of the proceedings require counsel? (Legal Advice and Assistance Regulations 1989, reg. 23)

The rule is that where assistance by way of representation has been granted and the solicitor thinks that the proper conduct of proceedings requires counsel, he may apply to the Area Director for approval.

NOTE: The result of not obtaining permission or of having permission refused is that costs will be assessed on the basis of the solicitor having conducted the case on his own, rather than a separate assessment of counsel's fee as would happen where approval has been given (Legal Advice and Assistance Regulations 1989, reg. 29(5) and (6), p. 56).

Will approval be given?

YES   if the case poses unusually complex evidential problems or novel or difficult points of law.

NO

    (i) if the reason for instructing counsel is:

        (*a*) that the case is contested, protracted or involves the cross-examination of witnesses or arguments on points of law;

        (*b*) the personal circumstances or convenience of the solicitor;

        (*c*) that the other side is represented by counsel.

    (ii) if it would be more appropriate to instruct a solicitor agent.

2.9 Should ABWOR be withdrawn? (Legal Advice and Assistance Regulations 1989, reg. 25)

The rule is that the Area Director is required to withdraw approval of ABWOR where he considers that the client no longer has reasonable grounds for taking, defending or being a party to the proceedings or continuing to do so; or that the client has required the proceedings to be conducted unreasonably so as to incur an unjustifiable expense to the legal aid fund or it is unreasonable for ABWOR to continue.

NOTES: On withdrawal the solicitor has to serve notice on his client, the court and other parties to the proceedings but withdrawal is no bar to future applications for assistance by way of representation.

There is an appeal to the area committee (Legal Advice and Assistance Regulations 1989, reg. 26, p.155). If the appeal is successful the solicitor has to serve another notice on the court and other parties to the proceedings.

The Area Director can act on information from any source—including the opponent. These grounds are the equivalent to the legal aid powers to discharge on merits (Civil Legal Aid (General) Regulations 1989, reg. 77, p. 199). There is no equivalent in ABWOR to the legal aid system of revocation or to the legal aid "show cause" procedure.

Will ABWOR be withdrawn?
YES

   (i) if information comes to light which if known at the time would have meant that the original application for ABWOR would have been refused;

   (ii) if circumstances have changed so that the applicant no longer has reasonable grounds for continuing or prospects of success;

  (iii) if the client is dead;

  (iv) if the solicitor is without instructions;

   (v) if the client has had a reconciliation with the opponent;

  (vi) if the client refuses to accept advice not to proceed;

 (vii) if the client has failed to pay his contribution;

(viii) if the client has had a financial windfall and can afford to continue the proceedings at his own expense;

  (ix) if the client consents; and

   (x) if there is any other good reason.

3. EMERGENCY CIVIL LEGAL AID APPLICATIONS

3.1 Will an applicant as a matter of urgency be granted civil legal aid? (Civil Legal Aid (General) Regulations 1989, regs. 19–25)

The rule is that any person who desires civil legal aid, as a matter of urgency, may apply to the Area Director.

The Area Director has power to issue a temporary or provisional certificate, known as an "emergency certificate" immediately without waiting for an assessment of means from the DSS.

He can only exercise that power if he has sufficient information to show the nature of the proceedings, the circumstances in which legal aid is required, and to be satisfied that the applicant is likely to fulfil the conditions under which full legal aid may be granted. This means that a full application giving all this information has to be submitted at the same time as the application for an emergency certificate. Details of the criteria governing the grant of full legal aid are set out in NFG 4, p. 47).

In addition, in emergency cases the Area Director must be satisfied that it is in the interests of justice that the applicant should, as a matter of urgency, be granted legal aid before issuing an emergency certificate. The following matters will fall to be considered under this head:

(a) *Is there a hearing date before expiry of the time a full legal aid application would take to process, and, if so, would an adjournment be possible without undue difficulty to the applicant, the opponent or the court?*

If **YES**   an emergency certificate is not appropriate; the adjournment should be arranged and the full application for a substantive certificate take its course.

(b) *Has there been any delay on the part of the solicitor or the applicant which has helped to create the emergency?*

If **YES**   it may not be reasonable to grant an emergency certificate.

(c) *Is the applicant's liberty threatened?*

If **YES**   it will almost always be in the interests of justice for the emergency certificate to be granted.

(d) *Would any delay cause the risk of miscarriage of justice, or unreasonable hardship to the applicant, or exceptional problems in handling the case?*

If **YES**   it will almost always be in the interests of justice for the emergency certificate to be granted.

3.2 What does an applicant have to know about emergency legal aid?

The applicant must be told:

(i) an emergency certificate is only intended to help an applicant about urgent matters and will not be a substitute for full legal aid, even if there is no limitation on condition on the certificate;

(ii) the applicant's means will still have to be assessed by the DSS so:

(a) if the applicant does not co-operate, this may result not only in no grant of full legal aid but also in withdrawal of the emergency certificate. This could mean the applicant having to pay all the legal costs personally,

(b) if the applicant turns out to be outside the eligibility limits or fails to pay any contribution, again the emergency legal aid may be withdrawn and the applicant may have to pay; and

(iii) the emergency certificate will normally only cover urgent legal work. It is no use the applicant expecting the solicitor to run the whole case on emergency legal aid.

3.3 Some examples of decisions in emergency cases

1 INJUNCTION—NON-MOLESTATION (DIVORCE AND JUDICIAL SEPARATION)

Emergency certificates for taking proceedings

Grant if there has been recent serious physical violence which is likely to be repeated—either to applicant or children.

Refuse

(i) if the injunction is not necessary because the respondent is already under an obligation not to molest (*e.g.* as a result of bail conditions in criminal proceedings);

(ii) if the incident complained of is merely anti-social behaviour or involves only damage to property.

Emergency certificates for defending proceedings

Grant

(i) if there are serious allegations claimed wholly or substantially;

(ii) if there is any question of inability to defend (*e.g.* because of illiteracy, mental handicap);

(iii) if there is a real danger of the respondent going to prison.

Refuse if the matter can be dealt with by undertakings being given.

2 INJUNCTION—OUSTER (DIVORCE AND JUDICIAL SEPARATION)

Emergency certificates for taking proceedings

Grant

(i) if in addition to the criteria under non-molestation (above) the applicant is in a refuge or temporary accommodation having been recently excluded from the house;

(ii) the applicant is the owner of the house from which the respondent is to be evicted;

(iii) the interests of the children require sole occupation of the house.

Refuse

(i) if the respondent has already left voluntarily and does not wish to return;

(ii) if the applicant left voluntarily and there is no real danger in returning without the protection of an injunction;

(iii) if the applicant has been out of occupation for some time (*e.g.* over 10 days).

Emergency certificates for defending proceedings

Grant if in addition to the criteria under non-molestation above there has been an *ex parte* ouster order made with no opportunity for the respondent to contest the issues.

Refuse if the respondent has left voluntarily and there is no good reason to return.

3 INJUNCTIONS—ASSAULT & TRESPASS (COMMON LAW)

NOTE: These injunctions, which are the only remedies available to those who are not married or living together as husband and wife, have to be framed in the county court as part of an action for damages. An emergency certificate will be limited to the steps necessary to obtain an injunction. Pursuit of the claim for damages will be considered as part of the substantive application only.

Emergency certificates for taking proceedings
Grant   in the same circumstances as for non-molestation injunction.
Refuse   in the same circumstances as for non-molestation injunction.

Emergency certificates for defending proceedings
Grant   in the same circumstances as for non-molestation injunctions.
Refuse   in the same circumstances as for non-molestation injunctions.

4 CUSTODY (MARRIED)

Emergency certificates for taking proceedings
Usually **Grant**   where child has been taken by the parent who does not have care and control.
Usually **Refuse**   if other parent has had *de facto* care of the child for some time, with no evidence of ill-treatment.

Emergency certificates for defending proceedings
Usually **grant**   unless the behaviour has been particularly unreasonable, *i.e.* that no reasonable explanation has been given for taking or failing to return the child.

5 CUSTODY (UNMARRIED)

Emergency certificates for taking proceedings
Usually **grant**   when the child has been taken by father, but an enquiry may be made as to whether any attempt has been made to collect the child.

Emergency certificates for defending proceedings
Usually **grant**   unless the behaviour has been particularly unreasonable, *i.e.* that no reasonable explanation has been given for taking or failing to return the child.

6 WARDSHIP

Emergency certificates for taking proceedings
Grant
  (i) if there is a threat to remove child from jurisdiction particularly if there is a likelihood of the child's passport being snatched or the chance of putting the child on the respondent's passport;
  (ii) if there is a threat of serious ill-treatment or neglect.

Refuse
  (i) if ordinary custody proceedings will provide sufficient protection;
  (ii) the child is in care.

Emergency certificates for defending proceedings
Usually **grant**   unless the behaviour has been particularly unreasonable, *i.e.* that no reasonable explanation has been given for taking or failing to return the child.

46

4. CIVIL LEGAL AID

4.1 Statutory framework and conditions—general guide

The statutory framework for civil legal aid is contained in Parts I and IV, sections 1, 2, and 14–18 of the Legal Aid Act 1988 (see p. 85 *et seq.*).

Details of the system are set out in the Civil Legal Aid (Matrimonial Proceedings) Regulations 1989 (see p. 137 *et seq.*); the Civil Legal Aid (General) Regulations 1989 (see p. 165 *et seq.*); and the Civil Legal Aid (Assessment of Resources) Regulations 1989 (see p. 231 *et seq.*).

The general principle of Part IV of the Legal Aid Act 1988 is that representation for specific proceedings is available to any person whose financial resources make him/her eligible, subject to such person satisfying the Board that he/she has reasonable grounds for taking, defending or being a party to proceedings which come within the Act, and that it is reasonable for representation to be granted.

Schedule 2 to the Act specifies the proceedings for which legal aid is available (see p. 123 *et seq.*). The Act defines the general scope of civil legal aid. Details of the system are set out in the regulations.

The Act uses new terminology. It specifies "representation" in civil courts and criminal courts instead of civil legal aid and criminal legal aid. The latter descriptions have been retained from the previous system for the purposes of these Notes for Guidance (and they still appear in the Act in the headings to Parts IV and V).

4.2 Matters for consideration by area offices on receipt of applications for legal aid

(a) Is civil legal aid available for the proceedings? (Legal Aid Act 1988, s.14)

The rule is that civil legal aid is a statutory system. Unless the application comes within the statutory provisions, civil legal aid will not be available. So the first basic question which every caseworker asks on receipt of an application is whether it comes within the system.

The availability of civil legal aid is defined normally by the court or other body which hears the proceedings. It is a matter which a solicitor should consider before submitting an application for legal aid. So the answers to the question of whether or not civil legal aid is available are:

YES

    (i) if the proceedings are in courts specified in Part I, paras. 1 and 2 of Schedule 2 to the Legal Aid Act 1988 (see p. 123);

    (ii) if the proceedings are before any of the tribunals specified in Part I of Schedule 2 to the Legal Aid Act 1988 (see p. 123), namely Employment Appeal Tribunal, Lands Tribunal and Commons Commissioners;

    (iii) if the proceedings are before the Restrictive Practices Court under Part III of the Fair Trading Act 1973 (Part I, para. 6 of Schedule 2 to the Legal Aid Act 1988, see p. 124);

NO

    (i) if the proceedings are excepted under Part II of Schedule 2 to the Legal Aid Act 1988 (see p. 124) namely, defamation (apart from defending a counter claim); relator actions; recover of penalties; election petitions; county court judgment summonses and other county court matters where only the time and mode of payment are in issue;

    (ii) if the proceedings are before a Coroners Court or the Court of Protection (not part of the court system mentioned in Part I of Schedule 2 to the Legal Aid Act 1988 (above);

    (iii) generally for undefended divorce (Civil Legal Aid (Matrimonial Proceedings) Regulations 1989, p. 137 *et seq.*; see, however, those regulations for restricted cases where legal aid may be available);

    (iv) for a grant of representation unless it is necessary to enable a legally aided action to be brought (Civil Legal Aid (General) Regulations 1989, reg. 46, p. 189);

(v) if proceedings are before an arbitrator except for a county court reference to arbitration, (but the existence of an arbitration clause in an insurance policy is not necessarily a bar to legal aid being granted where insurers are bound by the British Insurance Association and Lloyds Underwriters agreement 1956).

(b) Is the applicant a person to whom legal aid can be granted? (Legal Aid Act 1988, s.14)

The rule is that civil legal aid is available to "any person" subject to and in accordance with the Act.

The second general question which area staff have to answer therefore is whether the applicant is a person to whom legal aid can be granted. This is another matter the solicitor should bear in mind when submitting an application for legal aid since the application must be refused if the applicant is not within this category.

So the answers to whether the applicant is a person to whom legal aid can be granted are:

YES

    (i) if the applicant is an individual;

    (ii) if the applicant is a partner or member of a firm since a firm or partnership is not a body corporate or incorporate;

NO if the applicant is a body of persons corporate or unincorporate unless that body is concerned only in a representative fiduciary or official capacity (Legal Aid Act 1988, s.2(10), p. 90), *i.e.* where such a body would be exempt from any assessment of means.

4.3 Is the applicant within the financial eligibility limits?

See Eligibility Tables, pp. 9–12.

4.4 Has the applicant reasonable grounds for taking, defending or being a party to the proceedings (the legal merits test)? (Legal Aid Act 1988, s.15(2))

The rule is that a person shall not be granted civil legal aid for the purpose of any proceedings unless he satisfies the Board (*i.e.* the Area Director/area committee) that he has reasonable grounds for taking, defending or being a party to the proceedings.

This is the legal merits test. The use of the word "reasonable" in both this and the second test (the reasonableness test) may at first sight be confusing but for this test it means reasonable grounds for taking proceedings or reasonable grounds for being a party to proceedings rather than an overall concept of "reasonableness."

The Area Director must be satisfied that on the facts put forward and the law which relates to them, there is a case or defence which should be put before a court for a decision. The Area Director must assume for this purpose that the facts are proved. He/she sees only one side of the case, and is in no position to adjudicate on issues. The likelihood of success is also a factor which the Area Director must bear in mind but it is of the essence of litigation that there are two opposing points of view on which the court is required to adjudicate. Litigation is also notoriously uncertain so that any attempt to restrict legal aid to certainties or near certainties or even those cases with a probability of success would not only be doomed to failure (if the aim was 100 per cent. success rate) but would also be a denial to many applicants of an opportunity to obtain justice.

The aim therefore must be to achieve a balance between being over-cautious and not granting legal aid for cases where there is little or no hope of success. If legal aid is granted in hopeless cases it raises the expectations of assisted persons too high, forces opponents to defend their rights and wastes public money, perhaps doubly if costs are awarded against the fund. The decision is therefore one of balance. The consistent overall marker of an average success rate in the region of 85 per cent. over a number of years indicates the balance that has been struck.

So the answer to the question of whether there are reasonable grounds to proceed is:
YES

    (i) if there is an issue of fact or law which should be submitted to the court for a decision;

    (ii) if the solicitor would advise the applicant to take or defend proceedings privately, *i.e.* if he had means which were adequate to meet the likely costs of the case or would make payment of the likely costs possible although something of a sacrifice;

    (iii) if the applicant shows that, as a matter of law, he has reasonable grounds for taking or defending proceedings, i.e. that there is a case or defence which is likely to succeed, assuming the facts are proved.

An application must however not only satisfy this criterion on the legal merits but also the reasonableness test (see next section, NFG 4.5).

4.5 Is it reasonable in the particular circumstances of the case for the applicant to be granted civil legal aid (the reasonableness test)? (Legal Aid Act, s.15(3))

The rule is that a person may be refused legal aid if in the particular circumstances of the case if appears to the Board (*i.e.* the Area Director/area committee) unreasonable that it should be granted or more appropriate that ABWOR should be granted. This rule is in addition to and not an alternative to the legal merits test. The discretion is wide on the face of it but there are well recognised circumstances in which the decision has to be made, and the most common cases are set out below.

The question that has to be asked is whether it is reasonable for legal aid to be used (it has been framed in the positive form to avoid the use of double negatives in the answers) and the answers are as follows:
NO

    (i) if the application reveals some illegal motive or the conduct of the applicant is such as to be unacceptable to the court (but moral character on its own should not be a bar to grant);

    (ii) if the benefit to be achieved does not justify the costs of the proceedings (*e.g.* small claims) *but* this factor may be outweighed by the importance of the case; loss of a roof over one's head (housing rent arrears cases); loss of status, dignity or reputation (race relations, equal opportunities cases); the defence in a divorce case on the grounds that although the marriage has broken down the serious allegations by the petitioner are untrue;

    (iii) if the applicant has other rights and facilities making it unnecessary for him/her to obtain legal aid or has a reasonable expection of obtaining financial or other help from a body of which he is a member, *e.g.*:

        Trade Union;
        Commission for Racial Equality;
        Equal Opportunities Commission;
        AA/RAC, etc.;
        Estate (probate action);
        Firm where applicant is a member of a firm; but the terms and conditions including adequacy of alternative funding may be a crucial factor;

    (iv) if a solicitor would not normally be employed in such proceedings, *e.g.* arithmetical calculations in variation proceedings; mortgage arrears; application to suspend warrant of possession or execution; application for extra time to meet High Court judgment; application to register county court or High Court maintenance order in magistrates' court.
    [NOTE: A green form extension may be appropriate.]

(v) if the proceedings should be taken in a court other than the one specified in the application, *i.e.* where costs are lower but the proceedings still meet the needs of the applicant. This can apply in, *e.g.*;

maintenance
custody
adoption
protection;

(vi) if ABWOR is available for the proceedings and is more appropriate. This can only arise where both ABWOR and civil legal aid are available for the proceedings which will give the applicant the same remedies and the applicant is financially eligible under both schemes. ABWOR will be the choice because it is simpler and less expensive. The most common choice is between remedies relating to exclusion and protection orders in the magistrates' court as opposed to injunctions and exclusion orders in the High Court and the county court. If the magistrates' court proceedings give the applicant the protection he/she needs then it may be unreasonable to grant legal aid for High Court or county court proceedings, but reasonable to direct the applicant towards ABWOR;

(vii) if the defendant has no means to satisfy any judgment against him/her;

(viii) if the applicant would get no personal benefit out of the proceedings.

4.6 Do persons other than the applicant have an interest? (Civil Legal Aid (General) Regulations 1989, reg. 32)

When considering a civil legal aid application, the Area Director/area committee must take into account, in addition to the usual legal merits and reasonableness tests, whether there are persons with the same interest in the proceedings as the applicant.

If the application does not satisfy the merits test it will be refused in the normal way. If the application does satisfy the merits tests the first question that has to be asked is whether the other persons who have an interest are parties to the proceedings:

YES Regulation 32 will not normally be invoked since, in accordance with the usual taxation rules, costs will be apportioned and only those items which are solely attributable to the assisted person, together with a proportion of those costs which are common to all the parties, will be allowed against the legal aid fund.

NO

(i) the Area Director/area committee must consider whether the other persons have the "same" interest as the applicant as distinct from merely a "similar" interest. If they do not have the "same" interest, regulation 32 will not be invoked;

(ii) for persons to have the "same" interest, each person involved must be seeking an identical outcome to the proceedings, *e.g.* an order, injunction or declaration which would benefit each person without the need for them to issue separate proceedings;

(iii) persons seeking damages will not have the "same" interest, even if the claims arise from a single event, where the award of damages would be individual to each plaintiff and would vary with their personal circumstances;

(iv) there may be cases involving a number of persons where they have both the "same" and "similar" interests, *e.g.* an application for an order that the common parts of a block of flats be restored to their former state (the "same" interest) and an order that damages be paid to each plaintiff (a "similar" interest). Regulation 32 will only be invoked where the main purpose is to pursue the "same" interest claim.

If the other persons have the "same" interest the next question to be considered by the Area Director/area committee is whether the rights of the applicant would be substantially prejudiced by refusal of the application:

(i) if **NO** the application will be refused. The main factor when considering potential prejudice is whether other members of the interested group would proceed if legal aid were not granted. If either the other persons are not numerous, or the court has no power to authorise a representative action the Area Director will deal with the application by way of consideration of contributions from the others rather than refusal (see below);

(ii) if **YES** the application will be approved.

Where the application is approved, the Area Director must then consider whether it is reasonable that other persons having the "same" interest should contribute to the cost of the proceedings:

(i) if the applicant stands to gain significant personal benefit, no contribution from the others will be sought;

(ii) if a contribution is called for it will be based, if possible, on an assessment of the other person's means but, if not, on a proportional division of the estimated costs of the proceedings. Payment of the contribution together with any contribution payable by the applicant will be made one of the conditions of the offer of legal aid;

(iii) if the applicant has, without success, taken all reasonable steps to collect the contribution, the Area Director has power to redetermine the amount of any additional contribution.

5 THE STATUTORY CHARGE

5.1 Statutory authority and framework

The statutory provisions relating to the charge are contained in section 16 of the Legal Aid Act 1988 (see p. 99) and Part XI of the Civil Legal Aid (General) Regulations 1989 (see p. 202).

The underlying principle of the charge is to put the legally assisted person as far as possible in the same position in relation to proceedings as an unassisted person, whose first responsibility at the end of the proceedings is to pay whatever legal costs are not being paid by the other side. It prevents an assisted person from making a profit at the expense of legal aid and is a deterrent to running up costs unreasonably.

It is one of three financial obligations imposed on assisted person:

(i) to pay any assessed contribution out of income or capital;

(ii) to pay what the court considers reasonable towards the other side's costs; and

(iii) to pay his/her own legal costs out of any money or property recovered or preserved (the charge).

The application forms contain warnings about the effect of the charge, but the Board is firmly of the view that it is the solicitor's responsibility to ensure that the client is kept fully informed about the implications throughout the case.

As with all legal aid payments the solicitor's costs and counsel's fees are paid out of the legal aid fund, not out of the charge. The solicitor and counsel must therefore still look to the legal aid fund for payment even though the client may bear the ultimate responsibility.

5.2 Has the assisted person been successful wholly or in part in the proceedings or obtained an out of court settlement with the benefit of legal aid?

NO   the statutory charge cannot arise.

YES   the charge may arise so the remaining questions need to be considered.

5.3 Is there a net liability of the Legal Aid Board on the assisted person's account in respect of any proceedings?

(a) Calculate the total costs paid or payable to solicitor(s) and counsel on behalf of the assisted person, including green form costs for advice and assistance given in the same matter.

NOTE: When considering what sums are payable by the Board "in respect of any proceedings" remember:

1. "Proceedings" in matrimonial cases means the whole proceedings, *i.e.* action, cause or matter. So, if there is a transfer of property in one section of the proceedings the charge on that property will cover the costs of any other part of the proceedings for which legal aid was granted.

2. Where there is more than one legal aid certificate for related matters, proceed- ings are separate for the purpose of calculating the amount of the charge. There is no rollover from money or property recovered in one set of proceed- ings to cover the costs of any other proceedings.

3. Proceedings do not have to have been commenced. If a settlement is reached either before or during proceedings the charge will affect all property received by the assisted person whether or not it was claimed in the potential or actual proceedings.

(b) Having reached a decision on the total amount payable out of the legal aid fund, calculate the amount of costs (if any) paid by the other side.

NOTE: Does *(b)* exceed or equal *(a)*? If so there is *no* net liability and no charge. If *(a)* exceeds *(b)* then:

(c) Calculate the amount of the assisted person's legal aid contribution paid.

NOTE: Does the total of *(b)* and *(c)* exceed or equal *(a)*? If so, there is *no* net liability and no charge. If *(a)* still exceeds *(b)* and *(c)* there *is* a net liability and the charge may arise in respect of the balance.

5.4 Has money or property been "recovered" or "preserved" out of which the net liability can be met in whole or in part?

NO   the charge does not arise.

YES   the charge does arise.

What is "recovery"?

It is where the assisted person succeeds in claiming ownership of someone else's property or possession of his own property, *i.e.* at the end of the day there is a *gain* for the assisted person.

What is "preservation"?

It is where the assigning person succeeds in fending off a claim by someone else to his (the assisted person's) property or to possession of that other person's property, *i.e.* at the end of the day the assisted person keeps all or part of what he regards as his own.

NOTE: In either case:

1. Property includes money.

2. The property or money must have been the subject matter of the proceedings (but if a settlement is reached either before or during proceedings the charge will affect all property received by the assisted person whether or not it was claimed in the actual or potential proceedings (*Van Hoorn* v. *The Law Society* [1985] Q.B. 106).

3. The words mean the same as in the Solicitors' Acts 1934–1974, under which a solicitor may be able to obtain a charging order on property which he recovered or preserved for his client.

5.5 Does the case come within any of the exemptions?

There is no short cut to looking at the detailed exemptions set out in regulation 94 of the Civil Legal Aid (General) Regulations 1989 (see p. 204). They must be considered in each case.

NOTE:

1. The exemption for interim payments only applies while the payments remain interim. Once the final award of damages is made, interim damages are included in the calculation for the statutory charge.

2. Some of the exemptions in matrimonial proceedings relate solely to awards between spouses, so will not apply to awards made to intervening parties.

5.6 Enforcement

PROPERTY

Will the house have to be sold to pay the charge straightaway?

NO if the case comes within regulation 97 of the Civil Legal Aid (General) Regulations 1989 (see p. 207) *i.e.* the proceedings are under the Married Women's Property Act 1882, Matrimonial Causes Act 1973 or Inheritance (Provision for Family and Dependants) Act 1975 *and* the property is intended to be used as a home for the assisted person or his/her dependants:

(i) enforcement can be postponed and a charge registered against the property on payment of simple interest of 12 per cent. per annum;

(ii) payment will be made as and when the property is sold or the assisted person can make other arrangements to pay the amount due.

YES if the property is recovered or preserved in any other proceedings and the assisted person cannot raise the money in any other way to pay the Legal Aid Board.

MONEY

Will any money recovered or preserved have to be paid to the Legal Aid Board?

NO if the case comes within regulation 96 of the Civil Legal Aid (General) Regulations 1989 (see p. 206) *i.e* the proceedings are under the Married Women's Property Act 1882, Matrimonial Causes Act 1973 or Inheritance (Provision for Family and Dependants) Act 1975, *and* the money is by virtue of an order of the court or an agreement to be used to purchase a home for the assisted person or his/her dependants.

The charge can be registered against the new home, with payment of interest (see regulation 96 for full details of the report made to the Area Director).

YES   in any other case—all the money must be paid to the Legal Aid Board forthwith unless it is obvious that the money recovered or preserved will be more than the likely amount of the costs. In that case the solicitor can estimate the amount of costs, pay that amount to the Legal Aid Board with an undertaking that his or her bill will not exceed that amount. If the Area Director is satisfied that the fund will be safeguarded, the balance can be released to the assisted person; but the solicitor will not be paid more than the amount in the undertaking (Civil Legal Aid (General) Regulations 1989, reg. 90, p. 203).

WHEN DOES THE DUTY TO REPORT ARISE?

In the case of either property or money, the solicitor has a duty to inform the Area Director as soon as possible about money or property recovered or preserved so that the office can take adequate steps to enforce the charge and safeguard the fund.

DOES THE BOARD HAVE POWER TO TRANSFER THE CHARGE TO A SUBSTITUTED PROPERTY?

YES   the Board has all the power of a mortgagee but it is a discretion which will only be exercised in the following circumstances:

(i) there must be an existing charge registered against the original property;

(ii) the assisted person must satisfy the Board that:

the new property will have sufficient equity to meet the amount of the charge; and
the sale is necessary for reasons of health disability or employment; or
the new property is to be used as the sole residence of the assisted person with at least one dependent child living at home; and
a refusal to transfer the charge would cause hardship to the assisted person.

(iii) If there is a balance of proceeds of sale left after purchasing the new property this must be paid to the Board in part satisfaction of the charge.

DOES THE BOARD HAVE POWER TO WAIVE THE CHARGE ALTOGETHER?

NO   there is no power to waive the legal aid charge (as compared with the advice and assistance charge where it can be waived on the grounds of hardship).

5.7 Does the Board have power to refuse to pay solicitors' costs?

YES   the Board has power to defer payment of the solicitors' costs if there has been a loss to the fund because the solicitor has failed to comply with regulations.

(i) Regulation 102 of the Civil Legal Aid (General) Regulations 1989 provides that where an assisted person's solicitor has failed to comply with any provision of these regulations and as a result of his default or omission the fund incurs a loss:

(a) the appropriate area committee may defer payment of all or part of the solicitor's profit costs in connection with the proceedings to which the certificate relates until he has complied with such provisions; and

(b) if the Board refers the conduct of the solicitor to the Solicitors' Disciplinary Tribunal and the solicitor is disciplined, the Board may retain any sum, payment of which has been deferred under sub-paragraph (a), in accordance with the finding of the Tribunal.

(ii) The only profit costs, payment of which may be deferred, are those arising under the legal aid certificate in connection with which the solicitor's default or omission has occurred.

(iii) Payment of a solicitor's profit costs will, normally, only be deferred if he has failed to comply with any of the provisions in Part XI of the Civil Legal Aid (General) Regulations 1989.

(iv) As regulation 102 is compensatory, not punitive, deferment will not be of an amount in excess of the loss to the fund. The loss to the fund may comprise:

(a) the net liability of the fund as defined in section 16(9) of the Legal Aid Act 1988;

(b) any additional costs incurred by the legal aid fund, *e.g.* under regulation 91(1) of the Civil Legal Aid General Regulations; and

(c) the amount of any costs caught by section 16(5) of the Legal Aid Act 1988.

SPECIAL CASES

In some cases, where the solicitor has been in breach of statutory duty or negligent, proceedings may have to be taken against him. Even in such cases:

(i) counsel's fees will be paid; but

(ii) payment of disbursements may be withheld as credit against the claim for damages (withholding payment of disbursements in this way is not, however, deferring payment under regulation 102 of the Civil Legal Aid (General) Regulations 1989).

FAILURE TO COMPLY WITH REGULATION 90 OF THE CIVIL LEGAL AID (GENERAL) REGULATIONS 1989 (NOTIFICATION TO THE BOARD)

The most common default or omission giving rise to the application of regulation 102 is failure to comply with regulation 90. When considering regulation 90 it should be borne in mind that:

(i) property (which includes monies and costs) is recovered or preserved at the moment an action is disposed of either by compromise or judgment. It is at that moment that the statutory charge attaches. It continues to attach unless and until the judgment is reversed on appeal; and

(ii) regulation 90(1)(a) requires an assisted person's solicitor to inform the area director forthwith of any property (including monies and costs) recovered or preserved. This obligation to report arises immediately there is a compromise or judgment which gives rise to recovery or preservation.

HAS THERE BEEN A LOSS TO THE FUND?

Payment of profit costs will not be deferred under regulation 102 unless there has been a loss to the fund. This may depend upon whether (a) money or (b) other property was originally subject to the charge and whether the discretion to transfer the charge to substituted property would have arisen and been exercised:

MONIES (INCLUDING COSTS) SUBJECT TO THE STATUTORY CHARGE AND COSTS PAYABLE TO THE LEGAL AID FUND UNDER SECTION 16(5) OF THE LEGAL AID ACT 1988:

(i) where a solicitor does not report forthwith that monies were recovered or preserved under a compromise or order, and, as a result of the delay, the compromise or order is rendered worthless, there has been a loss to the fund;

(ii) where monies are recovered or preserved and paid to the assisted person or a third party, who dissipates them, there has been a loss to the fund;

(iii) where monies are recovered or preserved and not dissipated but used for the purchase of property, even if a charge or caution can be registered against that property, there has been a loss to the fund which has been deprived of its right to immediate enforcement. The loss to the fund can be made good when the property is sold and the solicitor can, then, be paid his profit costs.

PROPERTY (OTHER THAN MONIES OR COSTS) SUBJECT TO THE STATUTORY CHARGE

(i) Where property is recovered or preserved, but the solicitor does not report that fact forthwith and, as a result of the delay, the assisted person is able to sell the property and dissipate the proceeds, there has been a loss to the fund.

(ii) Where property is recovered or preserved but is then sold and the proceeds invested in new property against which a charge or caution can be registered then, if the circumstances pertaining when the original property was recovered or preserved were not such as to fall within the guidelines for exercise of the discretion to transfer the charge to substituted property, there may have been a loss to the fund. This will be a question of fact and whether, had the position been clear to the assisted person, he would have gone ahead with the transaction or not.

(iii) Where property is recovered or preserved as in (ii) above, but the circumstances are such that, although the discretion to transfer the charge to substituted property could have been exercised, as a matter of fact it would not have been exercised, there may have been a loss to the fund. Again (as in (ii) above) this is a question of fact.

(iv) Where property has been recovered or preserved as in (ii) above, but the circumstances are such as to fall within the guidelines for the exercise of the discretionary power to transfer the charge to substituted property, and the discretion would have been exercised in favour of the assisted person had the opportunity been given, there has been no loss to the fund.

REGISTRATION OF A CHARGE OR CAUTION WHEN PAYMENT OF PROFIT COSTS HAS BEEN DEFERRED

Where a charge against property is registered (perhaps with the assisted person's consent) in a case where payment of the solicitor's profit costs is being deferred because there has been a loss to the fund, the amount of the charge includes the amount of profit costs, payment of which has been deferred. The fund will be obliged to pay the profit costs when the loss to the fund has been made good. This will generally be upon the sale of the charged property.

BREACH OF STATUTORY DUTY OR NEGLIGENCE BY SOLICITOR

Solicitors sometimes recognise that their actions have caused loss to the fund and that, as a result, legal aid may have a cause of action against them. The legal aid office may well ask the solicitor to make good the loss. Counsel must still be paid out of the fund so, to make good the loss, the solicitor would have to send a cheque to cover counsel's fees and any payments on account which have been made (and, if his own profit costs have already been paid, a sum sufficient to satisfy the balance of the deficiency in the legal aid fund). This is entirely separate from the procedure under regulation 102.

6 APPLICATIONS FOR LEGAL AID FOR APPEALS

(a) Appeals to the House of Lords or appeals from magistrates' courts
Even where the proceedings in the court below were legally aided, a fresh application for a new certificate must be submitted to make or defend an appeal to the House of Lords or an appeal from a magistrates' court (Civil Legal Aid (General) Regulations 1989, reg. 46(2)).

(b) Other appeals

Where the proceedings in the court below have been legally aided, the certificate may be amended to include making or defending an appeal or making an interlocutory appeal, and applications for an amendment should be made to the appropriate Area Director as soon as possible. The defence of an interlocutory appeal is regarded as being included within the scope of the original certificate.

If there is no existing certificate covering proceedings in the court below, a full application must be made in respect of the appellate proceedings.

(c) Distinction between final and interlocutory appeals

The Notes to Order 59, rule 4 of the Rules of the Supreme Court deal with the distinction between final and interlocutory appeals and final and interlocutory orders. The test applied in *Bozson* v. *Altrincham U.D.C.* [1903] 1 K.B. 547 required the final order to dispose of the rights of the parties finally.

However a unanimous Court of Appeal held in *Salter Rex & Co.* v. *Ghosh* [1971] 2 Q.B. 597 that the test lies in the nature of the application made to the court rather than the order made (see also *White* v. *Brunton* [1984] Q.B. 570).

Orders for ancillary relief made in the Family Division are always interlocutory.

7 APPEALS TO THE DIVISIONAL COURT OF THE FAMILY DIVISION

Since the period of six weeks, prescribed by the Rules of the Supreme Court for serving notice and entering an appeal to the Divisional Court of the Family Division, frequently elapses before a certificate can be obtained, it is inevitable that many such appeals are out of time. To avoid this difficulty prompt notification should be given to the opposite side of the intention to appeal against the order and of the fact that application is being made for a legal aid certificate. The notice of appeal itself should contain an application to extend the time for appeal. This is particularly important if the respondent to the appeal is likely not to instruct solicitors or to take part in the appeal personally.

Experience shows that if these precautions are taken, the Divisional Court may be expected to give leave, without any prior application, for the necessary extension of time at the hearing of the appeal.

Where the applicant is in receipt of assistance by way of representation (ABWOR) for proceedings in a magistrates' court this will cover giving notice of appeal and applying for a case to be stated within the ordinary time for so doing and matters preliminary thereto.

8 APPEALS TO THE COURT OF APPEAL AND APPLICATIONS FOR EXTENSION OF TIME

Unnecessary delays in applying for legal aid to appeal to the Court of Appeal should be avoided because it is generally in the interest of all parties that an appeal should be heard as soon as possible.

A legal aid certificate to appeal, or an amendment of an existing certificate albeit initially limited to bespeaking those parts of the transcript relevant to the proposed appeal and then obtaining the opinion of counsel, can be granted by an Area Director very quickly. However, as thereafter the transcript has to be prepared, the opinion of counsel obtained and the matter reconsidered by the Area Director, the Board wishes to emphasise that, to avoid delay, application for legal aid or for an amendment of an existing certificate should be made as soon as possible after the conclusion of the original hearing and all other steps towards the hearing of an appeal, such as the bespeaking of the transcript and the instruction of counsel, should be undertaken with the utmost possible despatch.

A practical step that should be taken is to warn the individual shorthand writer concerned, at the end of the hearing, that an appeal is under consideration and that a transcript is likely to be required.

Similar precautions to those referred to in NFG 7 should be observed in respect of appeals to the Court of Appeal. Prompt notification should be given to the opposite side of the intention to appeal and of the fact that application is being made immediately either for a legal aid certificate or for an amendment to an existing certificate. In giving such notification the other party or parties should be asked if they will consent to an extension of time. It must be emphasised that the giving of the notification suggested does not absolve the party intending to appeal from prompt application for a certificate, or for an amendment.

It is understood that the Court of Appeal thinks that, where such a notification is given as is indicated above, the other party or parties should, and would normally be expected to, consent to an extension of time corresponding to the time allowed in High Court appeals; and should their failure so to consent necessitate an application for extension of time to the Court of Appeal, the Court might well, in the absence of special circumstances, order the other party or parties to pay the costs of the application.

In the notice suggested in NFG 7, for the Family Division it was also recommended that the notice of appeal itself should contain an application to extend the time for appeal; but this recommendation would not appear to be helpful in cases of appeal to the Court of Appeal.

9 APPEALS FROM PENSION APPEALS TRIBUNAL

An appeal from a decision of the Pensions Appeal Tribunal lies to the High Court. Accordingly, legal aid is available for such appeals. However, rule 28 of the Pensions Appeal Tribunal (England and Wales) Rules 1980 provides that the Tribunal shall meet the costs properly incurred by the applicant in connection with an appeal. As a result no benefit is likely to accrue to the applicant from the use of legal aid. Indeed, he could even be penalised if he is liable to pay a contribution, since he will be deprived of such contribution until the conclusion of the case. In these circumstances, where an application is received for legal aid in connection with such an appeal, the legal aid office will inquire of the applicant's solicitor about any possible benefit to the applicant from legal aid. If there is no such benefit the application will be referred to the Area Director with a view to refusal on the grounds of unreasonableness.

10 APPEALS TO THE EMPLOYMENT APPEAL TRIBUNAL

The procedure for making appeals to the Employment Appeal Tribunal is contained in the Employment Apeal Tribunal Rules 1980 (S.I. 1980 No. 2035) and a Practice Direction dated February 17, 1981 ([1981] 1 All E.R. 853).

The time for appeal is 42 days from the date when the decision of the Industrial Tribunal was sent to the appellant. Every notice of appeal not delivered within the time limit must be accompanied by an application for an extension of time setting out the reason for the delay. An application for an extension of time cannot be considered until a notice of appeal has been presented.

It is not necessarily a good excuse for delay in appealing that legal aid has been applied for, and in such cases the intending appellant should, at the earliest possible moment, and at the latest within the time limit for appealing, inform the registrar, and the other party, of his intentions and seek the latter's agreement to an extension of time for appealing.

11 CHOICE OF FORUM IN MATRIMONIAL PROCEEDINGS

By virtue of the Domestic Proceedings and Magistrates' Courts Act 1978 the grounds for obtaining financial provision and protection in a magistrates' court have been closely aligned with those on which the jurisdiction of the divorce court is based. There are, however, still significant differences and clients and their legal advisors will still have to choose the forum which is more appropriate to the client's needs.

The choice is a matter for clients and their legal advisers but there are certain factors which need to be taken into account by the Area Director if the proceedings are the subject of an aplication for legal aid.

(a) Multiplicity of proceedings should be avoided if at all possible. For example, it might well be unreasonable for legal aid to be granted to a client who wants a divorce and whose marriage has irretrievably broken down to apply in the first instance for maintenance or protection in the magistrates' court as a preliminary to the divorce proceedings.

(b) The divorce court will obviously be the correct forum to commence proceedings where the wider powers of that court on injunction applications or those relating to property or lump sum orders in excess of £1000 are necessary to deal with the client's case.

(c) Where, however, the magistrates' court is able to provide the relief the client is seeking, *i.e* where a protection order is sought or where resolution of ancillary matters is confined to (i) an application for a lump sum payment which is not likely to lead to an award of more than £1000; (ii) a maintenance payment classed as a small maintenance payment for taxation purposes; and (iii) no property settlement is sought, clients and their legal advisers will normally be expected to commence proceedings in the magistrates' court. The system of legal aid in the magistrates' court, ABWOR, has the added advantage of dispensing with the full legal aid assessment of means. It can, therefore usually be obtained much more quickly than a full legal aid certificate and speed is an importance factor in many of these cases.

12 SCOPE OF CERTIFICATE IN MATRIMONIAL PROCEEDINGS

These notes equally apply to a suit for nullity or judicial separation to the extent that the individual items or their equivalent apply in such a suit.

The interpretation of the wording of the legal aid certificate, with particular regard to its scope, must always be a matter for decision by the taxing officer concerned in the light of any representations made by the solicitor with the normal remedies by way of objection and review in the event of dissatisfaction. Without in any way fettering his discretion, the following notes, which have been agreed with the Senior Registrar of the Family Division, set out for the guidance of solicitors, the Board's views as to the scope of some common forms of certificate.

A. Certificates to prosecute or defend a suit for divorce
(1) *Principles*

(a) Subject to any limitation, restriction or condition expressed therein, a certificate covers all the steps which are normally necessary for the purpose of prosecuting or defending a suit.

(b) Unless extended by amendment, the certificate does not cover any step after the final decree other than applications for ancillary relief or custody or access made promptly after the final decree.

(c) The certificate will not cover any further steps in the decree proceedings if the cause at any time becomes undefended.

(2) *Matters regarded as within the scope of the usual form of certificate*

A certificate covering the prosecution or defence of proceedings for a decree of divorce is regarded as covering:

(i) filing supplemental pleadings;

(ii) raising or opposing an issue as to domicile;

(iii) making or opposing an application for maintenance pending suit;

(iv) satisfying the judge as to the arrangements to be made for a child of the family;

(v) an application to remove a child of the family from the jurisdiction of the court, provided it is made before the final decree;

(vi) an application for an injunction of one of the following types, provided it is made any time up to the final decree:

    (*a*) to prevent molestation of one spouse by the other,
    (*b*) to prevent the removal of a child of the family from the jurisdiction of the court,
    (*c*) to require a spouse to leave the matrimonial home,
    (*d*) to require the return of a child of the family to the person from whom it has been taken;

(vii) an application for custody of, or access to, a child provided it is made before, on or promptly after the final decree;

(viii) an issue as to the status of a child provided it is raised at any time up to the making of an order for ancillary relief in respect of that child which is made before, on or promptly after the final decree;

(ix) an application for an injunction to restrain the other spouse from dealing with property to defeat an order for ancillary relief, provided it is made at any time up to the making of an order for ancillary relief, in respect of a party or a child of the family, which is made before, on or promptly after the final decree;

(x) an application for rescission of a decree nisi consequent upon the reconciliation of the parties;

(xi) making or opposing an application to expedite the making absolute of a decree nisi;

(xii) making or opposing an application before or promptly after the final decree, for:

    (*a*) a periodical payments order,
    (*b*) a secured periodical payments order,
    (*c*) a lump sum order,
    (*d*) a transfer of property order,
    (*e*) a settlement of property order,
    (*f*) a variation of settlement order,

in respect of a party or a child of the family, excluding the trial by a judge of an issue as to conduct;

(xiii) an application made before the final decree for a variation order;

(xiv) making or opposing an application for a periodical payments order or a lump sum order in respect of a party or a child of the family when the applicant has been unsuccessful in the main suit;

(xv) the registration in a magistrates' court of an order for ancillary relief provided that the application is made not later than six months from the date of the order or the date of the final decree, whichever shall be the later;

(xvi) steps by a petitioner in connection with an application by the respondent under section 10(2) of the Matrimonial Causes Act 1973;

(xvii) an application under section 7 of the Matrimonial Causes Act 1973;

(xviii) attendance before a registrar on a summons for directions or pre-trial review.

(3) *Matters regarded as outside the scope of the usual form of certificate*

The legal aid regulations deal with the instances when it is necessary to obtain specific authority from the Area Director to obtain an amendment to the certificate in order to take certain steps in the proceedings. Unless such specific authority or amendment has been obtained, then, having regard to the principles enumerated in paragraph (1) above, a certificate to prosecute or (as a respondent spouse) to defend a suit for divorce will not cover the initiation or opposing, as appropriate, of the following steps in such proceedings:

(i) on the part of the petitioner:

  (a) filing an answer to a separate cross-petition by the respondent;
  (b) filing a second petition;

(ii) on the part of the respondent spouse:

  (a) making cross-charges in an answer, followed by a prayer for divorce or some alternative matrimonial relief;
  (b) filing a separate cross-petition;

(the cover afforded by such a certificate will be taken to extend to proceedings under a second petition or separate cross-petition which have taken place after an order for consolidation with the previous proceedings, but not otherwise)

(iii) an application for a variation order after the final decree;

(iv) the enforcement of an order for ancillary relief or costs;

(v) an application for alteration of a maintenance agreement;

(vi) an application for provision to be made out of the estate of a deceased former spouse;

(vii) an application for an avoidance of disposition order;

(viii) protracted negotiations subsequent to, and to give effect to, an order for access to a child;

(ix) an application by the unsuccessful party for the decree nisi to be made absolute;

(x) proceedings under section 17 of the Married Women's Property Act 1882;

(xi) opposing an intervention by the Queen's Proctor to show cause against the decree nisi being made absolute;

(xii) resisting the respondent's application under section 10(1) of the Matrimonial Causes Act 1973 for rescission of the decree;

(xiii) an application for committal for breach of an injunction.

(It is emphasised that the above list is not exhaustive).

(4) *Limitations and conditions*

Where a legal aid certificate has been granted to continue to prosecute or to defend a defended suit for divorce, it will provide that the certificate covers the decree proceedings so long as the cause remains defended.

The certificate will also contain the following limitations. Whilst the cause remains defended the certificate is limited to:

(i) all steps up to and including discovery of documents, and, thereafter;

(ii) the obtaining of counsel's opinion on the merits of the cause continuing as a contested cause.

Despite this limitation, attendance before the registrar on a summons for directions or a pre-trial review is within the scope of the certificate.

B. Certificates relating to matters other than prosecuting or defending a suit for divorce

Since April 1, 1977, legal aid may not be granted for decree proceedings in undefended divorce cases (except where the petition is directed to be heard in open court or by reason of physical or mental incapacity it is impracticable for an applicant to proceed without legal aid) but it is still available for a number of matters arising in the course of divorce proceedings (Legal Aid (Matrimonial Proceedings) Regulations 1989 (see NFG 13).

Legal aid certificates issued in respect of these other matters have hitherto varied in wording. If the certificate sets out particular matters which were covered, *e.g* an application for periodical payments or for a transfer of property order, the certificate covered only the particular matters specified. If the certificate was worded in general terms, *e.g.* to apply for ancillary relief, it included in its scope all those types of ancillary relief listed in rule 2(2) of the Matrimonial Causes Rules 1977 except for an avoidance of disposition order or a variation order made after a decree absolute.

The cost of matrimonial proceedings, particularly those funded out of legal aid, is steadily increasing. From many complaints received from assisted persons who find at the end of the proceedings that they are personally responsible for payment of legal costs because of the operation of the statutory charge (see NFG 5), it is clear that had they appreciated the position earlier they might have taken a different view about pursuing further proceedings, perhaps at unreasonable length, or at least would have taken those proceedings in the full realisation that they were at further risk financially. Accordingly, since February 1, 1984 all legal aid certificates issued in connection with ancillary relief in matrimonial proceedings have been limited initially to the securing of one substantive order only. This does not prevent applications to the appropriate Area Director for amendment of the certificate if legal aid is required for any further court hearing. On receipt of such an application for amendment, however, the Area Director will need to be satisfied about the necessity for the subsequent hearing and may also require to be provided with an estimate of the costs to date and an assurance that the effect of the statutory charge has been explained to the assisted person.

In connection with applications for custody or access or an order declaring that the court is satisfied as to arrangements for the welfare of the children of the family, legal aid may only be granted if there is reason to believe that such application will be opposed (regulation 2 of the Legal Aid (Matrimonial Proceedings) Regulations 1989, adding new paragraph 5A to Part II of Schedule 2 to the Legal Aid Act 1988 and see NFG 13). As from February 1, 1984 legal aid certificates concerning access in matrimonial proceedings have been limited initially to securing one substantive order for defined access. If legal aid is required for a subsequent hearing it will be necessary to apply to the appropriate Area Director for amendment of the certificate. The Area Director again may request information about the reasons for the subsequent hearing and the provision of an estimate of the costs to date and, in appropriate cases, an assurance that the operation of the statutory charge has been explained to the client.

Legal aid certificates relating to custody only will not necessarily be subject to the same limitations but will, of course, only be granted in cases where there is reason to believe that an application for custody will be opposed.

C. Proceedings for enforcement

A certificate granted for the purpose of enforcing an order for ancillary relief or costs will normally specify the process of enforcement to be adopted. In the absence of any such wording, it will be regarded as covering one application for enforcement only.

It should be remembered that by virtue of paragraph 5 of Part II of Schedule 2 to the Legal Aid Act 1988, legal aid is not available for proceedings for or consequent upon the issue of a judgment summons in the county court.

Where a maintenance order has been made for payment direct to a child, enforcement proceedings can only be taken by that child acting by next friend or guardian *ad litem* (*Shelley* v. *Shelley* [1952] P. 107). The parent's legal aid certificate cannot be amended to include such proceedings, which must be the subject of a separate legal aid application by the child. No separate application is, however, required in the case of an application to register an order in a magistrates' court as registration is regarded as part of the process of obtaining the order and not as procedure for enforcement.

Legal aid certificates, other than those to prosecute or defend a suit for divorce, will not cover the registration in a magistrates' court of an order for ancillary relief, unless specifically mentioned in the original certificate or any amendment thereto. Where an application is received relating to proceedings for enforcement or variation of such an order in the original court, the Area Director will require to be satisfied that there is good reason for not pursuing such proceedings in a magistrates' court following due registration.

13 UNDEFENDED DIVORCE AND LEGAL AID

Since April 1, 1977, legal aid has not been available for undefended divorce or judicial separation decree proceedings (Legal Aid (Matrimonial) Proceedings Regulations 1977). It may only be granted for such decree proceedings (a) if they become defended (either to the respondent to defend or to the petitioner to continue the proceedings after an answer has been filed); or (b) if the registrar directs the petition to be heard in open court (for example where the registrar is not satisfied on the merits of the case or on other matters such as domicile); or (c) if by reason of physical or mental incapacity it is impracticable for the applicant to proceed without legal aid.

Apart from decree proceedings, legal aid may be granted to make or oppose an application; (a) for an injunction (but the certificate will not cover the filing of a petition unless the court makes it a condition of the injunction); (b) for a substantive application for ancillary relief; (c) for an order relating to custody of or access to a child or the care and control of a child (but only where there is reason to believe that the application will be opposed); and (d) for an order declaring that the court is satisfied with arrangements for welfare of children (but only where there is reason to believe that the application will be opposed). (Legal aid cannot be granted under this provision where the proceedings are unopposed even if the judge is not satisfied and adjourns the hearing either for additional information to be provided or for a party to appear before him.)

There is a residual power to grant legal aid for the purposes of making or opposing any other application or satisfying the court on any other matter which raises a substantial question for determination by the court. This provision covers, for example, applications under section 10 of the Matrimonial Causes Act 1973 and applications where there are allied proceedings in another court or another jurisdiction.

Use of green form scheme
The following are examples of the work that a solicitor may be expected to carry out under a green form and within the limit of expenditure authorised by the general authority:

(i) preliminary advice on the grounds for divorce or judicial separation, the effects of a decree on status, the future arrangements for the children, the income and assets of the family and matters relating to housing and the matrimonial home;

(ii) drafting the petition and the statement of the arrangements for the children and where necessary typing or writing the entries on the forms;

(iii) advising on filing the documents at court and the consequential procedure, including service if no acknowledgment of service is filed;

(iv) advising a client when the acknowledgment of service is received as to the procedure for applying for directions for trial, and typing or writing the entries on the form of affidavit of evidence;

(v) advising as to attendances before the judge to explain the arrangements for the children and as to what, if any, evidence will be required by the judge other than that of the petitioner, but not attending court;

(vi) advising on obtaining the decree absolute.

The court record

The Matrimonial Causes Rules 1977 (as amended) provide for a solicitor's name and address to be given for service in a divorce petition, where the petitioner is receiving advice under the green form and is suing in person.

Court fees

Court fees will not be payable where the petitioner is not receiving legal aid but is receiving income support or family credit or advice and assistance under the green form scheme.

14 MAINTENANCE PROCEEDINGS IN MAGISTRATES' COURTS

1. In advising a client contemplating proceedings for a matrimonial order in a magistrates' court who will need legal aid, the solicitor may find it helpful to have regard to the following questions upon which the legal aid authority will need to be satisfied;

(i) whether in the circumstances of the case it is in the best interests of the client to seek a matrimonial order rather than some other form of matrimonial relief;

(ii) whether the magistrates are likely to make an order in favour of the client and, if so, whether it is likely that the order can be successfully enforced having regard to the financial resources and commitments of the proposed defendant; and

(iii) whether the advantage to the client or any children of the client which may be obtained is likely to be more than trivial.

2. Where the client is in receipt of income support, it is for her to decide whether to take maintenance proceedings, in the light of the advice she may receive from her solicitor as to the advantages of doing so. Whatever decision she takes, the Department of Social Security will ensure that she continues to receive the full benefit to which she is entitled. The fact that she is in receipt of income support does not prejudice her right to take maintenance proceedings or to get legal aid for the purpose where appropriate but, like any other applicant for legal aid, she will have to show that the proceedings are likely to be successful and that she will thereby obtain some personal benefit. All the considerations in paragraph 1 will apply, but even where there is no reasonable prospect of securing an order for more than the income support rates there may be potential benefit to the client from proceedings. For example, many women cease to receive income support on taking up employment. Where there are children concerned in the proceedings, issues of custody, welfare or paternity may well make proceedings necessary. Again, it may be in the client's interests to obtain a personal protection order.

3. Solicitors may wish to know that sometimes a woman's decision to take proceedings has followed a discussion with an officer of the Department of Social Security. A point in favour of proceedings in these cases is that the woman will have been given a leaflet setting out the options open to her and the Department will normally have satisfied itself that the man is able to pay maintenance. She will, therefore, have had an opportunity to consider the desirability of taking proceedings. Where, however, the woman is seeking maintenance on her own initiative, either before or very soon after claiming income support, no enquiries into the man's financial position will have been

made by the Department. In these circumstances the question of her proceedings should be considered without regard to the fact that she is or soon may be in receipt of income support.

15 MAINTENANCE IN DIVORCE PROCEEDINGS

1. Whether a wife who is receiving income support should take proceedings for maintenance for herself and for her children is a decision which she is entitled to make herself in the first instance. The Department of Social Security have produced a leaflet setting out the considerations which she might have in mind when making this decision.

2. It is wrong to say that the existence of social security benefit either enables, or entitles, a husband to throw on to social security the burden which he ought himself to bear, consistent with being left himself with a proper standard of living, *per* Russell L.J. in *Barnes* v. *Barnes* [1972] 3 All E.R. 872 at 876 (see also *Peacock* v. *Peacock* [1984] 1 W.L.R. 532).

3. A party to divorce proceedings who wishes to apply for a maintenance order should be expected to satisfy the Area Director that:—

   (i) the other party has sufficient means to pay; and

   (ii) that the applicant has reasonable grounds for seeking an order.

4. It is possible that some solicitors are not supplying sufficient information to enable an Area Director to make a decision whether the applicant has reasonable grounds for seeking an order. In particular the Area Director will need information about the financial resources of the party against whom an order is sought. There is a variety of reasons which might justify a wife who is in receipt of income support in taking maintenance proceedings.
For example:

   (i) she may consider the respondent can and ought to pay for the maintenance of the children;

   (ii) an applicant who has decided that she wishes to seek a maintenance order following the principle to which Russell L.J. referred in the *Barnes* case ought not to be refused legal aid merely because the amount of the order she is likely to obtain is less than her entitlement to income support.

These are merely examples, which are not in any way definitive, of the kind of circumstances where a wife in receipt of income support might be justified in taking maintenance proceedings.

5. Apart from the fact that an assisted person may well wish to get all her legal proceedings concluded with the hope of making a fresh start, she may well have been advised by her solicitor to apply for legal aid at a time when she is eligible for aid without contribution. A solicitor is entitled to advise a client to make an application for maintenance at the time which is most advantageous to her.

6. It may in any event be in the interest of the legal aid fund for all the proceedings which are likely to take place to be concluded within a reasonably short space of time. If there is a lapse of many months between the conclusion of the decree proceedings and the obtaining of a maintenance order it is more likely that the respondent will oppose the maintenance proceedings, and the expense of preparing for the maintenance proceedings may be greater than it would have been had all the steps necessary to collate the evidence for the decree proceedings and ancillary relief been carried out at once.

16 MATRIMONIAL CASES SET DOWN IN DEFENDED LIST

The policy of the Matrimonial Causes Act 1973 is to avoid defended suits in relation to the decree unless there are reasons why the suit should be defended in the interests of either party, and to ensure that normally the award of a decree will not compromise decisions over issues relating to custody of, access to, and maintenance of, children, and the other ancillary matters.

It is the duty of the Area Director to ensure that legally aided cases are not defended without good reason. To ensure this, certificates, whether to prosecute or defend divorce proceedings, should be limited so as to exclude a defended suit so that an application for amendment must be made before a case is set down in the defended list. Before a certificate is so amended enquiries should be made to ascertain whether, without detriment to the proper interests of the parties or either of them, the case can be disposed of as an undefended suit. Solicitors making application for an amendment should certify that in their opinion a defended case cannot be avoided, setting out the reasons upon which that opinion is based, the state of representations to achieve a settlement, and, if counsel's opinion has been obtained on the matter, indicating the view he has formed. If necessary, the Area Director should require submission of the pleadings, any opinion of counsel and other papers that may be relevant in reaching a decision as to whether or not the amendment should be made.

17 ADOPTION AND STEP-PARENTS

If an applicant for legal aid for adoption proceedings wishes to bring the proceedings in the High Court or county court the Area Director will wish to know why the cheaper course of bringing them in a magistrates' court cannot be followed. Although legal aid is not available for this purpose in the magistrates' court unless proceedings are contested, this will not by itself justify a grant of legal aid to bring proceedings in the High Court or county court, but such a grant might however be justifiable if a difficult point of law is involved.

Section 14 of the Adoption Act 1976 provides that where the married couple consist of a parent and step-parent of the child the court shall dismiss the application if it considers the matter would be better dealt with under section 42 (orders for custody, etc.) of the Matrimonial Causes Act 1973.

The effect of this provision was considered by Ormrod L.J., in two cases, *Re S. (Infants) (Adoption by Parent)* [1977] Fam. 173 and *Re S.* (1978) 9 Fam. Law 88.

In the first case his Lordship stated that the court would require considerably more investigation and information than is normal in adoption cases and in many cases evidence from the other natural parent should be given even if his or her consent had been obtained, or at least a detailed statement of his present attitude to, and past relationship with, the child would be required from the guardian *ad litem*. The motives of each of the adopters should be carefully examined and he stated it would be the duty of the guardian *ad litem* to draw the attention of the court to the disadvantages as well as the advantages of adoption and the possible effect on the step-parent should be borne in mind. The court would also have to consider whether it was more appropriate for a further application to be made under section 42 of the Matrimonial Causes Act 1973 to the court which dealt with the former divorce proceedings of the parents of the child concerned.

In the 1978 case, his Lordship conceded that section 10(3) of the Children Act 1975 (now covered by section 14 of the Adoption Act 1976) was a difficult section to interpret and apply but went on to say that it was the intention that the section should virtually prohibit adoption by a step-parent and parent. In the circumstances of the case before him, he made an adoption order, holding that the child was *de facto* a member of the adopting family and had been since the marriage and had never been a member of another family, (the natural father's only contact with the child had been for a few moments visit in the nursing home, the father having separated from the mother three months after marriage). Adoption in this case did not impose an artificial status.

When therefore applications for legal aid in adoption proceedings in the county court or High Court are made in step-parent cases, the Area Director will first enquire of the solicitors submitting the application their reasons for seeking an adoption order as opposed to one under section 42 of the Matrimonial Causes Act 1973, and the solicitors will be referred to section 14 and the two decisions of Ormrod L.J. If, notwithstanding the solicitor's wish to proceed with the application, the Area Director will have to take into account the representations of the solicitors and consider whether or not the matter should be dealt with more appropriately by way of application under section 42. If the Area Director is of the opinion that the circumstances warrant an application for adoption proceedings, it is considered that if a difficult point of law is involved a grant of legal aid would be justified to bring proceedings in a county court or the High Court notwithstanding that the magistrates' court has jurisdiction.

18 SCOPE OF CERTIFICATE—INCLUSION OF COPY CERTIFICATES WITH PAPERS DELIVERED TO COUNSEL

It is the duty of the solicitor acting for an assisted person to satisfy himself that the scope of the certificate issued to the client covers the proceedings contemplated and the steps to be taken. It is important that a copy of the form of offer and acceptance of legal aid (which sets out the terms of the certificate), or of the certificate itself, and also copies of all relevant authorities under regulations 59, 60 or 61 of the Civil Legal Aid (General) Regulations 1989 and any amendments of the certificate, should be included with the papers to counsel. Counsel will then be apprised of such authorities and of the specific wording of the certificate and of any limitation or special condition so that he can be satisfied that what he advises falls within the scope of the certificate. The observance of this duty will not, however, relieve the solicitor of his responsibility to ensure that what is done falls within the scope of the certificate.

In any case of doubt, counsel should b specifically asked to advise whether the proceedings or steps referred to in the instructions are covered.

The attention of solicitors acting for assisted persons is drawn to regulations 51 and 52 of the above Regulations which deal with the powers of an Area Director to amend a legal aid certificate. In the event of any items being disallowed on taxation by reason of the work done being outside the scope of the certificate or any authority required by regulations 59, 60 or 61 the costs thereby lost will not be reimbursed from the legal aid fund.

19 LEGAL AID FOR PROCEEDINGS IN THE HIGH COURT OR COUNTY COURT

Although certificates may limit proceedings to a county court, in marginal cases it will be left to the assisted person, on the advice of his or her solicitor and counsel, to take proceedings either in a county court or the High Court. When advising an assisted client it must be borne in mind that if proceedings are commenced in the High Court but, owing to the amount recovered, county court costs are awarded, the assisted person may suffer financial hardship. Costs payable from the legal aid fund will be taxed on the High Court scale and the difference between the two amounts must be met from any contribution determined or, if this is insufficient, may be the subject of a charge upon the damages recovered. Solicitors should, for that reason, exercise great care in the decisions made as to the forum.

20 CERTIFICATES LIMITING PROCEEDINGS TO A COUNTY COURT

Where a legal aid certificate relates only to proceedings in a county court, the certificate unless amended, will not cover proceedings after a transfer to the High Court.

If it is the assisted person who wishes to apply for a transfer of the proceedings to the High Court an application should be made to the Area Director to consider whether, in the event of the application being granted, he or she will be prepared to amend the certificate extending it to the continuation of the proceedings in the High Court. If an application for transfer is made by any other party, an application for amendment of the certificate should be made immediately after the order transferring the proceedings. In the absence of such an amendment the certificate will not cover any subsequent steps.

No amendment will be required on a transfer of proceedings from a county court to the High Court where the certificate does not specify a particular court.

21 NOTICE OF ISSUE OF CERTIFICATE

Under regulation 50 of the Civil Legal Aid (General) Regulations 1989, whenever an assisted person becomes a party to the proceedings, or a party to the proceedings becomes an assisted person, his or her solicitor shall forthwith serve all other parties with notice of the issue of the certificate. If at any time thereafter any other person becomes a party to the proceedings, similar notice must be served on such persons. For this purpose a garnishee is a party who should be served with notice if either the judgment creditor or the judgment debtor is an assisted person in respect of the proceedings in which judgment was obtained or in the proceedings by way of garnishee.

It has been the general practice not to give notice of any limitation to other parties in the proceedings, because disclosure of any limitation of the certificate might operate unfairly on the assisted person, since it might be thought by other parties to indicate a weakness in the assisted person's case. However, in *Scarth* v. *Jacobs-Paton*, *The Times*, November 1, 1978 the Court of Appeal said that where legal aid had been granted for an appeal but the certificate was limited to filing notice of appeal and obtaining leading counsel's favourable opinion, the respondent should be given notice of those limitations. The Court considered that the practice of not giving notice of limitations could cause hardship where an assisted person had lost an action brought by him and obtained legal aid for an appeal, because as soon as notice of appeal was filed, the appeal was set down for hearing and the respondent had immediately to incur the expense of preparing his case and instructing counsel. If the assisted person then discontinued the appeal as a result of an unfavourable opinion from counsel, the court would normally award costs in favour of the respondent, most of which might have to be borne by the legal aid fund.

As a result of this case, it has been decided that where a limited certificate or a limited amendment of a certificate is issued for appellate proceedings the main wording of the certificate (which is repeated in the notice given to other parties) should indicate the nature of the limitation. The same considerations, however, do not apply to non-appellate cases, for which the existing procedure of setting out a limitation in a certificate as a separate matter which does not need to be included in the notice served on the other parties is being continued.

A solicitor for an assisted person is also required to serve prescribed notice upon any other persons who are, or become, parties to the proceedings, of revocation or discharge of a legal aid certificate, the replacement of an emergency certificate by a full legal aid certificate and an amendment to a certificate, other than a financial amendment under regulation 52.

Where a person receives approval of assistance by way of representation in respect of proceedings in a magistrates' court, the solicitor is required to give notice as soon as practicable to any other party to the proceedings (Legal Advice and Assistance Regulations 1989, reg. 24). There is no prescribed form of notice in this case.

22 FILING OF CERTIFICATES AND NOTICES IN COURT

Under regulation 50(4) of the Civil Legal Aid (General) Regulations 1989, a solicitor is required, if the proceedings have begun, or otherwise upon their commencement, to send the certificate post to the appropriate court office or registry. Similarly the regulations provide that a solicitor must send to the appropriate court office or registry notice of revocation or discharge of the certificate, an extension of an emergency certificate or a certificate replacing an emergency certificate, and any amendment to a certificate.

The Court of Appeal has stated *obiter* in *Scarth* v. *Jacobs-Paton, The Times*, November 1, 1978 that when a certificate has been granted for an appeal that is expressed to be limited to filing notice of appeal and conditional on counsel's opinion, the other parties to the proceedings should be given notice of the limitation (see NFG 21).

23 DUTIES OF SOLICITORS AND COUNSEL

Apart from the duty now imposed upon solicitors by regulation 70(2) of the (Civil Legal Aid (General) Regulations 1989 to report when required, certifying the reasonableness of the continuance of legal aid for the proceedings, solicitors are reminded that even where a full legal aid certificate has been issued for the taking of, defending or being a party to proceedings, they should keep under constant review the reasonableness of such proceedings continuing at public expense. If a solicitor wastes costs by failure to conduct the proceedings with reasonable competence and expedition, the taxing officer has power to reduce his costs or even disallow them completely Civil Legal Aid (General) Regulations 1989, reg. 109).

The Area Director who issued the certificate has power to discharge a certificate, under regulation 70(3), on failure by a solicitor to report under regulation 70(2), in addition to his power to discharge it if it appears that the assisted person no longer has reasonable grounds for taking, defending or being a party to the proceedings, or that he or she requires the proceedings to be conducted unreasonably so as to incur an unjustifiable expense to the legal aid fund or that it appears unreasonable for him to continue to receive legal aid (Civil Legal Aid (General) Regulations 1989, reg. 77).

A solicitor or counsel, having reason to believe that the circumstances referred to in regulation 77 have arisen, must forthwith report the fact to the appropriate Area Director (Civil Legal Aid (General) Regulations 1989, reg. 67). In doing so, the solicitor and counsel are protected in respect of any breach of privilege Civil Legal Aid (General) Regulations 1989 (reg. 73). At that stage, solicitor and counsel should decide whether they wish to continue with the case. If they do not, the Area Director has power to allow the certificate to continue, subject to the instruction of a new solicitor, as an alternative to discharge. If they do decide not to continue with the case, reasons should be given to the Area Director.

Regulation 70(1) of the Civil Legal Aid (General) Regulations 1989 imposes a duty on an assisted person's solicitor and counsel to give the Area Director such information regarding the progress and disposal of the proceedings to which the certificate relates as the Area Director may, from time to time, require for the purpose of performing his or her functions under the scheme. This regulation also imposes new duties upon the solicitor, without being so required by the Area Director, to report where the assisted person declines to accept a reasonable offer of settlement or a sum which is paid into court and to notify the Area Director where a legal aid certificate is issued to another party to the proceedings.

It is also the duty of an assisted person's solicitor forthwith (a) to inform the Area Director of any property recovered or preserved for the assisted person; and (b) to pay to the Legal Aid Board all moneys received by him or her by virtue of an order or agreement made in the assisted person's favour (subject to the possibility of a direction being made by the Area Director that such lesser sum may be paid as would be sufficient to safeguard the legal aid fund (Civil Legal Aid (General) Regulations 1989, reg. 90)). For the further duties of the assisted person's solicitor in relation to the regulations governing the postponement in certain cases of the enforcement of the statutory charge which became effective from December 1, 1988 and are now contained in Part XI of the Civil Legal Aid (General) Regulations 1989 (see NFG 6).

24 ACCEPTANCE OF SUMS PAID INTO COURT

Assisted litigants are not always sufficiently warned of the consequence which may result from their refusal to accept sums paid into court.

The same principles apply in assisted and unassisted cases and, if an assisted person declines to accept a payment in, and in the event does not recover more than the sum paid in, costs as from the date of payment in are likely to be awarded against him. The provisions of section 17 of the Legal Aid Act 1988 apply in assessing the costs which the assisted person should reasonably pay, the payment of which might well result in the assisted person having to bear the full order for costs, as from the date of payment in, from his or her damages.

The sum recovered by the assisted person by way of damages is in any event subject to the statutory charge in respect of sums paid out of the legal aid fund for his own costs. Thus the result may be that out of damages which he in any even considered inadequate, the assisted person will have to bear not only his/her own costs but a considerable proportion of those incurred by the defendants. It will be appreciated that, unless the damages are substantial, the result could well be that the assisted person would recover nothing.

If an assisted person refuses to accept a payment into court which his advisers consider adequate, the solicitor nominated must report the position to the Area Director before proceeding further.

As to the position where in the proceedings costs are awarded on the county court scale, see NFG 19.

25 INSTRUCTING COUNSEL—LEADING COUNSEL

Under regulation 59 of the Civil Legal Aid (General) Regulations 1989, a solicitor acting for an assisted person may instruct counsel where it appears necessary for the proper conduct of proceedings. Unless authority has been given in the certificate or by the Area Director, counsel shall not be instructed in authorised summary proceedings nor shall Queen's Counsel or more than one counsel be instructed. When counsel entrusts a case to another counsel under section 32(1)(b) of the Legal Aid Act 1988 the leave of the Area Director is not required.

An authority given under regulation 59(1) for "briefing counsel" covers the brief itself and any necessary consultation on the brief after its delivery. It does not cover consultations or other work done on instructions prior to delivery of the brief. Where there is no *inter partes* taxation there is no discretion under regulation 63(3) of the Civil Legal Aid (General) Regulations 1989 to allow unauthorised costs incurred in instructing counsel (*Din* v. *Wandsworth London Borough Council* (*No. 3*) [1983] 1 W.L.R. 1171).

An application to instruct Queen's Counsel should be made in sufficient time to enable the Area Director to give the application proper and detailed consideration. Solicitors may be required to lodge papers relating to the action in support of the application.

When a junior who has been instructed takes silk, the Area Director will, on the application for authority for him to continue as a leader, take into consideration the following matters:

(a) Queen's Counsel is permitted, and should normally be willing at any time before the first anniversary of his appointment as Queen's Counsel, (*inter alia*) to settle pleadings and other documents, appear at the trial or at any hearing preceding the trial and do any other ordinary work of a junior in any proceedings in regard to which he was instructed to settle before his appointment.

(b) He may, at his discretion, continue to act as a junior (including settling pleadings, notices of appeal and other documents), appearing at any hearing (whether original or appellate) and doing any other ordinary work of a junior without limit of time, *inter alia*, in a civil suit if he was instructed therein before his appointment as Queen's Counsel and before the first anniversary of his appointment appeared as a junior at the trial or on an appeal therein.

(c) Save as aforesaid he should refuse to act as a junior in any matter or proceedings after the first anniversary of his appointment as Queen's Counsel unless, in his opinion, such a refusal would cause harm to the client. In such event he may, at his discretion, continue so to act for any purpose in regard to such matter or proceeding until the second anniversary of his appointment.

(d) In the event of Queen's Counsel not electing or being able to continue as a junior it is open to a solicitor to instruct a fresh junior.

If authority is given to continue the case as a leader, on any application for authority to instruct a junior Area Directors must bear in mind that in view of the abolition of the two-counsel rule, counsel may now accept instructions to appear as an advocate without a junior, but may decline if he considers he would be unable to conduct the case properly unless a junior was also instructed.

Where a certificate is granted for leading counsel alone he may settle pleadings or draft such other documents as necessary for the conduct of contentious proceedings as are normally drafted by junior counsel where he has agreed to appear as an advocate without a junior. If an authority is given to instruct leading counsel it should be made quite clear whether this includes the continued employment of junior counsel in addition to leading counsel or whether leading counsel alone should be employed.

26 COUNSEL'S FEES

It was agreed between the Council of the Law Society, the Senate of the Inns of Court, the Bar and the Supreme Court Taxing Office, that when a bill of costs is prepared for taxation in a legal aid case, any items in respect of counsel's fees should be inserted in accordance with a note of fees rendered by counsel to the instructing solicitor after the work to which the fees relate has been completed. Counsel is at liberty to supply to the instructing solicitor for the use of the taxing master, a memorandum about any factors in relation to the case which affect the amount of the fees for which counsel has asked and should, as a matter of courtesy, supply a memorandum to the taxing master if so requested by him.

The instructing solicitor should use his best endeavours to secure the allowance on the taxation of a proper fee for counsel and must inform counsel's clerk of any reduction in time to give an opportunity to apply for authority for the lodging of objections within the terms of regulation 113 of the Civil Legal Aid (General) Regulations 1989. If the instructing solicitor feels unable to support before the taxing master the amount of the fees for which counsel asks, the instructing solicitor should inform counsel beforehand.

It should be appreciated that, as the fees of counsel who have acted for assisted persons are paid out of the legal aid fund, they cannot be paid until the solicitor's bill of costs has been taxed or assessed by the Area Director under regulation 105 or 107 of the Civil Legal Aid (General) Regulations 1989 unless payment on account is made under the provisions of regulations 100 or 101.

Solicitors must attach counsel's fee notes to the copies of their taxed bills when passing them to area committees for payment.

Appeal against taxation
It is important that counsel is informed as soon as possible after taxation of any reduction in his fees as, if he is dissatisfied with the fee allowed, he must require his instructing solicitor to obtain the leave of the Area Director to carry in objections to the taxation and the solicitor must apply for leave within 14 days of the taxation giving notice of his application to the taxing officer and to the opposite party.

If counsel wishes to appeal to a judge by way of a review of the taxing officer's certificate he must first require his instructing solicitors to obtain the leave of the Legal Aid Board. The application to the judge must be made within 14 days of the signing of the certificate unless a longer period is allowed by the taxing office or the court.

Appeals against assessment

Where the Area Director has disallowed or reduced counsel's fees he or she has a duty to notify counsel accordingly. If counsel is dissatisfied and wishes to make representations so that his fees can be reconsidered by the area committee, he must make them in writing. They are made directly to the area committee and not through instructing solicitors.

Where counsel has been instructed but not assigned, the instructing solicitor should be given an opportunity of commenting on counsel's representations.

If counsel is dissatisfied with the decision of the area committee he may, within 21 days of that decision, apply to the area committee to certify a point of principle of general importance. If the area committee certify accordingly, counsel may, within 21 days of the certification, appeal in writing to the committee appointed by the Board. The position is similar under the Legal Advice and Assistance Regulations 1989 and the Legal Aid in Criminal and Care Proceedings (Costs) Regulations 1989, in respect of the review by the area committee of a determination of counsel's fees and an appeal to a committee appointed by the Board on certification by the area committee of a point of principle of general importance.

27 EXPERTS' AND WITNESSES' FEES AND UNUSUAL EXPENDITURE

Where it is necessary for the proper conduct of the proceedings for certain action to be taken, for example, the obtaining of a report, opinion or evidence of an expert or non-expert witness, or the incurring of unusual expenditure, an assisted person's solicitor may apply in advance to the Area Director for authority to incur the costs of taking such action (Civil Legal Aid (General) Regulations 1989, reg. 61). On taxation, no question can be raised as to the propriety of any step taken under such prior authority (Civil Legal Aid (General) Regulations 1989, reg. 63(1)). The Area Director must specify the number of reports, or the number of persons who may give expert evidence and the maximum fee to be paid, and will wish to know the total commitment, including the cost of obtaining a report and tendering evidence, before authorising the employment of an expert. When a financial limit on costs is included in the authority, on taxation no question as to the amount of costs up to that limit can be raised, provided the solicitor and assisted person acted in good faith (Civil Legal Aid (General) Regulations 1989, reg. 63(2)).

Authority will not normally be granted for the solicitor to meet the costs of the assisted person travelling to obtain a medical report because such costs are not normally recoverable on taxation. However, the Area Director may be prepared to grant prior authority in exceptional circumstances where the report is essential to the conduct of the case and the assisted person cannot afford the cost of travelling to obtain it.

28 THE AREA DIRECTOR CANNOT GIVE RETROSPECTIVE AUTHORITIES

In *Wallace* v. *Freeman Heating Co. Ltd.* [1955] 1 W.L.R. 172, Pearson J., having adjourned a summons to review a taxation into open court, agreed with the decision of the taxing master that he should disallow a sum in the solicitor's bill for the legally aided appellant of the costs of bespeaking a shorthand transcript of the proceedings in the court of first instance because the legal aid committee had not, when granting the legal aid certificate for the appeal, authorised the bespeaking of a transcript. Their retrospective approval, after the master had first disallowed the amount, was insufficient.

29 SOLICITOR'S LIEN—LEGAL AID CASES

When a legal aid certificate is amended to enable a new solicitor to have the conduct of an assisted person's case, the normal practice is for the original solicitor to hand the papers over to the new solicitor on an undertaking that at the end of the case, the new solicitor will either have a consolidated bill taxed or make the papers available to the original solicitor so that he may prepare a bill for taxation of his costs.

From time to time solicitors who have taken over the conduct of an assisted person's case have reported difficulties in obtaining the papers from their predecessors, who wish to safeguard their entitlement to their costs. There have been cases in which the original solicitor has claimed a lien on the papers pending payment of his costs and disbursements out of the legal aid fund.

As a matter of law, a solicitor's lien arises in respect of costs due for work done on the instructions of the client, for which the client has undertaken personal liability. Pre-certificate costs and disbursements (apart from those covered by a green form) will fall within this category, and this lien is protected by regulation 103 of the Civil Legal Aid (General) Regulations 1989.

However, once a legal aid certificate has been issued the situation is altered, since the assisted person's solicitor has a statutory right to be paid out of the legal aid fund, and may not take any payment other than from the legal aid fund (Legal Aid Act 1988, s.15; Civil Legal Aid (General) Regulations 1989, reg. 64).

The Board considers, therefore, that no lien arises in respect of costs and disbursement payable under a legal aid certificate, and that it is misleading to use the word "lien" in relation to such costs and disbursements.

Accordingly where, under a legal aid certificate, a change of solicitor is authorised by the Area Director, subject to (a) there being no lien in respect of pre-certificate costs and disbursements, and (b) an undertaking being given by the new solicitor as to the eventual taxation or assessment of costs, there is no reason why the papers should not be expeditiously transferred to the new solicitor.

30 REGULATION 64 OF THE CIVIL LEGAL AID (GENERAL) REGULATIONS 1989—*Littaur* v. *Steggles Palmer*

The case of *Littaur* v. *Steggles Palmer* [1986] 1 W.L.R. 780 is the first decision on the meaning of what is now regulation 64 of the Civil Legal Aid (General) Regulations 1989, which provides:

> "Where a certificate has been issued in connection with any proceedings, the assisted person's solicitor or counsel shall not receive or be a party to the making of any payment for work done in those proceedings during the currency of that certificate (whether within the scope of the certificate or otherwise) except such payments as may be made out of the fund."

In *Littaur*, the Court of Appeal confirmed that the purpose of what was then regulation 65 of the Legal Aid (General) Regulations 1980 was to prevent an abuse of legal aid. For example, regulation 65 prevented an assisted person's solicitor or counsel from claiming any payment in respect of proceedings covered by his legal aid certificate except such payments as may be made out of the legal aid fund; thus solicitors and counsel may not take their taxed or assessed legal aid costs or fees and take, in addition, a "topping-up" from the assisted person, or from anyone else. Neither may solicitors nor counsel avoid legal aid taxation or assessment once work has been carried out under a legal aid certificate. This is so even when proceedings have been concluded on terms which include the payment of an agreed sum in respect of costs to the assisted person and which the assisted person's solicitor and counsel (if any) is willing to accept in full satisfaction of the work done; there must still be an assessment of costs and fees (if any) (Civil Legal Aid (General) Regulations 1989 regs. 105(3)(b) and 106(1)). Solicitors and counsel may, of course, charge privately for work carried out before the issue and/or after the discharge of a legal aid certificate.

Generally, the proceedings covered by an assisted person's legal aid certificate will be the whole action in which he is represented, though certificates may bear limitations restricting the steps in the action which may be taken without the area committee's consent. For example:

"To continue to defend proceedings in the High Court of Justice, Queen's Bench Division 1986 No. 1234 instituted by ABC Limited and to counterclaim."

"LIMITED to close of pleadings."

However, certificates are sometimes issued:

(a) to cover only a specific step or steps in an action; and

(b) applications for legal aid are sometimes not granted in full.

For example, an application for legal aid to defend and counterclaim might be granted only to defend and the application in respect of the counterclaim might be refused. In *Littaur*, the Court of Appeal found that "proceedings" in what is now regulation 64 does not necessarily refer to the whole of an action but may refer (as it did in *Littaur*) only to a specific step in an action.

A certificate for a specific step
If a legal aid certificate is issued to cover only a specific step in an action, for example, "to apply within proceedings in the Queen's Bench Division between AB, plaintiff and YZ, defendant to purge the assisted person's contempt for breach of an order," and on completion of that specific step, no further steps in the action are expected, the assisted person's solicitor should apply promptly, with his client's agreement, for discharge of the certificate and serve the appropriate notices of discharge under regulation 82 of the Civil Legal Aid (General) Regulations 1989.

If further steps in the action are contemplated, the assisted person's solicitor should apply promptly for an amendment of the certificate. If the amendment is refused, but discharge of the certificate has not been effected or is not yet appropriate, regulation 64 does not prevent the solicitor from acting privately for his client in the steps for which the amendment had been sought and refused.

Certificates not granted in full
If an application for legal aid is only partially granted, for example, an application for legal aid to cover a defence and counterclaim is made but a certificate granted only to defend, then regulation 64 does not prevent the solicitor from acting privately for his client in that part of the action (the counterclaim) which is not covered by the legal aid certificate. Another example might be where an application for legal aid is made to cover defending divorce decree proceedings and representation as to ancillary relief, but legal aid is granted only to cover the latter; in these circumstances regulation 64 does not prevent the solicitor from acting privately for his client in defending the decree proceedings.

Before acting privately for a client in any steps in an action in which the client is legally aided, his solicitor should first either:

(i) ensure that an appropriate application for legal aid or for an amendment has been made and refused; or

(ii) have his client's consent either

(a) not to apply for legal aid for an amendment to cover the step or steps; or
(b) to act prior to the application being determined

and in either case should ensure that he (a) has his client's instructions to act privately, (b) explains what this will mean, and (c) advises his client that the legal aid area office will have to be informed.

Whenever a solicitor is instructed to act privately for a client in an action in which the client is legally aided, he should inform the appropriate area office in writing, as soon as possible explaining the reason. The very fact that an assisted person is also instructing his solicitor in a private capacity may be a matter which the Area Director should take into account when considering whether it is reasonable for the assisted person to continue to receive legal aid.

The Board is of the opinion that solicitors, whether or not they themselves undertake such work, should always consider whether a client would be likely to gain an advantage from the facilities available under the Legal Aid Act 1988, and should advise him accordingly. Although a solicitor is under no duty to insist on his client obtaining legal aid, failure to advise a client promptly of his rights tends to bring the legal aid scheme into disrepute and a solicitor must so conduct his affairs as not to bring the profession or the legal aid scheme into disrepute. A solicitor who persistently neglects to advise his client of his right after his oversight has been brought to his attention might well be in danger of disciplinary action. Quite apart from that, he could possibly be liable in negligence for breach of duty to his client if the circumstances were such that the client suffered quantifiable loss.

31 RIGHTS AND LIABILITIES OF PARTIES IN RESPECT OF COSTS IN LEGAL AID CASES

Broadly speaking, the principles as to costs in a legal aid case follow those that apply in ordinary cases but there are provisions that take account of the special circumstances of a legal aided case.

(a) If an assisted person succeeds in his action the court will make an order for costs upon precisely the same principles as would apply if legal aid were not involved. The assisted person has no beneficial entitlement to the costs (*The Debtor* v. *The Law Society* (*No. 5883 of 1979*), *The Times*, February 21, 1981 C.A.) and the party liable can obtain a discharge for them only if they are paid to the assisted person's solicitor and he is required to pay them into the legal aid fund.

It is the duty of an assisted person to claim costs if, in the same circumstances, a paying client would do so in his own interests.

(b) If the assisted person is unsuccessful he is, in principle, liable to an order for costs against him but he is protected by section 17(1) of the Legal Aid Act 1988 in respect of the *quantum* of such costs. His liability will not "exceed the amount (if any) which is a reasonable one for him to pay having regard to all the circumstances, including the financial resources of all the parties and their conduct in connection with the dispute." Thus, where the means of an assisted person are such that it would not be reasonable to require him to make any payment, the court will make a nil order. If, however, they are such that he can pay the full order or some part of it, the court, having taken account of the factors set out in section 17(1), will make the appropriate order. There are provisions for varying the *quantum* if the assisted person's financial resources subsequently increase but the assisted person has no right to apply for the variation of an order for costs made against him. A solicitor acting for an assisted person should provide the court with what information is required to make an appropriate order. The assisted person is further protected in that his house and its contents, and the tools of his trade, are exempt from execution to enforce any order against him for costs but, otherwise, such an order can be enforced in the normal way. The order is a personal one, as in the case of a paying client, and legal aid provides him no protection against his liability other than as stated.

(c) A successful unassisted opponent of an assisted party who, through the operation of section 17(1) is unable to recover from the assisted person the costs to which he would otherwise have been entitled is able, under section 18 of the Legal Aid Act 1988, to make application to the court for an order for payment to him by the Board of the whole or any part of the costs incurred by him in the proceedings. Such an order will be made if an order for costs would be made in the proceedings apart from this Act and the court is satisfied that it is just and equitable in all the circumstances that provision for the costs should be made out of public funds but the court is required, in every case, to consider what orders should be made for costs against the assisted party receiving legal aid and for determining his liability in respect of such costs. The party so claiming must establish that the proceedings in the court of first instance were instituted by the party receiving legal aid (see *Thew* (*R. & T.*) v. *Reeves* [1981] 3 W.L.R. 190) and the court must be satisfied that the unassisted party will suffer severe financial hardship unless the order is made. The phrase "severe financial hardship" was rigorously construed in the case of *Nowotnik* v. *Nowotnik* [1967] P. 83 but this decision was reversed in the case of *Hanning* v. *Maitland* (*No. 2*) [1970] 1 Q.B. 580. Lord Denning M.R. said that it "should not be construed so as to exclude the people of modest income or modest capital who would find it hard to bear their own costs." Since that decision the provision has been liberally interpreted. The requirement that the court should be satisfied that the unassisted party will suffer severe financial hardship refers only to cases in the court of first instance. In an appellate case the court is entitled to make an order for payment of costs out of the legal aid fund if satisfied that "it is just and equitable in all the circumstances of the case that provision for the costs" should be so made. For the meaning of the words "court of first instance" and "proceedings" see the decisions of the House of Lords in *Gayway Linings Ltd.* v. *Toczek* and *Megarity* v. *Ryan & Sons Ltd.* [1982] A.C. 81.

(d) Similar provisions are applied by section 12 of the Legal Aid Act 1988 in respect of the liability of a person receiving ABWOR by virtue of an order for costs made against him and by section 13 in respect of the liability of the Board for the costs of a successful unassisted party in proceedings in which a person receiving ABWOR is a party.

32 MONEYS PAYABLE TO AN ASSISTED PERSON

Regulation 87 of the Civil Legal Aid (General) Regulations 1988 requires all moneys payable by virtue of any agreement or order made in connection with the action, cause or matter to which the certificate relates to be paid to the assisted person's solicitor, or if he is no longer represented by a solicitor, to the Board. Only the solicitor, or as the case may be, the Board is capable of giving a good discharge for moneys so paid.

Cases, many of which relate to matrimonial proceedings, have occurred where a person ordered to pay the costs has made payment direct to the assisted person, often by way of additional sums when forwarding instalments of maintenance.

The Board takes the view that it is the duty of the assisted person's solicitor to bring to the notice of a party from whom costs are recoverable the express provisions of regulation 87 and to emphasise that only the solicitor for the assisted person or, as the case may be, the Board can give a good discharge for payments of this kind.

As a result of a case in which a solicitor paid a sum awarded by way of damages direct to his assisted client, contrary to the requirement of what is now regulation 90 of the Civil Legal Aid (General) Regulations 1989, the Council of the Law Society sought an opinion of leading counsel upon the question of liability. Leading counsel advised that a solicitor acting for an assisted person was under a clear statutory duty to pay over the moneys recovered in an action to the Law Society (now to the Board) and that, if he committed a breach of that duty, he would in counsel's view, be ordered by the court to make good the resulting loss suffered by the legal aid fund. Subject to the provisions of regulation 90, the Board is of the same view.

As to the Board's powers to defer payment of solicitors' profit costs see NFG 5.7, p. 54.

33 PROCEDURE ON TAXATION

1. *Form of bill*   A solicitor for an assisted person, in accordance with the order made by the court, must lodge in the taxing office a bill of costs, whether the assisted person was the successful or unsuccessful party in the proceedings. Together with the bill of costs and the documents usually lodged, there should be included the solicitor's copy of the legal aid certificate (copies of the offer and acceptance will not suffice) and any written authorities of the Area Director given pursuant to the Civil Legal Aid (General) Regulations 1989.

The solicitor for an assisted person who has obtained an order for costs to be paid by another party must lodge a six-column bill, of which the inner three columns should contain the *inter partes* costs and the outer columns any items of legal aid costs in excess of the *inter partes* costs to be taxed.

In the case of an assisted person who has not been awarded an order for costs to be paid by another party the solicitor should lodge a three-column bill.

2. *Allocaturs and certificates*   The allocatur or certificate relating to an assisted person who has obtained an order for the payment of his costs by another party will show:

(i) the total profit costs and disbursements allowed *inter partes*,

(ii) the legal aid costs allowed in accordance with the Act, which amount will be sub-divided into three parts, namely

(a) solicitor's profit costs;
(b) counsel's fees;
(c) other disbursements; and

(iii) the Value Added Tax payable.

It should be pointed out that the certificate belongs to the party by whom it is obtained, *i.e.* the successful party. When the certificate contains the costs of both parties to an action because both parties are assisted persons, the two solicitors should mutually agree about lodgment of the certificate with the Area Director or that one party should obtain an office copy for lodgment.

3. *Generally*   With the few exceptions made necessary by the Regulations, the taxation of bills should proceed with no regard to whether a party is assisted or not. The main differences in assisted cases will be that counsel's fees will not be marked on his brief or other documents and that any authorities will have to be produced on taxation. The absence of such authorities will not affect an *inter partes* taxation. In such case the relevant items may be allowed against the other party, but will not be allowed on the legal aid bill (but see *Ullah* v. *Hall Line Ltd.* [1959] 1 Lloyd's Rep. 238).

34 CRIMINAL LEGAL AID—ADMINISTRATIVE COMMITTALS

1. The Home Office has issued guidance (Circular No. 71/1986) to magistrates' courts and prosecuting agencies suggesting steps whereby defence solicitors could be enabled to take fuller advantage of the opportunity given by section 6(2) of the Magistrates' Courts Act 1980 (as amended by section 61 of the Criminal Justice Act 1982) not to attend committal proceedings involving only written statements.

2. The Home Office circular points out that where an accused person has a solicitor acting for him, examining justices may commit him for trial on written statements alone. The solicitor does not need to be present in court unless he or she disputes the sufficienty of the evidence disclosed in the written statements or there are other circumstances in which the defendant may need to be represented. The use of the dispensation in appropriate cases can reduce calls on defence solicitors' time and result in savings in payment from the legal aid fund to solicitors for attending committal proceedings.

3. The circular emphasises that to enable the procedure to work it is essential for the prosecution to provide written statements in good time before the date of hearing to enable the solicitor to take instructions from the accused person on the written statements and to decide whether or not an attendance is necessary.

4. The Legal Aid Board is of the opinion that, subject to the correct procedure being followed, solicitors should be expected to exercise the option not to attend court in appropriate cases. Accordingly they have decided that payment will not be made out of the legal aid fund for attendances at committal proceedings by either solicitors or counsel except in any of the following circumstances:

(i) where a submission is to be made of no case to answer or there is a need to take oral evidence from witnesses;

(ii) where there is to be an application for bail or for variation of the condition of bail;

(iii) where there is to be an application to lift reporting restrictions;

(iv) where there is to be an application in relation to the venue of the trial;

(v) where the written statements on which the committal will be based have been served less than 14 days before the date fixed for the committal proceedings;

(vi) where the solicitor has to attend to make an oral legal aid application to the magistrates' court or to make representation about the grant of legal aid for the Crown Court proceedings; or

(vii) where there is any other matter requiring the solicitor's or counsel's attendance at the hearing which may be reasonable in the particular circumstances of the case.

Solicitors will be expected, when submitting bills for payment to state precisely why attendance was necessary on each occasion.

5. Attached to the Home Office circular is a copy of a form of notice of non-attendance for use by defence solicitors wishing to inform the court that they will not be present at committal proceedings based on written statements alone. This form was prepared by the Home Office in consultation with the Law Society and issued to courts with the request that in cases where the defence solicitor has applied for legal aid the clerk to the justices should enclose a copy of the form with the court's response to the legal aid application.

35 COSTS OF THE OFFICIAL SOLICITOR

Where the Official Solicitor is acting for a person under a disability, he will not require an undertaking as to his costs from the solicitor to an assisted person but only an undertaking from the assisted person in respect of his costs limited to such amount as the court may order the assisted person to pay under section 17(1) of the Legal Aid Act 1988 and the Regulations made thereunder.

36 ABWOR FOR PROCEEDINGS BEFORE THE MENTAL HEALTH REVIEW TRIBUNAL

Eligibility and Assessment
ABWOR will be available to the person whose case or whose application to the Tribunal is, or is to be, the subject of the proceedings (Legal Advice and Assistance (Scope) Regulations 1989, reg. 9(a)). ABWOR would be available to a patient where the nearest relative has made the application.

The usual requirements will apply for obtaining the client's signature on the green form but regulation 14(3) of the Legal Advice and Assistance Regulation 1989 provides for a solicitor to accept an application for advice and assistance made on behalf of a patient. Applications for ABWOR should be made on the usual form (ABWOR 1).

Regulation 3(2) of the Legal Advice and Assistance (Amendment) Regulations 1990 disapplies regulations 22(5) of the Legal Advice and Assistance Regulations 1989 from ABWOR for Mental Health Review Tribunals and Board of Prison Visitors. It follows that ABWOR has to be approved unless it appears unreasonable that approval should be granted in the particular circumstances of the case in accordance with regulation 22(6) of the Legal Advice and Assistance Regulations 1989.

The solicitor should undertake the initial preparation of the case under the current green form limit. This should include obtaining the hospital's statement from the Regional Office of the Tribunal and an initial interview with the patient. If the hospital is at some distance from the solicitor's office, and it appears that the current limit may not be sufficient, an application should be made to the legal aid office for an extension to the financial limit.

Unless the ABWOR specifically authorises such work, prior permission must be obtained for a "report or opinion of an expert," *e.g.* a psychiatric report, or where "an act. . .involves unusually large expenditure" (see generally the Legal Advice and Assistance Regulations 1989, reg. 22(7)). Solicitors should therefore specify any report they wish to obtain when applying for ABWOR approval. It is expected that the solicitor will use his or her professional judgment to decide whether or not an independent psychiatric or other report is required. Any request to obtain a second independent psychiatric report, where, for instance, the solicitor or client considers the first report unsatisfactory, would also be dealt with under the same regulation. It is unlikely that approval will be given to the instruction of counsel (Legal Advice and Assistance Regulations 1989, reg. 23) as it will be expected that solicitors will usually be sufficiently experienced to render such a step unnecessary.

There is, at present, no requirement under the Legal Advice and Assistance Regulations or the Tribunal Regulations that the Tribunal should be notified of the granting of ABWOR and consequently that the patient will be represented. It would nevertheless be helpful if the Tribunal Office is notified.

Automatic Referral of Patients and Panel Solicitors
Section 68 of the Mental Health Act 1983 requires hospital managers to refer patients to the Tribunal where patients have not, of their own accord, applied to the Tribunal within the first six months or in the previous three years. These patients are likely to be the most seriously debilitated, lacking in awareness of their rights and the ability to initiate them.

The Department of Social Security has asked hospitals to implement this provision and they have issued a circular to Health Authorities asking them to ensure that hospitals inform patients of their rights and that patients be assisted to obtain legal help.

To assist hospitals in this task, a panel of solicitors who have considerable experience of Mental Health Review Tribunal work and who are competent to represent patients has been established. It should, however, be made absolutely clear that the existence of the panel will not in any way limit the patient's right to instruct the solicitor of his or her choice whether or not that solicitor is on the panel. The panel is supervised by the Law Society's Practice Directorate. Solicitors who wish to be considered for the panel should apply to The Legal Practice Directorate, The Law Society, 50–52 Chancery Lane, London WC2A 1SX. (Tel: 071–242–1222).

37 CARE PROCEEDINGS

When a child is made the subject of care proceedings, the child, the parents or any other party except the local authority may apply for legal aid to be represented in those proceedings under Part VI of the Legal Aid Act 1988 (s.28(1)). The full list of proceedings covered is set out in section 29(1)

(i) care proceedings under section 1 of the Children and Young Persons Act 1969 (the 1969 Act) or under section 21A of the Child Care Act 1980 (the 1980 Act);

(ii) variation and discharge of supervision or care orders under sections 15 or 21 of the 1969 Act;

(iii) appeals in such proceedings under sections 2(12), 3(8), 16(8) or 21(4) of the 1969 Act or section 21A of the 1980 Act;

(iv) applications under section 3 of the Children and Young Persons Act 1963 for an order directing the local authority to take proceedings under section 1 of the 1969 Act;

(v) proceedings over parental rights resolutions under sections 3, 5, or 67(2) of the 1980 Act;

(vi) proceedings about access under Part IA of the 1980 Act.

The authority to which application is made depends upon the court in which proceedings are taking place (Legal Aid Act 1988, s.27(4)):

(a) if the proceedings are in the juvenile court, apply to the court;

(b) for appeals to the Crown Court, apply to that court or the juvenile court whose order is being appealed against;

(c) for appeals to the High Court, apply to the Board

(d) for representation in applications for emergency orders, apply to a justice of the peace.

The procedure for applications, other than those to the Board, is mainly the same as for criminal legal aid and is set out in the Legal Aid in Criminal and Care Proceedings (General) Regulations 1989.

Subject to means, representation may be granted where it "appears desirable to do so in the interests of justice" (Legal Aid Act, s.28(2)). If it is refused by a juvenile court or justice of the peace, the applicant has no right to have the decision reviewed under regulation 15 Criminal and Care Proceedings Regulations (Criminal and Care Proceedings (General) Regulations 1989 reg. 60(3)). However, subject to means, representation *must* be granted where a juvenile is brought before the court under section 21A of the 1980 Act and wants to be represented.

Any doubts about granting representation should be resolved in favour of the applicant (Legal Aid Act, s.28(5)).

The normal criminal legal aid rules for assessing resources and means apply (Criminal and Care Proceedings (General) Regulations 1989, reg. 26 and Scheds. 3 and 4). However, a guardian *ad litem* is not "an appropriate contributor" (Criminal and Care Proceedings (General) Regulations 1989, reg. 57).

An application for civil legal aid should be made in the usual way on Form CLA1.

The Law Society has set up a national panel of solicitors who will provide representation and have a measure of expertise in child care cases. A list of solicitors on the panel and further information may be obtained from the Child Care Panel Adminisrator, The Legal Practice Directorate, The Law Society, 50–52 Chancery Lane, London WC2A 1SX. (Tel: 071–242–1222). Applicants for legal aid are, nonetheless, free to nominate any practising solicitor of their choice.

38 APPLICATIONS FOR BAIL TO THE HIGH COURT

Legal aid has always been available for applications for bail to the Judge in Chambers in the High Court. Nevertheless, the practice has grown up of not applying for legal aid on the assumption that an application is likely to be refused in view of the alternative Official Solicitor procedure.

The Official Solicitor Procedure should be used whenever it is appropriate to do so, as the grant of legal aid for an application to a Judge in Chambers in the High Court is a very much more expensive procedure. In cases where it is decided to apply for legal aid, the application should provide information relating to one or more of the following points:

(i) whether the defendant is in the custody of the magistrates' court (although legal aid is not restricted to such cases, defendants in the custody of the Crown Court can apply to that court for bail under criminal legal aid order);

(ii) the length of time the defendant may have to remain in custody pending trial;

(iii) whether the defendant has already applied for bail to the magistrates' court (bail is often granted on a second appearance when difficulties relating to sureties have been sorted out);

(iv) whether the defendant has been represented on previous applications for bail;

(v) whether it is suggested that the reasons given by the court for refusing bail were unreasonable or the grounds for refusing bail have altered;

(vi) whether an emergency legal aid certificate has previously been granted to the defendant in connection with the same case for an application to the Judge in Chambers in the High Court;

(vii) any special social or other reasons for making an application for bail.

39 LEGAL AID ABROAD

European Agreement on the Transmission of Applications for Legal Aid—Strasbourg January 27, 1977

Legal aid area offices receive a number of enquiries about legal aid abroad and practitioners may find it helpful to be reminded of the provisions of the European Agreement on the Transmission of Applications for Legal Aid which was ratified by the United Kingdom on January 17, 1978.

Other countries to have ratified the Agreement are Austria; Belgium; Denmark; Eire; France; Greece; Italy; Luxembourg; Norway; Portugal; Spain; Sweden; Turkey. Finland, which is not a member state of the Council of Europe, has acceded to the Agreement.

Under the Agreement, the Legal Aid Board is the Transmitting and Receiving Authority for England and Wales. This means that where a person requires legal aid for civil, commercial or administrative proceedings in one of the above countries, he may send his application to the Legal Aid Board which will transmit it to the appropriate authority in that country. Similarly, as the Receiving Authority, the Legal Aid Board accepts applications transmitted under the Agreement and passes them to the appropriate legal aid area office. (At present No. 1 legal aid area, London.)

Applications for transmission should be prepared in the same way and on the same forms (including form CLA 4) as applications for civil legal aid in England and Wales. Most countries will accept applications in English. However, France requires statements, medical reports (if submitted) and other documents to be accompanied by translations into French.

France also requires each application to be accompanied by a financial statement, in narrative form and in French, certified by the applicant's solicitor as being true to the best of his knowledge and belief. Austria requires applications to be accompanied by translations in German.

Advice and assistance under the green form scheme is available (subject to financial eligibility) for the preparation of applications for transmission under the Agreement including obtaining any necessary translations. Applications for transmission should be sent to The Legal Aid Board, Newspaper House, 8–16 Great New Street, London, EC4 3BN.

Legal Aid (Functions) Order 1989

Coming into force April 1, 1989

The Lord Chancellor, in exercise of the power conferred on him by section 3(4) of the Legal Aid Act 1988, hereby makes the following Order, a draft of which has, in accordance with section 36(2)(b) of that Act, been laid before and approved by resolution of each House of Parliament—

Citation and commencement

1. This Order may be cited as the Legal Aid (Functions) Order 1989 and shall come into force on April 1, 1989.

Functions under Part V of the Legal Aid Act 1988

2. The general function conferred on the Legal Aid Board by section 3(2) of the Legal Aid Act 1988 shall include all such functions mentioned in subsection (4)(b) of that section as are required to be exercised by the Board to enable it—

    (a) to determine under the Legal Aid in Criminal and Care Proceedings (General) Regulations 1989 as respects representation under Part V of that Act:

        (i) an application for review of a refusal by a magistrates' court to grant representation;

        (ii) a renewed application for amendment or withdrawal of a grant of representation, or for representation by counsel; and

        (iii) an application for prior authority to incur expenditure; and

    (b) to promote or assist in the promotion of publicity relating to the functions mentioned in that subsection.

Functions under Part VI of the Legal Aid Act 1988

3. The general function conferred on the Legal Aid Board by section 3(2) of the Legal Aid Act 1988 shall include all such functions mentioned in subsection (4)(c) of that section as are required to be exercised by the Board to enable it to determine under the Legal Aid in Criminal and Care Proceedings (General) Regulations 1989 as respects representations under Part VI of that Act—

    (a) a renewed application for amendment or withdrawal of a grant of representation; and

    (b) an application for prior authority to incur expenditure.

EXPLANATORY NOTE

(This note is not part of the Order)

This Order confers on the Legal Aid Board the functions required to enable area committees under the Legal Aid in Criminal and Care Proceedings Regulations 1989 (S.I. 1989/344) to determine the applications mentioned in articles 2 and 3.

In criminal proceedings the relevant applications are applications for review of refusals of representation by magistrates' courts, renewed applications for amendment or withdrawal of representation (or for representation by counsel), and applications for prior authority to incur expenditure.

In care proceedings the relevant applications are renewed applications for amendment or withdrawal of representation, and applications for prior authority to incur expenditure.

Article 2 also confers on the Board the functions required to enable it to promote publicity about Criminal Legal Aid.

Legal Aid Act 1988

CHAPTER 34

ARRANGEMENT OF SECTIONS

PART I

PRELIMINARY

PART II

LEGAL AID BOARD AND LEGAL AID

PART III

ADVICE AND ASSISTANCE

PART VII

GENERAL AND SUPPLEMENTARY

PART VIII

MISCELLANEOUS

Scottish provisions

Supplementary

SCHEDULES:

An Act to make new provision for the administration of, and to revise the law relating to, legal aid, advice and assistance.

[29th July 1988]

PART I

PRELIMINARY

Purpose of this Act

1. The purpose of this Act is to establish a framework for the provision under Parts II, III, IV, V and VI of advice, assistance and representation which is publicly funded with a view to helping persons who might otherwise be unable to obtain advice, assistance or representation on account of their means.

Interpretation

2.—(1) This section has effect for the interpretation of this Act.

(2) "Advice" means oral or written advice on the application of English law to any particular circumstances that have arisen in relation to the person seeking the advice and as to the steps which that person might appropriately take having regard to the application of English law to those circumstances.

(3) "Assistance" means assistance in taking any of the steps which a person might take, including steps with respect to proceedings, having regard to the application of English law to any particular circumstances that have arisen in relation to him, whether by taking such steps on his behalf (including assistance by way of representation) or by assisting him in taking them on his own behalf.

(4) "Representation" means representation for the purposes of proceedings and it includes—

(a) all such assistance as is usually given by a solicitor or counsel in the steps preliminary or incidental to any proceedings;

(b) all such assistance as is usually so given in civil proceedings in arriving at or giving effect to a compromise to avoid or bring to an end any proceedings; and

(c) in the case of criminal proceedings, advice and assistance as to any appeal;

and related expressions have corresponding meanings.

(5) Regulations may specify what is, or is not, to be included in advice or assistance of any description, or representation for the purposes of proceedings of any description, to which any Part or provision of a Part of this Act applies and the regulations may provide for the inclusion, in prescribed circumstances, of advice or assistance given otherwise than under this Act.

(6) Advice, assistance and representation under this Act, except when made available under Part II, is only by persons who are solicitors or barristers, but in the case of Part II, may be by other persons.

(7) In any particular case, advice, assistance and representation under this Act, except when made available under Part II, shall be by solicitor and, so far

as necessary counsel; but regulations may prescribe the circumstances in which representation is to be by counsel only or by solicitor only and regulate representation by more than one counsel.

(8) The Lord Chancellor may, if it appears to him to be necessary to do so for the purpose of fulfilling any obligation imposed on the United Kingdom or Her Majesty's Government in the United Kingdom by any international agreement, by order direct that such advice or assistance relating to the application of other laws than English law as is specified in the order shall be advice or assistance for any of the purposes of this Act.

(9) For the purposes of the application of subsection (8) above in the case of an obligation to provide for the transmission to other countries of applications for legal aid under their laws, the reference to advice or assistance relating to the application of other laws includes a reference to advice or assistance for the purposes of making and transmitting such an application.

(10) In this Act "person" does not include a body of persons corporate or unincorporate which is not concerned in a representative, fiduciary or official capacity so as to authorise advice, assistance or representation to be granted to such a body.

(11) In this Act "legally assisted person" means any person who receives, under this Act, advice, assistance or representation and, in relation to proceedings, any reference to an assisted party or an unassisted party is to be construed accordingly.

PART II

LEGAL AID BOARD AND LEGAL AID

The Legal Aid Board
3.—(1) There shall be established a body to be known as the Legal Aid Board (in this Act referred to as "the Board").

(2) Subject to subsections (3) and (4) below, the Board shall have the general function of securing that advice, assistance and representation are available in accordance with this Act and of administering this Act.

(3) Subsection (2) above does not confer on the Board any functions with respect to the grant of representation under Part VI for the purposes of proceedings for contempt.

(4) Subsection (2) above does not confer on the Board any of the following functions unless the Lord Chancellor so directs by order and then only to the extent specified in the order.

The functions referred to are—

    (a) determination of the costs of representation under Part IV;

    (b) functions as respects representation under Part V other than determination of the costs of representation for the purposes of proceedings in magistrates' courts;

    (c) functions as respects representation under Part VI for the purposes of care proceedings other than proceedings on an appeal from the decision of a juvenile court to the High Court;

(d) determination of the financial resources of persons for the purposes of this Act.

(5) Subject to subsection (6) below, the Board shall consist of no fewer than 11 and no more than 17 members appointed by the Lord Chancellor; and the Lord Chancellor shall appoint one of the members to be chairman.

(6) The Lord Chancellor may, by order, substitute, for the number for the time being specified in subsection (5) above as the maximum or minimum membership of the Board, such other number as he thinks appropriate.

(7) The Board shall include at least two solicitors appointed after consultation with the Law Society.

(8) The Lord Chancellor shall consult the General Council of the Bar with a view to the inclusion on the Board of at least two barristers.

(9) In appointing persons to be members of the Board the Lord Chancellor shall have regard to the desirability of securing that the Board includes persons having expertise in or knowledge of—

(a) the provision of legal services;

(b) the work of the courts and social conditions; and

(c) management.

(10) Schedule 1 to this Act shall have effect with respect to the Board.

Powers of the Board

4.—(1) Subject to the provisions of this Act, the Board may do anything—

(a) which it considers necessary or desirable to provide or secure the provision of advice, assistance and representation under this Act; or

(b) which is calculated to facilitate or is incidental or conducive to the discharge of its functions;

and advice, assistance and representation may be provided in different ways in different areas in England and Wales and in different ways in different fields of law.

(2) Without prejudice to the generality of subsection (1) above, the Board shall have power—

(a) to enter into any contract including, subject to subsection (7) below, any contract to acquire or dispose of land;

(b) to make grants (with or without conditions, including conditions as to repayment);

(c) to make loans;

(d) to invest money;

(e) to promote or assist in the promotion of publicity relating to the functions of the Board;

(f) to undertake any inquiry or investigation which the Board considers necessary or expedient in relation to the discharge of its functions; and

(g) to give the Lord Chancellor such advice as it may consider appropriate in relation to the provision of advice, assistance and representation under this Act.

(3) Subsection (1) above does not confer on the Board power to borrow money or to acquire and hold shares in bodies corporate or take part in forming bodies corporate.

(4) The powers to provide advice, assistance or representation under this Part and to secure its provision under this Part by means of contracts with, or grants or loans to, other persons or bodies—

    (a) shall not be exercisable unless the Lord Chancellor so directs and then only to the extent specified in the direction; and

    (b) if exercisable, shall be exercised in accordance with any directions given by him.

(5) The power to secure the provision of representation under Part IV by means of contracts with other persons shall only be exercisable in the classes of case prescribed in regulations.

(6) Advice, assistance and representation provided by the Board under this Part may be granted with or without limitations and may be amended, withdrawn or revoked.

(7) The power under subsection (2) above to enter into contracts to acquire or dispose of land shall not be exercised without the approval in writing of the Lord Chancellor.

(8) The Board may, from time to time, prepare and submit to the Lord Chancellor proposals for the assumption by it of any functions in relation to the provision of advice, assistance or representation under this Act.

Duties of the Board

5.—(1) The Board shall, from time to time, publish information as to the discharge of its functions in relation to advice, assistance and representation including the forms and procedures and other matters connected therewith.

(2) The Board shall, from time to time, furnish to the Lord Chancellor such information as he may require relating to its property and to the discharge or proposed discharge of its functions.

(3) It shall be the duty of the Board to provide to the Lord Chancellor, as soon as possible after 31st March in each year, a report on the discharge of its functions during the preceding twelve months.

(4) The Board shall deal in any report under subsection (3) above with such matters as the Lord Chancellor may from time to time direct.

(5) The Board shall have regard, in discharging its functions, to such guidance as may from time to time be given by the Lord Chancellor.

(6) Guidance under subsection (5) above shall not relate to the consideration or disposal, in particular cases, of—

    (a) applications for advice, assistance or representation;

    (b) supplementary or incidental applications or requests to the Board in connection with any case where advice, assistance or representation has been made available.

(7) For the purposes of subsection (2) above the Board shall permit any person authorised by the Lord Chancellor for the purpose to inspect and make copies of any accounts or documents of the Board and shall furnish such explanations of them as that person or the Lord Chancellor may require.

Board to have separate legal aid fund

6.—(1) The Board shall establish and maintain a separate legal aid fund.

(2) Subject to regulations, there shall be paid out of the fund—

(a) such sums as are, by virtue of any provision of or made under this Act, due from the Board in respect of remuneration and expenses properly incurred in connection with the provision, under this Act, of advice, assistance or representation;

(b) costs awarded to any unassisted party under section 13 or 18;

(c) any part of a contribution repayable by the Board under section 16(4) or 23(7); and

(d) such other payments for the purposes of this Act as the Lord Chancellor may, with the concurrence of the Treasury, determine.

(3) Subject to regulations, there shall be paid into the fund—

(a) any contribution payable to the Board by any person in respect of advice, assistance or representation under this Act;

(b) any sum awarded under an order of a court or agreement as to costs in any proceedings in favour of any legally assisted party which is payable to the Board;

(c) any sum which is to be paid out of property recovered or preserved for any legally assisted party to any proceedings;

(d) any sum in respect of the costs of an unassisted party awarded under section 13 or 18 which is repaid to the Board under that section;

(e) the sums to be paid by the Lord Chancellor in pursuance of section 42(1)(a); and

(f) such other receipts of the Board as the Lord Chancellor may, with the concurrence of the Treasury, determine.

Accounts and audit

7.—(1) The Board shall keep separate accounts with respect to—

(a) its legal aid fund; and

(b) the receipts and expenditure of the Board which do not relate to that fund;

and shall prepare in respect of each financial year a statement of accounts.

(2) The accounts shall be kept and the statement of accounts shall be prepared in such form as the Lord Chancellor may, with the approval of the Treasury, direct.

(3) The accounts shall be audited by persons to be appointed in respect of each financial year by the Lord Chancellor in accordance with a scheme of audit approved by him, and the auditors shall be furnished by the Board with copies of the statement and shall prepare a report to the Lord Chancellor on the accounts and statement.

(4) No person shall be qualified to be appointed auditor under subsection (3) above unless he is—

(a) a member of a body of accountants established in the United Kingdom and for the time being recognised for the purposes of section 389(1)(a) of the Companies Act 1985;

(b) authorised by the Secretary of State under section 389(1)(b) of that Act to be appointed auditor of a company; or

(c) a member of the Chartered Institute of Public Finance and Accountancy;

but a firm may be so appointed if each of its members is qualified to be so appointed.

(5) Upon completion of the audit of the accounts, the auditors shall send to the Lord Chancellor a copy of the statement of accounts and of their report, and the Lord Chancellor shall send a copy of the statement and of the report to the Comptroller and Auditor General.

(6) The Lord Chancellor and the Comptroller and Auditor General may inspect the accounts and any records relating to them.

(7) The Lord Chancellor shall lay before each House of Parliament a copy of every statement of accounts and reports of the auditors sent to him under subsection (5) above.

(8) In this section "financial year" means the period beginning with the day on which the Board is established and ending with 31st March next following and each subsequent period of 12 months ending with 31st March in each year.

PART III

ADVICE AND ASSISTANCE

Scope of this part

8.—(1) Subject to the provisions of this section, this Part applies to any advice or assistance and advice and assistance under this Part shall be available to any person subject to and in accordance with the provisions of this section and sections 9, 10 and 11.

(2) This Part only applies to assistance by way of representation if, and to the extent that, regulations so provide; and regulations may make such provision in relation to representation for the purposes of any proceedings before a court or tribunal or at a statutory inquiry.

(3) Advice or assistance of all descriptions or advice or assistance of any prescribed description is excluded from this Part, or is so excluded as regards any area, if regulations so provide; and if regulations provide for all descriptions to be excluded as regards all areas then, so long as the regulations so provide, this Part (other than this subsection) shall not have effect.

(4) Advice or assistance of any prescribed description is restricted to its provision to prescribed descriptions of persons if regulations so provide.

(5) This Part does not apply to advice or assistance given to a person in connection with proceedings before a court or tribunal or at a statutory inquiry at a time when he is being represented in those proceedings under any other Part of this Act.

Availability of, and payment for, advice and assistance

9.—(1) Advice and assistance to which this Part applies shall be available to any person whose financial resources are such as, under regulations, make him eligible for advice or assistance under this Part.

(2) If regulations so provide, advice or assistance to which this Part applies shall be available, in prescribed circumstances and subject to any prescribed conditions, to persons without reference to their financial resources.

(3) Subject to any prescribed exceptions, assistance by way of representation under this Part shall not be given without the approval of the Board.

(4) Approval under subsection (3) above may be given with or without limitations and may be amended, withdrawn or revoked.

(5) Except as provided by subsection (6) or (7) below, the legally assisted person shall not be required to pay to his solicitor any charge or fee.

(6) Except as provided by subsection (7) below, a legally assisted person shall, if his financial resources are such as, under regulations, make him liable to make a contribution, be liable to pay to his solicitor, in respect of the advice or assistance, charges or fees of such amount as is determined or fixed by or under the regulations.

(7) A legally assisted person to whom advice or assistance is made available by virtue of regulations under subsection (2) above shall, in circumstances prescribed by the regulations and, if the regulations apply only to persons of a prescribed description, he is a person of that description, be liable to pay to his solicitor, in respect of the advice or assistance, a fee of such amount as is fixed by or under the regulations (in lieu of a contribution under subsection (6) above).

Financial limit on prospective costs of advice or assistance

10.—(1) Where at any time (whether before or after the advice or assistance has begun to be given) it appears to a solicitor that the cost of giving advice or assistance to a person under this Part is likely to exceed the prescribed limit—

    (a) the solicitor shall determine to what extent that advice or assistance can be given without exceeding that limit; and

    (b) shall not give it (nor, as the case may be, instruct counsel to give it) so as to exceed that limit except with the approval of the Board.

(2) Approval under subsection (1)(b) above may be given with or without limitations and may be amended, withdrawn or revoked.

(3) For the purposes of this section the cost of giving advice or assistance shall be taken to consist of such of the following as are applicable in the circumstances, namely—

    (a) any disbursements, that is to say, expenses (including fees payable to counsel) which may be incurred by the solicitor or his firm in, or in connection with, the giving of the advice or assistance; and

    (b) any charges or fees (other than charges for disbursements) which would be properly chargeable by the solicitor or his firm in respect of the advice or assistance.

Payment for advice or assistance otherwise than through legally assisted person's contribution

11.—(1) This section applies to any charges or fees which, apart from section 9, would be properly chargeable in respect of advice or assistance given under this Part, in so far as those charges or fees are not payable by the legally assisted person in accordance with that section.

(2) Except in so far as regulations otherwise provide, charges or fees to which this section applies shall constitute a first charge for the benefit of the solicitor—

(a) on any costs which are payable to the legally assisted person by any other person in respect of the matter in connection with which the advice or assistance is given; and

(b) on any property which is recovered or preserved for the legally assisted person in connection with that matter.

(3) In so far as the charge created by subsection (2) above in respect of any charges or fees to which this section applies is insufficient to meet them, the deficiency shall, subject to subsection (5) below, be payable to the solicitor by the Board.

(4) For the purposes of subsection (2) above, it is immaterial, in the case of costs, whether the costs are payable by virtue of a judgment, order of a court or otherwise and, in the case of property, what its nature is and where it is situated and the property within the charge includes the legally assisted person's rights under any compromise or settlement arrived at to avoid proceedings or bring them to an end.

(5) For the purpose of determining what charges or fees would be properly chargeable, and whether there is a deficiency to be paid by the Board, charges or fees in respect of advice or assistance under this Part shall, in prescribed circumstances, be determined in such manner as may be prescribed.

Limit on costs against person receiving assistance by way of representation

12.—(1) Where a person receives any assistance by way of representation in any proceedings before a court or tribunal or at a statutory inquiry, then, except in so far as regulations otherwise provide, his liability by virtue of an order for costs made against him with respect to the proceedings shall not exceed the amount (if any) which is a reasonable one for him to pay having regard to all the circumstances, including the financial resources of all the parties and their conduct in connection with the dispute.

(2) Regulations shall make provision as to the court, tribunal or person by whom that amount is to be determined and the extent to which any determination of that amount is to be final.

(3) None of the following, namely, a legally assisted person's dwelling house, clothes, household furniture and the tools and implements of his trade shall—

(a) be taken into account in assessing his financial resources for the purposes of this section, or

(b) be subject to execution or any corresponding process in any part of the United Kingdom to enforce the order,

except so far as regulations may prescribe.

Costs of successful unassisted parties

13.—(1) This section applies to proceedings in which a person who receives assistance by way of representation is a party and which are finally decided in favour of an unassisted party.

(2) In any proceedings to which this section applies the court by which the proceedings are so decided may, subject to subsections (3) and (4) below, make an order for the payment by the Board to the unassisted party of the whole or any part of the costs incurred by him in the proceedings.

(3) Before making an order under this section, the court shall consider what order for costs should be made against the assisted party and for determining his liability in respect of such costs.

(4) An order under this section in respect of any costs may only be made if—

(a) an order for costs would be made in the proceedings apart from this Act;

(b) as respects the costs incurred in a court of first instance, those proceedings were instituted by the assisted party and the court is satisfied that the unassisted party will suffer severe financial hardship unless the order is made; and

(c) in any case, the court is satisfied that it is just and equitable in all the circumstances of the case that provision for the costs should be made out of public funds.

(5) Without prejudice to any other provision restricting appeals from any court, no appeal shall lie against an order under this section, or against a refusal to make such an order, except on a point of law.

(6) In this section "costs" means costs as between party and party, and includes the costs of applying for an order under this section; and where a party begins to receive the assistance after the proceedings have been instituted, or ceases to receive the assistance before they are finally decided or otherwise receives the assistance in connection with part only of the proceedings, the reference in subsection (2) above to the costs incurred by the unassisted party in the proceedings shall be construed as a reference to so much of those costs as is attributable to that part.

(7) For the purposes of this section proceedings shall be treated as finally decided in favour of the unassisted party—

(a) if no appeal lies against the decision in his favour;

(b) if an appeal lies against the decision with leave, and the time limited for application for leave expires without leave being granted; or

(c) if leave to appeal against the decision is granted or is not required, and no appeal is brought within the time limited for appeal;

and where an appeal against the decision is brought out of time the court by which the appeal (or any further appeal in those proceedings) is determined may make an order for the repayment by the unassisted party to the Board of the whole or any part of any sum previously paid to him under this section in respect of those proceedings.

(8) Where a court decides any proceedings in favour of the unassisted party and an appeal lies (with or without leave) against that decision, the court may, if it thinks fit, make or refuse to make an order under this section forthwith, but if an order is made forthwith it shall not take effect—

(a) where leave to appeal is required, unless the time limited for applications for leave to appeal expires without leave being granted;

(b) where leave to appeal is granted or is not required, unless the time limited for appeal expires without an appeal being brought.

(9) For the purposes of this section "court" includes a tribunal.

PART IV

CIVIL LEGAL AID

Scope of this part

14.—(1) This Part applies to such proceedings before courts or tribunals or at statutory inquiries in England and Wales as—

(a) are proceedings of a description for the time being specified in Part I of Schedule 2 to this Act, except proceedings for the time being specified in Part II of that Schedule; and

(b) are not proceedings for which representation may be granted under Part V,

and representation under this Part shall be available to any person subject to and in accordance with sections 15 and 16.

(2) Subject to subsection (3) below, Schedule 2 may be varied by regulations so as to extend or restrict the categories of proceedings for the purposes of which representation is available under this Part, by reference to the court, tribunal or statutory inquiry, to the issues involved, to the capacity in which the person seeking representation is concerned or otherwise.

(3) Regulations under subsection (2) above may not have the effect of adding any proceedings before any court or tribunal or at any statutory inquiry before or at which persons have no right, and are not normally allowed, to be represented by counsel or a solicitor.

(4) Regulations under subsection (2) above which extend the categories of proceedings for the purposes of which representation is available under this Part shall not be made without the consent of the Treasury.

Availability of, and payment for, representation under this Part

15.—(1) Subject to subsections (2) and (3) below, representation under this Part for the purposes of proceedings to which this Part applies shall be available to any person whose financial resources are such as, under regulations, make him eligible for representation under this Part.

(2) A person shall not be granted representation for the purposes of any proceedings unless he satisfies the Board that he has reasonable grounds for taking, defending or being a party to the proceedings.

(3) A person may be refused representation for the purposes of any proceedings if, in the particular circumstances of the case it appears to the Board—

(a) unreasonable that he should be granted representation under this Part, or

(b) more appropriate that he should be given assistance by way of representation under Part III;

and regulations may prescribe the criteria for determining any questions arising under paragraph (b) above.

(4) Representation under this Part may be granted by the Board with or without limitations and may be amended, withdrawn or revoked.

(5) Where the case is one in which the Board has power to secure the provision of representation under this Part by means of contracts with other

person, the grant of representation under this Part may be limited under subsection (4) above as regards the persons who may represent the legally assisted person to representation only in pursuance of a contract made with the Board.

(6) Except in so far as he is required under section 16 to make a contribution, a legally assisted person shall not be required to make any payment in respect of representation under this Part and it shall be for the Board to pay his solicitor for acting for him and to pay any fees of counsel for so acting.

(7) The Board's obligation under subsection (6) above is—

(a) in the case of representation provided in pursuance of a contract between the Board and the legally assisted person's solicitor, to make such payments as are due under the contract; and

(b) in the case of representation provided otherwise than in pursuance of such a contract, to make such payments as are authorised by regulations.

(8) Nothing in subsection (6) above affects the duty of the solicitor to pay in the first instance expenses incurred in connection with the proceedings that would ordinarily be paid in the first instance by a person's solicitor.

Reimbursement of Board by contributions and out of costs or property recovered

16.—(1) A legally assisted person shall, if his financial resources are such as, under regulations, make him liable to make such a contribution, pay to the Board a contribution in respect of the costs of his being represented under this Part.

(2) The contribution to be required of him by the Board shall be determined by the Board in accordance with the regulations and may take the form of periodical payments or one or more capital sums or both.

(3) The contribution required of a person may, in the case of periodical payments, be made payable by reference to the period during which he is represented under this Part or any shorter period and, in the case of a capital sum, be made payable by instalments.

(4) If the total contribution made by a person in respect of any proceedings exceeds the net liability of the Board on his account, the excess shall be repaid to him.

(5) Any sums recovered by virtue of an order or agreement for costs made in favour of a legally assisted person with respect to the proceedings shall be paid to the Board.

(6) Except so far as regulations otherwise provide—

(a) any sums remaining unpaid on account of a person's contribution in respect of the sums payable by the Board in respect of any proceedings; and

(b) a sum equal to any deficiency by reason of his total contribution being less than the net liability of the Board on his account,

shall be a first charge for the benefit of the Board on any property which is recovered or preserved for him in the proceedings.

(7) For the purposes of subsection (6) above it is immaterial what the nature of the property is and where it is situated and the property within the charge includes the rights of a person under any compromise or settlement arrived at

to avoid the proceedings or bring them to an end and any sums recovered by virtue of an order for costs made in his favour in the proceedings (not being sums payable to the Board under subsection (5) above).

(8) The charge created by subsection (6) above on any damages or costs shall not prevent a court allowing them to be set off against other damages or costs in any case where a solicitor's lien for costs would not prevent it.

(9) In this section references to the net liability of the Board on a legally assisted person's account in relation to any proceedings are references to the aggregate amount of—

(a) the sums paid or payable by the Board on his account in respect of those proceedings to any solicitor or counsel; and

(b) any sums so paid or payable for any advice or assistance under Part III in connection with those proceedings or any matter to which those proceedings relate,

being sums not recouped by the Board by sums which are recoverable by virtue of an order or agreement for costs made in his favour with respect to those proceedings or by virtue of any right of his to be indemnified against expenses incurred by him in connection with those proceedings.

(10) Where a legally assisted person has been represented in any proceedings in pursuance of a contract made with the Board on terms which do not differentiate between the remuneration for his and other cases, the reference in subsection (9)(a) above to the sums paid or payable by the Board on his account in respect of the proceedings shall be construed as a reference to such part of the remuneration payable under the contract as may be specified in writing by the Board.

Limit on costs against assisted party

17.—(1) The liability of a legally assisted party under an order for costs made against him with respect to any proceedings shall not exceed the amount (if any) which is a reasonable one for him to pay having regard to all the circumstances, including the financial resources of all the parties and their conduct in connection with the dispute.

(2) Regulations shall make provision as to the court, tribunal or person by whom that amount is to be determined and the extent to which any determination of that amount is to be final.

(3) None of the following, namely, a legally assisted person's dwelling house, clothes, household furniture and the tools and implements of his trade shall—

(a) be taken into account in assessing his financial resources for the purposes of this section, or

(b) be subject to execution or any corresponding process in any part of the United Kingdom to enforce the order,

except so far as regulations may prescribe.

Costs of successful unassisted parties

18.—(1) This section applies to proceedings to which a legally assisted person is a party and which are finally decided in favour of an unassisted party.

(2) In any proceedings to which this section applies the court by which the proceedings were so decided may, subject to subsections (3) and (4) below,

make an order for the payment by the Board to the unassisted party of the whole or any part of the costs incurred by him in the proceedings.

(3) Before making an order under this section, the court shall consider what order for costs should be made against the assisted party and for determining his liability in respect of such costs.

(4) An order under this section in respect of any costs may only be made if—

    (a) an order for costs would be made in the proceedings apart from this Act;

    (b) as respects the costs incurred in a court of first instance, those proceedings were instituted by the assisted party and the court is satisfied that the unassisted party will suffer severe financial hardship unless the order is made; and

    (c) in any case, the court is satisfied that it is just and equitable in all the circumstances of the case that provision for the costs should be made out of public funds.

(5) Without prejudice to any other provision restricting appeals from any court, no appeal shall lie against an order under this section, or against a refusal to make such an order, except on a point of law.

(6) In this section "costs" means costs as between party and party, and includes the costs of applying for an order under this section; and where a party beings to receive representation after the proceedings have been instituted, or ceases to receive representation before they are finally decided or otherwise receives representation in connection with part only of the proceedings, the reference in subsection (2) above to the costs incurred by the unassisted party in the proceedings shall be construed as a reference to so much of those costs as is attributable to that part.

(7) For the purposes of this section proceedings shall be treated as finally decided in favour of the unassisted party—

    (a) if no appeal lies against the decision in his favour;

    (b) if an appeal lies against the decision with leave, and the time limited for applications for leave expires without leave being granted; or

    (c) if leave to appeal against the decision is granted or is not required, and no appeal is brought within the time limited for appeal;

and where an appeal against the decision is brought out of time the court by which the appeal (or any further appeal in those proceedings) is determined may make an order for the repayment by the unassisted party to the Board of the whole or any part of any sum previously paid to him under this section in respect of those proceedings.

(3) Where a court decides any proceedings in favour of the unassisted party and an appeal lies (with or without leave) against that decision, the court may, if it thinks fit, make or refuse to make an order under this section forthwith, but if an order is made forthwith it shall not take effect—

    (a) where leave to appeal is required, unless the time limited for applications for leave to appeal expires without leave being granted;

    (b) where leave to appeal is granted or is not required, unless the time limited for appeal expires without an appeal being brought.

(9) For the purposes of this section "court" includes a tribunal.

PART V

CRIMINAL LEGAL AID

Scope of this part

19.—(1) This Part applies to criminal proceedings before any of the following—

(a) a magistrates' court;

(b) the Crown Court;

(c) the criminal division of the Court of Appeal or the Courts-Martial Appeal Court; and

(d) the House of Lords in the exercise of its jurisdiction in relation to appeals from either of those courts;

and representation under this Part shall be available to any person subject to and in accordance with sections 21, 22, 23, 24 and 25.

(2) Representation under this Part for the purposes of the proceedings before any court extends to any proceedings preliminary or incidental to the proceedings, including bail proceedings, whether before that or another court.

(3) Representation under this Part for the purposes of the proceedings before a magistrates' court extends to any proceedings before a juvenile court or other magistrates' court to which the case is remitted.

(4) In subsection (2) above in its application to bail proceedings, "court" has the same meaning as in the Bail Act 1976, but that subsection does not extend representation to bail proceedings before a judge of the High Court exercising the jurisdiction of that Court.

(5) In this Part—

"competent authority" is to be construed in accordance with section 20;

"Court of Appeal" means the criminal division of that Court;

"criminal proceedings" includes proceedings for dealing with an offender for an offence or in respect of a sentence or as a fugitive offender and also includes proceedings instituted under section 115 of the Magistrates' Courts Act 1980 (binding over) in respect of an actual or apprehended breach of the peace or other misbehaviour and proceedings for dealing with a person for a failure to comply with a condition of a recognizance to keep the peace or be of good behaviour;

"proceedings for dealing with an offender as a fugitive offender" means proceedings before a metropolitan stipendiary magistrate under section 9 of the Extradition Act 1870, section 7 of the Fugitive Offenders Act 1967 or section 6 of the Criminal Justice Act 1988; and

"remitted," in relation to a juvenile court, means remitted under section 56(1) of the Children and Young Persons Act 1933;

and any reference, in relation to representation for the purposes of any proceedings, to be proceedings before a court includes a reference to any proceedings to which representation under this Part extends by virtue of subsection (2) or (3) above.

Competent authorities to grant representation under this Part

20.—(1) Subject to any provision made by virtue of subsection (10) below, the following courts are competent to grant representation under this Part for the purposes of the following proceedings, on an application made for the purpose.

(2) The court before which any proceedings take place, or are to take place, is always competent as respects those proceedings, except that this does not apply to the House of Lords; and, in the case of the Court of Appeal and the Courts-Martial Appeal Court, the reference to proceedings which are to take place includes proceedings which may take place if notice of appeal is given or an application for leave to appeal is made.

(3) The Court of Appeal or, as the case may be, the Courts-Martial Appeal Court is also competent as respects proceedings on appeal from decisions of theirs to the House of Lords.

(4) The magistrates' court—

(a) which commits a person for trial or sentence or to be dealt with in respect of a sentence;

(b) which has been given a notice of transfer under section 4 of the Criminal Justice Act 1987 (transfer of serious fraud cases); or

(c) from which a person appeals against his conviction or sentence,

is also competent as respects the proceedings before the Crown Court.

(5) The magistrates' court inquiring into an offence as examining justices is also competent, before it decides whether or not to commit the person for trial, as respects any proceedings before the Crown Court on his trial.

(6) The Crown Court is also competent as respects applications for leave to appeal and proceedings on any appeal to the Court of Appeal under section 9(11) of the Criminal Justice Act 1987 (appeals against orders or rulings at preparatory hearings).

(7) On ordering a retrial under section 7 of the Criminal Appeal Act 1968 (new trials ordered by Court of Appeal or House of Lords on fresh evidence) the court ordering the retrial is also competent as respects the proceedings before the Crown Court.

(8) Any magistrates' court to which, in accordance with regulations, a person applies for representation when he has been arrested for an offence but has not appeared or been brought before a court is competent as respects the proceedings in relation to the offence in any magistrates' court.

(9) In the event of the Lord Chancellor making an order under section 3(4) as respects the function of granting representation under this Part for the purposes of proceedings before any court, the Board shall be competent as respects those proceedings, on an application made for the purpose.

(10) An order under section 3(4) may make provision restricting or excluding the competence of any court mentioned in any of subsections (2) to (8) above and may contain such transitional provisions as appear to the Lord Chancellor necessary or expedient.

103

Availability of representation under this Part

21.—(1) Representation under this Part for the purposes of any criminal proceedings shall be available in accordance with this section to the accused or convicted person but shall not be available to the prosecution except in the case of an appeal to the Crown Court against conviction or sentence, for the purpose of enabling an individual who is not acting in an official capacity to resist the appeal.

(2) Subject to subsection (5) below, representation may be granted where it appears to the competent authority to be desirable to do so in the interests of justice; and section 22 applies for the interpretation of this subsection in relation to the proceedings to which that section applies.

(3) Subject to subsection (5) below, representation must be granted—

    (a) where a person is committed for trial on a charge of murder, for his trial;

    (b) where the prosecutor appeals or applies for leave to appeal to the House of Lords, for the proceedings on the appeal;

    (c) where a person charged with an offence before a magistrates' court—
        (i) is brought before the court in pursuance of a remand in custody when he may be again remanded or committed in custody, and
        (ii) is not, but wishes to be, legally represented before the court (not having been legally represented when he was so remanded),

        for so much of the proceedings as relates to the grant of bail; and

    (d) where a person:
        (i) is to be sentenced or otherwise dealt with for an offence by a magistrates' court or the Crown Court, and
        (ii) is to be kept in custody to enable enquiries or a report to be made to assist the court,

        for the proceedings on sentencing or otherwise dealing with him.

(4) Subject to any provision made under section 3(4) by virtue of section 20(10), in a case falling within subsection (3)(a) above, it shall be for the magistrates' court which commits the person for trial, and not for the Crown Court, to make the grant of representation for his trial.

(5) Representation shall not be granted to any person unless it appears to the competent authority that his financial resources are such as, under regulations, make him eligible for representation under this Part.

(6) Before making a determination for the purposes of subsection (5) above in the case of any person, the competent authority shall, except in prescribed cases, require a statement of his financial resources in the prescribed form to be furnished to the authority.

(7) Where a doubt arises whether representation under this Part should be granted to any person, the doubt shall be resolved in that person's favour.

(8) Where an application for representation for the purposes of an appeal to the Court of Appeal or the Courts-Martial Appeal Court is made to a competent authority before the giving of notice of appeal or the making of an application for leave to appeal, the authority may, in the first instance, exercise its power to grant representation by making a grant consisting of advice on the question whether there appear to be reasonable grounds of appeal and assistance in the preparation of an application for leave to appeal or in the giving of a notice of appeal.

(9) Representation granted by a competent authority may be amended or withdrawn, whether by that or another authority competent to grant representation under this Part.

(10) Regulations may provide for an appeal to lie to a specified court or body against any refusal by a magistrates' court to grant representation under this Part and for that other court or body to make any grant of representation that could have been made by the magistrates' court.

(11) Subsection (3) above shall have effect in its application to a person who has not attained the age of eighteen as if the references in paragraphs (c) and (d) to remand in custody and to being remanded or kept in custody included references to being committed under section 23 of the Children and Young Persons Act 1969 to the care of a local authority or a remand centre.

Criteria for grant of representation for trial proceedings

22.—(1) This section applies to proceedings by way of a trial by or before a magistrates' court or the Crown Court or on an appeal to the Crown Court against a person's conviction.

(2) The factors to be taken into account by a competent authority in determining whether it is in the interests of justice that representation be granted for the purposes of proceedings to which this section applies to an accused shall include the following—

    (a) the offence is such that if proved it is likely that the court would impose a sentence which would deprive the accused of his liberty or lead to loss of his livelihood or serious damage to his reputation;

    (b) the determination of the case may involve consideration of a substantial question of law;

    (c) the accused may be unable to understand the proceedings or to state his own case because of his inadequate knowledge of English, mental illness or other mental or physical disability;

    (d) the nature of the defence is such as to involve the tracing and interviewing of witnesses or expert cross-examination of a witness for the prosecution;

    (e) it is in the interests of someone other than the accused that the accused be represented.

(3) The Lord Chancellor may, by order, vary the factors listed in subsection (2) above by amending factors in the list or by adding new factors to the list.

Reimbursement of public funds by contributions

23.—(1) When representation under this Part is granted to any person whose financial resources are such as, under regulations, make him liable to make a contribution, the competent authority shall order him to pay a contribution in respect of the costs of his being represented under this Part.

(2) Where the legally assisted person has not attained the age of sixteen, the competent authority may, instead of or in addition to ordering him to make a contribution, order any person—

    (a) who is an appropriate contributor in relation to him; and

    (b) whose financial resources are such as, under regulations, make him liable to make a contribution, to pay a contribution in respect of the costs of the representation granted to the legally assisted person.

(3) Regulations may authorise the making of a contribution order under subsection (1) or (2) above after the grant of representation in prescribed circumstances.

(4) The amount of the contribution to be required under subsection (1) or (2) above by the competent authority shall be such as is determined in accordance with the regulations.

(5) A legally assisted person or appropriate contributor may be required to make his contribution in one sum or by instalments as may be prescribed.

(6) Regulations may provide that no contribution order shall be made in connection with a grant of representation under this Part for the purposes of proceedings in the Crown Court, the Court of Appeal or the House of Lords in a case where a contribution order was made in connection with a grant of such representation to the person in question in respect of proceedings in a lower court.

(7) Subject to subsection (8) below, if the total contribution made in respect of the costs of representing any person under this Part exceeds those costs, the excess shall be repaid—

(a) where the contribution was made by one person only, to him; and

(b) where the contribution was made by two or more persons to them in proportion to the amounts contributed by them.

(8) Where a contribution has been made in respect of the costs of representing any person under this Part in any proceedings and an order for costs is made in favour of that person in respect of those proceedings, then, where sums due under the order for costs are paid to the Board or the Lord Chancellor under section 20(2) of the Prosecution of Offences Act 1985 (recovery regulations)—

(a) if the costs of the representation do not exceed the sums so paid, subsection (7) above shall not apply and the contribution shall be repaid;

(b) if the costs of the representation do exceed the sums so paid, subsection (7) above shall apply as if the costs of the representation were equal to the excess.

(9) References in subsection (8) above to the costs of representation include any charge or fee treated as part of those costs by section 26(2).

(10) In this Part—

"appropriate contributor" means a person of a description prescribed under section 34(2)(c); and

"contribution order" means an order under subsection (1) or (2) above.

Contribution orders: supplementary

24.—(1) Where a competent authority grants representation under this Part and in connection with the grant makes a contribution order under which any sum is required to be paid on the making of the order, it may direct that the grant of representation shall not take effect until that sum is paid.

(2) Where a legally assisted person fails to pay any relevant contribution when it is due, the court in which the proceedings for the purposes of which

he has been granted representation are being heard may, subject to subsection (3) below, revoke the grant.

(3) A court shall not exercise the power conferred by subsection (2) above unless, after affording the legally assisted person an opportunity of making representations in such manner as may be prescribed, it is satisfied—

(a) that he was able to pay the relevant contribution when it was due; and

(b) that he is able to pay the whole or part of it but has failed or refused to do so.

(4) In subsection (2) above "relevant contribution," in relation to a legally assisted person, means any sum—

(a) which he is required to pay by a contribution order made in connection with the grant to him of representation under this Part; and

(b) which falls due after the making of the order and before the conclusion of the proceedings for the purposes of which he has been granted such representation.

(5) Regulations with respect to contribution orders may—

(a) provide for their variation or revocation in prescribed circumstances;

(b) provide for their making in default of the prescribed evidence of a person's financial resources;

(c) regulate their making after the grant of representation;

(d) authorise the remission or authorise or require the repayment in prescribed circumstances of sums due or paid under such orders; and

(e) prescribe the court or body by which any function under the regulations is to be exercisable.

(6) Schedule 3 to this Act shall have effect with respect to the enforcement of contribution orders.

Payment of costs of representation under this Part

25.—(1) Where representation under this Part has been granted to any person the costs of representing him shall be paid—

(a) by the Lord Chancellor; or

(b) by the Board,

as the Lord Chancellor may direct.

(2) Subject to regulations, the costs of representing any person under this Part shall include sums on account of the fees payable to his counsel or solicitor and disbursements reasonably incurred by his solicitor for or in connection with his representation.

(3) The costs required by this section to be paid in respect of representing him shall not include any sum in respect of allowances to witnesses attending to give evidence in the proceedings for the purposes of which he is represented in any case where such allowances are payable under any other enactment.

Payment for advice or assistance where representation under this Part is subsequently granted

26.—(1) This section has effect where—

(a) advice or assistance under Part III is given to a person in respect of any matter which is or becomes the subject of criminal proceedings against him; and

(b) he is subsequently granted representation under this Part for the purposes of those proceedings.

(2) If the solicitor acting for the person under the grant of representation is the same as the solicitor who gave him the advice or assistance, any charge or fee in respect of the advice or assistance which, apart from this section, would fall to be secured, recovered or paid as provided by section 11 shall instead be paid under section 25 as if it were part of the costs of the representation.

(3) If a contribution order is made in connection with the grant of representation under this Part to him—

(a) any sum which he is required by virtue of section 9(6) or (7) to pay in respect of the advice or assistance (whether or not already paid) shall be credited against the contribution to be made by him under the contribution order; and

(b) section 25 shall have effect in a case to which subsection (2) above applies as if the charges and fees properly chargeable in respect of the advice or assistance were part of the costs of the representation under this Part and as if any such sum as is mentioned in paragraph (a) above which he has paid were part of the contribution made under the contribution order.

PART VI

LEGAL AID IN SPECIAL CASES

Care proceedings

Representation in care proceedings: scope and competent authorities

27.—(1) This section and section 28 apply, subject to subsection (2) below, to the following proceedings (referred to as "care proceedings"), that is to say—

(a) proceedings under section 1 of the 1969 Act or under section 21A of the 1980 Act (care proceedings);

(b) proceedings under section 15 or 21 of the 1969 Act (variation and discharge of supervision or care orders);

(c) proceedings under section 2(12), 3(8), 16(8) or 21(4) of the 1969 Act or section 21A of the 1980 Act (appeals in such proceedings);

(d) proceedings under section 3 of the Children and Young Persons Act 1963 (application by parent or guardian for an order directing a local authority to take proceedings under section 1 of the 1969 Act);

(e) proceedings under section 3, 5 or 67(2) of the 1980 Act (proceedings in connection with resolutions by local authorities with respect to the assumption of parental rights and duties); and

(f) proceedings under Part 1A of the 1980 Act (access orders);

and representation for the purposes of care proceedings to which this section applies shall be available to any person subject to and in accordance with section 28.

(2) Subsection (1) above may be varied by regulations so as to restrict the categories of proceedings for the purposes of which representation is available under this section and section 28.

(3) Representation for the purposes of care proceedings before a juvenile court extends to the proceedings before any juvenile court to which the case is remitted.

(4) Subject to any provision made by virtue of subsection (6) below, the authorities competent, on an application made for the purpose, to grant representation for the purposes of care proceedings are—

(a) as respects proceedings before a juvenile court, the court;

(b) as respects appeals from decisions of juvenile courts to the Crown Court, the Crown Court or the juvenile court from which the appeal is brought;

(c) as respects appeals from decisions of juvenile courts to the High Court, the Board;

(d) as respects proceedings before a justice of the peace under section 12E of the 1980 Act (applications for emergency orders), the justice of the peace.

(5) In the event of the Lord Chancellor making an order under section 3(4) as respects the function of granting representation for the purposes of any care proceedings, the Board shall be competent as respects those proceedings, on an application made for the purpose.

(6) An order under section 3(4) may make provision restricting or excluding the competence of any authority mentioned in subsection (4) above and may contain such transitional provisions as appear to the Lord Chancellor necessary or expedient.

(7) In this section and section 28—

"the 1969 Act" means the Children and Young Persons Act 1969;

"the 1980 Act" means the Child Care Act 1980; and

"remitted" in relation to a juvenile court, means remitted under section 2(11) of the 1969 Act.

Care proceedings: availability

28.—(1) Representation for the purposes of care proceedings to which this section applies shall be available to any person, other than a local authority, who is a party to the proceedings.

(2) Subject to subsection (4) below, representation may be granted where it appears to the competent authority to be desirable to do so in the interests of justice.

(3) Subject to subsection (4) below, representation must be granted where a child—

(a) is brought before a juvenile court under section 21A of the 1980 Act; and

(b) is not legally represented before the court but wishes to be.

(4) Representation shall not be granted to any person unless it appears to the competent authority that his financial resources are such as, under regulations, make him eligible for representation.

(5) Where a doubt arises whether representation should be granted to any person, the doubt shall be resolved in that person's favour.

(6) Representation granted by a competent authority may be amended or withdrawn, whether by that or another authority competent to grant representation.

(7) Regulations may provide for an appeal to lie to a specified court or body against any refusal by a juvenile court to grant representation for the purposes of care proceedings and for that other court or body to make any grant of representation that could have been made by the juvenile court.

Contempt proceedings

Representation in contempt proceedings

29.—(1) This section applies to any proceedings where a person is liable to be committed or fined—

(a) by a magistrates' court under section 12 of the Contempt of Court Act 1981;

(b) by a county court under section 14, 92 or 118 of the County Courts Act 1984;

(c) by any any superior court for contempt in the face of that or any other court;

and in this Act "proceedings for contempt" means so much of any proceedings as relates to dealing with a person as mentioned in paragraph (a), (b) or (c) above.

(2) In any proceedings for contempt against a person the court may order that he be granted representation under this section for the purposes of the proceedings if it appears to the court to be desirable to do so in the interests of justice.

(3) In this section, "superior court" means the Court of Appeal, the High Court, the Crown Court, the Courts-Martial Appeal Court, the Restrictive Practices Court, the Employment Appeal Tribunal and any other court exercising in relation to its proceedings powers equivalent to those of the High Court, and includes the House of Lords in the exercise of its jurisdiction in relation to appeals from courts in England and Wales.

Supplementary

Supplementary

30.—(1) In Part V, the following provisions—

(a) section 23 and 24 together with Schedule 3; and

(b) section 25,

shall apply for the purposes of representation in care proceedings to which sections 27 and 28 apply as they apply for the purposes of representation under that Part in criminal proceedings with the modification mentioned below.

(2) The modification referred to above is the substitution for paragraphs 9(b) and 10(2)(b) of Schedule 3 of the following sub-paragraph—

"(b) references to the proceedings for the purposes of which a grant of representation has been made include, where the proceedings result in the giving of a direction under section 2(11) of the Children and Young Persons Act 1969 (duty in care proceedings to direct that the infant be brought before a juvenile court acting for the area in which he resides), the proceedings before the court before which the legally assisted person is brought in pursuance of the direction."

(3) In Part V, section 25 shall apply for the purposes of representation in proceedings for contempt as it applies for the purposes of representation under that Part in criminal proceedings.

PART VII

GENERAL AND SUPPLEMENTARY

Act not generally to affect position of legal representatives or other parties

31.—(1) Except as expressly provided by this Act or regulations under it—

(a) the fact that the services of counsel or a solicitor are given under this Act shall not affect the relationship between or rights of counsel, solicitor and client or any privilege arising out of such relationship; and

(b) the rights conferred by this Act on a person receiving advice, assistance or representation under it shall not affect the rights or liabilities of other parties to the proceedings or the principles on which the discretion of any court or tribunal is normally exercised.

(2) Without prejudice to the generality of subsection (1)(b) above, for the purpose of determining the costs of a legally assisted person in pursuance of an order for costs or an agreement for costs in his favour (other than an order under Part II of the Prosecution of Offences Act 1985) the services of his solicitor and counsel shall be treated as having been provided otherwise than under this Act and his solicitor shall be treated as having paid counsel's fees.

(3) A person who provides advice, assistance or representation under this Act shall not take any payment in respect of the advice, assistance or representation except such payment as is made by the Board or authorised by, or by regulations under, this Act.

(4) The revocation under this Act of a grant (or, in the case of Part III, of approval for a grant) of advice, assistance or representation to a legally assisted person shall not affect the right of any legal representative of his, arising otherwise than under a contract, to remuneration for work done before the date of the revocation.

111

Selection and assignment of legal representatives

32.—(1) Subject to the provisions of this section, a person entitled to receive advice or assistance or representation may select—

(a) the solicitor to advise or assist or act from him, and

(b) if the case requires counsel, his counsel,

from among the solicitors and counsel willing to provide advice, assistance or representation under this Act.

(2) Where the Board limits a grant of representation under Part IV to representation in pursuance of a contract made by the Board, it may, as it thinks fit, assign to the legally assisted person a solicitor or a solicitor and counsel or direct that he may only select a solicitor from among those with whom such a contract subsists.

(3) A person's right to select his solicitor or counsel is subject, in the case of representation under Part V, to regulations under subsection (8) below.

(4) Subsection (1) above does not confer any right of selection in relation to proceedings under section 29 for the purposes of proceedings for contempt.

(5) Where a court grants representation to a person for the purposes of proceedings for contempt, it may assign to him for the purposes of the proceedings any counsel or solicitor who is within the precincts of the court at the time.

(6) The selection by or assignment to a person of solicitor or counsel shall not prejudice the law and practice relating to the conduct of proceedings by a solicitor or counsel or the circumstances in which a solicitor or counsel may refuse or give up a case or entrust it to another.

(7) Regulations may provide that the right conferred by subsection (1) above shall be exercisable only in relation to solicitors who are for the time being members of a prescribed panel.

(8) Regulations may provide as respects representation under Part V that subsection (1) above shall not apply in cases of any prescribed description and that in any such case a prescribed authority shall assign solicitor or counsel or solicitor and counsel in accordance with regulations under section 2(7) to the person entitled to receive such representation.

(9) No solicitor or counsel who is for the time being excluded from legal aid work under section 47(2) of the Solicitors Act 1974 (powers of Solicitors Disciplinary Tribunal) or section 42 of the Administration of Justice Act 1985 (exclusion of barristers from legal aid work) may be selected or assigned under this section.

(10) Notwithstanding subsection (1) above, a solicitor who has been selected to act for a person under that subsection may himself select to act for that person, as the solicitor's agent, any other solicitor who is not for the time being excluded from selection.

Legal aid complaints against barristers and their exclusion from legal aid work

33.—(1) The following sections shall be substituted for sections 41 and 42 of the Administration of Justice Act 1985—

"**Application to legal aid complaints against barristers of disciplinary provisions** 41.—(1) The disciplinary provisions applicable to barristers shall apply to legal aid complaints relating to the conduct of barristers as they apply to other complaints about their conduct.

(2) Subject to any exclusion or restriction made by those provisions, any disciplinary tribunal which hears a legal aid complaint relating to the conduct of a barrister may, if it thinks fit and whether or not it makes any other order, order that any fees—

(a) otherwise payable in connection with his services under or in accordance with the Legal Aid Act 1988, or

(b) otherwise chargeable in connection with his services in respect of advice or assistance made available under Part III of that Act, shall be reduced or cancelled.

(3) Accordingly, in so far as any of sections 9, 11, 15(6) and (7) and 25(2) of the Legal Aid Act 1988 (which relate to remuneration for legal aid work) has effect in relation to any fees reduced or cancelled by an order under subsection (2) above, it shall so have effect subject to the provisions of that order.

(4) An appeal shall lie in the case of an order under subsection (2) above in the same manner as an appeal would lie in the case of any other order of such a tribunal.

(5) The reference in subsection (2) above to a disciplinary tribunal is a reference to a tribunal acting under the disciplinary provisions applicable to barristers and it includes a reference to a member exercising any functions of the tribunal delegated to him.

Exclusion of barristers from legal aid work   42.—(1) Subject to any exclusion or restriction made by the disciplinary provisions applicable to barristers, where a disciplinary tribunal hears a charge of professional misconduct or breach of professional standards against a barrister, it may order that he shall be excluded from legal aid work, either temporarily or for a specified period, if it determines that there is good reason for the exclusion arising out of—

(a) his conduct in connection with any such services as are mentioned in section 40(1); or

(b) his professional conduct generally.

(2) Subsection (4) of section 41 shall apply to an order under subsection (1) as it applies to an order under subsection (2) of that section.

(3) The disciplinary provisions applicable to barristers shall include provision enabling a barrister who has been excluded from legal aid work under this section to apply for an order terminating his exclusion from such work.

(4) In this section—

(a) the reference to a disciplinary tribunal shall be construed in accordance with section 41(5); and

(b) references to a person being excluded from legal aid work are references to his being excluded from those who may be selected or assigned under section 32 of the Legal Aid Act 1988."

Regulations

34.—(1) The Lord Chancellor may make such regulations as appear to him necessary or desirable for giving effect to this Act or for preventing abuses of it.

(2) Without prejudice to the generality of subsection (1) above, any such regulations may—

(a) make provision as to the matters which are or are not to be treated as distinct matters for the purposes of advice or assistance under Part III, as to the proceedings which are or are not to be treated as distinct proceedings for the purposes of representation under Part IV, and as to the apportionment of sums recoverable or recovered by virtue of any order for costs made generally with respect to matters or proceedings treated as distinct;

(b) regulate the procedure of any court or tribunal in relation to advice, assistance or representation under this Act or orders for costs made thereunder and authorise the delegation (subject to appeal) or the exercise of their functions by members, officers or other courts or the judges or members of other courts;

(c) regulate the availability of advice, assistance or representation (other than for the purposes of proceedings for contempt) and the making of contributions towards its provision by reference to the financial resources or, in prescribed cases, the aggregate financial resources, of persons and provide for the courts, persons or bodies who are to determine the financial resources of persons and the persons who are to be required or permitted to furnish information for those purposes;

(d) provide for the cases in which a person may be refused advice, assistance or representation or have the grant of it withdrawn or revoked by reason of his conduct when seeking or receiving advice, assistance or representation (whether in the same or a different matter);

(e) make provision for the remuneration and payment of the expenses of solicitors and counsel and for the courts, persons or bodies by whom, and the manner in which, any determinations which may be required for those purposes are to be made, reviewed or appealed;

(f) make provision for the recovery of sums due to the Board and for making effective the charge created by this Act on property recovered or preserved for a legally assisted person and regulating the release or postponement of the enforcement of any charge (however created) in favour of the Board.

(3) Regulations may also modify this Act for the purposes of its application to prescribed description of persons or in prescribed circumstances.

(4) Without prejudice to subsection (3) above, regulations may also modify this Act for the purposes of its application—

(a) in cases where its modification appears to the Lord Chancellor necessary for the purpose of fulfilling any obligation imposed on the United Kingdom or Her Majesty's Government in the United Kingdom by any international agreement; or

(b) in relation to proceedings for securing the recognition or enforcement in England and Wales of judgments given outside the United Kingdom for whose recognition or enforcement in the United Kingdom provision is made by any international agreement.

(5) Regulations made for the purposes mentioned in subsection (2)(b) above may include provisions—

(a) as to the determination of costs incurred in connection with proceedings not actually begun; and

(b) as to the cases in which and extent to which a person receiving advice, assistance or representation may be required to give security for costs, and the manner in which it may be so given.

(6) Regulations made for the purposes mentioned in subsection (2)(c) above may provide that the income or capital of a person in receipt of prescribed social security benefits is to be taken as not exceeding a prescribed amount.

(7) Regulations made for the purposes mentioned in subsection (2)(e) above may include provisions—

(a) imposing conditions for the allowance of remuneration and expenses;

(b) attaching financial penalties in the event of appeals or reviews of determinations being unsuccessful;

(c) authorising the making of interim payments of remuneration or in respect of expenses.

(8) Regulations made for the purposes mentioned in subsection (2)(f) above may include provisions—

(a) for the enforcement for the benefit of the Board of an order or agreement for costs made in favour of a legally assisted person;

(b) for making a solicitor's right to payment by the Board wholly or partly dependent on his performance of the duties imposed on him by regulations made for the purposes of that paragraph; and

(c) requiring interest to be charged at a prescribed rate in circumstances where enforcement of a charge in favour of the Board is postponed.

(9) The Lord Chancellor, in making regulations for the purposes mentioned in subsection (2)(e) above as respects any description of legal aid work, shall have regard, among the matters which are relevant, to—

(a) the time and skill which it requires;

(b) the general level of fee income arising from it;

(c) the general level of expenses of barristers and solicitors which is attributable to it;

(d) the number and general level of competence of barristers and solicitors undertaking it;

(e) the effect of the regulations on the handling of the work; and

(f) the cost to public funds of any provision made by the regulations.

(10) Before making regulations for the purposes mentioned in subsection (2)(e) above, the Lord Chancellor shall consult the General Council of the Bar and the Law Society.

(11) Regulations under this Act may make different provision for different description of advice, assistance or representation, for different cases or classes of case, for different areas or for other different circumstances and for different descriptions of persons.

(12) Before making regulations as to the procedure of any court or tribunal, the Lord Chancellor shall so far as practicable consult any rule committee or

similar body by whom or on whose advice rules of procedure for the court or tribunal may be made apart from this provision or whose consent or concurrence is required to any such rules so made.

(13) No regulations shall be made under this section which include provision for the purposes mentioned in subsection (2)(c) or (e) above except with the consent of the Treasury.

(14) In subsection (6) above "social security benefits" means any benefit provided under section 20(1) of the Social Security Act 1986 (income-related benefits).

Advisory Committee

35.—(1) the existing advisory committee shall continue in being to advise the Lord Chancellor on such questions relating to the provision of advice, assistance or representation under this Act as he may from time to time refer to them and to make recommendations or furnish comments to him on such matters as they consider appropriate.

(2) Appointments to the committee by the Lord Chancellor, whether by way of replacing existing members or making additional appointments, shall be made so as to secure that the committee is constituted of persons having knowledge of the work of the courts and social conditions.

(3) The Lord Chancellor may pay to the members of the advisory committee such travelling and other allowances as he may, with the consent of the Treasury, determine; and any expenses of the Lord Chancellor under this subsection shall be defrayed out of money provided by Parliament.

(4) It shall be the duty of the advisory committee to provide to the Lord Chancellor, as soon as possible after 31st March in each year, a report containing any advice, recommendations or comments of theirs on questions or matters arising during the preceding twelve months.

(5) The Lord Chancellor shall lay before each House of Parliament a copy of the annual report of the committee made to him under subsection (4) above.

(6) The Lord Chancellor may, by order dissolve the advisory committee on such day as is specified in the order and on that day this section shall cease to have effect except as regards the defrayal out of money provided by Parliament of the allowances falling to be paid thereafter under subsection (3) above.

(7) In this section "the existing advisory committee" means the advisory committee in existence under section 21 of the Legal Aid Act 1974 at the passing of this Act.

Orders and regulations: general

36.—(1) Any power under this Act to make an order or regulations shall be exercisable by statutory instrument.

(2) As respects orders under this Act other than orders under section 47—

(a) except in the case of an order under section 3(4) and 35(6), any instrument containing the order shall be subject to annulment in pursuance of a resolution of either House of Parliament;

(b) in the case of an order under section 3(4) or 35(6), no such order shall be made unless a draft of it has been laid before and approved by resolution of each House of Parliament.

(3) As respects regulations under this Act—

(a) except in the case of regulations under section 8, 14(2) and 32(7), any instrument containing the regulations shall be subject to annulment in pursuance of a resolution of either House of Parliament;

(b) in the case of regulations under section 8, 14(2) or 32(7), no such regulations shall be made unless a draft of them has been laid before and approved by resolution of each House of Parliament.

Laying of Board's annual reports before Parliament

37. The Lord Chancellor shall lay before each House of Parliament a copy of the annual report of the Board made to him under section 5(3).

Restriction of disclosure of information

38.—(1) Subject to the following provisions of this section, no information furnished for the purposes of this Act to the Board or any court or other person or body of persons upon whom functions are imposed or conferred by regulations and so furnished in connection with the case of a person seeking or receiving advice, assistance or representation shall be disclosed otherwise than—

(a) for the purpose of enabling or assisting the Lord Chancellor to perform his functions under or in relation to this Act;

(b) for the purpose of enabling the Board to discharge its functions under this Act;

(c) for the purpose of facilitating the proper performance by any court, tribunal or other person or body of persons of functions under this Act;

(d) with a view to the institution of, or otherwise for the purpose of, any criminal proceedings for an offence under this Act;

(e) in connection with any other proceedings under this Act; or

(f) for the purpose of facilitating the proper performance by any tribunal of disciplinary functions as regards barristers or solicitors.

(2) This section does not apply to information in the form of a summary or collection of information so framed as not to enable information relating to any particular person to be ascertained from it.

(3) Subsection (1) above shall not prevent the disclosure of information for any purpose with the consent of the person in connection with whose case it was furnished and, where he did not furnish it himself, with that of the person or body of persons who did.

(4) A person who, in contravention of this section, discloses any information furnished to the Board or any court or other person or body of persons for the purposes of this Act shall be liable on summary conviction to a fine not exceeding level 4 on the standard scale.

(5) Proceedings for an offence under this section shall not be brought without the written consent of the Attorney General.

(6) For the avoidance of doubt it is hereby declared that information furnished to counsel or a solicitor as such by or on behalf of a person seeking or receiving advice, assistance or representation under this Act is not information furnished to the Board or a person upon whom functions are imposed or conferred as mentioned in subsection (1) above.

Proceedings for misrepresentation, etc.

39.—(1) If any person seeking or receiving advice, assistance or representation under this Act—

(a) intentionally fails to comply with regulations as to the information to be furnished by him; or

(b) in furnishing any information required by regulations knowingly makes any false statement or false representation,

he shall be liable on summary conviction to a fine not exceeding level 4 on the standard scale or to imprisonment for a term not exceeding three months or to both.

(2) Notwithstanding anything in the Magistrates' Courts Act 1980, proceedings in respect of an offence under subsection (1) above may be brought at any time within the period of six months beginning with the date on which evidence sufficient in the opinion of the prosecutor to justify a prosecution comes to his knowledge.

(3) Nothing in subsection (2) above shall authorise the commencement of proceedings for an offence at a time more than two years after the date on which the offence was committed.

(4) A county court shall have jurisdiction to hear and determine any action brought by the Board to recover the loss sustained by it on account of its legal aid fund by reason of—

(a) the failure of a person seeking or receiving advice, assistance or representation to comply with regulations as to the information to be furnished by him; or

(b) a false statement or false representation made by such a person in furnishing information for the purposes of this Act,

notwithstanding that the claim in the action is for a greater amount than that which for the time being is the county court limit for the purposes of section 15 of the County Courts Act 1984.

Adaptation of rights of indemnity in cases of advice, assistance or representation in civil proceedings

40.—(1) This section shall have effect for the purpose of adapting in relation to Parts III and IV any right (however and whenever created or arising) which a person may have to be indemnified against expenses incurred by him.

(2) In determining for the purposes of any such right the reasonableness of any expenses, the possibility of avoiding them or part of them by taking advantage of Part III or Part IV shall be disregarded.

(3) Where a person having any such right to be indemnified against expenses incurred in connection with any proceedings receives in connection with those proceedings advice, assistance or representation then (without prejudice to the effect of the indemnity in relation to his contribution, if any, under section 9 or 16) the right shall ensure also for the benefit of the Board as if any expenses incurred by the Board on his account in connection with the advice, assistance or representation had been incurred by him.

(4) Where a person's right to be indemnified enures for the benefit of the Board under subsection (3) above in a case where he has been represented in pursuance of a contract made with the Board on terms which do not differentiate between the remuneration for his and other cases, the reference in

that subsection to any expenses incurred by the Board on his account shall be construed as a reference to such part of the remuneration payable under the contract as may be specified in writing by the Board.

(5) Where—

(a) a person's right to be indemnified against expenses incurred in connection with any proceedings arises by virtue of an agreement and is subject to any express condition conferring on those liable under it any right with respect to the bringing or conduct of the proceedings; and

(b) those liable have been given a reasonable opportunity of exercising the right so conferred and have not availed themselves of the opportunity,

the right to be indemnified shall be treated for the purpose of subsection (3) above as not being subject to that condition.

(6) Nothing in subsections (3) and (5) above shall be taken as depriving any person or body of persons of the protection of any enactment or, except as provided in subsection (5), as conferring any larger right to recover money in respect of any expenses than the person receiving advice, assistance or representation would have had if the expenses had been incurred by him.

Application to Crown

41. This Act binds the Crown.

Finance

42.—(1) The Lord Chancellor shall pay to the Board out of money provided by Parliament—

(a) such sums as are required (after allowing for payments by the Board into its legal aid fund under paragraphs (a), (b), (c), (d) and (f) of section 6(3)) to meet the payments which, under subsection (2) of that section, are to be paid by the Board out of that fund; and

(b) such sums as he may, with the approval of the Treasury, determine are required for the other expenditure of the Board.

(2) The Lord Chancellor may, with the approval of the Treasury—

(a) determine the manner in which and times at which the sums referred to in subsection (1)(a) above shall be paid to the Board; and

(b) impose conditions on the payment of the sums referred to in sub-section (1)(b) above.

Definitions

43. In this Act—

"advice," "assistance" and "representation" have the meanings assigned to them by section 2(2), (3) and (4) respectively subject, however, to the other provisions of that section;

"the Board" has the meaning assigned to it by section 3(1);

"determination," in relation to the costs of advice or assistance or representation for the purposes of proceedings, includes taxation and assessment;

"financial resources," in relation to any person, includes any valuable facility which is available to him;

"order for costs" includes any judgment, order, decree, award or direction for the payment of the costs of one party to any proceedings by another party, whether given or made in those proceedings or not;

"prescribed" means prescribed by relations made by the Lord Chancellor under this Act;

"proceedings for contempt" has the meaning assigned to it by section 29(1);

"regulations" means regulations made by the Lord Chancellor under this Act;

"sentence," in relation to a person, includes any order made on his conviction of an offence;

"solicitor" means solicitor of the Supreme Court;

"statutory inquiry" has the meaning assigned to it by section 19(1) of the Tribunals and Inquiries Act 1971; and

"tribunal" includes an arbitrator or umpire, however appointed, and whether the arbitration takes place under a reference by consent or otherwise.

PART VIII

MISCELLANEOUS

Scottish provisions

Scottish provisions
44. The Legal Aid (Scotland) Act 1986 shall have effect subject to the amendments specified in Schedule 4 to this Act.

Supplementary

Amendments, repeals and transitional provisions
45.—(1) The enactments specified in Schedule 5 to this Act shall have effect subject to the amendments there specified.

(2) Subject to subsection (4) below, the enactments specified in Schedule 6 to this Act are repealed to the extent specified in the third column of that Schedule.

(3) Where any enactment amended or repealed by subsection (1) or (2) above extends to the United Kingdom or any part of it, the amendment or repeal has a corresponding extent.

(4) Schedule 7 to this Act shall have effect for the purpose of making the transitional and saving provisions set out there.

Amendments of Legal Aid Act 1974 pending repeal

46. The Legal Aid Act 1974 shall have effect subject to the amendments specified in Schedule 8 to this Act.

Short title, commencement and extent

47.—(1) This Act may be cited as the Legal Aid Act 1988.

(2) Subject to subsections (3) and (4) below, this Act shall come into force on such day as the Lord Chancellor appoints by order and different days may be appointed for different provisions.

(3) Section 44 and Schedule 4 shall come into force on such day as the Secretary of State appoints by order and different days may be appointed for different provisions.

(4) Sections 35 (together with the repeal of section 21 of the Legal Aid Act 1974) and 465 shall come into force on the date on which this Act is passed.

(5) An order under subsection (2) or (3) above may contain such transitional and saving provisions as appear to the Lord Chancellor or, as the case may be, the Secretary of State necessary or expedient.

(6) This Act, with the exception of sections 12(3) and 17(3), section 44 and Schedule 4 and the amendments or repeals of the enactments referred to in section 45(3), extends to England and Wales only and section 44 and Schedule 4 cxtcnd to Scotland only.

SCHEDULES

SCHEDULE 1

The Legal Aid Board

Incorporation and Status

1. The Board shall be a body corporate.

2. The Board shall not be regarded as the servant or agent of the Crown or as enjoying any status, immunity or privilege of the Crown; and the Board's property shall not be regarded as property of, or held on behalf of, the Crown.

Tenure of Members

3. Subject to paragraphs 4 and 5 any member of the Board shall hold and vacate office in accordance with the terms of his appointment, but a person shall not be appointed a member of the Board for a period of more than 5 years.

4.—(1) The chairman or a member may resign office by giving notice in writing to the Lord Chancellor, and if the chairman ceases to be a member he shall cease to be the chairman.

(2) A person who ceases to be the chairman or a member shall be eligible for reappointment.

5. The Lord Chancellor may terminate the appointment of a member of the Board if satisfied that—

    (a) he has become bankrupt or made an arrangement with his creditors;

    (b) he is unable to carry out his duties as a Board member by reason of physical or mental illness;

    (c) he has been absent from meetings of the Board for a period longer than six consecutive months without the permission of the Board; or

    (d) he is otherwise unable or unfit to discharge the functions of a member of the Board.

Members' interests

6.—(1) Before appointing a person to be a member of the Board, the Lord Chancellor shall satisfy himself that that person will have no such financial or other interest as is likely to affect prejudicially the exercise or performance by him of his functions as a member of the Board.

(2) The Lord Chancellor shall from time to time satisfy himself with respect to every member of the Board that he has no such interest as is referred to in sub-paragraph (1) above.

(3) Any person whom the Lord Chancellor proposes to appoint as, and who has consented to be, a member of the Board, and any member of the Board, shall, whenever requested by the Lord Chancellor to do so, supply him with such information as the Lord Chancellor considers necessary for the performance by the Lord Chancellor of his duties under this paragraph.

7.—(1) A member of the Board who is in any way directly or indirectly interested in a contract made or proposed to be made by the Board shall disclose the nature of his interest at a meeting of the Board; and the disclosure shall be recorded in the minutes of the Board, and the member shall not take any part in any deliberation or decision of the Board with respect to that contract.

(2) For the purposes of sub-paragraph (1) above, a general notice given at a meeting of the Board by a member of the Board to the effect that he is a member of a specified company or firm and is to be regarded as interested in any contract which may, after the date of the notice, be made with the company or firm shall be regarded as a sufficient disclosure of his interest in relation to any contract so made.

(3) A member of the Board need not attend in person at a meeting of the Board in order to make any disclosure which he is required to make under this paragraph if he takes reasonable steps to secure that the disclosure is made by a notice which is brought up and read out at the meeting.

Remuneration of members

8.—(1) The Board may—

> (a) pay to its members such remuneration; and
>
> (b) make provision for the payment of such pensions, allowances or gratuities to or in respect of its members,

as the Lord Chancellor may, with the approval of the Treasury, determine.

(2) Where a person ceases to be a member of the Board otherwise than on the expiry of his term of office, and it appears to the Lord Chancellor that there are special circumstances which make it right for that person to receive compensation, the Lord Chancellor may, with the consent of the Treasury, direct the Board to make that person a payment of such amount as the Lord Chancellor may, with the consent of the Treasury, determine.

Staff

9.—(1) The Board shall appoint a person to be the chief executive of the Board who shall be responsible to the Board for the exercise of its functions.

(2) The Board may appoint such other employees as it thinks fit.

(3) The Board may only appoint a person to be its chief executive or the holder of any other employment of a specified description after consultation with, and subject to the approval of, the Lord Chancellor.

(4) The reference in sub-paragraph (3) above to employment of a specified description is a reference to any employment for the time being specified by the Lord Chancellor in a direction given for the purposes of that sub-paragraph.

(5) An appointment under this paragraph may be made on such terms and conditions as the Board, with the approval of the Lord Chancellor and consent of the Treasury, may determine.

10.—(1) The Board shall make, in respect of such of its employees as, with the approval of the Lord Chancellor and the consent of the Treasury, it may determine such arrangements for providing pensions, allowances or gratuities, including pensions, allowances or gratuities by way of compensation for loss of employment, as it may determine.

(2) Arrangements under sub-paragraph (1) above may include the establishment and administration, by the Board or otherwise, of one or more pension schemes.

(3) If an employee of the Board—

(a) becomes a member of the Board; and

(b) was by reference to his employment by the Board a participant in a pension scheme established and administered by it for the benefit of its employees,

the Board may determine that his service as a member shall be treated for the purposes of the scheme as service as an employee of the Board whether or not any benefits are to be payable to or in respect of him by virtue of paragraph 8.

(4) Where the Board exercises the power conferred by sub-paragraph (3) above, any discretion as to the benefits payable to or in respect of the member concerned which the scheme confers on the Board shall be exercised only with the approval of the Lord Chancellor and consent of the Treasury.

Proceedings

11.—(1) Subject to anything in regulations, the Board may regulate its own proceedings.

(2) The Board may make such arrangements as it considers appropriate for the discharge of its functions, including the delegation of specified functions and shall make such arrangements for the delegation of functions to committees and persons as may be prescribed.

(3) Subject to anything in regulations, committees may be appointed and may be dissolved by the Board, and may include, or consist entirely of, persons who are not members of the Board.

(4) A committee shall act in accordance with such directions as the Board may from time to time give, and the Board may provide for anything done by a committee to have effect as if it had been done by the Board.

(5) The validity of any proceedings of the Board or of any committee appointed by the Board shall not be affected by any vacancy among its members or by any defect in the appointment of any member.

Instruments

12.—(1) The fixing of the seal of the Board shall be authenticated by the chairman or another member of the Board and by some other person authorised either generally or specially by the Board to act for that purpose.

(2) A document purporting to be duly executed under the seal of the Board, or to be signed on the Board's behalf, shall be received in evidence and, unless the contrary is proved, be deemed to be so executed or signed.

Allowances

13. The Board may pay to the members of any committee such fees and allowances as the Lord Chancellor may, with the consent of the Treasury, determine.

SCHEDULE 2

Civil Proceedings: Scope of Part IV Representation

Part I

Description of Proceedings

1. Proceedings in, or before any person to whom a case is referred in whole or in part by, any of the following courts, namely:

(a) the House of Lords in the exercise of its jurisdiction in relation to appeals from courts in England and Wales;

(b) the Court of Appeal;

(c) the High Court;

(d) any county court.

2. The following proceedings in a magistrates' court, namely—

(a) proceedings under the Guardianship of Minors Acts 1971 and 1973;

(b) proceedings under section 43 of the National Assistance Act 1948, section 22 of the Maintenance Orders Act 1950, section 4 of the Maintenance Orders Act 1958, or section 18 of the Supplementary Benefits Act 1976;

(c) proceedings in relation to an application for leave of the court to remove a child from a person's custody under section 27 or 28 of the Adoption Act 1976 or proceedings in which the making of an order under Part II or section 29 or 55 of the Adoption Act 1976 is opposed by any party to the proceedings;

(d) proceedings under Part I of the Maintenance Orders (Reciprocal Enforcement) Act 1972 relating to a maintenance order made by a court of a country outside the United Kingdom;

(e) proceedings under Part II of the Children Act 1975;

(f) proceedings for or in relation to an order under Part I of the Domestic Proceedings and Magistrates' Courts Act 1978.

3. Proceedings in the Employment Appeal Tribunal.

4. Proceedings in the Lands Tribunal.

5. Proceedings before a Commons Commissioner appointed under section 17(1) of the Commons Registration Act 1965.

6. Proceedings in the Restrictive Practices Court under Part III of the Fair Trading Act 1973, and any proceedings in that court in consequence of an order made, or undertaking given to the court, under that Part of that Act.

PART II
EXCEPTED PROCEEDINGS

1. Proceedings wholly or partly in respect of defamation, but so that the making of a counterclaim for defamation in proceedings for which representation may be granted shall not of itself affect any right of the defendant to the counterclaim to representation for the purposes of the proceedings and so that representation may be granted to enable him to defend the counterclaim.

2. Relator actions.

3. Proceedings for the recovery of a penalty where the proceedings may be taken by any person and the whole or part of the penalty is payable to the person taking the proceedings.

4. Election petitions under the Representation of the People Act 1983.

5. In a county court, proceedings for or consequent on the issue of a judgment summons and, in the case of a defendant, proceedings where the only question to be brought before the court is as to the time and mode of payment by him of a debt (including liquidated damages) and costs.

6. Proceedings incidental to any proceedings excepted by this Part of this Schedule.

SCHEDULE 3
CRIMINAL PROCEEDINGS: ENFORCEMENT OF CONTRIBUTION ORDERS
PART I
ORDERS MADE BY A COURT

Collecting court

1. In this Part "collecting court," in relation to a contribution order, means a magistrates' court specified in the order; and the court so specified shall be:

(a) in a case where the court making the order is itself a magistrates' court, that court;

(b) in a case where the order is made on an appeal from a magistrates' court, or in respect of a person who was committed (whether for trial or otherwise by a magistrates' court) to the Crown Court, the court from which the appeal is brought or, as the case may be, which committed him; and

(c) in any other case, a magistrates' court nominated by the court making the order.

Enforcement proceedings

2.—(1) Any sum required to be paid by a contribution order shall be recoverable as if it had been adjudged to be paid by an order of the collecting court, subject to and in accordance with the provisions of this paragraph.

(2) Sections 17 (not more than one committal for same arrears) and 18 (power to review committal) of the Maintenance Orders Act 1958 shall apply as if a contribution order were a maintenance order.

(3) The collecting court may exercise, in relation to a contribution order, the power conferred by section 75 of the Magistrates' Courts Act 1980 (power to dispense with immediate payment); and for the purposes of that section any provisions made by the authority which made the order as to time for payment, or payment by instalments, shall be treated as made by the collecting court.

(4) The following provisions of the Magistrates' Courts Act 1980 shall apply as if a contribution order were enforceable as an affiliation order:

section 80 (application of money found on defaulter to satisfy sum adjudged);

section 93 (complaint for arrears);

section 94 (effect of committal on arrears); and

section 95 (power to remit arrears).

(5) Any costs awarded under section 64 of the Magistrates' Courts Act 1980 on the hearing of a complaint for the enforcement of a contribution order shall be enforceable as a sum required to be paid by that order.

3.—(1) Without prejudice to paragraph 2, any sum required to be paid by a contribution order shall be enforceable by the High Court or a county court as if the sum were due to the clerk of the collecting court in pursuance of a judgment or order of the High Court or county court, as the case may be.

(2) The clerk of the collecting court shall not take proceedings by virtue of this paragraph unless authorised to do so by the court.

(3) This paragraph shall not authorise—

(a) the enforcement of a sum required to be paid by a contribution order by issue of a writ of fieri facias or other process against goods or by imprisonment or attachment of earnings; or

(b) the enforcement by a county court of payment of any sum exceeding the amount which for the time being is the county court limit for the purposes of section 15 of the County Courts Act 1984.

4.—(1) Any expenses incurred by the clerk of a magistrates' court in recovering any sum required to be paid by a contribution order shall be treated for the purposes of Part VI of the Justices of the Peace Act 1979 as expenses of the magistrates' courts committee.

(2) Any sum paid to a clerk of a magistrates' court in or towards satisfaction of a liability imposed by a contribution order shall be paid by him to the Lord Chancellor and section 61(4) of the Justices of the Peace Act 1979 (regulations as to accounts of justices' clerks) shall apply in relation to sums payable to the Lord Chancellor under

this sub-paragraph as it applies in relation to sums payable to the Secretary of State under that section.

Transfer of enforcement proceedings to different court
5.—(1) Where in relation to any contribution order it appears to the collecting court that the person subject to it is residing in a petty sessions area other than that for which the court acts, the court may make an order under this paragraph ("a transfer order") with respect to the contribution order specifying the other petty sessions area.

(2) Where a court makes a transfer order in relation to any contribution order—

(a) payment under the contribution order shall be enforceable in the petty sessions area specified in the transfer order; and

(b) as from the date of the transfer order, a magistrates' court for that petty sessions area shall be substituted for the court which made the transfer order as the collecting court in relation to the contribution order.

Limitations on enforcement by proceedings
6. Any sum due under a contribution order shall not be recoverable, and payment of any such sum shall not be enforced, under paragraph 2 or 3 until—

(a) the conclusion of the proceedings for the purposes of which the relevant grant of representation was made; or

(b) if earlier, the revocation or withdrawal of the relevant grant of representation.

7. Where a contribution order has been made in respect of a member of Her Majesty's armed forces and the Secretary of State notifies the collecting court that any sum payable under the order will be recovered by deductions from the person's pay, the collecting court shall not enforce payment of any sum unless and until the Secretary of State subsequently notifies it that the person is no longer a member of those forces and that sum has not been fully recovered.

Power to defer enforcement proceedings
8. The collecting court may defer recovering any sum due under a contribution order if—

(a) an appeal is pending in respect of the proceedings for the purposes of which the relevant grant of representation was made; or

(b) the person granted representation has been ordered to be retried.

Interpretation
9. In this Part:

(a) "relevant grant of representation," in relation to a contributiln order, means the grant of representation in connection with which the order was made; and

(b) references to the proceedings for the purposes of which a grant of representation has been made include, where the proceedings are proceedings before a magistrates' court which result:

(i) in the legally assisted person being committed to the Crown Court for trial or sentence, or

(ii) in his case being remitted to a juvenile court in pursuance of section 56(1) of the Children and Young Persons Act 1933,

the proceedings before the Crown Court or that juvenile court.

PART II

ORDERS MADE BY THE BOARD

Limitations on enforcement by proceedings
10.—(1) Any sum due under a contribution order shall not be recoverable, and payment of any such sum shall not be enforced until:

(a) the conclusion of the proceedings for the purposes of which the relevant grant of representation was made; or

(b) if earlier, the revocation or withdrawal of the relevant grant of representation.

(2) In this paragraph—

(a) "relevant grant of representation," in relation to a contribution order, means the grant of representation in connection with which the order was made; and

(b) the reference to the proceedings for the purposes of which the relevant grant of representation was made includes, where the proceedings are proceedings before a magistrates' court which result:
   (i) in the legally assisted person being committed to the Crown Court for trial or sentence, or
   (ii) in his case being remitted to a juvenile court in pursuance of section 56(1) of the Children and Young Persons Act 1933,
   the proceedings before the Crown Court or that juvenile court.

11. Where a contribution order has been made in respect of a member of Her Majesty's armed forces and the Secretary of State notifies the Board that any sum payable under the order will be recovered by deductions from the person's pay, the Board shall not enforce payment of any sum unless and until the Secretary of State subsequently notifies it that the person is no longer a member of those forces and that sum has not been fully recovered.

SCHEDULE 4

AMENDMENTS OF LEGAL AID (SCOTLAND) ACT 1986 (c. 47)

PART I

Direct payment of fees and outlays by legally assisted person
1. In section 4(2) (payments out of the Scottish Legal Aid Fund):

(a) in paragraph (a), after the word "due" there shall be inserted the words "out of the Fund;"

(b) in paragraph (c), the words "for the purposes of this Act" are repealed.

2. In section 16—

(a) subsection (1) is repealed;

(b) in subsection (2), the words "In this section and" are repealed.

3. In section 17 (contributions, etc.)—

(a) in subsection (1), for the words from "by the Board" to "the Fund" there shall be substituted the word "to contribute to the fees and outlays incurred by them (or on their behalf)";

(b) subsections (3) to (8) are repealed;

(c) at the end there shall be added the following subsections—

"(9) Except insofar as regulations made under this section otherwise provide—

(a) any award of expenses to a legally assisted person; and
(b) any property (wherever situated) recovered or preserved for him in the proceedings for which he is legally assisted,
shall be paid initially to the Fund, to be applied towards:
   (i) the fees and outlays incurred by or on behalf of the legally assisted person in those proceedings;
   (ii) recouping any sums paid out of the fund on his behalf in respect of

advice and assistance in relation to those proceedings or to any matter to which those proceedings relate.

(10) Where the solicitor acting for a legally assisted person is employed by the Board for the purposes of Part V of this Act, references in subsection (1) above and in section 33 of this Act to "fees and outlays" include references to sums which would have been payable to that solicitor had he not been so employed.

(11) Nothing in subsection (9) above shall prejudice the power of the court to allow any damages or expenses to be set off.

(12) An account of expenses which:

(a) has been agreed between the board and the solicitor acting for the legally assisted person; or

(b) has been taxed,

shall not be liable to taxation by an auditor of court in any proceedings."

4. In section 32(a) (restriction on payment etc.), the words, "out of the Fund" are repealed.

5. In section 33 (fees and outlays of solicitors and counsel) in subsection (1), for the words from "out" to the end there shall be substituted the words—

"in respect of any fees or outlays properly incurred by him in so acting—

(a) by the person concerned, to the extent to which a contribution has been determined for him under section 17 of this Act;

(b) to the extent that such fees and outlays exceed any such contribution out of the Fund in accordance with section 4(2)(a) of this Act."

6. In section 36(2) (regulations), in paragraph (b) at end add—

"and the power to substitute different amounts for the amount specified in section 10(2) of this Act includes power to substitute different amounts in relation to different cases or classes of case."

PART II

Liability of legally assisted person for expenses to be assessed in all cases

7. In section 18 (expenses)—

(a) subsection (1) is repealed;

(b) in subsection (2), for the words "in proceedings to which this section applies," there shall be substituted the words "in any proceedings."

8. In section 19(1) (expenses out of the Fund), for the words "to which this section applies" there shall be substituted the words "to which a legally assisted person is party and which are finally decided in favour of an unassisted party."

9. In section 20(1) (supplementary), for the words "sections 18 and" there shall be substituted the word "section."

PART III

Board's property to be rateable

10. In Schedule 1, paragraph 2(4) is repealed.

SCHEDULE 5

MINOR AND CONSEQUENTIAL AMENDMENTS

Public Records Act 1958 (c. 51)

1. In Schedule 1 to the Public Records Act 1958 (definition of public records), there shall be inserted at the end of Part I of the Table at the end of paragraph 3 the following entry—

| "Lord Chancellor's Department. | Legal Aid |
| | Board." |

Parliamentary Commissioner Act 1967 (c. 13)
2. In Schedule 2 to the Parliamentary Commissioner Act 1967 (which lists the bodies subject to the jurisdiction of the Parliamentary Commissioner), there shall be inserted (at the appropriate place in alphabetical order) the following entry—

"Legal Aid Board."

Attachment of Earnings Act 1971 (c. 32)
3. In section 25(1) of the Attachment of Earnings Act 1971, for the words "section 7 or 8(2) of the Legal Aid Act 1982" there shall be substituted the words "section 23 of the Legal Aid Act 1988."

House of Commons Disqualification Act 1975 (c. 24)
4. In Part III of Schedule 1 to the House of Commons Disqualification Act 1975 (other disqualifying offices), there shall be inserted (at the appropriate places in alphabetical order) the following entries—

"Chairman of the Legal Aid Board."

"Member of the Legal Aid Board."

Northern Ireland Assembly Disqualification Act 1975 (c. 25)
5. In Part III of Schedule 1 to the Northern Ireland Assembly Disqualification Act 1975 (other disqualifying offices), there shall be inserted (at the appropriate places in alphabetical order) the following entries—

"Chairman of the Legal Aid Board."

"Member of the Legal Aid Board."

Sex Discrimination Act 1975 (c. 65)
6. In section 75(4) of the Sex Discrimination Act 1975—

(a) for the words "Legal Aid Act 1974" there shall be substituted the words "Legal Aid Act 1988"; and

(b) for the words "any of those Acts for payment of any sum into the legal aid fund" there shall be substituted the words "either of those Acts for payment of any sum to the Legal Aid Board or into the Scottish Legal Aid Fund."

Race Relations Act 1976 (c. 74)
7. In section 66(6) of the Race Relations Act 1976—

(a) for the words "Legal Aid Act 1974" there shall be substituted the words "Legal Aid Act 1988"; and

(b) for the words "any of those Acts for payment of any sum into the legal aid fund" there shall be substituted the words "either of those Acts for payment of any sum to the Legal Aid Board or into the Scottish Legal Aid Fund."

Child Care Act 1980 (c. 5)
8. In section 21A of the Child Care Act 1980, after subsection (8), there shall be inserted the following subsection—

"(9) In this section "legal aid" means representation for the purposes of care proceedings under Part VI of the Legal Aid Act 1988."

Magistrates' Courts Act 1980 (c. 43)
9. In section 92(1)(b) of the Magistrates' Courts Act 1980, for the words "section 7 or 8(2) of the Legal Aid Act 1982" there shall be substituted the words "section 23 of the Legal Aid Act 1988."

Supreme Court Act 1981 (c. 54)
10. In section 47(7) of the Supreme Court Act 1981, for the words "legal aid contribution order made under section 7 or 8(2) of the Legal Aid Act 1982" there shall be substituted the words "contribution order made under section 23 of the Legal Aid Act 1988."

Telecommunications Act 1984 (c. 12)
11. In section 52 of the Telecommunications Act 1984, the following subsection shall be substituted for subsection (5)—

"(5) A charge conferred by subsection (4) above is subject to:

(a) any charge under the Legal Aid Act 1988 and any provision of that Act for payment of any sum to the Legal Aid Board;

(b) any charge or obligation for payment in priority to other debts under the Legal Aid (Scotland) Act 1986 and any provision of that Act for payment of any sum into the Scottish Legal Aid Fund; or

(c) any charge under the Legal Aid, Advice and Assistance (Northern Ireland) Order 1981 and any provision of that Order for payment of any sum into the legal aid fund."

Prosecution of Offences Act 1985 (c. 23)
12. In section 19(2)(b) of the Prosecution of Offences Act 1985, the words "(including any legal aid order)" shall be omitted and at the end of that paragraph there shall be inserted the words "or any grant of representation for the purposes of the proceedings which has been made under the Legal Aid Act 1988."

13. In section 20(2) of that Act, for the words "out of the legal aid fund or" there shall be substituted the words "by the Legal Aid Board or out of."

14. In section 21(1) of that Act, for the definition of "legally assisted person" there shall be substituted the following—

" 'legally assisted person,' in relation to any proceedings, means a person to whom representation under the Legal Aid Act 1988 has been granted for the purposes of the proceedings".

15. In section 21 of that Act, after subsection (4), there shall be inserted the following subsection—

"(4A) Where one party to any proceedings is a legally assisted person then:

(a) for the purposes of sections 16 and 17 of this Act, his costs shall be taken not to include either the expenses incurred on his behalf by the Legal Aid Board or the Lord Chancellor or, if he is liable to make a contribution under section 23 of the Legal Aid Act 1988, any sum paid or payable by way of contribution; and

(b) for the purposes of sections 18 and 19 of this Act, his costs shall be taken to include the expenses incurred on his behalf by the Legal Aid Board or the Lord Chancellor (without any deduction on account of any contribution paid or payable under section 23 of the Legal Aid Act 1988), but, if he is liable to make such a contribution his costs shall be taken not to include any sum paid or payable by way of contribution."

Child Abduction and Custody Act 1985 (c. 60)
16. In section 11 of the Child Abduction and Custody Act 1985, for the words "Part I of the Legal Aid Act 1974" there shall be substituted the words "Part III or IV of the Legal Aid Act 1988."

Administration of Justice Act 1985 (c. 61)
17. In section 40 of the Administration of Justice Act 1985 (preliminary provisions concerning legal aid complaints), for the words from the beginning of paragraph (a) to

the end there shall be substituted the words "the provision for any person of services under the Legal Aid Act 1988 including, in the case of a solicitor, provision for any person of such services in the capacity of agent for that person's solicitor."

18. In section 43 of that Act (jurisdiction and powers of Solicitors Disciplinary Tribunal in relation to complaints against solicitors)—

(a) in subsection (3), for paragraphs (a), (b) and (c) there shall be substituted the following—

"(a) otherwise payable under or in accordance with the Legal Aid Act 1988, or
(b) otherwise chargeable in respect of advice or assistance made available under Part III of that Act"; and

(b) in subsection (4), for paragraphs (a) and (b) there shall be substituted the words "any of sections 9, 11, 15(6) and (7) and 25(2) of, or any provision made under, the Legal Aid Act 1988."

19. In section 44 of that Act—

(a) in subsection (3), in the inserted subsection (2A), for the words from the beginning of paragraph (a) to the end there shall be substituted the words:

"(a) his conduct, including conduct in the capacity of agent for another solicitor, in connection with the provision for any person of services under the Legal Aid Act 1988; or
(b) his professional conduct generally;" and

(b) in subsection (4), in the inserted subsection (6), for the words from "each" to the end there shall be substituted the words "those who may be selected or assigned for the purpose of providing for any person services under the Legal Aid Act 1988."

Housing Act 1985 (c. 68)

20. In section 170(5) of the Housing Act 1985:

(a) for the words "Legal Aid Act 1974" there shall be substituted the words "Legal Aid Act 1988;" and

(b) for the words "into the legal aid fund" there shall be substituted the words "to the Legal Aid Board."

Family Law Act 1986 (c. 55)

21. Section 64 of the Family Law Act 1986 (family proceedings rules) shall cease to have effect.

Criminal Justice Act 1987 (c. 38)

22. In section 4(1) of the Criminal Justice Act 1987, for the words "section 28(7A) of the Legal Aid Act 1974" there shall be substituted the words "section 20(4) of the Legal Aid Act 1988."

SCHEDULE 6

REPEALS

Chapter	Short title	Extent of repeal
1967 c. 80.	The Criminal Justice Act 1967.	Section 90.
1974 c. 4.	The Legal Aid Act 1974.	The whole Act.
1974 c. 47.	The Solicitors Act 1974.	Section 75(d). In Schedule 3, paragraph 10.
1975 c. 72.	The Children Act 1975.	Section 65.

Chapter	Short title	Extent of repeal
		In Schedule 3, paragraph 82.
1976 c. 36.	The Adoption Act 1976.	In Schedule 3, paragraph 18.
1976 c. 63.	The Bail Act 1976.	Section 11.
1976 c. 71.	The Supplementary Benefits Act 1976.	In Schedule 7, paragraphs 33 and 35.
1977 c. 38.	The Administration of Justice Act 1977.	In Schedule 1, Part I.
1977 c. 45	The Criminal Law Act 1977.	In Schedule 12, the entry relating to the Legal Aid Act 1974.
1978 c. 22.	The Domestic Proceedings and Magistrates' Courts Act 1978.	In Schedule 2, paragraphs 45 and 52.
1979 c. 26.	The Legal Aid Act 1979.	The whole Act.
1979 c. 55.	The Justices of the Peace Act 1979.	In Schedule 2, paragraph 27.
1980 c. 5.	The Child Care Act 1980.	In Schedule 5, paragraph 36.
1980 c. 30.	The Social Security Act 1980.	In Schedule 4, paragraph 9.
1980 c. 43.	The Magistrates' Courts Act 1980.	In Schedule 7, paragraphs 126 to 129.
1981 c. 49.	The Contempt of Court Act 1981.	Section 13. In Schedule 2, Part I.
1982 c. 27.	The Civil Jurisdiction and Judgments Act 1982.	Section 40(1).
1982 c. 44.	The Legal Aid Act 1982.	The whole Act.
1982 c. 48.	The Criminal Justice Act 1982.	Section 25(2). Section 29(3). Section 60(4).
1983 c. 41.	The Health and Social Services and Social Security Adjudications Act 1983.	In Schedule 1, paragraph 3.
1984 c. 42.	The Matrimonial and Family Proceedings Act 1984.	In Schedule 1, paragraph 18.
1984 c. 60.	The Police and Criminal Evidence Act 1984.	Section 59.
1985 c. 23.	Prosecution of Offences Act 1985.	Section 16(8). In section 19(2)(b), the words "(including any legal aid order)". In section 21(1), the definition of "legal aid order".
1985 c. 61.	The Administration of Justice Act 1985.	Sections 45 and 46. In Schedule 7, paragraphs 1 to 3.
1986 c. 28.	The Children and Young Persons (Amendment) Act 1986.	Section 3(3).
1986 c. 47.	The Legal Aid (Scotland) Act 1986.	In section 4(2)(c), the words "for the purposes of this Act".

Chapter	Short title	Extent of repeal
		In section 16, subsection (1) and, in subsection (2), the words "in this section and".
		In section 17, subsections (3) to (8).
		Section 18(1).
		In section 32(1), the words ", out of the Fund".
		In Schedule 1, paragraph 2(4).
1986 c. 50.	The Social Security Act 1986.	In Schedule 10, paragraphs 46, 47 and 56.
1986 c. 55.	The Family Law Act 1986.	Section 64.
1987 c. 38.	The Criminal Justice Act 1987.	In Schedule 2, paragraphs 7 and 8.

SCHEDULE 7

TRANSITION

Preliminary

1. In this Schedule—

"the 1974 Act" means the Legal Aid Act 1974; and

"the appointed day" means the day appointed by the Lord Chancellor under section 47(2) of this Act for the coming into force of section 3(2) thereof.

The Legal Aid Fund

2.—(1) On the appointed day the legal aid fund ("the Old Fund") maintained by the Law Society under section 17 of the 1974 Act shall be wound up.

(2) If, as at the appointed day, after taking account of all receipts and expenses of the Law Society attributable to their functions under the 1974 Act and the Legal Aid Act 1982 ("the 1982 Act"), there is in relation to the Old Fund any surplus or deficit—

(a) such surplus shall be paid by the Law Society to the Lord Chancellor; and

(b) such deficit shall be made up by payment to the Law Society by the Lord Chancellor of the amount of the deficit.

(3) Notwithstanding their repeal by this Act—

(a) sections 15(9) and 18 of the 1974 Act shall continue to have effect for the purposes of requiring the Law Society to account for the Old Fund and to report on the discharge of its functions under that Act up to the appointed day; and

(b) section 17(5) of that Act shall continue to have effect for the purposes of any determination as to the expenses of receipts of the Law Society;

and, if the appointed day falls on a day which is not the last day of the financial year (for the purposes of the said section 18), references in those sections to the financial year shall be construed as references to the period commencing on the day immediately following the end of the last complete financial year and ending with the appointed day.

(4) The Lord Chancellor shall pay to the Law Society such expenses incurred after the appointed day in connection with their functions under sections 15(9) and 18 of the 1974 Act as appear to him to be reasonable.

(5) Any payments received by the Lord Chancellor under sub-paragraph (2)(a) above shall be paid by him into the legal aid fund established by the Board under section 6.

(6) Any amount required to be paid by the Lord Chancellor under sub-paragraph (2)(b) or (4) above shall be defrayed out of money provided by Parliament.

Rights, obligations and property

3.—(1) Subject to paragraph 2, on the appointed day all rights, obligations and property of the Law Society which are referable to its functions under the 1974 Act and the 1982 Act shall become rights, obligations and property of the Board.

(2) Any payments which are required to be made into or out of the Old Fund in connection with legal aid or advice or assistance under the 1974 Act shall, on and after the appointed day, be paid to or by the Board.

Transfer of functions

4.—(1) Any grant of legal aid under Part I of the 1974 Act which is in force immediately before the appointed day shall, on and after the appointed day, have effect as a grant by the Board of representation under Part IV of this Act.

(2) Any approval given in connection with the grant of legal aid or advice or assistance under Part I of the 1974 Act which is in force immediately before the appointed day shall, on and after the appointed day, have effect as an approval by the Board in connection with the corresponding advice, assistance or representation under Part III or IV of this Act.

(3) Anything which, immediately before the appointed day, is in the process of being done by or in relation to the Law Society in connection with any function which it has relating to legal aid or advice or assistance under Part I of the 1974 Act, may be continued, on and after the appointed day, by or in relation to the Board.

Legal aid contribution orders

5. Notwithstanding their repeal by this Act, the provisions of the 1974 Act and the 1982 Act with respect to legal aid contribution orders shall continue to have effect in relation to any such order made in connection with a legal aid order made by virtue of section 28(11A) of the 1974 Act (legal aid for proceedings for contempt).

The Board: transfers of employment

6.—(1) The Board shall make, not later than such date as the Lord Chancellor may determine, an offer of employment by the Board to such of the persons employed immediately before that date by the Law Society for the purpose of their functions under the 1974 Act as fall within such descriptions as the Lord Chancellor designates for the purposes of this paragraph or are persons whom the Board wishes to employ.

(2) The terms of the offer shall be such that they are, taken as a whole, not less favourable to the person to whom the offer is made than the terms on which he is employed on the date on which the offer is made.

(3) An offer made in pursuance of this paragraph shall not be revocable during the period of three months commencing with the date on which it is made.

7.—(1) Where a person becomes an employee of the Board on acceptance of an offer made under paragraph 6, then, for the purposes of the Employment Protection (Consolidation) Act 1978, his period of employment with the Law Society shall count as a period of employment by the Board, and the change of employment shall not break the continuity of the period of employment.

(2) Where an offer is made under paragraph 6 to any person, none of the agreed redundancy procedures applicable to employees of the Law Society shall apply to him.

(3) Where a person employed by the Law Society ceases to be so employed—

(a) on becoming a member of the staff of the Board on accepting an offer under paragraph 6; or

(b) having unreasonably refused such an offer;

Part VI of the Employment Protection (Consolidation) Act 1978 shall not apply to him and he shall not be treated for the purposes of any scheme in force under section 19 of the 1974 Act as having been retired on redundancy.

(4) Where a person to whom an offer under paragraph 6 has been made continues in employment in the law Society after having not unreasonably refused that offer he shall be treated for all purposes as if no offer under paragraph 6 had been made to him.

8.—(1) Any dispute as to whether an offer purporting to be made under paragraph 6 complies with that paragraph shall be referred to and be determined by an industrial tribunal.

(2) An industrial tribunal shall not consider a complaint referred to it under sub-paragraph (1) above unless the complaint is presented to the tribunal before the end of the period of 3 months beginning with the date of the offer of employment or within such further period as the tribunal considers reasonable in a case where it is satisfied that it was not reasonably practicable for the complaint to be presented before the end of the period of 3 months.

(3) An appeal shall lie to the Employment Appeal Tribunal on a question of law arising from the decision of, or in proceedings before, an industrial tribunal under this paragraph.

(4) Except as mentioned in sub-paragraph (3) above, no appeal shall lie from the decision of an industrial tribunal under this paragraph.

9.—(1) In the event of the Board assuming under section 3(4) any of the functions specified in that subsection the Lord Chancellor shall by regulations make such provision corresponding to paragraphs 6, 7 and 8 in respect of employees to whom this paragraph applies as appears to him to be appropriate.

(2) This paragraph applies to persons employed—

(a) in civil service of the State; or

(b) by a magistrates' courts committee,

and so employed wholly or mainly in connection with the functions referred to in sub-paragraph (1) above.

Pensions
10. Any arrangements made by the Law Society under section 19 of the 1974 Act in respect of any pension shall be treated on and after the appointed day (so far as may be necessary to preserve their effect) as having been made under paragraph 10(2) of Schedule 1 to this Act, and any pension scheme administered by the Law Society immediately before the appointed day shall be deemed to be a pension scheme established and administered by the Board under that paragraph and shall continue to be administered accordingly.

Representation in affiliation proceedings: transitory provision
11. Until the repeal of the Affiliation Proceedings Act 1957 by the Family Law Reform Act 1987 takes effect, Schedule 2 to this Act shall be taken to include proceedings in the Crown Court or a magistrates' court for or in relation to an affiliation order within the meaning of the Affiliation Proceedings Act 1957.

SCHEDULE 8

Transitory Amendments of Legal Aid Act 1974

Preliminary
1. In this Schedule "the 1974 Act" means the Legal Aid Act 1974.

Regulation of charges on property
2. In section 20(2)(e) of the 1974 Act (regulation of charge on property):

(a) after the words "receiving advice or assistance or legal aid" there shall be inserted the words "and regulating the release or postponement of the enforcement of any charge (however created) for the benefit of the legal aid fund"; and

(b) at the end there shall be inserted the words; "and

(iii) requiring interest to be charged at a prescribed rate in circumstances where enforcement of a charge for the benefit of the legal aid fund is postponed."

Remuneration

3. In section 39 of the 1974 Act, for subsection (3) (fair remuneration in criminal and certain other legal aid cases) there shall be substituted the following:

"(3) The Lord Chancellor, in making regulations under this section as to the amounts payable to counsel or solicitors undertaking any description of legal aid work under this Part of this Act, shall have regard, among the matters which are relevant, to:

(a) the time and skill which it requires;

(b) the general level of fee income arising from it;

(c) the general level of expenses of barristers and solicitors which is attributable to it;

(d) the number and general level of competence of barristers and solicitors undertaking it;

(e) the effect of the regulations on the handling of the work; and

(f) the cost to public funds of any provision made by the regulations.".

4.—(1) In Schedule 2 to the 1974 Act (remuneration in civil legal aid cases):

(a) in paragraph 1(1), for the words "95 per cent. of the" there shall be substituted the words "the full"; and

(b) in paragraph 2(1), for the words "95 per cent. of the" there shall be substituted the words "the full."

(2) The amendments made by this paragraph have effect in relation to any case in which the order or direction for taxation is made on or after the date on which this Act is passed.

Civil Legal Aid (Matrimonial Proceedings) Regulations 1989

Coming into force April 1, 1989

The Lord Chancellor, in exercise of the powers conferred on him by sections 14(2) and 43 of the Legal Aid Act 1988(a), hereby makes the following Regulations of which a draft has, in accordance with section 36(3)(b) of that Act, been laid before and approved by resolution of each House of Parliament.

Citation, commencement and revocation

1.—(1) These regulations may be cited as the Civil Legal Aid (Matrimonial Proceedings) Regulations 1989 and shall come into force on April 1, 1989.

(2) The Legal Aid (Matrimonial Proceedings) Regulations 1977 are hereby revoked.

Proceedings for divorce or judicial separation

2. After paragraph 5 of Part II of Schedule 2 to the Legal Aid Act 1988 there shall be added the following new paragraph:

"**5A.** Proceedings for a decree of divorce or judicial separation unless the cause is defended, or the petition is directed to be heard in open court, or it is not practicable by reason of physical or mental incapacity for the applicant to proceed without representation; except that representation shall be available for the purpose of making or opposing an application—

(a) for an injunction;

(b) for ancillary relief, excluding representation for the purpose only of inserting a prayer for ancillary relief in the petition;

(c) for an order relating to the custody of (or access to) a child, or the education or care or supervision of a child, excluding representation for the purpose only of making such an application where there is no reason to believe that the application will be opposed;

(d) for an order declaring that the court is satisfied as to arrangements for the welfare of the children of the family, excluding representation for the purpose only of making such an application where there is no reason to believe that the application will be opposed; or

(e) for the purpose of making or opposing any other application, or satisfying the court on any other matter which raises a substantial question for determination by the court."

EXPLANATORY NOTE
(This note is not part of the Regulations)
These regulations replace the Legal Aid (Matrimonial Proceedings) Regulations 1977 (S.I. 1977/447). Regulation 2 adds a new paragraph to Part II of Schedule 2 to the Legal Aid Act 1988, excluding (with certain exceptions) from the scope of Part IV of the Act, representation in proceedings for divorce or judicial separation.

Legal Advice and Assistance (Scope) Regulations 1989

Coming into force April 1, 1989

ARRANGEMENT OF REGULATIONS

The Lord Chancellor, in exercise of the powers conferred on him by sections 8 and 43 of the Legal Aid Act 1988, hereby makes the following Regulations of which a draft has, in accordance with section 36(3)(b) of that Act, been laid before and approved by resolution of each House of Parliament—

PART I

GENERAL

Citation and Commencement

1. These Regulations may be cited as the Legal Advice and Assistance (Scope) Regulations 1989 and shall come into force on April 1, 1989.

Interpretation

2. In these Regulations, unless the context otherwise requires—

"ABWOR" means assistance by way of representation;

"the Act" means the Legal Aid Act 1988;

"board of visitors" means a board of visitors appointed by the Secretary of State under section 6(2) of the Prison Act 1952;

"client" means a person seeking or receiving advice or assistance or on whose behalf advice or assistance is sought;

"conditional sale agreement" has the meaning assigned to it in section 189 of the Consumer Credit Act 1974;

"conveyancing services" has the meaning assigned to it in section 11 of the Administration of Justice Act 1985;

"mental disorder" has the meaning assigned to it in section 1 of the Mental Health Act 1983;

"rental purchase agreement" has the meaning assigned to it in section 88 of the Housing Act 1980;

"will" has the meaning assigned to it in section 1 of the Wills Act 1837;

PART II

EXCLUSIONS FROM PART III OF THE ACT

Conveyancing Services

3.—(1) Subject to paragraphs (2) and (3), advice and assistance consisting of conveyancing services are excluded from Part III of the Act.

(2) Paragraph (1) does not exclude from Part III of the Act advice or assistance relating to a rental purchase agreement or a conditional sale agreement for the sale of land.

(3) Paragraph (1) does not exclude from Part III of the Act advice or assistance consisting of such conveyancing services as are necessary in order to give effect to an order of the court or, in proceedings under the Matrimonial

Causes Act 1973 or the Matrimonial and Family Proceedings Act 1984, the terms of an agreement.

Wills

4.—(1) Except as provided by paragraph (2), advice and assistance in the making of wills are excluded from Part III of the Act.

(2) Advice and assistance in the making of a will are not excluded by paragraph (1) from Part III of the Act where they are given to a client who is:

(a) aged 70 or over; or

(b) blind (or partially sighted), deaf (or hard of hearing), or dumb, or who suffers from mental disorder of any description, or who is substantially and permanently handicapped by illness, injury or congenital deformity; or

(c) a parent or guardian within the meaning of section 87 of the Child Care Act 1980 of a person to whom any description in (b) applies, where the client wishes to provide in the will for that person; or

(d) the mother or father of a minor who is living with the client, where the client is not living with the minor's other parent, and the client wishes to appoint a guardian for that minor under section 4 of the Guardianship of Minors Act 1971.

Transition

5. Where advice or assistance has been given before these Regulations come into force, nothing in this Part shall affect further advice or assistance given in relation to the same matter.

PART III

ABWOR

Application of Part III of the Act to ABWOR

6. Part III of the Act does not apply to ABWOR except as provided in this Part.

Proceedings in magistrates' courts

7.—(1) Part III of the Act applies to ABWOR given—

(a) to a client for the purposes of the proceedings in magistrates' courts specified in the Schedule;

(b) at a hearing in any proceedings in a magistrates' court to a party who is not receiving and has not been refused representation in connection with those proceedings, where the court—

(i) is satisfied that the hearing should proceed on the same day;

(ii) is satisfied that that party would not otherwise be represented; and

(iii) requests a solicitor who is within the precincts of the court for purposes other than the provision of ABWOR in accordance with this sub-paragraph, or approves a proposal from such a solicitor, that he provide that party with ABWOR; or

(c) to a person in connection with an application for a warrant of further detention, or for an extension of such a warrant, made in respect of that person to a magistrates' court under section 43 or 44 of the Police and Criminal Evidence Act 1984**(b)**.

(2) Subject to paragraph (3), Part III of the Act also applies, in criminal proceedings in magistrates' courts where the client has not previously received and is not otherwise receiving representation or ABWOR in connection with the same proceedings, to ABWOR given to a client—

(a) in making an application for bail;

(b) at an appearance in court where the client is in custody and wishes the case to be concluded at that appearance, unless the solicitor who is advising him considers that the case should be adjourned in the interests of justice or of the client;

(c) who is before the court as a result of a failure to obey an order of the court, where such failure may lead to his being at risk of imprisonment;

(d) who is not in custody and who in the opinion of the solicitor requires ABWOR.

(3) Paragraph (2) does not apply to committal proceedings, to proceedings in which the client pleads not guilty, nor, unless the solicitor considers the circumstances to be exceptional, to proceedings in connection with a non-imprisonable offence.

(4) Part III also applies to ABWOR given to a defendant in proceedings in a magistrates' court where the defendant is before the court as a result of a failure to pay a fine or other sum which he was ordered on conviction to pay, and such failure may lead to his being at risk of imprisonment.

Proceedings in county courts

8. Part III of the Act applies to ABWOR given by a solicitor at a hearing in any proceedings in a county court to a party who is not receiving and has not been refused representation in connection with those proceedings, where the court—

(a) is satisfied that the hearing should proceed on the same day;

(b) is satisfied that that party would not otherwise be represented; and

(c) requests a solicitor who is within the precincts of the court for purposes other than the provision of ABWOR in accordance with this regulation, or approves a proposal from such a solicitor, that he provide that party with ABWOR.

Other Proceedings

9. Part III of the Act applies to ABWOR given—

(a) to a person in proceedings before a Mental Health Review Tribunal under the Mental Health Act 1983 whose case or whose application to the Tribunal is or is to be the subject of the proceedings;

(b) to a prisoner in proceedings before a board of visitors who has been permitted by the board of visitors to be legally represented in those proceedings.

SCHEDULE

PROCEEDINGS IN MAGISTRATES' COURTS IN WHICH ABWOR IS AVAILABLE

1. In this Schedule "proceedings in a magistrates' court" includes giving notice of appeal or applying for a case to be stated within the ordinary time for so doing, and matters preliminary thereto.

2. The proceedings in which Part III of the Act applies to ABWOR under regulation 7(1)(a) are proceedings—

(a) for or in relation to an affiliation order within the meaning of the Affiliation Proceedings Act 1957;

(b) for or in relation to an order under Part I of the Domestic Proceedings and Magistrates' Courts Act 1978;

(c) under the Guardianship of Minors Act 1971 and 1973;

(d) under section 43 of the National Assistance Act 1948, section 22 of the Maintenance Orders Act 1950, section 4 of the Maintenance Orders Act 1958, section 18 of the Supplementary Benefits Act 1976, or section 24 of the Social Security Act 1986;

(e) in relation to an application for leave of the court to remove a child from a person's custody under section 27 or 28 of the Adoption Act 1976 or proceedings in which the making of an order under Part II or section 29 or 55 of the Adoption Act 1976 is opposed by any party to the proceedings;

(f) under Part I of the Maintenance Orders (Reciprocal Enforcement) Act 1972 relating to a maintenance order made by a court of a country outside the United Kingdom;

(g) under Part II of the Children Act 1975;

EXPLANATORY NOTE
(This note is not part of the Regulations)

These Regulations replace, with amendments, the provisions in the Legal Advice and Assistance Regulations (No. 2) 1980 (S.I. 1980/1898) which prescribe the scope of advice and assistance (including assistance by way of representation). The other provisions of those Regulations are replaced, with amendments, by the Legal Advice and Assistance Regulations 1989 (S.I. 1989/340).

The main changes are to disapply (with certain exceptions) the provisions of Part III of the Act from advice and assistance consisting of conveyancing services (regulation 3) or in the making of wills (regulation 4).

In accordance with section 8(2) of the Legal Aid Act 1988, the Regulations apply Part III of the Act to assistance by way of representation (as to proceedings in magistrates' courts, regulation 7; as to proceedings in county courts, regulation 8; as to proceedings before Mental Health Review Tribunals and proceedings before boards of prison visitors, regulation 9).

Legal Advice and Assistance Regulations 1989*

Coming into force April 1, 1989

ARRANGEMENTS OF REGULATIONS

* As amended by the Legal Advice and Assistance (Amendment) Regulations 1989 (S.I. 1989 No. 560) and the Legal Advice and Assistance (Amendment) Regulations 1990 (S.I. 1990 No. 486).

The Lord Chancellor, in exercise of the powers conferred on him by sections 2, 9, 10, 11, 34, and 43 of the Legal Aid Act 1988(**a**), having consulted the General Council of the Bar, the Law Society, the County Court Rule Committee and the Magistrates' Courts Rule Committee, and with the consent of the Treasury, hereby makes the following Regulations:—

Citation, commencement, and transitional provisions

1.—(1) These Regulations may be cited as the Legal Advice and Assistance Regulations 1989 and shall come into force on April 1, 1989.

(2) Where a review under paragraph (7) of regulation 29 relates to a claim made before June 1, 1989, paragraphs (8) and (9) of that regulation shall not apply and the solicitor may appeal in writing within 21 days of receipt of notification of the decision on the review to a committee appointed by the Board.

Revocations

2. The Regulations specified in Schedule 1 are hereby revoked.

Interpretation

3.—(1) In these Regulations, unless the context otherwise requires—

"ABWOR" means assistance by way of representation;

"the Act" means the Legal Aid Act 1988;

"appropriate area committee" means the area committee in whose area an application for advice and assistance, or a claim for costs has been dealt with by an Area Director;

"area committee" has the meaning assigned to it in the Civil Legal Aid (General) Regulations 1989;

"Area Director" has the meaning assigned to it in the Civil Legal Aid (General) Regulations 1989;

"assessed deficiency" means the amount by which the sum allowed to the solicitor by the Area Director in assessing his claim under regulation 29 exceeds any contribution payable by the client to the solicitor under section 9 of the Act together with the value of any charge arising under section 11 of the Act;

"board of visitors" means a board of visitors appointed by the Secretary of State under section 6(2) of the Prison Act 1952;

"child" means a person under the age that is for the time being the upper limit of compulsory school age by virtue of section 35 of the Education Act 1944 together with any Order in Council made under that section;

"client" means a person seeking or receiving advice and assistance or on whose behalf advice and assistance is sought;

"costs" means the cost of giving advice or assistance, including disbursements, charges and fees;

"Costs Regulations" means the Legal Aid in Criminal and Care Proceedings (Costs) Regulations 1989;

"extension" means the grant of prior authority to exceed the limit prescribed under section 10(1) of the Act and, where appropriate, the grant of prior authority to exceed any further limit imposed under regulation 21(3) or 22(8);

"family credit" means family credit under the Social Security Act 1986;

"fund" means the legal aid fund;

"income support" means income support under the Social Security Act 1986;

"patient" means a person who by reason of mental disorder within the meaning of the Mental Health Act 1983 is encapable of managing and administering his property and affairs;

"Scope Regulations" means the Legal Advice and Assistance (Scope) Regulations 1989;

"serious service offence" means an offence under any of the Army Act 1955, the Air Force Act 1955, or the Naval Discipline Act 1957 which cannot be dealt with summarily or which appears to an interviewing service policeman to be serious;

"volunteer" means a person who, for the purpose of assisting with an investigation, attends voluntary at a police station or at any other place where a constable is present or accompanies a constable to a police station or any such other place without having been arrested.

(2) Any reference in these Regulations to a regulation or Schedule by number means the regulation or Schedule so numbered in these Regulations.

Limit on cost of advice and assistance

4.—(1) Subject to paragraph (2), the limit applicable under section 10(1) of the Act is—

(a) in respect of advice and assistance given in accordance with regulation 6(1), £90;

(b) in respect of advice and assistance provided to a petitioner for divorce or judicial separation which includes advice or assistance in the preparation of the petition, three times the relevant sum specified for preparation in the table in paragraph 1(1)(a) of Part 1 of Schedule 1 to the Costs Regulations;

(c) in respect of all other advice and assistance, twice the relevant sum referred to in sub-paragraph (b);

(2) Section 10(1) of the Act shall not apply to—

(a) advice or assistance specified in regulation 5(1)(b) of the Legal Advice and Assistance at Police Stations (Remuneration) Regulations 1989**(j)** where the interests of justice require such advice or assistance to be given as a matter of urgency; or

(b) ABWOR provided under arrangements made by the Board under regulation 7; or

(c) advice or assistance given under arrangements made by the Board under regulation 8.

ABWOR relating to applications for further detention

5.—ABWOR to which Part III of the Act applies by virtue of regulation 7(1)(c) of the Scope Regulations (application for warrant of further detention) shall be available without reference to the client's financial resources.

Provision of advice and assistance at police stations, etc.

6.—(1) A solicitor may give advice and assistance to any person who—

(a) is arrested and held in custody at a police station or other premises; or

(b) is being interviewed in connection with a serious service offence; or

(c) is a volunteer.

(2) Subject to any arrangements made by the Board under paragraph (3), an application for advice and assistance in the circumstances specified in paragraph (1) may be made by telephone to the solicitor from whom the advice and assistance is sought.

(3) The Board may make arrangements for solicitors designated by the Board to attend at police stations or other premises in order to provide advice and assistance under paragraph (1).

(4) Advice and assistance given under this regulation shall be available without reference to the client's financial resources.

ABWOR in criminal proceedings in magistrates' courts

7.—(1) The Board may make arrangements for the provision of ABWOR to which Part III of the Act applies by virtue of regulation 7(2) and (4) of the Scope Regulations.

(2) Arrangements under paragraph (1) may provide for solicitors designated by the Board to attend at magistrates' courts.

(3) ABWOR under this regulation shall be available without reference to the client's financial resources.

Advice and assistance in criminal proceedings in magistrates' courts

8.—(1) Arrangements under regulation 7 may provide for a solicitor who gives ABWOR in accordance with them also to give—

(a) advice to a defendant who is in custody;

(b) advice to a defendant who is before the court as a result of a failure to pay a fine or other sum which he was ordered on conviction to pay, or to obey an order of the court, where such failure may lead to his being at risk of imprisonment;

(c) advice, where in the opinion of the solicitor the defendant requires it, to a defendant who is not in custody;

(d) assistance to a defendant to make an application for representation under the Act in respect of any subsequent appearance of the defendant before the court.

(2) Advice and assistance given under this regulation shall be available without reference to the client's financial resources.

Applications for advice and assistance

9.—(1) An application for advice and assistance to which this regulation applies shall be made in accordance with its provisions to the solicitor from whom the advice and assistance is sought.

(2) This regulation applies to all advice and assistance except—

(a) advice or assistance given under regulation 6 or 8; and

(b) ABWOR given under regulation 7, or to which Part III of the Act applies by virtue of regulation 7(1)(c) of the Scope Regulations (warrants of further detention).

(3) Subject to regulations 10 and 15, the application under paragraph (1) shall be made by the client in person.

(4) Where a client makes an application under paragraph (1) he shall provide the solicitor with the information necessary to enable the solicitor to determine—

(a) his disposable capital;

(b) where appropriate, whether he is in receipt of income support or family credit, and

(c) where he is not in receipt of income support or family credit, his disposable income.

(5) Where an application under paragraph (1) is for advice or assistance relating to the making of a will, the client shall provide the solicitor with the information necessary to enable the solicitor to determine whether the advice or assistance would fall within regulation 4(2) of the Scope Regulations.

(6) The information required by this regulation shall be furnished on a form approved by the Board.

Attendance on behalf of a client

10.—(1) Where a client cannot for good reason attend on the solicitor in order to apply for advice and assistance in accordance with paragraph (3) of regulation 9, he may authorise another person to attend on his behalf.

(2) Where a person authorised in accordance with paragraph (1) attends on a solicitor, he shall furnish the solicitor with the information necessary to enable the solicitor to determine—

(a) the client's disposable capital;

(b) where appropriate, whether the client is in receipt of income support or family credit; and

(c) where the client is not in receipt of income support or family credit, the client's disposable income.

(3) Where the application is for advice or assistance relating to the making of a will, the person authorised in accordance with paragraph (1) shall provide the solicitor with the information necessary to enable the solicitor to determine whether the advice or assistance would fall within regulation 4(2) of the Scope Regulations.

(4) The information required by this regulation shall be furnished on a form approved by the Board.

Eligibility for advice and assistance to which regulation 9 applies

11.—(1) A client is eligible for advice and assistance (excluding ABWOR) to which regulation 9 applies if his weekly disposable income does not exceed the highest amount for the time being specified in the first column of the table in Schedule 3, and his disposable capital does not exceed £935.

(2) A client is eligible for ABWOR to which regulation 9 applies if his weekly disposable income does not exceed the highest amount for the time

being specified in the first column of the table in Schedule 3, and his disposable capital does not exceed £3,000.

Amended by the Legal Advice and Assistance (Amendment) Regulations 1990 (S.I. 1990 No. 486).

Contributions to the cost of advice and assistance to which regulation 9 applies

12.—(1) Subject to paragraph (2), the contribution which a client is liable to make under section 9(6) of the Act is as set out in Schedule 3.

(2) A client whose weekly disposable income does not exceed the lowest sum for the time being specified in the first column of the table in Schedule 3 is not liable to make any contribution under section 9(6) of the Act.

Assessment of disposable income, disposable capital and maximum contribution

13.—(1) Subject to paragraphs (2) and (3), a solicitor to whom an application under regulation 9 is made shall assess the disposable income and disposable capital of the client and, where appropriate, of any person whose financial resources may be treated as those of the client in accordance with Schedule 2.

(2) Where the solicitor is satisfied that any of the persons whose disposable incomes are to be assessed under paragraph (1) is directly or indirectly in receipt of income support or family credit, he shall take that person's disposable income as not exceeding the lowest sum for the time being specified in the first column of the table in Schedule 3.

(3) Where, in the case of an application for ABWOR to which regulation 9 applies, the solicitor is satisfied that any of the persons whose disposable capital is to be assessed under paragraph (1) is directly or indirectly in receipt of income support, he shall take that person's disposable capital as not exceeding the capital sum specified in regulation 11(2).

(4) The solicitor shall also determine the maximum contribution, if any, payable to him by the client under section 9(6) of the Act in accordance with the provisions of Schedule 3.

(5) The solicitor shall not provide advice and assistance to any person until either the form referred to in regulation 9(6) has been signed by the client or, where appropriate, the form referred to in regulation 10(4) has been signed on behalf of the client, and in any case, until the solicitor has assessed disposable income and disposable capital in accordance with paragraph (1).

Children and patients

14.—(1) A solicitor shall not, except where paragraph (2) applies, accept an application for advice and assistance from a child unless he has been authorised to do so by the Area Director and the Area Director shall withhold such authority unless he is satisfied that it is reasonable in the circumstances that the child should receive advice and assistance.

(2) A solicitor may accept an application for advice and assistance from a child who—

(a) is arrested and held in custody at a police station or other premises;

(b) is being interviewed in connection with a serious service offence; or

(c) is a volunteer;

where the solicitor is satisfied that the application cannot reasonably be made by any of the persons specified in paragraph (3)(a), (c) or (d).

(3) A solicitor may accept an application for advice and assistance on behalf of a child or patient from—

(a) in the case of a child, his parent or guardian or other person in whose care he is; or

(b) in the case of a patient, a receiver appointed under Part VII of the Mental Health Act 1983 or the patient's nearest relative or guardian within the meaning of Part II of the Mental Health Act 1983; or

(c) in the case of a child or patient, a person acting for the purposes of any proceedings as his next friend or guardian *ad litem*; or

(d) in the case of a child or a patient, any other person where the Area Director is satisfied that it is reasonable in the circumstances and has given prior authority for the advice and assistance to be given to such other person on behalf of the child or patient.

Clients resident outside England and Wales

15.—Where the client resides outside England and Wales, the Area Director may give the solicitor prior authority to accept a postal application for advice and assistance if the Area Director is satisfied that it is reasonable in the circumstances to do so.

Advice and assistance from more than one solicitor

16.—(1) A person shall not, except where regulation 6, 7 or 8 applies, be given advice and assistance for the same matter by more than one solicitor without the prior authority of the Area Director, and such authority may be given on such terms and conditions as the Area Director may in his discretion see fit to impose.

(2) Where regulation 6 applies, a person may be given advice and assistance for the same matter by more than one solicitor without the prior authority of the Area Director, provided that the cost of that advice and assistance shall not exceed the cost that would have been incurred had it been given by one solicitor.

Separate matters

17. Where two or more separate matters are involved, each matter shall be the subject of a separate application for advice and assistance provided that matters connected with or arising from proceedings for divorce or judicial separation, whether actual or prospective between the client and his spouse, shall not be treated as separate matters for the purpose of advice and assistance.

Refusal of advice and assistance

18. A solicitor may for good cause either refuse to accept an application for advice and assistance or (having accepted an application) decline to give, or to continue to give advice and assistance and may, if he thinks fit, refuse to disclose his reasons for doing so to the client or person seeking advice and assistance on his behalf; but he shall give the Area Director such information about such a refusal as the Area Director may require.

152

Power to require information

19. The Area Director may require a solicitor who has given advice and assistance to furnish such information as he may from time to time require for the purposes of his functions under these Regulations; and the solicitor shall not be precluded, by reason of any privilege arising out of the relationship between solicitor and client, from disclosing such information to him.

Entrusting functions to others

20. Subject to any arrangements made by the Board under regulations 6, 7 or 8, nothing in these Regulations shall prevent a solicitor from entrusting any function under these Regulations to a partner of his or to a competent and responsible representative of his who is employed in his office or is otherwise under his immediate supervision.

Extensions

21.—(1) Subject to regulation 22(8), and except where regulation 6, 7 or 8 applies, where it appears to the solicitor that the cost of giving advice or assistance is likely to exceed the limit applicable under section 10(1) of the Act, he shall apply to the Area Director for an extension and shall furnish such information as may enable him to consider and determine that application.

(2) Where an Area Director receives an application in accordance with paragraph (1) he shall consider—

(a) whether it is reasonable for the advice and assistance to be given; and

(b) whether the estimate of the costs to be incurred in giving advice and assistance is reasonable.

(3) If the Area Director is satisfied that it is reasonable for the advice or assistance to be given and that the estimate of the costs to be incurred in giving it is reasonable, he shall grant an extension and shall prescribe such higher limit as he thinks fit and may limit the advice and assistance to such subject matter as he thinks fit.

Applications for approval of ABWOR

22.—(1) The approval of the Board shall not be required for ABWOR to be given in accordance with arrangements made by the Board under regulation 7.

(2) The approval of the Board shall not be required for ABWOR to which Part III of the Act applies by virtue of regulation 7(1)(b), 7(1)(c), or 8 of the Scope Regulations.

(3) Subject to paragraph (1), where it appears to the solicitor that the client needs ABWOR to which Part III of the Act applies by virtue of regulation 7(1)(a), 7(2) or 9 of the Scope Regulations, he shall apply to the Area Director for approval.

(4) The application for approval shall be on a form approved by the Board and the solicitor shall supply such information as may enable the Area Director to consider and determine it.

(5) An application for approval, except in respect of ABWOR to which Part III of the Act applies by virtue of regulation 9 of the Scope Regulations, shall be refused unless it is shown that the client has reasonable grounds for taking, defending or being a party to the proceedings to which it relates.

(6) An application for approval may be refused if it appears unreasonable that approval should be granted in the particular circumstances of the case.

(7) The Area Director may grant an application for approval in whole or in part and may impose such conditions as to the conduct of the proceedings to which his approval relates as he thinks fit, and in particular it shall be a condition of every approval that the prior permission of the Area Director shall be required—

(a) to obtain a report or opinion of an expert; or

(b) to tender expert evidence; or

(c) to perform an act which is either unusual in its nature or involves unusually large expenditure;

unless such permission has been included in the grant of approval.

(8) An approval of ABWOR shall include an extension in respect of the matter to which it relates and, without prejudice to paragraph (7), the Area Director may prescribe such higher limit as he thinks fit.

Amended by the Legal Advice and Assistance (Amendment) Regulations 1990 (S.I. 1990 No. 486).

Counsel
23. Where it appears to the solicitor that the proper conduct of proceedings in respect of which ABWOR has been granted under regulation 22 requires the instruction of counsel, he may apply to the Area Director for approval and the Area Director shall grant approval if he considers that the proper conduct of the proceedings requires counsel.

Notification of approval of assistance by way of representation
24. Where ABWOR has been approved in respect of proceedings specified in regulation 7(1)(a) of the Scope Regulations and the client becomes a party to proceedings or is already a party to proceedings the solicitor shall as soon as practicable give notice of the approval to any other party to the proceedings and the court in which the proceedings are pending.

Withdrawal of approval of assistance by way of representation
25.—(1) The Area Director shall withdraw approval of ABWOR granted under regulation 22 from such date as he considers appropriate where, as a result of information which has come to his knowledge, he considers that:

(a) in respect of proceedings specified in regulation 7(1)(a) of the Scope Regulations, the client no longer has reasonable grounds for taking, defending or being a party to the proceedings, or for continuing to do so; or

(b) the client has required the proceedings to be conducted unreasonably so as to incur an unjustifiable expense to the fund; or

(c) it is unreasonable in the particular circumstances that the client should continue to receive ABWOR.

(2) When approval of ABWOR is withdrawn, the Area Director shall notify the solicitor who shall forthwith—

(a) inform his client; and

(b) in respect of proceedings specified in regulation 7(1)(a) of the Scope Regulations, if proceedings have been commenced, send a copy of the notice to the court and to any other party to the proceedings to which the approval related.

(3) Withdrawal of approval shall not affect or prejudice any subsequent application for representation or for approval of ABWOR in respect of the same proceedings.

Appeals against refusal of ABWOR, etc.

26.—(1) Where the Area Director—

(a) refuses an application under regulation 22 for the approval of ABWOR; or

(b) refuses authority in respect of any of the matters set out in paragraph (7)(a) to (c) of regulation 22; or

(c) withdraws approval of ABWOR under regulation 25;

the client may appeal to the appropriate area committee.

(2) An appeal shall be made by giving notice on a form approved by the Board within 14 days of the Area Director's decision to refuse the application or authority or withdraw approval.

Determination of appeals

27.—(1) The area committee shall, on an appeal under regulation 26, reconsider the application for approval or authority or the circumstances set out in paragraph (1)(a) to (c) of regulation 25 and shall—

(a) dismiss the appeal; or

(b) in the case of an application for approval or authority, grant the application subject to such terms and conditions as the committee thinks fit; or

(c) in the case of a decision to withdraw approval, quash that decision.

(2) The decision of the area committee on an appeal shall be final and it shall give notice in writing of its decision, and the reasons for it, to the client and to any solicitor acting for him.

(3) Where the Area Director's decision to withdraw approval is quashed on appeal by the area committee, the solicitor shall, in respect of proceedings specified in regulation 7(1)(a) of the Scope Regulations, notify any other party to the proceedings and the court, if any, in which the proceedings are pending.

Collection and refund of contributions

28.—(1) Where a client is required to make a contribution in respect of the cost of advice or assistance, the solicitor may collect that contribution in such instalments as may be agreed between him and the client and where the total contribution is likely to exceed the cost of giving advice or assistance, he shall not require the client to pay a sum higher than would be expected to defray his reasonable costs.

(2) Where the reasonable costs of the advice or assistance are less than any contribution made by the client, the solicitor shall refund the balance.

Costs payable out of the fund

29.—(1) Where the reasonable costs of the advice or assistance, including charges for disbursements, exceed any contribution payable by the client to the solicitor under section 9 of the Act together with the value of any charge arising under section 11 of the Act, the solicitor shall, except where paragraph (2) applies, submit a claim to the Area Director requesting payment of the deficiency.

(2) A claim for charges or fees properly chargeable for advice and assistance given in the circumstances specified in regulation 6 shall be made in accordance with the Legal Advice and Assistance at Police Stations (Remuneration) Regulations 1989.

(3) A claim for the costs of advice and assistance given in accordance with arrangements made by the Board under regulation 7 or 8 shall be made in accordance with the Legal Advice and Assistance (Duty Solicitor) (Remuneration) Regulations 1989.

(4) Where the claim does not relate to ABWOR in respect of which counsel has been instructed, the Area Director shall assess it and pay the assessed deficiency, if any, to the solicitor.

(5) Where the claim relates to ABWOR in respect of which counsel has been instructed and the Area Director considers that the proper conduct of the proceedings required counsel, or the instruction of counsel has been approved under regulation 23, the Area Director shall—

    (a) assess the solicitor's claim excluding counsel's fee, and pay the assessed deficiency, if any, to the solicitor; and

    (b) assess counsel's fee and pay him the amount so allowed less the amount, if any, by which the value of any charge arising under section 11 of the Act together with the amount of any contribution payable by the client under section 9(6) of the Act exceeds the amount allowed to the solicitor on the assessment of his claim.

(6) Where the claim relates to ABWOR in respect of which counsel has been instructed without obtaining prior approval under regulation 23, and the Area Director considers that the proper conduct of the proceedings did not require counsel, the Area Director shall—

    (a) determine the assessed deficiency on the basis that counsel had not been instructed and the solicitor had conducted the case on his own;

    (b) allow the amount which it would have allowed counsel under paragraph (5) above and pay counsel what it would have paid him under that paragraph to the extent of the assessed deficiency; and

    (c) pay the balance of the net assessed deficiency if any to the solicitor.

(7) If any solicitor or counsel is dissatisfied with any decision of the Area Director as to the payment of an assessed deficiency in the costs of advice and assistance, he may within 21 days of receipt of notification of that decision make written representations to the appropriate area committee; and that committee shall review the assessment of the Area Director whether by confirming, increasing or decreasing the amount assessed by the Area Director.

(8) A solicitor or counsel who is dissatisfied with the decision of an area committee on a review under paragraph (7) may within 21 days of receipt of notification of the decision apply to that committee to certify a point of principle of general importance.

(9) Where an area committee certifies a point of principle of general importance the solicitor or counsel may, within 21 days of receipt of notification of that certification, appeal in writing to a committee appointed by the Board against the decision of the area committee under paragraph (7).

(10) On an appeal under this regulation the committee appointed by the Board may reverse, affirm or amend the decision of the area committee under paragraph (7).

Basis of assessments

30.—(1) In any assessment or review of a claim for costs made under these Regulations the amount to be allowed shall, subject to paragraph (2), be assessed in accordance with the provisions of regulation 6 of and Schedule 1, Part I, paragraph 1(a) to the Costs Regulations as if the work done was work to which those provisions applied.

(2) Where the claim is in respect of ABWOR to which regulation 5 applies and which is given in unsocial hours (as defined in regulation 2 of the Legal Advice and Assistance at Police Stations (Remuneration) Regulations 1989), by a solicitor designated in accordance with arrangements made by the Board under regulation 6(3), the amount to be allowed under paragraph (1) shall be increased by one third.

Amended by the Legal Aid Advice and Assistance (Amendment) Regulations 1989 (S.I. 1989 No. 560).

Recovery of costs

31.—(1) Where any sum is payable to the client by virtue of an order for costs made in connection with proceedings for which ABWOR has been approved under regulation 22, the sum shall be paid to the clerk to the justices, who shall pay it to the Board; and only the clerk to the justices shall be able to give a good discharge for it.

(2) The Board shall, except where a payment has been made under paragraph (3), pay to the solicitor such portion of the sum paid to the Board under paragraph (1) as corresponds to the charge created in his favour on that sum by section 11(2)(a) of the Act, and pay any balance to the client.

(3) The Board may in addition to any payment under regulation 29, pay the solicitor a sum not greater than the sum payable to the Board under paragraph (1) and where such a payment is made, the Board shall require the solicitor to assign his charge under section 11(2)(a) of the Act to the Board.

Exceptions to charge on property recovered or preserved

32. The provisions of section 11(2)(b) of the Act shall not apply to the matters specified in Schedule 4.

Authority not to enforce the charge

33.—Where in the opinion of the solicitor—

(a) it would cause grave hardship or distress to the client to enforce the charge on any money or property recovered or preserved for him; or

(b) the charge on any property recovered or preserved could be enforced only with unreasonable difficulty because of the nature of the property, the solicitor may apply to the appropriate area committee for authority not to enforce, either wholly or in part, the charge and, if the committee gives authority, any deficiency in the solicitor's costs shall be computed as if section 11(2)(b) of the Act did not apply to that money or property or to such part of it as the committee may have authorised.

Costs awarded against a client

34.—Where proceedings have been concluded in which a client is or was in receipt of ABWOR and an order for costs has been made against him in those proceedings, the amount of his liability for costs (if any) shall be determined in accordance with Schedule 5.

Costs of successful unassisted parties out of the fund

35.—Before making any order under section 13 of the Act, the Court shall afford the Area director who dealt with the application under regulation 22 an opportunity to make representations.

False statements, etc.

36.—Where a client has wilfully failed to comply with the provisions of these Regulations as to the information to be furnished by him or, in furnishing such information, has knowingly made a false statement or false representation, and after the failure occurred or the false statement or false representation was made the client received advice or assistance, the appropriate area committee may declare that the advice or assistance so given was not given under the Act and these Regulations and, if it does, shall so inform the client and the solicitor; and thereafter the Board shall be entitled to recover from the client any sums paid out of the fund in respect of the advice and assistance so given.

SCHEDULES

SCHEDULE 1

Regulations revoked	References
The Legal Advice and Assistance Regulations (No. 2) 1980.	S.I. 1980/1898.
The Legal Advice and Assistance (Amendment) Regulations 1982.	S.I. 1982/1592.
The Legal Advice and Assistance (Amendment) (No. 2) Regulations 1983.	S.I. 1983/470.
The Legal Advice and Assistance (Financial Conditions) Regulations 1983.	S.I. 1983/618.
The Legal Advice and Assistance (Amendment) (No. 3) Regulations 1983.	S.I. 1983/1142.
The Legal Advice and Assistance (Financial Conditions) (No. 2) Regulations 1983.	S.I. 1983/1784.
The Legal Advice and Assistance (Prospective Cost) (No. 2) Regulations 1983.	S.I. 1983/1785.

The Legal Advice and Assistance (Amendment) (No. 5) Regulations 1983.	S.I. 1983/1935.
The Legal Advice and Assistance (Amendment) (No. 6) Regulations 1983.	S.I. 1983/1963.
The Legal Advice and Assistance (Amendment) Regulations 1984.	S.I. 1984/241.
The Legal Advice and Assistance (Amendment) (No. 2) Regulations 1984.	S.I. 1984/637.
The Legal Advice and Assistance (Amendment) Regulations 1985.	S.I. 1985/1491.
The Legal Advice and Assistance (Prospective Cost) Regulations 1985.	S.I. 1985/1840.
The Legal Advice and Assistance (Amendment) (No. 2) Regulations 1985.	S.I. 1985/1879.
The Legal Advice and Assistance (Amendment) Regulations 1986.	S.I. 1986/275.
The Legal Advice and Assistance (Financial Conditions) (No. 2) Regulations 1987.	S.I. 1987/396.
The Legal Advice and Assistance (Financial Conditions) Regulations 1988.	S.I. 1988/666.
The Legal Advice and Assistance (Financial Conditions) (No. 2) Regulations 1988.	S.I. 1988/459.
The Legal Advice and Assistance (Amendment) Regulations 1988.	S.I. 1988/461.

SCHEDULE 2
ASSESSMENT OF RESOURCES

1. In this Schedule, unless the context otherwise requires—

"capital" means the amount or value of every resource of a capital nature;

"income" means the total income from all sources which the person concerned has received or may reasonably expect to receive in respect of the seven days up to and including the date of his application;

"the person concerned" means the person whose disposable capital and disposable income are to be assessed.

2. The provisions of this Schedule apply to a man and a woman who are living with each other in the same household as husband and wife as they apply to the parties to a marriage.

3. Any question arising under this Schedule shall be decided by the solicitor to whom the client has applied and that solicitor, in deciding any such question, shall have regard to any guidance which may from time to time be given by the Board as to the application of this Schedule.

4. The disposable capital and disposable income of the person concerned shall be the capital and income as assessed by the solicitor after deducting any sums which are to be left out of account or for which allowance is to be made under the provisions of this Schedule.

5. The resources of any person who, under section 26(3) and (4) of the Social Security Act 1986 is liable to maintain a child or who usually contributes substantially to a child's maintenance, or who has care and control of the child, not being a person who has such care and control by reason of any contract or for some temporary purpose, may be treated as the resources of the child, if, having regard to all the circumstances, including the age and resources of the child and to any conflict of interest it appears just and equitable to do so.

6. If it appears to the solicitor that the person concerned has, with intent to reduce the amount of his disposable capital or disposable income, whether for the purpose of making himself eligible for advice and assistance, reducing his liability to pay a contribution in respect of the costs of advice and assistance or otherwise—

(a) directly or indirectly deprived himself of any resources; or

(b) converted any part of his resources into resources which are to be left out of account wholly or partly;

the resources of which he has so deprived himself or which he has so converted shall be treated as part of his resources or as not so converted as the case may be.

Amended by the Legal Advice and Assistance (Amendment) Regulations 1990 (S.I. 1990 No. 486).

7.—(1) In computing the capital and income of the person concerned, there shall be left out of account the value of the subject matter of any claim in respect of which he is seeking advice or assistance.

(2) In computing the capital and income of the person concerned, the resources of any spouse of his shall be treated as his resources unless—

(i) the spouse has a contrary interest in the matter in respect of which he is seeking advice and assistance, or

(ii) the person concerned and his spouse are living separate and apart, or

(iii) in all the circumstances of the case it would be inequitable or impractical to do so.

8. In computing the capital of the person concerned—

(a) there shall be left out of account the value of the main or only dwelling in which he resides and the value of his household furniture and effects, of his clothes and of tools and implements of his trade;

(b) where the person concerned resides in more than one dwelling in which he has an interest there shall be taken into account in respect of the value to him of any interest in a dwelling which is not the main dwelling any sum which may be obtained by borrowing money on the security thereof;

(c) where the person concerned has living with him one or more of the following persons, namely, a spouse whose resources are required to be aggregated with his, a dependent child or a dependent relative wholly or substantially maintained by him, a deduction shall be made of £335 in respect of the first person, £200 in respect of the second and £100 in respect of each further person.

9. In computing the income of the person concerned—

(a) there shall be left out of account—

(i) any income tax paid or payable on income treated under the provisions of this Schedule as his income;

(ii) contributions estimated to have been paid under the Social Security Acts 1975–1988 or any scheme made under those Acts during or in respect of the seven days up to and including the date of the application for advice and assistance;

(b) there shall be a deduction in respect of the spouse of the person concerned, if the spouses are living together, in respect of the maintenance of any dependent child and in respect of the maintenance of any dependent relative of the person concerned, being (in either of such cases) a member of his or her household, at the following rates—

(i) in the case of a spouse at a rate equivalent to 25 per cent. above the amount specified for the time being in column (3) of paragraph 6 of Part IV of Schedule 4 to the Social Security Act 1975 (increase for adult dependant of category A retirement pension);

(ii) in the case of a dependent child or a dependent relative, at a rate equivalent to 25 per cent. above the amount specified for the time being in paragraph 2 of Part I of Schedule 2 to the Income Support (General) Regulations 1987 appropriate to the age of the child or relative.

10. If the person concerned is making bona fide payments for the maintenance of a spouse who is living apart, of a former spouse, of a child or relative who is not (in any such case) a member of the household of the person concerned, there shall be a deduction of such payment as was or will be made in respect of the seven days up to and including the date of the application for advice and assistance.

11. Where it appears to the solicitor that there has been some error or mistake in the assessment of the disposable income, disposable capital or maximum contribution of the person concerned, he may reassess the disposable income or disposable capital or maximum contribution or, as the case may be, amend the assessment and in the latter case the amended assessment shall for all purposes be substituted for the original assessment.

SCHEDULE 3

CONTRIBUTIONS BY CLIENTS

The contribution payable by a client under section 9(6) of the Act where his disposable income falls within a range specified in the first column of the following table, is the amount specified in relation to that range in the second column.

Disposable income	Maximum contribution
Exceeding £64 but not exceeding £72 a week	£5
Exceeding £72 but not exceeding £78 a week	£12
Exceeding £78 but not exceeding £84 a week	£19
Exceeding £84 but not exceeding £90 a week	£25
Exceeding £90 but not exceeding £96 a week	£32
Exceeding £96 but not exceeding £102 a week	£38
Exceeding £102 but not exceeding £108 a week	£45
Exceeding £108 but not exceeding £114 a week	£51
Exceeding £114 but not exceeding £120 a week	£58
Exceeding £120 but not exceeding £125 a week	£64
Exceeding £125 but not exceeding £130 a week	£70
Exceeding £130 but not exceeding £135 a week	£75

Amended by the Legal Advice and Assistance Regulations 1990 (S.I. 1990 No. 486).

SCHEDULE 4

EXCEPTIONS TO CHARGE ON PROPERTY RECOVERED OR PRESERVED

The provisions of section 11(2)(b) of the Act shall not apply to—

(a) any periodical payment of maintenance, which for this purpose means money or money's worth paid towards the support of a spouse, former spouse, child or any other person for whose support the payer has previously been responsible or has made payments;

(b) any property recovered or preserved for the client as a result of advice and assistance given to him by the solicitor which comprises the client's main or only dwelling, or any household furniture or tools of trade;

(c) (without prejudice to (b) above) the first £2,500 of any money or of the value of any property recovered or preserved by virtue of—

(i) an order made or deemed to be made, under the provisions of section

23(1)(c) or (f), 23(2), 24, 27(6)(c) or (f), or 35 of the Matrimonial Causes Act 1973;

(ii) an order made, or deemed to be made, under the provisions of section 2 or 6 of the Inheritance (Provision for Family and Dependants) Act 1975;

(iii) an order made, or deemed to be made, under section 17 of the Married Women's Property Act 1882; or

(iv) an order made, or deemed to be made, under the provisions of section 4(2)(b) of the Affiliation Proceedings Act 1957; or

(v) an order for the payment of a lump sum made, or deemed to be made, under the provisions of section 60 of the Magistrates' Courts Act 1980; or

(vi) an order made, or deemed to be made, under the provisions of section 2(1)(b) or (d), 6(1) or (5), 11(2)(b) or (3)(b) or 20(2) of the Domestic Proceedings and Magistrates' Courts Act 1978; or

(vii) an order made, or deemed to be made, under section 9(2)(b), 10(1)(b)(ii), 11(b)(ii) of the Guardianship of Minors Act 1971 or under section 11B, 11C or 11D of that Act; or

(viii) an order made, or deemed to be made, under section 34(1)(c) or 35 of the Children Act 1975; or

(ix) an agreement which has the same effect as an order made, or deemed to be made, under any of the provisions specified in this sub-paragraph;

(d) one-half of any redundancy payment within the meaning of Part VI of the Employment Protection (Consolidation) Act 1978 recovered or preserved for the client;

(e) any payment of money in accordance with an order made under section 136 of the Employment Protection (Consolidation) Act 1978 by the Employment Appeal Tribunal;

(f) any sum, payment or benefit which, by virtue of any provision of or made under an Act of Parliament, cannot be assigned or charged.

SCHEDULE 5

Costs Awarded Against a Client

1. No costs attributable to the period during which a client was in receipt of ABWOR shall be recoverable from him until the court has determined the amount of his liability in accordance with section 12 of the Act:

Provided that where the ABWOR does not relate to or has been withdrawn so that it no longer relates to the whole of the proceedings the court shall nevertheless make a determination in respect of that part of the proceedings to which the approval of ABWOR relates.

2. The court may, if it thinks fit, refer to the clerk to the justices for investigation any question of fact relevant to the determination, requiring him to report his findings on that question to the court.

3. In determining the amount of the client's liability his dwelling-house, clothes, household furniture and the tools and implements of his trade shall be left out of account to the like extent as they are left out of account by the solicitor in determining the client's disposable capital.

4. Any person, not being himself a client, who is a party to proceedings to which the client is a party may, at any time before the judgment, lodge with the clerk to the justices an affidavit exhibiting thereto a statement setting out the rate of his own income and amount of his own capital and any other facts relevant to the determination of his means in accordance with section 12 of the Act and shall serve a copy thereof together with the exhibit upon the client's solicitor and such affidavit and exhibit shall be evidence of the facts stated therein.

5. The court may, if it thinks fit, order the client and any party who has filed an affidavit in accordance with paragraph (4) of this Schedule to attend for oral examination as to his means and as to any other facts relevant to the determination of the amount of the client's liability and may permit any party to give evidence and call witnesses thereon.

6. The court may direct—

(a) that payment under the order for costs shall be limited to such amount payable in instalments or otherwise as the court thinks reasonable having regard to all the circumstances; or

(b) where the court thinks it reasonable for payment under sub-paragraph (a) not to be made immediately, that payment under the order for costs be suspended either until such date as the court may determine or sine die.

7. The party in whose favour an order is made may within six years from the date thereof apply to the court for the order to be varied on the grounds that—

(a) material additional information as to the client's means, being information which could not have been obtained by that party with reasonable diligence at the time the order was made, is available; or

(b) there has been a change in the client's circumstances since the date of the order,

and on any such application the order may be varied as the court thinks fit but save as aforesaid the determination of the court shall be final.

8. Where an order for costs is made against a client who is concerned in the proceedings solely in a representative, fiduciary or official capacity, he shall have the benefit of section 12(1) of the Act and his personal resources shall not (unless there is reason to the contrary) be taken into account for that purpose, but regard shall be had to the value of the property or estate, or the amount of the fund out of which he is entitled to be indemnified.

9. Where a client is a child, his means for the purpose of determining his liability for costs under section 12(1) of the Act shall be taken as including the means of any person whose disposable income and disposable capital has, by virtue of Schedule 2 been included in assessing the child's resources.

10. Where an order for costs is made against a next friend or guardian *ad litem* of a client who is a child or patient, he shall have the benefit of section 12(1) of the Act in like manner as it applies to a client, and the means of the next friend or guardian *ad litem* shall be taken as being the means of the child as defined in paragraph 9 or, as the case may be, of the patient.

EXPLANATORY NOTE
(This note is not part of the Regulations)

These Regulations replace, with amendments, the Legal Advice and Assistance Regulations (No. 2) 1980 (S.I. 1980/1898) (as amended) (except their provisions as to the scope of advice and assistance), which are replaced, with amendments, by the Legal Advice and Assistance (Scope) Regulations 1989 (S.I. 1989/560).

The main changes reflect the transfer of responsibility for administration of legal aid from the Law Society to the Legal Aid Board established by the Legal Aid Act 1988.

Other important changes are—

(a) to enable the Board to make duty solicitor arrangements replacing those made by the Law Society under the Legal Aid (Duty Solicitor) Scheme 1988 (regulations 6(3) and 7);

(b) to require the provision of information to enable the solicitor to determine whether advice or assistance relating to the making of a will would fall within the scope of Part III of the Act (regulations 9(5), 10(3));

(c) to require the Board to be given an opportunity to make representations before any order for costs against the Board is made under section 13 of the Act (regulation 35);

(d) to set out in the Regulations the financial limits on advice and assistance which can be given without the approval of the Board (regulation 4);

(e) to set out in the Regulations all the provisions for eligibility for advice and assistance and contributions (regulations 11 to 13 and Schedules 2 and 3);

(f) to provide for the purposes of eligibility and contributions that the resources of a man and a woman living together as husband and wife are to be treated as if they were married (paragraph 2 of Schedule 2); and

(g) to provide (subject to the transitional provision in regulation 1(2)) for the assessment of costs by Area Directors, for reviews of such assessments by area committees, and for appeals from such reviews to a committee appointed by the Board (regulation 29).

Civil Legal Aid (General) Regulations 1989

Coming into force April 1, 1989

ARRANGEMENT OF REGULATIONS

PART I

GENERAL

PART II

APPLICATIONS FOR CERTIFICATES

Part XIII

Costs Awarded Against an Assisted Person

Part XIV

Costs of Unassisted Parties out of the Fund

PART XV

PARTICULAR COURTS AND TRIBUNALS

The Lord Chancellor, in exercise of the powers conferred on him by sections 2(7), 6(2), (3), 15(3), 16(6), 17, 31, 34 and 43 of and paragraph 11 of Schedule 1 to the Legal Aid 1988 and all other powers enabling him in that behalf, after consulting the General Council of the Bar, the Law Society, the Supreme Court Rule Committee, the County Court Rule Committee, the Matrimonial Causes Rule Committee and the Magistrates' Courts Rule Committee and with the consent of the Treasury, hereby makes the following Regulations:—

PART I

GENERAL

Citation, commencement, revocations and transitional provisions

1.—(1) These Regulations may be cited as the Civil Legal Aid (General) Regulations 1989 and shall come into force on April 1, 1989.

(2) The Regulations specified in Schedule 1 are hereby revoked.

(3) Where a review by an area committee under regulation 104, 105 or 106 relates to an assessment made before June 1, 1989, paragraphs (5) and (6) of regulation 105 shall not apply and the assisted person's solicitor or counsel may, within 21 days of the area committee's decision, appeal in writing to a committee appointed by the Board.

Scope

2. These Regulations apply for the purposes of the provision of civil legal aid under Part IV of the Legal Aid Act 1988.

Interpretation

3.—(1) In these Regulations, unless the context otherwise requires—

"the Act" means the Legal Aid Act 1988;

"affidavit of costs and resources" means an affidavit which includes the matters specified in Schedule 2 and which is sworn by a person in support of his application for an order under section 18 of the Act;

"appropriate area committee" means the area committee in whose area an application for a certificate has been granted or refused and includes an area committee to whose area an application has been transferred under these Regulations;

"area committee" means an area committee appointed by the Board in accordance with regulation 4;

"Area Director" means an Area Director appointed by the Board in accordance with regulation 4 and includes any person duly authorised to act on his behalf;

"assessment officer" means a person authorised by the Secretary of State to assess the disposable income, disposable capital and maximum contribution of the person concerned;

"assisted person" means a person in respect of whom a certificate issued under these Regulations is in force and, for the purposes of Part XI only, includes a person in respect of whom a certificate has been, but is no longer, in force;

"authorised summary proceedings" means proceedings in a magistrates' court for which legal aid is available by virtue of Part I of Schedule 2 to the Act;

"certificate" means a legal aid certificate issued in accordance with these Regulations (or any regulations revoked by these Regulations) and includes an amendment to a certificate issued under Part VII and, unless the context otherwise requires, an emergency certificate;

"contribution" means the contribution payable under section 16(1) of the Act in respect of the costs of representation;

"court" includes:

(a) in relation to proceedings tried or heard at first instance by a master or taxing master or the Supreme Court, a registrar of the Family Division of the High Court, a district registrar or the registrar of a county court, that master of registrar;

(b) in relation to proceedings on appeal to the Court of Appeal the registrar of civil appeals;

"disposable capital" and "disposable income" mean the amounts of capital and income available for the making of a contribution after capital and income have been computed in accordance with the Civil Legal Aid (Assessment of Resources) Regulations 1989;

"EEC lawyer" has the same meaning as in the European Communities (Services of Lawyers) Order 1978;

"emergency certificate" means a certificate issued under Part III of these Regulations;

"fund" means the legal aid fund;

"legal aid" means representation under Part IV of the Act;

"legal aid area" has the meaning assigned by regulation 4(1);

"legal executive" means a fellow of the Institute of Legal Executives;

"master" in relation to an application for an order under section 18 of the Act in respect of proceedings in or on appeal from the Chancery or Queen's Bench Division of the High Court, means a taxing master of the Supreme Court or a district registrar of the High Court; and in relation to such an application made in respect of proceedings in or on appeal from the Family Division of the High Court, means a registrar of the said Division or a district registrar of the High Court;

"matrimonial proceedings" means—

(a) any proceedings with respect to which rules may be made under section 50 of the Matrimonial Causes Act 1973; or

(b) any proceedings in a county court under section 17 of the Married Women's Property Act 1882 or section 1 of or Schedule 1 to the Matrimonial Homes Act 1983; or

(c) any proceedings under the Domestic Violence and Matrimonial Proceedings Act 1976;

"maximum contribution" means the amount assessed by the assessment officer as the maximum amount which an assisted person may be liable to pay on account of his contribution;

"patient" means a person who, by reason of mental disorder within the meaning of the Mental Health Act 1983, is incapable of managing and administering his property and affairs;

"standard basis" and "indemnity basis," in relation to the taxation of costs, have the meanings assigned by Order 62, rule 12 of the Rules of the Supreme Court 1965;

"substantive certificate" means a certificate issued to replace an emergency certificate which is still in force.

(2) Any reference in these Regulations to a regulation or Schedule by number means the regulation or Schedule so numbered in these Regulations.

(3) References in these Regulations to costs shall, unless the context otherwise requires, be construed as including references to fees, charges, disbursements, expenses and remuneration.

Area Committees, Area Directors and legal aid areas

4.—(1) The Board shall, for the purposes of administering the Act, appoint—

(a) area committees; and

(b) Area Directors,

in respect of areas (in these Regulations referred to as "legal aid areas") to be specified by the Board.

(2) Area committees and Area Directors so appointed shall exercise functions respectively delegated to them by the Board or conferred on them by these Regulations.

Powers exercisable by courts

5. Where the power to do any act or exercise any jurisdiction or discretion is conferred by any provision of these Regulations on a court, it may, unless it is exercisable only during the trial or hearing of the action, cause or matter, be exercised—

(a) in respect of proceedings in a county court or the Family Division of the High Court, by the registrar;

(b) in respect of proceedings in the Chancery or Queen's Bench Division of the High Court, by a judge, master or district registrar;

(c) in respect of proceedings in the Court of Appeal, by a single judge of that Court or by the registrar of civil appeals;

(d) in respect of proceedings in the House of Lords, by the Clerk of the Parliaments;

(e) by any person who, under any enactment or rules of court, is capable of exercising the jurisdiction of the court in relation the the proceedings in question.

Powers exercisable by Area Directors

6.—(1) Where an area committee is required or entitled to perform any function under these Regulations, that function may, subject to paragraph (2), be performed on behalf of that committee by the Area Director.

(2) Paragraph (1) shall not empower an Area Director to determine an appeal under regulation 39.

Computation of time

7.—(1) Where, under these Regulations, an act is required to be done within a specified period after or from a specified date, the period of time so fixed starts immediately after that date.

(2) The period within which an act is required or authorised to be done under these Regulations may, if the Area Director thinks fit, be extended and any such period may be extended although the application for extension is not made until after the expiration of the period.

Service of notices

8.—(1) Where by virtue of these Regulations any document is required to be served (whether the expression "serve" or the expression "send" or "send by post" or any other expression is used) the document may be served—

(a) if the person to be served is acting in person, by delivering it to him personally or by delivering it at, or sending it by post to, his address for service or, if he has no address for service:

   (i) by delivering the document at his residence or by sending it by post to his last known residence, or
   (ii) in the case of a proprietor of a business, by delivering the document at his place of business or by sending it by post to his last known place of business;

(b) if the person to be served is acting by a solicitor:

   (i) by delivering the document at, or by sending it by post to, the solicitor's address for service, or
   (ii) where the solicitor's address for service includes a numbered box at a document exchange, by leaving the document at that document exchange or at a document exchange which transmits documents daily to that document exchange.

(2) Any document which is left at a document exchange in accordance with paragraph (1)(b)(ii), shall, unless the contrary is proved, be deemed to have been served on the second day after the day on which it is left.

Availability of documents to the court

9. Any document sent to a court office or registry or filed or exhibited under the provisions of these Regulations may, on request, be made available for the use of the court at any stage of the proceedings.

PART II

APPLICATIONS FOR CERTIFICATES

Applications to be made to Area Directors

10. Any person who wishes to be granted legal aid for the purposes of proceedings may apply for a certificate—

(a) if resident in the United Kingdom, to any Area Director; or

(b) if resident elsewhere, to the Area Director of one of the legal aid areas nominated by the Board for this purpose.

Form and lodgment of application

11. Every application—

(a) shall be made in writing on a form approved by the Board or in such other written form as the Area Director may accept; and

(b) shall be lodged with the Area Director.

Contents of application

12.—(1) Every application shall—

(a) state the name of the solicitor selected by the applicant to act for him;

(b) contain such information and be accompanied by such supporting documents (including any welfare report) as may be necessary to enable:

(i) the Area Director to determine the nature of the proceedings in respect of which legal aid is sought and whether it is reasonable that representation should be granted; and

(ii) the assessment officer to assess the disposable income, disposable capital and maximum contribution of the applicant.

(2) An applicant for legal aid in connection with authorised summary proceedings may, with a view to expediting the issue to him of a certificate, lodge with the Area Director (when he applies for a certificate or at any time before it is issued) an undertaking on a form approved by the Board to pay any contribution that may be assessed under the Civil Legal Aid (Assessment of Resources) Regulations 1989.

(3) An applicant shall, if required to do so for the purpose of providing additional material, supply such further information or documents as may be required or attend for an interview and, for this purpose, "applicant" includes a person to whom a certificate has been issued on a form of undertaking given under paragraph (2).

Applications by persons resident outside United Kingdom

13.—(1) Subject to paragraph (2), where the applicant resides outside the United Kingdom and cannot be present in England or Wales while his application is considered, his application shall be—

(a) written in English or in French; and

(b) except where the applicant is a member of Her Majesty's armed forces, sworn—

    (i) if the applicant resides within the Commonwealth or the Republic of Ireland, before any justice of the peace or magistrate or any person for the time being authorised by law in the place where he resides to administer an oath for any judicial or other legal purpose, or

    (ii) if the applicant resides elsewhere, before a British consular officer or any other person for the time being authorised to exercise the functions of such an officer or having authority to administer an oath in that place; and

(c) accompanied by a statement in writing, signed by some responsible person who has knowledge of the facts, certifying that part of the application which relates to the applicant's disposable income and disposable capital.

(2) The requirements of paragraph (1) may be waived by the Area Director where compliance with them would cause serious difficulty, inconvenience or delay and the application otherwise satisfies the requirements of regulations 11 and 12.

Child Abduction and Custody Act 1985

14.—(1) A person whose application under the Hague Convention or the European Convention has been submitted to the Central Authority in England and Wales pursuant to section 3(2) or section 14(2) of the Child Abduction and Custody Act 1985 and on whose behalf a solicitor in England and Wales has been instructed in connection with the application—

(a) shall be eligible to receive legal aid whether or not his financial resources are such as to make him eligible to receive it under regulations made under the Legal Aid Act 1988;

(b) shall not be refused legal aid by virtue of subsections (2) and (3) of section 15 of the said Act of 1988; and

(c) shall not be required to pay a contribution to the legal aid fund;

and these Regulations (with the exception of those provisions relating to assessment of disposable income and capital, eligibility on their merits and payment of contribution) shall apply accordingly.

(2) In this regulation the "Hague Convention" means the convention defined in section 1(1) of the Child Abduction and Custody Act 1985 and the "European Convention" means the convention defined in section 12(1) of that Act.

Registration of certain foreign orders and judgments

15.—(1) This regulation applies to any person who—

(a) appeals to a magistrates' court against the registration of or the refusal to register a maintenance order made in a Hague Convention country pursuant to the Maintenance Orders (Reciprocal Enforcement) Act 1972; or

(b) applies for the registration of a judgment under section 4 of the Civil Jurisdiction and Judgments Act 1982.

(2) Subject to paragraph (3), a person to whom this regulation applies—

(a) shall be eligible to receive legal aid whether or not his financial resources are such as to make him eligible to receive it under regulations made under the Legal Aid Act 1988;

(b) shall not be refused legal aid by virtue of subsections (2) and (3) of section 15 of the said Act of 1988;

(c) shall not be required to pay a contribution to the legal aid fund,

and these Regulations (with the exception of those provisions relating to assessment of disposable income and capital, eligibility on the merits and payment of contribution) shall apply accordingly.

(3) A person shall not be given legal aid under this regulation in respect of any appeal or application as is mentioned in paragraph (1) unless he benefited from complete or partial legal aid or exemption from costs or expenses in the country in which the maintenance order was made or the judgment was given.

(4) In this regulation, "Hague Convention country" has the same meaning as in the Reciprocal Enforcement of Maintenance Orders (Hague Convention Countries) Order 1979 and "the Maintenance Orders (Reciprocal Enforcement) Act 1972" means that Act as applied with such exceptions, adaptations and modifications as are specified in the said 1979 Order.

Application on behalf of minors and patients

16.—(1) Subject to paragraph (5), an application for legal aid for a minor or patient shall be made on his behalf by a person of full age and capacity and:

(a) where the application relates to proceedings which are required by rules of court to be brought or defended by a next friend or guardian *ad litem*, the person making the application shall be the next friend or guardian *ad litem*; or,

(b) where the application relates to proceedings which have not actually begun, the person who, subject to any order of the court, intends to act in either of those capacities when the proceedings begin, shall make the application.

(2) Except where an application is made by the Official Solicitor, the Area Director shall not issue a certificate applied for by a person on behalf of a minor or patient unless that person has signed an undertaking to pay to the Board (if required to do so) any sums which, by virtue of any provision of the Act or of these Regulations, the Area Director may require an assisted person of full age and capacity to pay upon the issue or during the currency or upon the discharge or revocation of a certificate.

(3) Any certificate issued to a minor or patient shall be in his name, stating the name of the person who has applied for it on his behalf.

(4) In any matter relating to the issue, amendment, revocation or discharge of a certificate issued to a minor or patient, and in any other matter which may arise between an assisted person who is a minor or patient and the Area Director, the person who is named in the certificate as the next friend or guardian *ad litem* of the minor or patient shall be treated for all purposes (including the receipt of notices) as the agent of the minor or patient.

(5) An Area Director may, where the circumstances appear to make it desirable, waive all or any of the requirements of the preceding paragraphs of this regulation.

Power to transfer application to another area office

17. If it appears to an Area Director that an application could, without prejudice to the applicant, be more conveniently or appropriately dealt with in another area office, the papers relating to the application shall be transferred to that other office.

Reference to the assessment officer for assessment of resources

18.—(1) Except where he has previously refused the application, the Area Director shall refer to the assessment officer so much of it as is relevant to the assessment of the applicant's disposable income and disposable capital; and (subject to paragraph (2) and regulation 21) no application shall be approved until the assessment officer has assessed the applicant's disposable income, disposable capital and maximum contribution in accordance with the Civil Legal Aid (Assessment of Resources) Regulations 1989.

(2) Where an Area Director approves an application relating to proceedings:

(a) in the House of Lords or on appeal from a magistrates' court in any action, cause or matter in which the applicant was an assisted person in the court below; or

(b) by way of a new trial ordered by a court in any action, cause or matter in which the applicant was an assisted person;

he shall not require the assessment officer to re-assess the assisted person's disposable income and disposable capital.

PART III

EMERGENCY CERTIFICATES

Application for emergency certificate

19.—(1) Any person who desires legal aid as a matter of urgency may apply to any Area Director for an emergency certificate on a form approved by the Board or in such other manner as the Area Director may accept as sufficient in the circumstances of the case.

(2) Subject to paragraph (3), an application for an emergency certificate shall contain such information and be accompanied by such documents as may be necessary to enable the Area Director to determine the nature of the proceedings for which legal aid is sought and the circumstances in which it is required and whether—

(a) the applicant is likely to fulfil the conditions under which legal aid may be granted under the Act and these Regulations; and

(b) it is in the interests of justice that the applicant should, as a matter of urgency, be granted legal aid;

and the applicant shall furnish such additional information and documents (if any) as may be sufficient to constitute an application for a certificate under Part II of these Regulations.

(3) If it appears to the Area Director that the applicant cannot at the time of making the application reasonably furnish the information required under paragraph (2), or any part of it, that Area Director shall nevertheless have the power to issue an emergency certificate subject to such conditions as to the furnishing of additional information as he thinks fit.

Refusal of emergency certificate

20. An application for an emergency certificate may be refused—

(a) on one of the grounds on which a substantive certificate may be refused under regulation 34; or

(b) on the ground that the applicant is unlikely to fulfil the conditions under which legal aid may be granted; or

(c) on the ground that it is not in the interests of justice that legal aid be granted as a matter of urgency.

Issue and effect of emergency certificate

21.—(1) An Area Director shall have power to approve an application made under regulation 19 and to issue an emergency certificate without reference to the assessment officer.

(2) An emergency certificate shall not be issued in respect of authorisied summary proceedings.

(3) Where an Area Director issues an emergency certificate, he shall send the emergency certificate (together with a copy) to the solicitor selected by the applicant, and a copy of the certificate to the applicant.

(4) An emergency certificate shall have the same effect in all respects as a substantive certificate and any person holding an emergency certificate shall, while it is in force, be deemed for the purposes of the proceedings to which the emergency certificate relates to be an assisted person.

Duration of emergency certificate

22. An emergency certificate shall remain in force until—

(a) it is discharged or revoked in accordance with Part X of these Regulations; or

(b) it is merged in a substantive certificate under regulation 23; or

(c) the expiry of any period (including any extension of that period granted under regulation 24(1)) allowed for the duration of the emergency certificate.

Merger in substantive certificate

23.—(1) Where a substantive certificate is issued, the emergency certificate shall merge in the substantive certificate and the substantive certificate shall take effect from the date upon which the emergency certificate was issued in respect of the proceedings specified in the emergency certificate.

(2) Where an emergency certificate is merged in a substantive certificate, the substantive certificate shall state—

(a) the date of issue of the emergency certificate; and

(b) that the emergency certificate has been continuously in force from that date until the date of the substantive certificate.

Extension and expiry of emergency certificate

24.—(1) The Area Director (whose decision shall be final) may extend the period allowed for the duration of an emergency certificate where—

(a) the applicant is offered a substantive certificate in respect of the proceedings to which the emergency certificate relates and either fails to signify his acceptance or appeals against the terms of the offer; or

(b) the application for a substantive certificate in respect of the proceedings to which the emergency certificate relates has been refused and either notice of appeal has been given to the appropriate area committee within the time limits laid down by regulation 36 or the time limit for doing so has not expired; or

(c) there are exceptional circumstances.

(2) Where an emergency certificate is extended under paragraph (1)(a) or (b), no further work may be done or steps taken under the certificate.

Notification of extension of emergency certificate

25.—(1) Where an emergency certificate is extended, the Area Director shall:

(a) forthwith issue a notice to that effect;

(b) send the notice (together with a copy) to the solicitor acting for the person to whom the emergency certificate was issued; and

(c) send a copy of the notice to the person to whom the emergency certificate was issued.

(2) It shall be the duty of the solicitor to notify forthwith any counsel whom he may have instructed that the certificate has been extended.

(3) A solicitor who receives notice that an emergency certificate has been extended under regulation 24 shall, if proceedings have begun or otherwise upon their commencement—

(a) send a copy of the notice by post to the appropriate court office or registry; and

(b) serve notice of the fact upon any other persons who are parties to the proceedings;

and, if any other person becomes a party to the proceedings, serve a similar notice upon that person.

PART IV

DETERMINATION OF APPLICATIONS

Power to notify other parties of application

26.—(1) On receiving an application for a certificate, the Area Director may, if he thinks fit—

(a) notify any party to the proceedings in respect of which the application is made; and

(b) ask that party whether he is willing to delay taking any further step in, or in relation to, the proceedings until the application has been determined.

(2) When the Area Director has determined the application, he shall so inform any party notified under this regulation.

Financial eligibility
27.—(1) Where the assessment officer assesses that an applicant has disposable income of an amount which makes him ineligible for legal aid, the Area Director shall refuse the application.

(2) Where the assessment officer assesses that an applicant, having disposable income of an amount which makes him eligible for legal aid, has disposable capital of an amount which renders him liable to be refused legal aid, the Area Director shall refuse the application if it appears to him that the probable costs of the applicant in the proceedings in respect of which the application was made would not exceed the contribution payable by the applicant.

Eligibility on the merits
28. Without prejudice to the generality of section 15(2) or (3) of the Act, an application for a certificate shall only be approved after the Area Director has considered all the questions of fact or law arising in the action, cause or matter to which the application relates and the circumstances in which the application was made.

Refusal where advantage trivial or on account of nature of proceedings
29. Without prejudice to regulatons 28 and 32, an application may be refused where it appears to the Area Director that—

(a) only a trivial advantage would be gained by the applicant from the proceedings to which the application relates; or

(b) on account of the nature of the proceedings a solicitor would not ordinarily be employed.

Refusal where other rights or facilities available
30.—(1) Without prejudice to regulation 28, an application may be refused where it appears to the Area Director that—

(a) the applicant has available to him rights or facilities which make it unnecessary for him to obtain legal aid; or

(b) the applicant has a reasonable expectation of obtaining financial or other help from a body of which he is a member,

and that he has failed to take all reasonable steps to enforce or obtain such rights, facilities or help (including permitting the Area Director to take those steps on his behalf).

(2) Where it appears that the applicant has a right to be indemnified against expenses incurred in connection with any proceedings, it shall not, for the

purposes of paragraph (1), be deemed to be a failure to take reasonable steps if he has not taken proceedings to enforce that right, whether for a declaration as to that right or otherwise.

Determination of contribution

31.—(1) The Area Director shall, when determining an application, also determine the sums for the time being payable on account of the applicant's contribution and, in so doing, shall have regard to the probable cost of the proceedings.

(2) Where the probable cost of the proceedings exceeds any maximum contribution which has been assessed, the Area Director shall determine the maximum contribution as the sum payable on account of the applicant's contribution.

(3) Save as otherwise provided by these Regulations, the sum determined under paragraph (1) shall not exceed the maximum contribution which has been assessed.

Proceedings in which others have an interest

32.—(1) When determining an application, the Area Director shall consider whether it is reasonable and proper for persons concerned jointly with or having the same interest as the applicant to defray so much of the costs as would be payable from the fund in respect of the proceedings if a certificate were issued.

(2) In determining an application made by, or on behalf of, a person in connection with an action, cause or matter in which—

    (a) numerous persons have the same interest; and

    (b) in accordance with rules of court, one or more persons may sue or be sued, or may be authorised by a court to defend any such action, cause or matter on behalf of or for the benefit of all persons so interested,

the Area Director shall consider whether the rights of the applicant would be substantially prejudiced by the refusal of his application.

(3) Where an application has been approvd and the Area Director considers that it is reasonable that persons concerned jointly with or having the same interest as the applicant should contribute to the cost of the proceedings, he shall add the amount which would be payable by such persons to the sums (if any) payable by the applicant under regulation 31 and shall so notify him under regulation 43(2).

(4) The Area Director may subsequently redetermine the amount of any additional sums payable under paragraph (3) where he is satisfied that the applicant has, without success, taken all reasonable steps (including permitting the Area Director to take those steps on his behalf) to obtain such payment.

Application in representative, fiduciary or official capacity

33. Where an application is made in a representative, fiduciary or official capacity, the Area Director—

    (a) shall take into account the value of any property or estate or the amount of any fund out of which the applicant is entitled to be indemnified and the financial resources of any persons (including the applicant if appropriate) who might benefit from the proceedings; and

(b) may (without prejudice to regulation 28) either—

    (i) approve the application, subject to the payment from the property or resources specified in sub-paragraph (a) of any sums which he may in his discretion determine, or

    (ii) refuse the application, if he concludes that to do so would not cause hardship.

PART V

REFUSAL OF APPLICATIONS

Notification of refusal

34.—(1) Where an application for a certificate is refused on one or more of the following grounds, namely, that—

(a) the assessment officer has assessed that the applicant has disposable income which makes him ineligible for legal aid; or

(b) the assessment officer has assessed that the applicant, having disposable income of an amount which makes him eligible for legal aid, has disposable capital of an amount which renders him liable to be refused legal aid and it appears to the Area Director that, without legal aid, the probable costs to the applicant of the proceedings in respect of which the application was made would not exceed the sums payable by the applicant on account of his contribution; or

(c) the proceedings to which the application relates are not proceedings for which legal aid may be given; or

(d) the applicant has not shown that he has reasonable grounds for taking, defending or being a party to the proceedings; or

(e) it appears unreasonable that the applicant should receive legal aid in the particular circumstances of the case,

the Area Director shall notify the applicant of the grounds on which the application has been refused and inform him of the circumstances in which he may appeal to the appropriate area committee for the decision to be reviewed.

(2) Where an application is refused on either of the grounds specified in sub-paragraphs (d) and (e) of paragraph (1), the notification given under that paragraph shall include a brief statement of the reasons why that ground applies to the applicant's case.

Right of appeal against refusal

35.—(1) Where an Area Director refuses an application for a certificate or an applicant is dissatisfied with the terms upon which the Area Director would be prepared to issue it, the applicant may, subject to paragraph (2), appeal to the appropriate area committee.

(2) No appeal shall lie to an area committee from—

(a) an assessment of the assessment officer, or

(b) any decision by an Area Director as to the sums payable on account of the applicant's contribution or the method by which they shall be paid except a decision as to sums payable under regulation 32(3) or 33.

Time and form of appeal

36. Every appeal shall be brought by giving to the appropriate Area Committee, within 14 days of the date of notice of refusal of a certificate or of the terms upon which a certificate would be issued (or such longer period as the appropriate area committee may allow), notice of appeal in writing either on a form approved by the Board or in such other written form as the Area Director may accept as sufficient in the circumstances of the case.

Nature of appeal

37. Every appeal shall be by way of reconsideration of the application.

Representation at appeal or other final application

38.—(1) Upon an appeal the appellant may—

(a) furnish further statements, whether oral or in writing, in support of his application; and

(b) conduct the appeal himself, with or without the assistance of any person whom he may appoint for the purpose, or be represented by counsel or a solicitor or legal executive.

(2) With any necessary modifications, paragraph (1)(a) shall apply to any appeal to an area committee and, subject to regulation 58(3), paragraph (1)(b) shall apply to any appeal to an area committee on which the committee finally determines the applicant's right to receive legal aid.

Determination of appeal

39.—(1) The area committee shall determine the appeal in such manner as seems to it to be just and, without prejudice to the generality of the foregoing, may—

(a) dismiss the appeal; or

(b) direct the Area Director to offer a certificate subject to such terms and conditions as the area committee thinks fit;

(c) direct the Area Director to settle terms and conditions on which a certificate may be offered; or

(d) refer the matter, or any part of it, back to the Area Director for his determination or report.

(2) Any decision of an area committee with regard to an appeal shall be final, and it shall give notice of its decision, and the reasons for it, to the appellant and to any solicitor acting for him on a form approved by the Board.

Repeated refusal of certificates

40.—(1) Where a person has applied for and been refused a certificate on three separate occasions and it appears to the Area Director to whom such person applies that his conduct may amount to an abuse of the facilities provided by the Act, then the Area Director may report the matter to the appropriate area committee.

(2) If a report under paragraph (1) has been made, the area committee may:

(a) enquire whether any other area office has received an application from the person named in the report;

(b) call for a report as to the circumstances of any other such application; and

(c) if it considers that the person named in the report has abused the facilities provided by the Act, report thereon to the Board, making such recommendations as seem to the area committee to be just.

Power to make prohibitory directions

41.—(1) The Board, on receipt of a report made under regulation 40(2)(c), shall give the person named in it an opportunity of making (either by himself or by some other person acting on his behalf) representations in writing on the matter, and shall make such other enquiries as seem to be necessary; and, if they are satisfied that his conduct has amounted to an abuse of the facilities provided by the Act, may make a direction (in this regulation referred to as a "prohibitory direction") that no consideration shall, for a period not exceeding five years, be given by any Area Director either—

(a) to any future application by that person for a certificate with regard to any particular matter; or

(b) in exceptional circumstances, to any future application by him whatsover.

(2) The Board may in its discretion—

(a) include within the terms of any prohibitory direction any receiver, next friend or guardian *ad litem* who applies for a certificate on behalf of the person referred to in the prohibitory direction; and

(b) at any time vary or revoke any prohibitory direction in whole or in part.

(3) Where the Board makes a prohibitory direction, it shall inform the Lord Chancellor and shall, if so requested, give him its reasons for making it.

PART VI

ISSUE AND EFFECT OF CERTIFICATES

Issue of certificate where no contribution may be payable

42. Where an application is approved relating to proceedings where an undertaking under regulation 12(2) has been given or where no contribution is (for the time being) payable, the Area Director shall—

(a) issue a certificate;

(b) send the certificate (together with a copy) to the solicitor selected by the applicant; and

(c) send a copy of the certificate to the applicant together with a notice drawing the applicant's attention to the provisions of sections 16(6) and 17(1) of the Act.

Offer of certificate where contribution payable

43.—(1) Where an application is approved for any proceedings where a contribution will be payable, the Area Director shall require—

(a) any sums payable out of capital to be paid forthwith if the sum is readily available or, if it is not, by such time as seems to him reasonable in all the circumstances; and

(b) any sums payable out of income to be paid by such instalments as he may direct.

(2) The Area Director shall notify the applicant—

(a) of the sums payable under regulation 31; and

(b) of the terms upon which a certificate will be issued to him;

and draw to his attention the provisions of sections 16(1) and (6) and 17(1) of the Act.

Undertaking to account for sums received from third parties

44. Where the applicant—

(a) appears to be a member of an organisation or body which might reasonably be expected to give him financial assistance in meeting the cost of the proceedings for which the applicant has applied for legal aid; and

(b) does not appear to have any right to be indemnified by that organisation or body against expenses incurred in connection with those proceedings,

the Area Director shall require the applicant, as a term upon which the certificate will be issued, to sign an undertaking to pay to the Board (in addition to any sums payable under regulations 31 and 32) any sum which he receives from that organisation or body on account of the cost of those proceedings.

Acceptance and issue of certificate where contribution payable

45.—(1) An applicant who desires that a certificate should be issued to him on the terms notified to him by an Area Director shall, within 28 days of being so notified—

(a) signify his acceptance of those terms on a form approved by the Board and lodge it with the Area Director; and

(b) if those terms require the payment of any sums of money, give an undertaking, on a form approved by the Board, to pay those sums by the method stated in the terms and, if any sum is required to be paid before the certificate is issued, make that payment accordingly.

(2) When an applicant has complied with so many of the requirements of paragraph (1) as are relevant to his case, the Area Director shall issue a certificate and send it to the solicitor selected by the applicant.

(3) Where an application is approved relating to authorised summary proceedings in which an undertaking under regulation 12(2) has been given, the Area Director may defer issuing a certificate until a contribution has been paid.

Scope of certificates

46.—(1) A certificate may be issued in respect of the whole or part of proceedings and may be extended to cover appellate proceedings other than those mentioned in paragraph (2).

(2) A certificate shall not be extended to cover proceedings in the House of Lords or on appeal from a magistrates' court.

(3) A certificate shall not relate to more than one action, cause or matter except in the case of—

    (a) authorised summary proceedings; or

    (b) matrimonial proceedings; or

    (c) proceedings under the Guardianship of Minors Act 1971 or the Guardianship Act 1973 and proceedings under the Domestic Violence and Matrimonial Proceedings Act 1976;

    (d) an application for a grant of representation which is necessary to enable the action; which is the subject matter of the certificate, to be brought;

    (e) an application under section 33 of the Supreme Court Act 1981 or section 52 of the County Courts Act 1984 and subsequent court proceedings; or

    (f) proceedings which, under the Act, may be taken to enforce or give effect to any order or agreement made in the proceedings to which the certificate relates; and, for the purposes of this sub-paragraph, proceedings to enforce or give effect to an agreement or order shall include proceedings in bankruptcy or to wind-up a company.

Certificates to specify parties to proceedings

47. A certificate other than one relating to matrimonial proceedings or authorised summary proceedings shall specify the parties to the proceedings in respect of which it is issued.

Power to restrict costs allowable to distant solicitor

48.—(1) Where the solicitor selected by the applicant to whom a certificate is issued carries on his practice at a place which is so far away from where his services will be required in acting under the certificate that his selection will result in significantly greater expense to the fund than would have been incurred if the applicant had selected another solicitor, the certificate may provide that the solicitor shall not be entitled to payment in respect of any additional costs or disbursements incurred by reason of the fact that he does not carry on his practice at or near the place where his services are required in acting under the certificate.

(2) Where a certificate includes a provision under paragraph (1), payment of such additional costs or disbursements shall not be allowed on determination of the costs.

Effect of certificates

49. Any document purporting to be a certificate issued in accordance with these Regulations shall, until the contrary is proved, be deemed to be a valid certificate issued to the person named in it and for the purposes there set out and shall be received in evidence without further proof.

Notification of issue of certificates

50.—(1) Whenever an assisted person becomes a party to proceedings, or a party to proceedings becomes an assisted person, his solicitor shall forthwith—

(a) serve all other parties to the proceedings with notice of the issue of a certificate; and

(b) if at any time thereafter any other person becomes a party to the proceedings, forthwith serve a similar notice on that party.

(2) Copies of the notices referred to in paragraph (1) shall form part of the papers for the use of the court in the proceedings.

(3) Where an assisted person's solicitor—

(a) commences any proceedings for the assisted person in a county court; or

(b) commences proceedings in accordance with Order 112, rule 3 or 4 of the Rules of the Supreme Court 1965 or rule 101 or 103 of the Matrimonial Causes Rules 1977;

and at the same time files a copy of the notice to be served in accordance with paragraph (1), a copy of that notice shall be annexed to the originating process for service.

(4) A solicitor who receives a certificate from an Area Director shall, if proceedings have begun, or otherwise upon their commencement, send a copy of it by post to the appropriate court office or registry.

(5) Paragraphs (1) to (4) shall not apply to authorised summary proceedings and, where an assisted person is a party to such proceedings, his solicitor shall, before or at the first hearing that takes place after the certificate has been issued, file the certificate with the clerk to the justices.

PART VII

AMENDMENT OF CERTIFICATE AND ADJUSTMENT OF CONTRIBUTION

Power to amend certificates

51. The Area Director may amend a certificate where in his opinion—

(a) there is some mistake in the certificate; or

(b) it has become desirable for the certificate to extend to

(i) proceedings; or

(ii) other steps; or

(iii) subject to regulation 46 (3), other proceedings; or

(iv) proceedings which under the Act may be taken to enforce or give effect to any order or agreement made in the proceedings in respect of which the certificate was issued; or

(v) the bringing of an interlocutory appeal; or

(vi) proceedings in the Court of Justice of the European Communities on a reference to that Court for a preliminary ruling; or

(vii) representation by an EEC lawyer; or

(c) it has become desirable to add or substitute parties to the proceedings in respect of which the certificate was issued; or

(d) it has become desirable for the certificate to extend to any steps having the same effect as a cross-action or as a reply thereto, or a cross-appeal; or

(e) it has become desirable for the certificate not to extend to certain of the proceedings in respect of which it was issued; or

(f) a change of solicitor should be authorised.

Power to alter contribution and amend certificate

52.—(1) Without prejudice to the provisions of the Civil Legal Aid (Assessment of Resources) Regulations 1989, where the assisted person's disposable income and disposable capital have been assessed, the Area Director may, if he considers it to be desirable, request the assessment officer to re-assess the assisted person's financial resources and maximum contribution.

(2) Where the Area Director has determined the assisted person's contribution at a sum which is less than the maximum contribution and it appears likely that the costs incurred or likely to be incurred under the certificate may exceed the contribution which has been determined, he shall increase the amount payable on account of the assisted person's contribution to the amount or likely amount of the costs or to the amount of the maximum contribution, whichever is the lesser of the two.

(3) Without prejudice to regulation 51, the Area Director shall amend the certificate where he re-determines the amount payable on account of the assisted person's contribution whether as a result of a re-assessment pursuant to paragraph (1) or of an increase in contribution under paragraph (2) or otherwise.

Making and determination of applications for amendment

53. Parts II and V of these Regulations shall apply, with any necessary modifications, to applications for the amendment of certificates as they apply to applications for certificates.

Procedure on issue of amendment

54.—(1) Where an Area Director amends a certificate, he shall send two copies of the amendment to the assisted person's solicitor and one copy to the assisted person.

(2) A solicitor who receives an amendment sent to him under paragraph (1) shall forthwith—

(a) if proceedings have begun or otherwise upon their commencement, send a copy of the amendment by post to the appropriate court office or registry; and

(b) except in the case of an amendment made under regulation 52, serve notice of the fact upon all other parties to the proceedings, and, if any other person becomes a party to the proceedings, serve similar notice upon that person.

(3) The copy of the amendment sent to the appropriate court office or registry shall form part of the papers for the court in the proceedings.

(4) Paragraphs (2) and (3) shall not apply to authorised summary proceedings, and, where an assisted person is a party to such proceedings, his solicitor shall, before or at the first hearing that takes place after the amendment has been issued, file the amendment with the clerk to the justices.

Right to show cause on application to remove limitation
55. An Area Director shall not refuse an application to amend a certificate (other than an emergency certificate) by removing a limitation imposed upon it until—

(a) notice has been service on the assisted person that the application may be refused and his certificate discharged and that he may show cause why the application should be granted; and

(b) the assisted person has been given an opportunity to show cause why his application should be granted.

Procedure on refusal of amendment
56. Where an Area Director refuses an application for the amendment of a certificate, he shall notify the assisted person's solicitor in writing, stating his reasons for so doing.

Right of appeal against refusal of amendment
57.—(1) Where an Area Director refuses an application for the amendment of a certificate, the assisted person may appeal to the appropriate area committee.

(2) An appeal shall be brought by giving notice on a form approved by the Board within 14 days of the Area Director's decision to refuse the application.

Determination of appeal against refusal of amendment
58.—(1) Subject to paragraph (3), the area committee shall, on an appeal under regulation 57, reconsider the application and determine the appeal in such manner as seems to it to be just and, without prejudice to the generality of the foregoing, may—

(a) dismiss the appeal; or

(b) direct the Area Director to amend the certificate in such manner as the area committee thinks fit.

(2) Any decision of an area committee with regard to an appeal shall be final, and it shall give notice of its decision, and the reasons for it, to the assisted person and to his solicitor in a form approved by the Board.

(3) Nothing in this regulation or regulation 53 shall require the area committee to allow the assisted person to conduct an appeal under this regulation himself or to be represented on any such appeal if the area committee considers that such steps are unnecessary.

PART VIII

AUTHORITY TO INCUR COSTS

Instructing counsel

59. (1) Where it appears to an assisted person's solicitor that the proper conduct of the proceedings so requires, he may instruct counsel; but, unless authority has been given in the certificate or by the Area Director—

(a) counsel shall not be instructed in authorised summary proceedings; and

(b) a Queen's Counsel or more than one counsel shall not be instructed.

(2) Any instructions delivered to counsel under paragraph (1) shall:

(a) include a copy of the certificate (and any amendments to it) and any authority to incur costs under this Part of these Regulations;

(b) be endorsed with the legal aid reference number; and

(c) in the case of authorised summary proceedings, show the authority for counsel to be instructed;

but no fees shall be marked on any set of papers so delivered.

Power of Board to give general authority

60. The Board may give general authority to solicitors acting for assisted persons in any particular class of case to incur costs by—

(a) obtaining a report or opinion from one or more experts or tendering expert evidence;

(b) employing a person to provide a report or opinion (other than as an expert); or

(c) requesting transcripts of shorthand notes or tape recordings of any proceedings;

and, if such authority is given, the Board shall specify the maximum fee payable for any such report, opinion, expert evidence or transcript.

Other cases where authority may be sought

61.—(1) Where it appears to an assisted person's solicitor to be necessary for the proper conduct of the proceedings to incur costs by taking any of the steps specified in paragraph (2), he may, unless authority has been given in the certificate, apply to the Area Director for such authority.

(2) The steps referred to in paragraph (1) are—

(a) obtaining a report or opinion of an expert or tendering expert evidence in a case of a class not included in any general authority given under regulation 60; or

(b) paying a person, not being an expert witness, a fee to prepare a report and, if required, to give evidence in a case of a class not included in any general authority given under regulation 60; or

    (c) in a case of a class included in a general authority given under regulation 60, paying a higher fee than that specified by the Board or obtaining more reports or opinions or tendering more evidence (expert or otherwise) than has been specified; or

    (d) performing an act which is either unusual in its nature or involves unusually large expenditure; or

    (e) bespeaking any transcripts of shorthand notes or tape recordings of any proceedings not included in any general authority given under regulation 60.

(3) Where the Area Director gives authority for the taking of any step referred to in paragraph (2)(a) to (d), he shall specify the number of reports or opinions that may be obtained or the number of persons who may be authorised to give expert evidence and the maximum fee to be paid to each.

Reasons to be given for refusing authority
62. If an Area Director refuses an application for authority made under regulation 59 or 61, he shall give written reasons for his decision.

Effect of obtaining and failing to obtain authority
63.—(1) Subject to paragraph (2), no question as to the propriety of any step or act in relation to which prior authority has been obtained under regulation 59, 60 or 61 shall be raised on any taxation of costs.

(2) Where costs are incurred in accordance with and subject to the limit imposed by a prior authority given under regulation 59, 60 or 61, no question shall be raised on any taxation as to the amount of the payment to be allowed for the step or act in relation to which the authority was given unless the solicitor or the assisted person knew or ought reasonably to have known that the purpose for which the authority was given had failed or become irrelevant or unnecessary before the costs were incurred.

(3) Without prejudice to regulation 59, where costs are incurred in instructing a Queen's Counsel or more than one counsel, without authority to do so having been given in the certificate or under regulation 59(1), no payment in respect of those costs shall be allowed on any taxation unless it is also allowed on an inter partes taxation.

(4) Where costs are incurred in instructing counsel or in taking any step or doing any act for which authority may be given under regulation 60 or 61, without authority to do so having been given in the certificate or under regulation 59, 60 or 61, payment in respect of those costs may still be allowed on taxation.

Restriction on payment otherwise than from the fund
64. Where a certificate has been issued in connection with any proceedings, the assisted person's solicitor or counsel shall not receive or be party to the making of any payment for work done in those proceedings during the currency of that certificate (whether within the scope of the certificate or otherwise) except such payments as may be made out of the fund.

PART IX

CONDUCT OF PROCEEDINGS

Restrictions on entrusting case to others

65.—(1) No solicitor or counsel acting for an assisted person shall entrust the conduct of any part of the case to any other person except another solicitor or counsel selected under section 32(1) of the Act.

(2) Nothing in paragraph (1) shall prevent a solicitor from entrusting the conduct of any part of the case to a partner of his or to a competent and responsible representative of his employed in his office or otherwise under his immediate supervision.

Duty to report changes of circumstances

66. The assisted person shall forthwith inform his solicitor of any change in his circumstances or in the circumstances of his case, which he has reason to believe might affect the terms or the continuation of his certificate.

Duty to report abuse of legal aid

67.—(1) Where an assisted person's solicitor or counsel has reason to believe that the assisted person has—

(a) required his case to be conducted unreasonably so as to incur an unjustifiable expense to the fund or has required unreasonably that the case be continued; or

(b) intentionally failed to comply with any provision of regulations made under the Act concerning the information to be furnished by him or in furnishing such information has knowingly made a false statement or false representation,

the solicitor or counsel shall forthwith report the fact to the Area Director.

(2) Where the solicitor or counsel is uncertain whether it would be reasonable for him to continue acting for the assisted person, he shall report the circumstances to the Area Director.

Power of court to refer abuse to Area Director

68.—(1) Subject to paragraph (2), at any time during the hearing of any proceedings to which an assisted person is a party, the court may, on the application of the Board or of its own motion, make an order referring to the Area Director the question whether the assisted person's certificate should continue where the court considers that the assisted person has—

(a) in relation to any application for a certificate, made an untrue statement as to his financial resources or had failed to disclose any material fact concerning them, whether the statement was made or the failure occurred before or after the issue of the certificate and notwithstanding that it was made or occurred in relation to an application to another area office in connection with the same proceedings; or

(b) intentionally failed to comply with these Regulations by not furnishing to his solicitor or the Area Director any material information concerning anything other than his financial resources; or

(c) knowingly made an untrue statement in furnishing such information;

and the court shall notify the Area Director of the terms of any order so made.

(2) No order shall be made under paragraph (1) by reason of any such mis-statement or failure as is referred to in paragraph (1)(a) if the assisted person satisfies the court that he used due care or diligence to avoid such mis-statement or failure but the assisted person's solicitor shall nevertheless report the circumstances to the Area Director.

Duty to report on refusing or giving up case

69.—(1) A solicitor shall inform the Area Director of his reasons for refusing to act or for giving up a case after being selected.

(2) Counsel, where he has been selected to act or is acting for an assisted person, shall inform the Area Director of his reasons for refusing to accept instructions or for giving up the case or shall, if required so to do, inform that Area Director of his reasons for entrusting it to another.

(3) Without prejudice to any other right of a solicitor or counsel to give up a case, any solicitor or counsel may give up an assisted person's case in the circumstances specified in regulation 67.

(4) Where any solicitor or counsel exercises his right to give up an assisted person's case in the circumstances specified in regulation 67, the solicitor shall make a report to the Area Director of the circumstances in which that right was exercised.

(5) Where the Area Director to whom a report is made under paragraph (4) does not discharge or revoke the assisted person's certificate, he shall require the assisted person to select another solicitor to act for him.

Duty to report progress of proceedings

70.—(1) An assisted person's solicitor and his counsel (if any) shall give the Area Director such information regarding the progress and disposal of the proceedings to which the certificate relates as the Area Director may from time to time require for the purpose of performing his functions under these Regulations and, without being required so to do, the assisted person's solicitor shall—

(a) make a report where the assisted person declines to accept a reasonable offer of settlement or a sum which is paid into court;

(b) notify the Area Director where a legal aid certificate is issued to another party to the proceedings.

(2) Without prejudice to the generality of paragraph (1), an assisted person's solicitor shall, when required so to do by the Board, make a report to the Area Director, on a form approved by the Board, specifying the grounds on which he certifies that it is reasonable for the assisted person to continue to receive legal aid in respect of the proceedings to which the certificate relates.

(3) Where an assisted person's solicitor fails to make a report under paragraph (2) within 21 days of the Board's request, the Area Director shall—

(a) give notice to him and to the assisted person that the legal aid certificate may be discharged; and

(b) invite the assisted person to show cause why the certificate should not be discharged,

and the provisions of Part X of these Regulations shall apply, with any necessary modifications, where notice is given under sub-paragraph (a) above.

Duty to report death, etc., of assisted person
71. A solicitor who has acted or is acting for an assisted person shall, on becoming aware that the assisted person—

(a) has died; or

(b) has had a bankruptcy order made against him, report that fact to the Area Director.

Duty to report completion of case
72. A solicitor shall report forthwith to the Area Director either—

(a) upon the completion of the case if he has completed the work authorised by the certificate; or

(b) if, for any reason, he is unable to complete the work.

Privilege, etc., not to prevent disclosure
73.—(1) No solicitor or counsel shall be precluded, by reason of any privilege arising out of the relationship between counsel, solicitor and client, from disclosing to an Area Director or an area committee any information, or from giving any opinion, which he is required to disclose or give to the Area Director or that committee under the Act or these Regulations, or which may enable them to perform their functions under the Act or these Regulations.

(2) For the purpose of providing information under the Act or these Regulations or to enable an Area Director or an area committee to perform its functions under the Act or these Regulations, any party may disclose to an Area Director or an area committee communications in relation to the proceedings concerned sent to or by the assisted person's solicitor, whether or not they are expressed to be "without prejudice."

PART X

REVOCATION AND DISCHARGE OF CERTIFICATES

Effect of revocation or discharge
74.—(1) An Area Director may terminate a certificate by revoking or discharging it under this Part of these Regulations.

(2) Subject to this Part of these Regulations, a person whose certificate is revoked shall be deemed never to have been an assisted person in relation to those proceedings except for the purposes of section 18 of the Act; and a

person whose certificate is discharged shall, from the date of the discharge, cease to be an assisted person in the proceedings to which the certificate related.

Revocation or discharge of emergency certificate

75.—(1) The Area Director shall revoke an emergency certificate where the assessment officer assesses that the person to whom it was issued has disposable income of an amount which makes him ineligible for legal aid.

(2) The Area Director shall revoke an emergency certificate where the assessment officer assesses that the person to whom it was issued, having disposable income of an amount which makes him eligible for legal aid, has disposable capital of an amount which renders him liable to be refused legal aid, and it appears to the Area Director that, without legal aid, the probable cost to him of the proceedings in respect of which the emergency certificate was issued would not exceed the contribution which would be payable by him.

(3) The Area Director may revoke or discharge an emergency certificate if he is satisfied that the assisted person has failed to attend for an interview or to provide information or documents when required to do so under these Regulations, or has failed to accept an offer of a substantive certificate.

(4) The Area Director may revoke or discharge an emergency certificate upon the expiry of such period (including any extension of that period granted under regulation 24(1)) as he may have allowed for the duration of the certificate.

(5) No emergency certificate shall be revoked under paragraph (3) until—

(a) notice has been served on the assisted person and his solicitor that the Area Director may do so and that the assisted person may show cause why the certificate should not be revoked; and

(b) the assisted person has been given an opportunity to show cause why his certificate should not be revoked.

(6) Where notice is served under paragraph (5), no further work may be done or steps taken under the certificate unless authorised by the Area Director.

Discharge of certificate on financial grounds

76.—(1) The Area Director shall discharge a certificate (other than an emergency certificate) from such date as he considers appropriate where the assessment officer assesses that the person to whom it was issued has disposable income of an amount which makes him ineligible for legal aid.

(2) The Area Director shall discharge a certificate (other than an emergency certificate) from such date as he considers appropriate where the assessment officer assesses that the person to whom it was issued, having disposable income of an amount which makes him eligible for legal aid, has disposable capital of an amount which renders him liable to be refused legal aid, and it appears to the Area Director that, without legal aid, the probable cost to him of continuing the proceedings in respect of which the certificate was issued would not exceed the contribution which would be payable.

(3) Where the Area Director considers that the current financial circumstances of the assisted person are such that he could afford to proceed without legal aid, he may, with a view to discharging the certificate, require the assessment officer to assess the assisted person's current financial resources

in accordance with the Civil Legal Aid (Assessment of Resources) Regulations 1989 and may discharge the certificate from such date as he considers appropriate.

Discharge on the merits

77.—(1) The Area Director shall discharge a certificate from such date as he considers appropriate where, as a result of information which has come to his knowledge, he considers that—

    (a) the assisted person no longer has reasonable grounds for taking, defending or being a party to the proceedings, or for continuing to do so; or

    (b) the assisted person has required the proceedings to be conducted unreasonably so as to incur an unjustifiable expense to the fund; or

    (c) it is unreasonable in the particular circumstances that the assisted person should continue to receive legal aid.

Power to revoke or discharge for abuse of legal aid

78.—(1) Subject to paragraph (2), the Area Director may revoke or discharge a certificate where, as a result of information which has come to his knowledge, whether by a reference from the court under regulation 68 or otherwise, it appears to the Area Director that the assisted person has—

    (a) in relation to any application for a certificate, made an untrue statement as to his financial resources or has failed to disclose any material fact concerning them, whether the statement was made or the failure occurred before or after the issue of the certificate and notwithstanding that it was made or occurred in relation to an application to another area office in connection with the same proceedings; or

    (b) intentionally failed to comply with these Regulations by not furnishing to the Area Director or the solicitor any material information concerning any matter other than his financial resources; or

    (c) knowingly made an untrue statement in furnishing such information.

(2) No certificate shall be revoked or discharged under paragraph (1) by reason of any such mis-statement or failure as is referred to in paragraph (1)(a) if the assisted person satisfies the Area Director that he used due care or diligence to avoid such mis-statement or failure.

Power to revoke or discharge for failure to provide information, etc.

79. The Area Director may revoke or discharge a certificate if he is satisfied that the assisted person has failed to attend for an interview or to provide information or documents when required to do so under these Regulations.

Further power to discharge

80. The Area Director may discharge a certificate from such date as he considers appropriate—

(a) with the consent of the assisted person; or

(b) where the assisted person has been required to make a contribution and any payment in respect of it is more than 21 days in arrears; or

(c) on being satisfied, by the report of the assisted person's solicitor or otherwise, that—

    (i) the assisted person has died; or

    (ii) the assisted person has had a bankruptcy order made against him; or

    (iii) the proceedings to which the certificate relates have been disposed of; or

    (iv) the work authorised by the certificate has been completed.

Opportunity to show cause against revocation or discharge

81.—(1) Except where a certificate is discharged or revoked under regulation 75 or discharged under regulation 76 or 80(a), (b), (c)(i), (iii) or (iv), no certificate shall be revoked or discharged until—

(a) notice has been served on the assisted person that the Area Director may revoke or discharge his certificate (as the case may be) and that he may show cause why it should not be revoked or discharged; and

(b) the assisted person has been given an opportunity to show cause why his certificate should not be revoked or discharged.

(2) Where an Area Director revokes or discharges a certificate after notice has been given under paragraph (1), the assisted person may appeal to the appropriate area committee against such revocation or discharge and the provisions of regulations 36 to 39 shall, with the necessary modifications, apply to the conduct of such appeals.

(3) Any decision with regard to an appeal under paragraph (2) shall be final, and the area committee shall give notice of its decision and the reasons for it to the appellant and to any solicitor acting for him on a form approved by the Board.

Notification of revocation or discharge

82.—(1) Where an Area Director revokes or discharges an assisted person's certificate, he shall, unless the costs have already been determined, forthwith issue a notice of revocation or a notice of discharge (as the case may be), and shall send the notice (together with a copy) to his solicitor, and shall (except where the certificate has been discharged because the assisted person has died) send a further copy of the notice to the assisted person.

(2) A solicitor who receives a notice of revocation or a notice of discharge sent to him under paragraph (1) shall either forthwith, or if an appeal has been brought under regulation 81(2) which has been dismissed, forthwith upon receipt by him of a notice of dismissal—

(a) service notice of such revocation or discharge upon any other persons who are parties to the proceedings; and

(b) inform any counsel, and if proceedings have been commenced, send a copy of the notice by post to the appropriate court office or registry.

(3) The copy of the notice sent to the appropriate court office or registry shall form part of the papers for the use of the court in the proceedings.

(4) Paragraphs (2) and (3) shall not apply to authorised summary proceedings and, where an assisted person is a party to such proceedings, his solicitor shall before or at the first hearing that takes place after the notice of revocation or discharge (as the case may be) has been issued, file the notice with the clerk to the justices.

(5) Where the Area Director has considered revoking or discharging a certificate in consequence of information brought to his knowledge by any person, he may, if he thinks fit, inform that person whether or not the certificate has been revoked or discharged.

Effect of revocation or discharge on retainer

83.—(1) Upon receipt by him of a notice of revocation or discharge of a certificate, the retainer of any solicitor and counsel selected by or acting on behalf of the assisted person shall, subject to paragraph (2), either forthwith determine or, if an appeal had been brought under regulation 81(2) which had been dismissed, forthwith determine after receipt by him of a notice of such dismissal.

(2) If an Area Director revokes or discharges a certificate and proceedings have commenced, the retainer of the solicitor shall not determine until he has sent to the appropriate court office or registry, and has served, any notice required by regulation 82.

Costs to be taxed or assessed on revocation or discharge

84. Upon the determination of a retainer under regulation 83—

> (a) the costs of the proceedings to which the certificate related, incurred by or on behalf of the person to whom it was issued, shall, as soon as is practicable after the determination of the retainer, be submitted for taxation or assessment; and

> (b) the fund shall remain liable for the payment of any costs so taxed or assessed.

Operation of statutory charge

85.—(1) Where a certificate has been revoked or discharged, section 16(6) of the Act (which provides for a charge upon property recovered or preserved for an assisted person) shall apply to any property recovered or preserved as a result of the person whose certificate has been revoked or discharged continuing to take, defend or be a party to the proceedings to which the certificate related.

(2) For the purpose of paragraph (1), the reference to a person whose certificate has been discharged shall, where the certificate has been discharged under regulation 80(c)(i) or (ii), include his personal representatives, his trustee in bankruptcy or the Official Receiver, as the case may be.

Right to recover costs and contribution

86.—(1) Where a certificate has been revoked—

> (a) the Board shall have the right to recover from the person to whom the certificate was issued the costs paid or payable under regulation 84(b) less any amount received from him by way of contribution; and

(b) the solicitor who has acted under the certificate shall have the right to recover from that person the difference between the amount paid or payable out of the fund and the full amount of his solicitor and own client costs.

(2) Where a certificate has been discharged, the person to whom the certificate was issued shall remain liable for the payment of his contribution (if any) as determined or redetermined, up to the amount paid or payable by the Board under regulation 84(b) and, where he continues to take, defend or be a party to the proceedings to which the certificate related, section 17(1) of the Act shall apply in so far as the costs were incurred while he was an assisted person.

PART XI

PROPERTY AND COSTS RECOVERED FOR ASSISTED PERSONS

Money recovered to be paid to solicitor or the Board

87.—(1) Subject to regulations 89 and 94, all moneys payable to an assisted person—

(a) by virtue of any agreement or order made in connection with the action, cause or matter to which his certificate relates, whether such agreement was made before or after the proceedings were taken; or

(b) being moneys payable in respect of the action, cause or matter to which his certificate relates upon the distribution of property of a person who had been adjudicated bankrupt or has entered into a deed of arrangement, or of a company in liquidation; or

(c) being moneys which were paid into court by him or on his behalf in any proceedings to which his certificate relates and which have been ordered to be repaid to him; or

(d) being moneys standing in court to the credit of any proceedings to which his certificate relates,

shall be paid or repaid, as the case may be, to the solicitor of the assisted person or, if he is no longer represented by a solicitor, to the Board, and only the solicitor, or, as the case may be, the Board, shall be capable of giving a good discharge for moneys so payable.

(2) Where the assisted person's solicitor has reason to believe that an attempt may be made to circumvent the provisions of paragraph (1), he shall inform the Board.

Notice to trustee in bankruptcy, etc.

88.—(1) Where moneys become payable under regulation 87(b), the solicitor or the Board, as the case may be, shall send to the trustee in bankruptcy, the trustee or assignee of the deed of arrangement or the liquidator of the company in liquidation, as the case may be; notice that a certificate has been issued to the assisted person.

(2) A notice sent under paragraph (1) shall operate as a request by the assisted person for payment of the moneys payable under regulation 87(b) to

the assisted person's solicitor or the Board, as the case may be, and shall be a sufficient authority for that purpose.

Exceptions to regulation 87

89. Notwithstanding the requirements of regulations 87—

(a) payment of any sum under an order for costs in favour of an assisted person in authorised summary proceedings shall be made to the clerk to the justices, who shall pay it to the Board or as the Board shall direct, and only the clerk to the justices shall be able to give a good discharge therefor; and

(b) where any moneys recovered or preserved for an assisted person in any proceedings have been paid into or remain in court and invested for the benefit of the assisted person, such part of those moneys as is not subject to the charge created by section 16(6) of the Act in accordance with regulation 93 may be paid to the assisted person.

Solicitor to pay moneys recovered to the Board

90.—(1) An assisted person's solicitor shall forthwith—

(a) inform the Area Director of any property recovered or preserved for the assisted person and send to him a copy of the order or agreement by virtue of which the property was recovered or preserved; and

(b) subject to paragraphs (2) and (4), pay all moneys received by him under the terms of the order or agreement made in the assisted person's favour to the Board.

(2) Where the Area Director considers that the rights of the fund will thereby be safeguarded, he may direct the assisted person's solicitor to—

(a) pay to the Board under paragraph (1)(b) only such sums as, in the opinion of the Area Director, should be retained by the Board in order to safeguard the rights of the fund under any provisions of the Act and these Regulations; and

(b) pay any other moneys to the assisted person.

(3) Where in proceedings under any of the enactments referred to in regulation 96(1) the property recovered or preserved for the assisted person includes—

(a) property which by order of the court or under the terms of any agreement reached is to be used as a home for the assisted person or his dependants; or

(b) money which by order of the court or under the terms of any agreement reached is to be used to purchase a home for the assisted person or his dependants,

the assisted person's solicitor shall forthwith so inform the Area Director.

(4) If the Area Director considers and directs that the provisions of regulation 96 apply to any sum of money, paragraph (1)(b) above shall not apply to it and the assisted person's solicitor shall release the money only in accordance with the provisions of regulation 96.

Enforcement of orders, etc., in favour of assisted person

91.—(1) Where in any proceedings to which an assisted person is a party—

(a) an order or agreement is made providing for the recovery or preservation of property for the benefit of the assisted person and, by virtue of the Act, there is a first charge on the property for the benefit of the Board; or

(b) an order or agreement is made for the payment of costs to the assisted person,

the Board may take such proceedings in its own name as may be necessary to enforce or give effect to such an order or agreement.

(2) An assisted person may, with the consent of the appropriate Area Director, take proceedings (being proceedings for which representation may be granted under the Act) to give effect to an order or agreement referred to in regulation 87(a).

(3) Where the Board takes proceedings, it may authorise any person to swear an affidavit, file a proof, receive a dividend or take any other step in the proceedings in its name and the costs incurred by the Board in any such proceedings shall be a first charge on any property or sum so recovered.

Retention and payment out of moneys by the Board

92. Upon receipt of moneys paid to it under this Part of these Regulations, the Board shall retain—

(a) subject to regulation 103, any sum paid under an order or agreement for costs made in the assisted person's favour in respect of the period covered by his certificate;

(b) a sum equal to the amount (if any) by which any property recovered or preserved is charged for the benefit of the Board by virtue of section 16(6) of the Act; and

(c) any costs of proceedings taken by the Board under regulation 91(1);

and shall pay the balance to the assisted person.

Operation of statutory charge on moneys in court

93. Where any moneys recovered or preserved for an assisted person in any proceedings are ordered to be paid into or remain in court and invested for the benefit of the assisted person, the charge created by section 16(6) of the Act shall attach only to such parts of those moneys as, in the opinion of the Area Director, will be sufficient to safeguard the rights of the Board under any provisions of the Act or these Regulations and the Area Director shall notify the court in writing of the amount so attached.

Exemptions from the statutory charge

94. The charge created by section 16(6) of the Act shall not apply to—

(a) any interim payment made in accordance with an order made under Order 29, rule 11 or 12 of the Rules of the Supreme Court 1965, or Order 13, rule 12 of the County Court Rules 1981, or in accordance with an agreement having the same effect as such an order;

(b) any sum or sums ordered to be paid under section 5 of the Inheritance (Provision for Family and Dependants) Act 1975;

(c) any periodical payment of maintenance which, for this purpose, means money or money's worth paid towards the support of a spouse, former spouse, child or any other person for whose support the payer has previously been responsible or has made payments;

(d) the first £2,500 of any money, or of the value of any property, recovered or preserved by virtue of—

(i) an order made, or deemed to be made, under the provisions of section 23(1)(c) or (f), 23(2), 24, 27(6)(c) or (f), or 35 of the Matrimonial Causes Act 1973; or

(ii) an order made, or deemed to be made, under the provisions of section 2 or 6 of the Inheritance (Provision for Family and Dependants) Act 1975 or any provision repealed by that Act; or

(iii) an order made, or deemed to be made, after September 30, 1977, under section 17 of the Married Women's Property Act 1882; or

(iv) an order made, or deemed to be made, under the provisions of section 4(2)(b) of the Affiliation Proceedings Act 1957; or

(v) an order for the payment of a lump sum made, or deemed to be made, under the provisions of section 60 of the Magistrates' Courts Act 1980; or

(vi) an order made, or deemed to be made, under the provisions of section 2(1)(b) or (d), 6(1) or (5), 11(2)(b) or (3)(b) or 20(2) of the Domestic Proceedings and Magistrates' Courts Act 1978; or

(vii) an order made, or deemed to be made, under section 9(2)(b), 10(1)(b)(ii) or 11(b)(ii) of the Guardianship of Minors Act 1971 or under section 11B, 11C, or 11D of that Act; or

(viii) an order made, or deemed to be made, under section 34(1)(c) or 35 of the Children Act 1975; or

(ix) an agreement made after March 1, 1981 which has the same effect as an order made, or deemed to be made under any of the provisions specified in sub-paragraph (d)(i) to (viii); or

(e) where the certificate was issued before May 3, 1976, any money or property, of whatever amount or value, recovered or preserved by the virtue of an order made, or deemed to be made, under any of the provisions specified in sub-paragraph (d)(i) or (ii) before August 1, 1976 or which, if made on or after that date, gives effect to a settlement entered into before that date;

(f) any payment made in accordance with an order made by the Employment Appeal Tribunal, or in accordance with a settlement entered into after November 1, 1983 which has the same effect as such an order; or

(g) any sum, payment or benefit which, by virtue of any provision of, or made under, an Act of Parliament, cannot be assigned or charged.

Vesting and enforcement of charges

95.—(1) Any charge on property recovered or preserved for an assisted person arising under section 16(6) of the Act or created by virtue of regulation 96, 97 or 98 shall vest in the Board.

(2) The Board may enforce any such charge in any manner which would be available to a chargee in respect of a charge given inter partes, but the Board

shall not agree to the release or postponement of the enforcement of any such charge except where regulation 96, 97 or 98 applies and then only in accordance with the provisions of those regulations.

(3) Any such charge shall according to its nature—

(a) in the case of unregistered land, be a Class B land charge within the meaning of section 2 of the Land Charges Act 1972;

(b) in the case of registered land, be a registrable substantive charge; or

(c) in a case in which the conditions specified in section 54(1) of the Land Registration Act 1925 are met, be protected by lodging a caution in accordance with the provisions of that section,

and references to registration in regulations 96 to 98 shall be construed as references to registration or protection in accordance with paragraph (a), (b) or (c) of this regulation.

(4) Without prejudice to the provisions of the Land Registration Act 1925 and the Land Charges Act 1972, all conveyances and acts done to defeat, or operating to defeat, and such charge shall, except in the case of a bona fide purchaser for value without notice, be void as against the Board.

Postponement of enforcement of charges over money

96.—(1) This regulation applies where in proceedings under—

(a) the Married Women's Property Act 1882;

(b) the Matrimonial Causes Act 1973; or

(c) the Inheritance (Provision for Family and Dependents) Act 1975**(e)**,

there is recovered or preserved for the assisted person a sum of money which by order of the court or under the terms of any agreement reached is to be used for the purpose of purchasing a home for himself or his dependants.

(2) Where the assisted person—

(a) wishes to purchase a home in accordance with the order or agreement; and

(b) agrees in writing on a form approved by the Board to comply with the conditions set out in paragraph (3),

the Board may, if the Area Director is satisfied that the property to be purchased will provide adequate security for the sum referred to in paragraph (3)(b), agree to defer enforcing any charge over that sum.

(3) The conditions referred to in paragraph (2) are that—

(a) the property to be purchased shall be subject to a charge executed in favour of the Board and registered in accordance with regulation 95(3); and

(b) from the date on which the charge is first registered, simple interest shall accrue for the benefit of the Board at the rate of 12 per cent. per annum (or such other rate as may from time to time be prescribed) on such sum as, but for the provisions of this regulation, the Board would have retained under regulation 92(b) in respect of its charge over the property to which this regulation applies.

(4) Where the Board has agreed to defer enforcement under paragraph (2), the assisted person's solicitor may release any money received by him under

regulation 87 and which is the subject of the order or agreement, to the vendor or the vendor's representative on completion of the purchase of the property purchased in accordance with the order or agreement.

(5) Where—

(a) the Area Director has directed (under regulation 90(4)) that this regulation applies; and

(b) no agreement to defer enforcement under paragraph (2) above has been made,

the assisted person's solicitor may release any money received by him under regulation 87 and which is the subject of the order or agreement to another solicitor or to a person providing conveyancing services to whom section 22(1) of the Solicitors Act 1974(**a**) does not apply, who has given an undertaking to, and on a form approved by, the Board that he will fulfil the obligations imposed by this regulation on the assisted person's solicitor.

(6) Where the assisted person's solicitor releases any money under paragraph (4) or (5), he shall so inform the Area Director as soon as practicable and either—

(a) provide the Area Director with sufficient information to enable him to register a charge on the property purchased in accordance with the order or agreement; or

(b) send to the Area Director a copy of any undertaking given under paragraph (5).

(7) Where any sum of money retained by the assisted person's solicitor by virtue of this regulation has not been used for the purchase of a home after a period of one year from the date of the order or agreement under which it was recovered or preserved for the assisted person, the assisted person's solicitor shall pay that sum to the Board.

Postponement of enforcement of charges over land

97.—(1) This regulation applies where, in proceedings under any of the enactments referred to in regulation 96(1), there is recovered or preserved for the assisted person property which, by order of the court or under the terms of any agreement reached, is to be used as a home for the assisted person or his dependants.

(2) Where the Area Director considers that the provisions of this regulation apply to any property, he shall so direct.

(3) Where the Area Director has directed that this regulation applies to property and the assisted person—

(a) wishes to use the property as a home for himself or his dependants; and

(b) agrees in writing on a form approved by the Board to comply with the condition set out in paragraph (4),

the Board may, if the Area Director is satisfied that the property will provide adequate security for the sum referred to in paragraph (4), agree to defer enforcing of any charge over that property.

(4) The condition referred to in paragraph (3) is that from the date on which the charge is first registered where that date is after December 1, 1988, simple

interest shall accrue for the benefit of the Board at the rate of 12 per cent. per annum (or such other rate as may from time to time be prescribed) on such sum as, but for the provisions of this regulation, the Board would have retained under regulation 92(b) in respect of the property to which this regulation applies.

(5) Where, in a case to which this regulation applies, the charge in favour of the Board has not yet been registered in accordance with regulation 95(3) and the assisted person—

(a) wishes to purchase a different property in substitution for the property which is the subject of the order or agreement referred to in paragraph (1); and

(b) agrees in writing on a form approved by the Board to comply with the conditions set out in paragraph (6),

the Board may, if the Area Director is satisfied that the property to be purchased will provide adequate security for the sum referred to in paragraph (4), agree to defer enforcing any charge over that property.

(6) The conditions referred to in paragraph (5) are that—

(a) the property to be purchased shall be subject to a charge executed in favour of the Board and registered in accordance with regulation 95(3); and

(b) from the date on which the charge is first registered where that date is after December 1, 1988, simple interest shall accrue for the benefit of the Board at the rate referred to in paragraph (4) on the sum referred to in that paragraph.

Substitution of charged property

98.—(1) This regulation applies where a charge has been registered in favour of the Board in pursuance of an agreement made under regulation 96 or 97.

(2) Where, in a case to which this regulation applies—

(a) the assisted person wishes to purchase a different property in substitution for that over which a charge already exists;

(b) the assisted person agrees in writing on a form approved by the Board to comply with the conditions set out in paragraph (3); and

(c) the Area Director is satisfied that the property to be purchased will provide adequate security for the sum referred to in regulation 96(3)(b) or regulation 97(4), as the case may be,

the Board may agree to release that charge.

(3) The conditions referred to in paragraphs (2) and (4) are that—

(a) the property to be purchased shall be subject to a charge executed in favour of the Board and registered in accordance with regulation 95(3); and

(b) where simple interest has accrued, it shall continue to accrue for the benefit of the Board at the rate prescribed for the time being for the purposes of regulation 96(3)(b) on the sum referred to in that regulation or in regulation 97(4), as the case may be.

(4) Where, after a charge has been registered in favour of the Board in pursuance of an agreement made under this regulation—

(a) the assisted person wishes to purchase a different property in substitution for the property over which that charge exists;

(b) the assisted person agrees in writing on a form approved by the Board
to comply with the conditions set out in paragraph (3) above; and

(c) the Area Director is satisfied that the property to be purchased will
provide adequate security for the sum referred to in regulation
96(3)(b) or regulation 97(4), as the case may be,

the Board may agree to release that charge.

Payment and recovery of interest

99.—(1) Where interest is payable by the assisted person pursuant to the
provisions of regulations 96, 97 or 98, such interest shall continue to accrue
until the sum referred to in regulation 96(3)(b) or regulation 97(4), as the case
may be, is paid and the Board shall not seek to recover interest until such
payment is made.

(2) The Board may take such steps as may be necessary to enforce, give
effect to or terminate any agreement made under regulation 96, 97 or 98.

(3) Nothing in regulations 96 to 99 shall prevent the assisted person from
making interim payments of interest or capital in respect of any sum referred
to in regulation 96(3)(b) or 97(4), whether such payments are made at regular
intervals or not, and any such payment of capital shall reduce those sums
accordingly except that no interim payment shall be used to reduce any such
sum while interest on that sum remains outstanding.

PART XII

COSTS OF ASSISTED PERSONS

Payment on account

100.—(1) A solicitor acting for an assisted person under a certificate to which
this regulation applies may submit a claim to the Financial Controller of the
Board on a form approved by the Board for the payment of sums on account of
profit costs incurred in connection with the proceedings to which the certificate relates.

(2) Counsel instructed on behalf of an assisted person under a certificate to
which this regulation applies may submit a claim to the Financial Controller
of the Board on a form approved by the Board for the payment of sums on
account of his fees for work done in connection with the proceedings to
which the certificate relates.

(3) A claim may be made under this regulation in relation to a certificate:

(a) which was issued on or after October 1, 1986, after a period of 18
months has elapsed since the date on which the certificate was
issued;

(b) which was issued before October 1, 1986, after a period of 30 months
has elapsed since the date on which the certificate was issued.

(4) Further claims may be made under this regulation in relation to—

(a) a certificate to which paragraph (3)(a) applies, after periods of 12 months and 24 months have elapsed since the date on which a claim could first be made;

(b) a certificate to which paragraph (3)(b) applies, after a period of 12 months has elapsed since the date on which a claim could first be made.

(5) The maximum payment to be made for each claim under paragraph (1) or (2) in any one financial year shall be—

for the financial year 1989/90	38%
for the financial year 1990/91	46%
for the financial year 1991/92	54%
for the financial year 1992/93	62%
for the financial year 1993/94	70%
for the financial year 1994/95 and thereafter	75%

(6) Where a solicitor's retainer has been determined and another solicitor (who is not a member of the same firm) is acting on behalf of the assisted person, the appropriate area committee may authorise payment of a sum on account of the original solicitor's costs where it appears unlikely that the costs will be taxed within six months of the date on which the retainer was determined.

(7) The making of a payment under this regulation shall not release a solicitor from any obligation under these Regulations to submit his costs and counsel's fees for taxation or assessment on conclusion of the case.

(8) Where, after taxation or assessment, payments made under this regulation are found to exceed the final costs of the case, the solicitor or counsel (if any) shall, on demand, repay the balance due to the fund and, where the total costs exceed any payment made under this regulation, the balance shall be paid from the fund.

Payment on account of disbursements, in cases of hardship, etc.

101.—(1) Without prejudice to regulation 100, a solicitor acting for an assisted person may apply to the appropriate area committee for the payment of a sum on account of

(a) disbursements incurred or about to be incurred in connection with the proceedings to which the certificate relates;

(b) profit costs or counsel's fees where the proceedings to which the certificate relates have continued for more than 12 months and it appears unlikely that an order for taxation will be made within the next 12 months and delay in the taxation of those costs or fees will cause hardship to the solicitor or counsel.

(2) Without prejudice to regulation 100, where—

(a) the proceedings to which the certificate related have concluded or the solicitor is otherwise entitled to have his costs taxed; and

(b) counsel acting for the assisted person has not received payment in respect of his fees for at least six months since the event which gave rise to the right to taxation,

counsel may apply to the appropriate area committee for payment of 75 per cent. of the amount claimed on account of his fees for work done in connection with the proceedings to which the certificate related.

Deferment of solicitor's profit costs

102. Where an assisted person's solicitor has failed to comply with any provision of these Regulations and, as a result of his default or omission, the fund incurs loss—

(a) the appropriate area committee may defer payment of all or part of the solicitor's profit costs in connection with the proceedings to which the certificate relates until he has complied with such provisions; and

(b) if the Board refers the conduct of the solicitor to the Solicitors' Disciplinary Tribunal and the solicitor is disciplined, the Board may retain any sum, payment of which has been deferred under sub-paragraph (a), in accordance with the finding of the Tribunal.

Legal aid granted after costs incurred

103.—(1) Where, after proceedings have been instituted in any court, a party becomes an assisted person in relation to those proceedings, the provisions of section 17(1) of the Act shall apply only to so much of the costs of the proceedings as are incurred while a certificate is in force.

(2) Any solicitor who has acted on behalf of the assisted person in the proceedings to which a certificate relates before the date of the certificate, and any solicitor who has a lien on any documents necessary for the proceedings and who has delivered them up subject to his lien, may give notice of that fact to the appropriate area committee.

(3) Subject to paragraph (4), if moneys are recovered for the assisted person, the Board shall pay to any solicitor who has given notice under paragraph (2) out of the sum so recovered the costs to which he would have been entitled following a solicitor and own clients taxation.

(4) In any case where the sums so recovered are insufficient to pay the solicitor's costs in full in accordance with paragraph (3) and also to meet the sums paid out or payable out of the fund on the assisted person's account, the sums recovered in the proceedings shall be divided between the fund and the solicitor in the same proportions as the solicitor's costs and the cost to the fund bear to the aggregate of the two, and the first charge for the benefit of the Board imposed by virtue of section 16(6) of the Act on property recovered or preserved in the proceedings shall take effect accordingly.

(5) In any case in which the amount of—

(a) the costs payable to a solicitor under this regulation; or

(b) the inter partes costs incurred during the period in which the certificate was in force,

have not been ascertained on taxation, they shall, for the purpose of this regulation, be assessed by the appropriate area committee and, where the committee makes an assessment under this regulation, it shall do so with a view to allowing, for the costs referred to in sub-paragraph (a) above, such costs as the solicitor would have been entitled to on a solicitor and own client taxation and, for the costs referred to in sub-paragraph (b) above, such costs as would have been allowed on a taxation on the standard basis.

(6) For the purposes of this regulation, work done by a solicitor—

(a) immediately prior to the issue of an emergency certificate; and

211

(b) at a time when no application for an emergency certificate could be made because the appropriate area office was closed,

shall be deemed to be work done while such a certificate is in force if the solicitor applies for an emergency certificate at the first available opportunity and the application is granted.

Remuneration of counsel and solicitors in the Crown Court and magistrates' courts

104.—(1) The sums to be allowed to solicitors and counsel in connection with authorised summary proceedings or proceedings in the Crown Court for which legal aid is available under Part IV of the Act shall be assessed by the Area Director.

(2) Any assessment or review under this regulation shall be made in accordance with the provisions of regulation 6 of and Schedule 1 Part I paragraph 1(a) to the Legal Aid in Criminal and Care Proceedings (Costs) Regulations 1989 as if the work done was work to which those provisions apply.

(3) Paragraphs (4) to (8) of regulations 105 shall apply where costs are assessed by an Area Director under paragraph (1) as they apply to an assessment under that regulation.

(4) Subject to paragraph (3), regulations 105 to 110 shall not apply to costs in respect of authorised summary proceedings or proceedings in the Crown Court for which legal aid is available under Part IV of the Act.

Assessment of costs

105.—(1) In this regulation and in regulation 106, "assessment" means an assessment of costs with a view to ensuring that the amounts of costs to be allowed are those which would be allowed on a taxation on the standard basis under rules of court.

(2) Where the retainer of an assisted person's solicitor or counsel is determined before proceedings are actually begun and there has been no subsequent change of solicitor or counsel under the certificate, the amount of the solicitor's costs and counsel's fees (if any) shall be assessed by the Area Director.

(3) Where proceedings have begun and—

(a) the solicitor is of the opinion that the total amount which he and counsel (if any) would receive after taxation on the standard basis would not be more than £500; or

(b) the case of an assisted person (who is not such a person as is referred to in Order 62, rule 16, of the Rules of the Supreme Court 1965) has been settled after the commencement of proceedings without any direction of the court as the costs on terms that include provision for an agreed sum in respect of costs to be paid to the assisted person which the solicitor and counsel (if any) is willing to accept in full satisfaction of the work done; or

(c) there are special circumstances where a taxation would be against the interest of the assisted person or would increase the amount payable from the fund; or

(d) after a direction or order that the assisted person's costs shall be taxed on the standard basis, the solicitor incurs costs for the purpose of recovering moneys payable to the fund,

the solicitor may apply to the Area Director for an assessment of the amount of his costs and counsel's fees (if any) in respect of the work done.

(4) If any solicitor or counsel is dissatisfied with any decision on an assessment in accordance with paragraph (2) or (3), he may, within 21 days of that decision, make written representations to the appropriate area committee; and that committee shall review the assessment of the Area Director whether by confirming, increasing or decreasing the amount assessed by the Area Director.

(5) A solicitor or counsel who is dissatisfied with the decision of an area committee on a review under paragraph (4) may, within 21 days of the decision, apply to that committee to certify a point of principle of general importance.

(6) Where an area committee certifies a point of principle of general importance, the solicitor or counsel may, within 21 days of the certification, appeal in writing to a committee appointed by the Board against the decision of the area committee under paragraph (4).

(7) On an appeal under paragraph (6) the committee appointed by the Board may reverse, affirm or amend the decision of the area committee under paragraph (4).

(8) The assisted person's solicitor shall within seven days after an assessment or review under this regulation notify counsel in writing where the fees claimed on his behalf have been reduced or disallowed on assessment or review.

Agreement in respect of costs

106.—(1) Where, in proceedings to which an assisted person (or a former assisted person) has been a party and which have been brought to an end by a judgment, decree or final order, there has been an agreement as to the costs to be paid by any other party to the assisted person (or former assisted person) which that person's solicitor and counsel (if any) is willing to accept in full satisfaction of the costs of the work done, the amount of those costs shall be assessed by the Area Director.

(2) Where costs are to be assessed in the circumstances specified in paragraph (1), the Area Director may, if he thinks fit, request the taxing officer of the court in which the proceedings were conducted to assess the costs on the standard basis without a taxation.

(3) Paragraphs (4) to (8) of regulation 105 shall apply where costs are assessed by an Area Director under paragraph (1) as they apply to an assessment under that regulation.

Taxation of costs

107.—(1) The costs of proceedings to which an assisted person is a party shall be taxed in accordance with any direction or order given or made in the proceedings irrespective of the interest (if any) of the assisted person in the taxation; and, for the purpose of these Regulations, an order for the taxation of the costs of a review of taxation or of the costs of an appeal from a decision of a judge on such a review shall be deemed to be a final order.

(2) Any certificate or notice of revocation or discharge, or a copy of any such certificate or notice, shall be made available on the taxation.

(3) Where in any proceedings to which an assisted person is a party—

(a) judgment is signed in default, the judgment shall include a direction that the costs of any assisted person shall be taxed on the standard basis;

(b) the court gives judgment or makes a final decree or order in the proceedings, the judgment, decree or order shall include a direction (in addition to any other direction as to taxation) that the costs of any assisted person shall be taxed on the standard basis;

(c) the plaintiff accepts money paid into court, the costs of any assisted person shall be taxed on the standard basis.

(4) Where in any proceedings to which an assisted person or a former assisted person is a party and—

(a) the proceedings are, or have been, brought to an end without a direction having been given, whether under paragraph (3) or otherwise, as to the assisted person's costs being taxed on the standard basis; or

(b) a judgment or order in favour of an opposing party, which includes a direction that the assisted person's costs be so taxed, has not been drawn up or, as the case may be, entered by him; or

(c) a retainer is determined under regulation 83 in such circumstances as to require a taxation in accordance with the provisions of these Regulations;

the costs of that person shall be taxed on the standard basis on production of a copy of the notice of discharge or revocation of the certificate at the appropriate taxing office.

Failure to apply for taxation

108. Where, in any proceedings to which a former assisted person was a party, an order or agreement was made for the payment to him of costs and he has failed to ask for the costs to be taxed or his certificate is discharged before taxation, the Board may authorise the making of the application for taxation on his behalf and the costs of the application and of taxation shall be deemed to be costs in the proceedings to which the certificate related.

Disallowance or reduction of costs

109.—(1) Without prejudice to Order 62, rules 10 and 11 of the Rules of the Supreme Court 1965 or to Order 38, rule 1(3) of the County Court Rules 1981, on any taxation of an assisted person's costs in connection with proceedings (except authorised summary proceedings and proceedings in the Crown Court), any costs wasted by failure to conduct the proceedings with reasonable competence and expedition shall be disallowed or reduced, and where the solicitor has without good reason delayed putting in his bill for taxation the whole of the costs may be disallowed or reduced.

(2) No costs shall be disallowed or reduced under paragraph (1) until notice has been served by the taxing officer on the solicitor whose name appears on the assisted person's certificate and, in a case where those costs relate to counsel's fees, on the assisted person's counsel, requiring the solicitor or, as

the case may be, counsel to show cause orally or in writing why those costs should not be allowed or reduced.

Solicitor's duty to safeguard the interests of the fund
110. It shall be the duty of an assisted person's solicitor to safeguard the interests of the fund on any inter partes taxation pursuant to an order for costs made in favour of the assisted person where that person may himself have no interest in the result of the taxation, and for this purpose to take such steps as may appear to the solicitor to be necessary to obtain a review of taxation under regulation 113 or 114.

Costs of applications, reports, etc., under these Regulations
111. Costs incurred by reason of any application made under Part VIII, and of any report made by an assisted person's solicitor under Part IX, of these Regulations shall be taxed on the standard basis and costs incurred by reason of regulation 25, 50, 54, 82 or 124 shall be costs in the cause.

Duty to inform counsel
112.—(1) The assisted person's solicitor shall within seven days after the taxation (or provisional taxation) notify counsel in writing where the fees claimed on his behalf have been reduced or disallowed on taxation, and shall endorse the bill of costs with the date on which such notice was given or that no such notice is necessary.

(2) Where the bill of costs is endorsed that no notice under paragraph (1) is necessary, the taxing officer may issue the certificate or allocatur but, where such a notice has been given, the taxing officer shall not issue the certificate or allocatur until 14 days have elapsed from the date so endorsed.

Application to carry in objections to the taxation
113.—(1) In this regulation, in regulation 114 and in regulation 116, "legal aid taxation" means the taxation of a solicitor's bill to his own client where that bill is to be paid out of the fund.

(2) Where—

(a) an assisted person is dissatisfied with any decision of a taxing officer (except a decision under regulation 106) as to the amount which he is entitled to recover by virtue of an order or agreement for costs made in his favour or for which he is liable by virtue of an order for costs made against him; or

(b) the assisted person's solicitor is dissatisfied with any decision of the taxing officer:

(i) on an inter partes taxation pursuant to an order for costs made in favour of the assisted person, or

(ii) on a legal aid taxation,

the solicitor shall apply to the appropriate area committee for authority to carry in objections to the taxation; and if the area committee gives authority (but not otherwise) the solicitor may carry in objections in accordance with rules of court.

Application to judge to review taxation
114. Where the assisted person or his solicitor, as the case may be, is dissatisfied with the decision of the taxing officer on any matter to which objection

has been taken under regulation 113, the solicitor shall apply to the Board for authority to have the taxation reviewed; and, if the Board gives authority (but not otherwise), the solicitor may apply (or instruct counsel to apply) to a judge to review the taxation in accordance with rules of court.

Appeal from review of taxation

115.—(1) Subject to paragraph (2) and notwithstanding that the assisted person may have no interest in the appeal or would, but for regulation 118, have an interest adverse to that of his solicitor, an assisted person's solicitor:

    (a) may, with the authority of the Board, appeal from the decision of the judge on a review of taxation under regulation 114; or

    (b) shall be entitled to be heard on an appeal brought by any other party,

and, on any such appeal, the solicitor may appear by counsel.

(2) Nothing in this regulation shall be deemed to confer a right of appeal in proceedings to which an assisted person is not a party where no such right exists.

(3) Where an assisted person's solicitor applies for authority under paragraph (1), he shall do so before the expiration of the time allowed by rules of court for an appeal from the decision of a judge and, for this purpose, the time so allowed shall be extended by one month.

Counsel dissatisfied with taxation

116.—(1) Where counsel acting for an assisted person is dissatisfied with any decision on a legal aid taxation, it shall be the duty of the assisted person's solicitor to report the matter to the appropriate area committee or to the Board, as the case may be, and, if the committee or the Board give authority to do so—

    (a) to carry in objections to the taxation;

    (b) to apply to a judge to review the taxation; or

    (c) to appeal from the decision of the judge,

as the case may be, and regulations 113 to 115 and 120 shall apply as if the solicitor were the person dissatisfied.

(2) Paragraph (1) shall apply to a provisional taxation with the necessary modifications and in particular with the insertion of the words "to inform the taxing officer that he wishes to be heard on the taxation and to attend on the taxation," after the words "the assisted person's solicitor."

Objection by other party

117. If, in proceedings to which an assisted person is a party, any other party carries in objections to the inter partes taxation or applies to a judge to review that taxation, the assisted person's solicitor may be heard on the objections or review notwithstanding that the assisted person himself may have no interest in the taxation.

Assisted person having no interest or adverse interest in taxation

118. Where the assisted person has no interest in the taxation or would, but for the provisions of this regulation, have an interest adverse to that of his solicitor—

216

(a) it shall be the duty of the solicitor carrying in objections under regulation 113 or applying for a review under regulation 114 to ensure that all matters which are proper to be taken into account in consideration of the objections or on the review are placed before the taxing officer or the judge, as the case may be;

(b) the assisted person shall not be required to make any contribution to the fund on account of the costs of any proceedings arising under regulations 113 to 117 or in consequence of any order made in such proceedings; and

(c) the charge created by section 16(6) of the Act shall not apply in relation to any resulting increase in the net liability of the fund arising out of the costs of any proceedings under regulations 113 to 117 or in consequence of any order made in such proceedings.

Assisted person having financial interest in taxation

119. Without prejudice to the provisions of regulation 118, where the assisted person has a financial interest in the taxation—

(a) it shall be the duty of his solicitor to explain to him the extent of his interest in the taxation and the steps which can be taken to safeguard that interest and, if the assisted person so requests, to give notice in accordance with rules of court to the taxing officer that the assisted person has such an interest;

(b) the assisted person shall not be required to make any contribution to the fund on account of the costs of the taxation proceedings;

(c) the charge created by section 16(6) of the Act shall not apply in relation to any resulting increase in the net liability of the fund arising out of the costs of the taxation proceedings.

Costs to be paid out of the fund

120. Any proceedings under regulations 113 to 119 shall be deemed to be proceedings to which the assisted person's certificate relates, whether or not it has been discharged or revoked, and the costs of such proceedings shall be paid out of the fund.

Time limits, etc.

121.—(1) Subject to regulation 112 where any party to a taxation is an assisted person, the certificate or allocatur shall not, unless the parties agree, be signed until 21 days after the taxing officer's decision; and where an assisted person's solicitor applies under regulation 113 or 114 (or under regulation 116) for authority to carry in objections or to have a taxation reviewed, he shall do so before the expiration of the time allowed under rules of court for applying to the taxing officer for review of the taxation and the time so allowed shall, for this purpose, be extended by one month, or such longer period as the taxing officer may allow.

(2) Notice of any application made under regulation 113, 114 or 116 shall be given to the taxing officer and to any opposing party.

Appointment of solicitor to intervene

122.—(1) The Lord Chancellor may appoint a solicitor to intervene in any review by a judge of a taxation of the costs of proceedings to which an assisted person is a party, and any such appointment may be made in respect of a particular review or may extend to any review of taxation during the period for which the solicitor is appointed.

(2) Whenever the Board gives authority to an assisted person's solicitor to apply to a judge to review a taxation, it shall notify the Lord Chancellor and inform him of the name and address of the assisted person's solicitor.

(3) If, in proceedings to which an assisted person is a party, any other party applies to a judge to review the inter partes taxation or the assisted person's solicitor applies to a judge to review any such taxation as is referred to in regulation 113, the assisted person's solicitor shall so inform the Board and the Board shall notify the Lord Chancellor and inform him of the name and address of the assisted person's solicitor and, where the subject of the review is an inter partes taxation, the name and address of the solicitor acting for the other party.

(4) The solicitor appointed by the Lord Chancellor to intervene in a review of taxation shall be entitled to production of all documents relevant to the matters in issue before the judge and to delivery of copies thereof and to appear by counsel and be heard on the review, with a view to ensuring that all considerations which are proper to be taken into account are placed before the court, whether they relate to the interests of the fund or of the assisted person or to the remuneration of solicitors and counsel acting for assisted persons.

(5) On any review in which a solicitor appointed by the Lord Chancellor has intervened, the judge may make such order as may be just for the payment to or by that solicitor of the costs incurred by him or any other party, and any sum due to the solicitor by virtue of any such order shall be paid by him to the Board and any sum so payable by the solicitor shall be paid out of the fund, and the solicitor shall be entitled to receive from the fund the costs he has incurred on the intervention.

(6) A solicitor appointed by the Lord Chancellor under paragraph (1) may appeal from the decision of the judge on a review of taxation under regulation 115 and paragraphs (2) to (5) above shall apply to such an appeal as it applies to a review.

PART XIII

COSTS AWARDED AGAINST AN ASSISTED PERSON

Security for costs given by assisted person
123. Where in any proceedings an assisted person is required to give security for costs, the amount of such security shall not exceed the amount which could be ordered under section 17(1) of the Act.

Assisted person's liability for costs
124.—(1) Where proceedings have been concluded in which an assisted person (including, for the purpose of this regulation, a person who was an assisted person in respect of those proceedings) is liable or would have been liable for costs if he had not been an assisted person, no costs attributable to the period during which his certificate was in force shall be recoverable from

him until the court has determined the amount of his liability in accordance with section 17(1) of the Act.

(2) Where the assisted person's certificate does not relate to, or has been amended so that it no longer relates to the whole of the proceedings, the court shall nevertheless make a determination under section 17(1) of the Act in respect of that part of the proceedings to which the certificate relates.

(3) The amount of an assisted person's liability for costs shall be determined by the court which tried or heard the proceedings.

Affidavit of means by unassisted party

125.—(1) Any person, not being himself an assisted person, who is a party to proceedings (other than authorised summary proceedings) to which an assisted person is a party, may file in the appropriate court office or registry an affidavit exhibiting a statement setting out the rate of his own income and amount of his own capital and any other facts relevant to the determination of his means in accordance with section 17(1) of the Act.

(2) Any person filing an affidavit under paragraph (1) shall serve a copy of it, together with the exhibit, upon the assisted person's solicitor, who shall forthwith serve him with a copy of the certificate and shall send a copy of the affidavit to the Area Director.

Determination of liability for costs

126. In determining the amount of the assisted person's liability for costs—

(a) his dwelling-house, clothes, household furniture and the tools and implements of his trade shall be left out of account to the like extent as they are left out of account by the assessment officer in determining his disposable income and disposable capital; and

(b) any document which may have been sent to the court office or registry or filed or exhibited under these Regulations shall, subject to regulation 128, be evidence of the fact stated therein.

Postponement, adjournment or referral of determination

127. The court may, if it thinks fit—

(a) postpone or adjourn the determination for such time and to such place (including chambers) as the court thinks fit; or

(b) refer to a master, registrar or the Clerk of the Parliaments or (in the case of an appeal from a decision of the Crown Court or a court of summary jurisdiction) to the chief clerk or clerk to the justices of the court from which the appeal is brought, for investigation (in chambers or elsewhere) any question of fact relevant to the determination, and require him to report his findings on that question to the court.

Oral examination of parties

128.—(1) The court may, if it thinks fit, order the assisted person and any party who has filed an affidavit pursuant to regulation 125 to attend for oral examination as to his means and as to any other facts (whether stated in any document before the court or otherwise) which may be relevant to the determination of the amount of the assisted person's liability for costs and may permit any party to give evidence and call witnesses.

(2) Where the court has made an order under regulation 127(b), the person to whom the matter has been referred for investigation may exercise the power conferred on the court by this regulation.

Order for costs

129. The court may direct—

(a) that payment under the order for costs shall be limited to such amount, payable in instalments or otherwise (including an amount to be determined on taxation), as the court thinks reasonable having regard to all the circumstances; or

(b) where the court thinks it reasonable that no payment should be made immediately or that the assisted person should have no liability for payment, that payment under the order for costs be suspended either until such date as the court may determine or indefinitely.

Variation of order for costs

130. The party in whose favour an order for costs is made may, within six years from the date on which it was made, apply to the court for the order to be varied on the ground that—

(a) material additional information as to the assisted person's means, being information which could not have been obtained by that party with reasonable diligence at the time the order was made, is available; or

(b) there has been a change in the assisted person's circumstances since the date of the order;

and on any such application the order may be varied as the court thinks fit; but save as aforesaid the determination of the court shall be final.

Assisted person acting in representative, fiduciary or official capacity

131. Where an order for costs is made against an assisted person who is concerned in the proceedings in a representative, fiduciary or official capacity, he shall have the benefit of section 17(1) of the Act and his personal resources shall not (unless there is reason to the contrary) be taken into account for that purpose, but regard shall be had to the value of the property or estate, or the amount of the fund out of which he is entitled to be indemnified.

Assisted person a minor

132. Where a minor is an assisted person, his means for the purpose of determining his liability for costs under section 17(1) of the Act shall be taken as including the means of any person whose resources have been taken into account under the Civil Legal Aid (Assessment of Resources) Regulations 1989(a) by the assessment officer in assessing the disposable income and disposable capital of the minor.

Order against next friend or guardian ad litem

133. Where an order for costs is made against a next friend or guardian *ad litem* of an assisted person who is a minor or patient, he shall have the benefit of section 17(1) of the Act as it applies to an assisted person and the means of the next friend or guardian *ad litem* shall, for the purposes of regulation 132, be taken as being the means of the minor or, as the case may be, of the patient.

PART XIV

COSTS OF UNASSISTED PARTIES OUT OF THE FUND

Time and form of application

134.—(1) An application for an order under section 18 of the Act may be made at any time and in any manner in which an application for an order for costs might be made in respect of the same proceedings if none of the parties were receiving legal aid.

(2) Any proceedings in respect of which a separate certificate could properly be issued shall be treated as separate proceedings for the purposes of section 18 of the Act.

Unassisted party acting in representative, fiduciary or official capacity

135. Where an unassisted party is concerned in proceedings only in a representative, fiduciary or official capacity, then for the purposes of section 18(4)(b) of the Act the court shall not take into account his personal resources, but shall have regard to the value of the property, estate or fund out of which the unassisted party is entitled to be indemnified and may in its discretion also have regard to the resources of the persons, if any, including the unassisted party where appropriate, who are beneficially interested in that property, estate or fund.

Appearance by unassisted party and Area Director

136.—(1) The unassisted party and the Area Director may appear at any hearing or inquiry under Parts XIII and XIV of these Regulations.

(2) The Area Director may, instead of appearing, submit written representations concerning the application and such representations shall be:

(a) supported by an affidavit sworn by the Area Director; and

(b) sent to the proper officer of the court, with a copy to the unassisted party, not less than seven days before the hearing or inquiry to which they relate.

Applications in respect of magistrates' court proceedings

137.—(1) Where an application for an order under section 18 of the Act is made in respect of authorised summary proceedings, the court, instead of making an order forthwith, may in its discretion either—

(a) adjourn the hearing of the application; or

(b) dismiss the application.

(2) If the court adjourns the hearing of the application, the unassisted party shall swear an affidavit of costs and resources containing the matters specified in Schedule 2, which he shall produce at the adjourned hearing and, not

less than 21 days before the adjourned hearing, the unassisted party shall serve notice of the date and time of the hearing on the Area Director, with a copy of his affidavit of costs and resources together with any exhibits and supporting documents.

Applications in respect of county court proceedings
138. On application for an order under section 18 of the Act made in respect of proceedings in or on appeal from a county court, the court shall not make an order under that section forthwith, but may in its discretion—

    (a) refer the application to the registrar for hearing and determination; or

    (b) adjourn the application; or

    (c) dismiss the application,

and, in this regulation and regulations 139 to 142, "registrar" means the registrar of the county court in which the proceedings were tried or determined or from which the appeal was brought.

Procedure where application referred to registrar for determination
139. Where a court in accordance with regulation 138(a) refers an application to the registrar for hearing and determination—

    (a) the provisions of regulation 142 shall apply as if the registrar were the court and the court had adjourned the hearing of the application to a date to be fixed; and

    (b) the unassisted party or the Area Director may appeal to the judge on a point of law from the registrar's determination within 14 days of the date on which it was given.

Reference to registrar for inquiry and report
140. The court may, if it adjourns the hearing of an application in accordance with regulation 138(b), make an order referring it to the registrar for inquiry and report; and, if such an order is made—

    (a) the court shall serve a copy of its order on the unassisted party;

    (b) within 21 days of the court making its order (or such longer time as the court may allow), the unassisted party shall file an affidavit of costs and resources (with any exhibits and supporting documents) together with a copy; and

    (c) the court shall serve a copy of its order and of the unassisted party's affidavit of costs and resources filed under sub-paragraph (b) on the Area Director.

Procedure on inquiry and report
141.—(1) As soon as a copy of the order of the court and the affidavit of costs and resources have been served on the Area Director in accordance with regulation 140(1)(c), the registrar shall give the unassisted party and the Area Director not less than 21 days' notice of the date and time when he proposes to conduct his inquiry.

(2) In exercising his functions under this regulation, the registrar shall have the same powers as a taxing officer has in the exercise of his functions under the County Court Rules 1981.

(3) On completing his inquiry, the registrar shall report to the court in writing, and shall at the same time send a copy of his report to the unassisted party and the Area Director.

(4) When the court has received the registrar's report, it shall give the unassisted party and the Area Director 21 days' notice of the day appointed for the hearing and determination of the application in chambers.

Procedure where application adjourned

142. If the court adjourns the hearing of an application in accordance with regulation 138(b) but does not refer it to the registrar for inquiry and report:

(a) within 21 days of the adjournment, the unassisted party shall file an affidavit of costs and resources (with any exhibits and supporting documents) together with a copy; and

(b) not less than 21 days before the adjourned hearing, the court shall serve on the Area Director notice of the date fixed together with a copy of the affidavit of costs and resources filed under sub-paragraph (a).

Applications in respect of proceedings in the Supreme Court and House of Lords

143.—(1) On an application for an order under section 18 of the Act made in respect of proceedings in the Supreme Court (except proceedings on appeal from a county court) or in the House of Lords, the court shall not make an order forthwith, but may in its discretion—

(a) refer the application to a master or registrar for hearing and determination; or

(b) adjourn the hearing of the application; or

(c) dismiss the application,

and, in relation to proceedings in the Court of Appeal, "registrar" means the registrar of civil appeals, or, in respect of appeals from the Employment Appeal Tribunal or from the Restrictive Practices Court, the registrar of that Tribunal or Court, as the case may be.

(2) Where the application is referred to a registrar under paragraph (1)(a), the provisions of regulations 139 and 142 shall apply with any necessary modifications.

Procedure where application referred to master for determination

144. Where the court in accordance with regulation 143(1)(a) refers the application to a master for hearing and determination—

(a) the provisions of regulation 147 shall apply as if the master were the court and the court had adjourned the hearing of the application to a date to be fixed; and

(b) the master shall have the same powers as a taxing officer has in the exercise of his functions under Order 62 of the Rules of the Supreme Court 1965; and

(c) the unassisted party or the Area Director may appeal to a judge in chambers on a point of law within 14 days from the determination of the master.

Reference to master for inquiry and report

145. The court may, if it adjourns the hearing of an application in accordance with regulation 143(1)(b), make an order referring it to the master for inquiry and report; and if, such an order is made, then within 21 days of the court making the order (or such longer time as the master may allow) the unassisted party shall:

(a) file an affidavit of costs and resources;

(b) lodge a copy of the order of the court and of his affidavit of costs and resources, together with original exhibits and any other documents necessary to support the affidavit, with the master; and at the same time

(c) serve a copy of the order of the court and of his affidavit of costs and resources (and of any exhibits and supporting documents) on the Area Director.

Procedure on inquiry and report

146.—(1) Where the unassisted party has complied with the requirements of regulation 145, the master shall give the unassisted party and the Area Director not less than 21 days' notice of the date and time when he proposes to conduct his inquiry.

(2) In exercising his functions under this regulation, the master shall have the same powers as a taxing officer has in the exercise of his functions under Order 62 of the Rules of the Supreme Court 1965.

(3) On completing his inquiry, the master shall report to the court in writing, and shall at the same time send a copy of his report to the unassisted party and to the Area Director.

(4) When the court has received the report of the master, the unassisted party shall seek an appointment for the hearing and determination of the application in chambers, and shall give the Area Director not less than 21 days' notice of the date and time so fixed.

Procedure where application adjourned

147. If the court adjourns the hearing of an application in accordance with regulation 143 but does not refer it for inquiry and report, then—

(a) within 21 days of the adjournment, the unassisted party shall file an affidavit of costs and resources together with original exhibits and any other documents necessary to support the affidavit; and

(b) not less than 21 days before the adjourned hearing, the unassisted party shall serve notice on the Area Director of the date and time of the adjourned hearing together with a copy of his affidavit of costs and resources (and of any exhibits and supporting documents).

PART XV

PARTICULAR COURTS AND TRIBUNALS

The Lands Tribunal

148.—(1) In this regulation—

"the tribunal" means the Lands Tribunal established by section 1(1)(b) of the Lands Tribunal Act 1949 and

"the registrar" means the registrar of the tribunal.

(2) Except in so far as otherwise provided by this regulation, these Regulations shall apply to applications for legal aid for proceedings in the tribunal and in the conduct of all proceedings in it for which a certificate is granted in like manner as they apply to applications for legal aid for, and the conduct of, proceedings in any court.

(3) Where any power to do any act or exercise any jurisdiction or discretion is conferred by these Regulations on a court it shall be exercised by the tribunal and may, unless it is exercisable only during the hearing of the proceedings, be exercised by the registrar.

(4) Notwithstanding anything in regulation 105 or 107, the following provisions shall have effect in relation to proceedings in the tribunal to which an assisted person is a party:

(a) where a final decision is given in writing by the tribunal, it shall, in addition to any direction as to costs, contain a direction that the costs of any assisted person shall be taxed on the standard basis and the costs shall be so taxed by the registrar;

(b) where the proceedings are brought to an end without a direction having been given under sub-paragraph (a), the costs of any assisted person shall be taxed by the registrar on the standard basis; and

(c) in taxing the costs of any assisted person the registrar shall have power to determine as the appropriate scale for the taxation, one of the scales of costs for the time being prescribed by the County Court Rules 1981.

The Employment Appeal Tribunal

149.—(1) In this regulation—

"the Appeal Tribunal" means the Employment Appeal Tribunal established under section 135(1) of the Employment Protection (Consolidation) Act 1988; and

"the registrar" means the registrar of the Appeal Tribunal and includes any officer of the Appeal Tribunal authorised to act on behalf of the registrar.

(2) Except in so far as otherwise provided by this regulation, these Regulations shall apply to applications for legal aid for proceedings in the Appeal Tribunal and to the conduct of all proceedings in it for which a certificate is granted, in the same way as they apply to applications for legal aid for, and the conduct of, proceedings in any court.

(3) Where any power to do any act or exercise any jurisdiction or discretion is conferred by these Regulations on a court, it shall in relation to proceedings in the Appeal Tribunal, be exercised by the Tribunal and may, unless it is exercisable only during the hearing of the proceedings by a judge or member of the Appeal Tribunal or by the Appeal Tribunal as required to be constituted by paragraph 16 of Schedule 11 to the Employment Protection (Consolidation) Act 1978, be exercised by the registrar.

(4) Where it appears to the Area Director that an application for a certificate relates to proceedings in the Appeal Tribunal which are likely to be conducted in Scotland, he shall transmit the application forthwith to the Chief Executive of the Legal Aid Board in Scotland and shall notify the applicant and his solicitor accordingly.

(5) Where it appears to the Area Director doubtful whether the proceedings to which an application for a certificate relates will be conducted in the Appeal Tribunal in England and Wales or in Scotland, he shall request the registrar to determine that question and that determination shall be binding upon the Area Director.

(6) Where a certificate has been issued and there is a change of circumstances regarding the conduct of the proceedings in that, by direction of the Appeal Tribunal, they will be wholly or partly conducted in Scotland—

(a) the certificate shall remain in force;

(b) the assisted person shall continue to be represented in the proceedings in Scotland by the solicitor who represented him in England and that solicitor may instruct either a member of the English or the Scottish Bar; and

(c) no question as to the propriety of appearing in Scotland shall be raised on a taxation or on an assessment in accordance with regulation 105.

(7) The costs of an assisted person in respect of proceedings in the Appeal Tribunal shall be assessed in accordance with regulation 105 or taxed on the standard basis by a taxing master of the Supreme Court and the provisions of Order 62 of the Rules of the Supreme Court 1965 shall apply, with the necessary modifications, to the taxation of those costs as if the proceedings in the Appeal Tribunal were a cause or matter in the Supreme Court.

The Commons Commissioners

150.—(1) In this regulation, "a commissioner" means a Commons Commissioner appointed under section 17(1) of the Commons Registration Act 1965.

(2) Except in so far as otherwise provided by this regulation, these Regulations shall apply to applications for legal aid for proceedings before a commissioner and to the conduct of all proceedings before him for which a certificate is granted, in the same way as they apply to applications for legal aid for, and the conduct of, proceedings in any court.

(3) Where any power to do any act or exercise any jurisdiction or discretion is conferred on a court by these Regulations, it shall, in relation to proceedings before a commissioner, be exercised by him.

(4) The costs of an assisted person in respect of proceedings before a commissioner shall be taxed (or assessed) as if they were costs of proceedings in a county court.

The Restrictive Practice Court

151.—(1) In this regulation—

"the Court" means the Court established by section 1 of the Restrictive Practices Court Act 1976, and

"the proper officer of the Court" shall have the same meaning as in the Restrictive Practices Court Rules 1976.

(2) Except in so far as otherwise provided by this regulation, these Regulations shall apply to applications for legal aid for proceedings in the Court under Part III of the Fair Trading Act 1973 and to any proceedings in the Court in consequence of an order made, or undertaking given to the Court, under that Part of the Act, and to the Conduct of all such proceedings for which a certificate is granted, in the same way as they apply to applications for legal aid for, and the conduct of, proceedings in any court.

(3) Where any power to do any act or exercise any jurisdiction or discretion is conferred by these Regulations on a court it shall in relation to proceedings in the Court be exercised by that Court and may, unless it is exercisable only during the hearing of any proceedings by a judge or by the Court, be exercisable by the proper officer of the Court.

(4) Where it appears to the Area Director that an application for a certificate relates to proceedings in the Court which are likely to be conducted in Scotland or Northern Ireland, he shall transmit the application forthwith to the Chief Executive of the Legal Aid Board in Scotland or the Secretary of the Legal Aid Department of the Incorporated Law Society of Northern Ireland, as the case may be, and shall notify the applicant and his solicitor accordingly.

(5) Where it appears to the Area Director doubtful whether the proceedings to which an application for a certificate relates will be conducted in the Court in England and Wales or in Scotland or Northern Ireland, he shall request the proper officer of the Court to determine that question and that determination shall be binding upon the Area Director.

(6) Where a certificate has been issued and there is a change of circumstances regarding the conduct of the proceedings in that, by order of the Court, they will be wholly or partly conducted in Scotland or Northern Ireland—

(a) the certificate shall remain in force; and

(b) for any proceedings in Scotland—
   (i) the assisted person shall continue to be represented in the proceedings by the solicitor who represented him in England and Wales and that solicitor may instruct a member of the English or the Scottish Bar; and
   (ii) no question as to the propriety of appearing in Scotland shall be raised on a taxation or on an assessment in accordance with regulation 105; and

(c) for any proceedings in Northern Ireland, the assisted person shall continue to be represented in the proceedings by the solicitor who represented him in England and Wales and that solicitor shall instruct as his agent a solicitor on the panel maintained by the Incorporated Law Society of Northern Ireland of solicitors willing to act for assisted persons before the Court.

(7) The costs of an assisted person in respect of proceedings in the Court shall be assessed in accordance with regulation 105 or taxed on the standard basis by a taxing master of the Supreme Court, and the provisions of Order 62 of the Rules of the Supreme Court 1965 shall apply, with the necessary modifications, to the taxation of those costs as if the proceedings in the Court were a cause or matter in the Supreme Court.

SCHEDULES

SCHEDULE 1
REGULATIONS REVOKED

Title	Reference
The Legal Aid (General) Regulations 1980	S.I. 1980/1894
The Legal Aid (General) (Amendment) Regulations 1981	S.I. 1981/173
The Legal Aid (General) (Amendment) Regulations 1982	S.I. 1982/1892
The Legal Aid (General) (Amendment) Regulations 1983	S.I. 1983/424
The Legal Aid (General) (Amendment) (No. 2) Regulations 1983	S.I. 1983/1483
The Legal Aid (General) (Amendment) Regulations 1986	S.I. 1986/272
The Legal Aid (General) (Amendment) (No. 2) Regulations 1986	S.I. 1986/1186
The Legal Aid (General) (Amendment) (No. 3) Regulations 1986	S.I. 1986/2135
The Legal Aid (General) (Amendment) Regulations 1988	S.I. 1988/460
The Legal Aid (General) (Amendment) (No. 2) Regulations 1988	S.I. 1988/1938

SCHEDULE 2
MATTERS TO BE INCLUDED IN AN AFFIDAVIT OF COSTS AND RESOURCES

1. An estimate of the unassisted party's inter partes costs of the proceedings in respect of which his application is made, supported by—

(a) particulars of the estimated costs in the form of a summary bill of costs; and

(b) all necessary documentary evidence to substantiate each item in the bill.

2. A statement, supported by evidence, of the unassisted party's financial resources of every kind during the period beginning three years before his application is made, and of his estimated future financial resources and expectations.

3. A declaration that to the best of his knowledge and belief the unassisted party has not, and at any relevant time has not had and will not have any financial resources or expectations not specified in the statement described in paragraph 2 above.

4. A declaration that the unassisted party has not at any time deliberately forgone or deprived himself of any financial resources or expectations with a view to furthering his application.

5. A statement supported by evidence of the unassisted party's reasonable financial commitments during the period covered by his statement described in paragraph 2 above, including, if desired, his estimated solicitor and own client costs of the proceedings in respect of which his application is made.

6.—(1) If the unassisted party has, or at any relevant time has had, a spouse, his statements and declarations described in paragraphs 2 to 5 above shall also take account of and (to the best of this knowledge and belief) specify that spouse's financial resources, expectations and commitments, unless he or she had a contrary interest to the unassisted party in the proceedings in respect of which his application is made, or the unassisted party and his spouse are or at the relevant time were living separate and apart, or for some other reason it would be either inequitable or impracticable for the unassisted party to comply with the requirements of his paragraph.

(2) Paragraph (1) shall apply to a man and woman who are living with each other in the same household as husband and wife as it applies to the parties to a marriage.

7. Full particulars of any application for legal aid made by the unassisted party in connection with the proceedings in respect of which his application is made, including the date and reference number of any such application and the Area Director to whom it was made.

EXPLANATORY NOTE
(This note is not part of The Regulations)

These Regulations replace, with amendments, the Legal Aid (General) Regulations 1980 (as subsequently amended). The main changes made reflect the transfer of responsibility for administration of the legal aid scheme from the Law Society to the Legal Aid Board established by the Legal Aid Act 1988.

Other important changes are—

(a) to require an assisted person's solicitor, where the Board makes such a request, to certify that it is reasonable for the assisted person to continue to receive legal aid (regulation 70(2), (3));

(b) to make provision for payments on account of costs and fees incurred by solicitors and counsel and of disbursements (regulations 100, 101);

(c) to make fresh provision for the deferment of solicitors' profit costs (regulation 102);

(d) to provide for work done immediately prior to the issue of an emergency certificate to be deemed in certain circumstances to be work done under the certificate (regulation 103(6));

(e) to provide (subject to the transitional provision in regulation 1(3)) for the assessment of costs by Area Directors, for reviews of such assessments by area committees, and for appeals from such reviews to a committee appointed by the Board (regulations 104, 105 and 106);

(f) to require solicitors to inform counsel where counsel's fees are reduced or disallowed on assessment or taxation (regulations 105(8), 106(3) and 112); and

(g) to enable assisted persons who have a financial interest in the taxation of costs to take steps to safeguard their interest (regulation 119).

Civil Legal Aid (Assessment of Resources) Regulations 1989*

Coming into force April 1, 1989

ARRANGEMENT OF REGULATIONS

---

* As amended by the Civil Legal Aid (Assessment of Resources) (Amendment) Regulations 1990 (S.I. 1990 No. 484) with effect from April 9, 1990 unless otherwise stated.

The Lord Chancellor, in exercise of the powers conferred on him by sections 15(1), 16, 34 and 43 of the Legal Aid Act 1988 and with the consent of the Treasury, hereby makes the following Regulations:—

Citation and commencement
1. These Regulations may be cited as the Civil Legal Aid (Assessment of Resources) Regulations 1989 and shall come into force on 1st April 1989.

Revocations
2. The Regulations specified in Schedule 1 are hereby revoked.

Interpretation
3.—(1) In these Regulations, unless the context otherwise requires—

"the Act" means the Legal Aid Act 1988;

"area committee," "Area Director" and "assessment officer" have the meanings assigned to them by the Civil Legal Aid (General) Regulations 1989;

"certificate" means a legal aid certificate issued in accordance with the Civil Legal Aid (General) Regulations 1989;

"child" means a person—

(a) under the age that is for the time being the upper limit of compulsory school age within the meaning of the Education Act 1944(**c**); or

(b) over the limit of compulsory school age and either receiving full-time instruction at an educational establishment or undergoing training for a trade, profession; or vocation;

"contribution" and "maximum contribution" have the meanings assigned to them by the Civil Legal Aid (General) Regulations 1989;

"disposable capital" and "disposable income" have the meanings assigned to them by regulation 4;

"income" includes:

(a) benefits,

(b) privileges, and

(c) any sum payable (whether voluntarily or under a court order, the terms of any instrument or otherwise) for the purpose of the maintenance of a child;

"legal aid" means representation under Part IV of the Act;

"make an assessment," in relation to the assessment officer, means to assess the disposable income, disposable capital and maximum contribution of the person concerned;

"period of computation" means the period of 12 months next ensuing from the date of the application for a certificate, or such other period of 12 months as in the particular circumstances of any case the assessment officer may consider to be appropriate;

"person concerned" means the person—

(a) whose disposable income and disposable capital are to be assessed or reassessed; or

(b) whose resources are to be treated as the resources of any other person under these Regulations.

(2) Any reference in these Regulations to a regulation or Schedule by number means the regulation or Schedule so numbered in these Regulations.

Computation of disposable capital, disposable income and maximum contribution

4.—(1) Subject to the provisions of these Regulations, the assessment officer shall—

(a) take into account the financial resources of the person concerned; and

(b) compute his income and capital in accordance with Schedules 2 and 3;

and, in these Regulations, "disposable income" and "disposable capital" mean the amounts of income and capital available for the making of a contribution after the person concerned's income and capital have been computed in accordance with those Schedules.

(2) Subject to paragraph (3) below, legal aid shall be available to a person whose disposable income does not exceed £6,350 a year but a person may be refused legal aid where—

(a) his disposable capital exceeds £6,310; and

(b) it appears to the Area Director that he could afford to proceed without legal aid.

(3) Where the subject matter of the dispute in respect of which the legal aid application has been made includes a claim in respect of personal injuries, legal aid shall be available to a person whose disposable income does not exceed £7,000 a year but a person may be refused legal aid where—

(a) his disposable capital exceeds £8,000; and

(b) it appears to the Area Director that he could afford to proceed without legal aid.

(4) The maximum contribution which a person who desires to receive legal aid shall be liable to make is—

(a) where his disposable income exceeds £2,645 a year, a contribution in respect of disposable income not greater than one quarter of the excess;

(b) where his disposable capital exceeds £3,000, a contribution in respect of disposable capital not greater than the excess.

(5) In this regulation "personal injuries" includes any death and any disease or other impairment of a person's physical or mental condition.

Amended by the Civil Legal Aid (Assessment of Resources) (Amendment) Regulations 1990 (S.I. 1990 No. 484).

Subject matter of dispute

5.—(1) In computing the income or capital of the person concerned, there shall be excluded the value of the subject matter of the dispute in respect of which the legal aid application has been made.

(2) Periodical payments of maintenance (whether made voluntarily or otherwise) shall not be treated as the subject matter of the dispute for the purposes of paragraph (1).

Application in representative, fiduciary or official capacity
6. Where an application for legal aid is made by a person who is concerned in the proceedings only in a representative, fiduciary or official capacity, the assessment officer shall, in computing the income and capital of that person and the amount of any contribution to be made—

(a) where so requested by the Area Director, assess the value of any property or estate or the amount of any fund out of which that person is entitled to be indemnified and the disposable income, disposable capital and maximum contribution of any persons (including that person if appropriate), who might benefit from the outcome of the proceedings; and

(b) except in so far as they are assessed under paragraph (a), disregard the personal resources of that person.

Resources of spouses, etc.
7.—(1) Subject to paragraph (2), in computing the income and capital of the person concerned the resources of his or her spouse shall be treated as his or her resources.

(2) The resources of the spouse of the person concerned shall not be treated as his or her resources if—

(a) the spouse has a contrary interest in the dispute in respect of which the legal aid application is made; or

(b) the person concerned and the spouse are living separate and apart.

(3) Paragraphs (1) and (2) above and Schedules 2 and 3 shall apply to a man and a woman who are living with each other in the same household as husband and wife as it applies to the parties to a marriage.

Resources of an applicant who is a child
8.—[*Omitted by the Civil Legal Aid (Assessment of Resources) (Amendment) Regulations 1990 (S.I. 1990 No. 484).*]

Deprivation or conversion of resources
9. Where it appears to the assessment officer that the person concerned has with intent to reduce the amount of his disposable income or disposable capital, whether for the purpose of making himself elegible for legal aid, reducing his liability to pay a contribution towards legal aid or otherwise—

(a) directly or indirectly deprived himself of any resources; or

(b) converted any part of his resources into resources which under these Regulations are to be wholly or partly disregarded, or in respect of which nothing is to be included in determining the resources of that person;

the resources of which he has so deprived himself or which he has so converted shall be treated as part of his resources or as not so converted as the case may be and, for this purpose, resources which are to be wholly or partly disregarded shall include the repayment of money borrowed on the security of a dwelling.

Amended by the Civil Legal Aid (Assessment of Resources) (Amendment) Regulations 1990 (S.I. 1990 No. 484).

Notification of the assessment officer's decision

10.—(1) The assessment officer shall make an assessment of the disposable capital, disposable income and maximum contribution of the person concerned.

(2) The assessment made under paragraph (1) shall be communicated in writing to the Area Director and the assessment officer may draw attention to any special circumstances affecting the manner in which any contribution is to be made.

Duty of the person concerned to report change in financial circumstances

11. The person concerned shall inform the Area Director of any change in his financial circumstances which has occurred since the original assessment was made and which he has reason to believe might affect the terms on which the certificate was granted or its continuation.

Re-assessment on change of circumstances

12.—(1) Where:

(a) it appears that the circumstances upon which the assessment officer has assessed the disposable income or disposable capital of the person concerned have altered so that:

(i) his disposable income may have increased by an amount greater than £750 or decreased by an amount greater than £300; or

(ii) his disposable capital may have increased by an amount greater than £750;

or

(b) new information which is relevant to the assessment has come to light;

the assessment officer shall re-assess that person's disposable income or disposable capital and maximum contribution, as the case may be, unless it appears to him to be unlikely that any significant change in that person's liability to make a contribution will result from such a re-assessment.

(2) For the purpose of making a re-assessment under paragraph (1), the amount and value of every resource of a capital nature acquired since the date of the legal aid application shall be ascertained as at the date of receipt of that resource.

Further assessment of resources outside the original period of computation

13.—(1) Where a certificate is still in force after the expiration of the period of computation and the Area Director considers that the current financial circumstances of the person concerned are such that he could afford to proceed without legal aid, he may request the assessment officer to make a further assessment of the current disposable income and current disposable capital of the person concerned with a view to discharging the certificate.

(2) Where a request under paragraph (1) is made, the assessment officer shall make a further assessment in accordance with the provisions of Schedules 2 and 3 and, for this purpose—

(a) the period of computation shall be the period of twelve months following the date of the Area Director's request; and

(b) the amount and value of every resource of a capital nature acquired since the date of the legal aid application shall be ascertained as at the date of receipt of that resource.

Amendment of assessment due to error or mistake

14. Where it appears to the assessment officer that—

(a) there has been some error or mistake in the assessment of a person's disposable income, disposable capital or maximum contribution or in any computation or estimate upon which such assessment was based; and

(b) it would be just and equitable to correct the error or mistake,

the officer may make an amended assessment which shall, for all purposes, be substituted for the original assessment and have effect in all respects as if it were the original assessment.

Power of assessment officer to estimate the resources of the person concerned

15.—(1) Where the Area Director informs the assessment officer that the person concerned requires a certificate as a matter of urgency and the officer is not satisfied that he can make an assessment and communicate it to the Area Director by the time that he is requested so to do, the officer may, on the basis of the information then available to him, make an estimate of the disposable income and disposable capital of the person concerned and of his maximum contribution.

(2) The assessment officer shall communicate any estimate made under paragraph (1) to the Area Director in writing and, until the making of a full assessment, the estimate shall be treated as if it were an assessment and section 17(1) of the Act and regulation 4(2) to (4) above shall have effect as if the disposable income, disposable capital and maximum contribution of the person concerned were of the amounts specified in the estimate.

(3) In any case in which the assessment officer makes an estimate under paragraph (1) he shall, upon receiving such additional information as he may require, make an assessment and shall communicate it to the Area Director in writing and the assessment shall for all purposes take the place of the estimate.

Amended by the Civil Legal Aid (Assessment of Resources) (Amendment) Regulations 1990 (S.I. 1990 No. 484).

SCHEDULES

SCHEDULE 1

REGULATIONS REVOKED

Title	Reference
The Legal Aid (Assessment of Resources) Regulations 1980	S.I. 1980/1630
The Legal Aid (Assessment of Resources) (Amendment) Regulations 1983	S.I. 1983/423
The Legal Aid (Assessment of Resources) (Amendment) Regulations 1986	S.I. 1986/276
The Legal Aid (Assessment of Resources) (Amendment) Regulations 1988	S.I. 1988/467
The Legal Aid (Financial Conditions) Regulations 1988	S.I. 1988/667

SCHEDULE 2

COMPUTATION OF INCOME

1. The income of the person concerned from any source shall be taken to be the income which that person may reasonably expect to receive (in cash or in kind) during the period of computation and, in the absence of other means of ascertaining it, shall be taken to be the income received during the preceding year.

2. The income in respect of any emolument, benefit or privilege which is received otherwise than in cash shall be estimated at such sum as in all the circumstances is just and equitable.

3.—(1) The income from a trade, business or gainful occupation other than an employment at a wage or salary shall be deemed to be the profits there from which have accrued or will accrue to the person concerned in respect of the period of computation, and, in computing such profits, the assessment officer may have regard to the profits of the last accounting period of such trade, business or gainful occupation for which accounts have been prepared.

(2) In ascertaining the profits under paragraph (1), there shall be deducted all sums necessarily expended to earn those profits, but no deduction shall be made in respect of the living expenses of that person or of any member of his family or household, except in so far as such member of his family or household is wholly or mainly employed in such trade or business and such living expenses form part of his remuneration.

4.—(1) In computing the income of the person concerned, there shall be deducted the total amount of tax which it is estimated would be payable by the person concerned if his income (as computed in accordance with paragraphs 1 to 3 above but not taking into account the provisions of regulation 5) were his income for a fiscal year and his liability for tax in that year were to be ascertained by reference to that income and not by reference to his income in any other year or period.

(2) For the purposes of this paragraph, tax shall be estimated at the rate provided by and after making all appropriate allowances, deductions or reliefs in accordance with the statutory provisions relating to income tax in force for the fiscal year in which the legal aid application is made.

4A. In computing the income of the person concerned, there shall be deducted any sums payable (net of community charge benefit) by the person concerned in respect of the personal community charge to which he is subject by virtue of section 2 of the Local Government Finance Act 1988.

Amended by the Civil Legal Aid (Assessment of Resources) (Amendment) Regulations 1990 (S.I. 1990 No. 484), with effect from April 1, 1990.

5. Where the person concerned or his spouse is in receipt of income support paid under the Social Security Act 1986, the person concerned shall, for the period during which income support is received, be deemed to have a disposable income which does not exceed the figure for the time being specified in regulation 4(4)(a).

Amended by the Civil Legal Aid (Assessment of Resources) (Amendment) Regulations 1990 (S.I. 1990 No. 484) with effect from April 1, 1990.

6. There shall be disregarded—

(a) attendance allowance paid under the Social Security Acts 1975–1988(**b**);

(b) mobility allowance paid under the Social Security Acts 1975–1988;

(c) constant attendance allowance paid as an increase to a disablement pension under section 61 of the Social Security Act 1975(**c**); and

(d) any payment made out of the social fund under section 32 of the Social Security Act 1986(**d**).

7. Where the income of the person concerned consists, wholly or in part, of a wage or salary from employment, there shall be deducted—

(a) the reasonable expenses of travelling to and from his place of employment;

(b) the amount of any payments reasonably made for membership of a trade union or professional organisation; and

(c) where it would be reasonable so to do, an amount to provide for the care of any dependant child living with the person concerned during the time that person is absent from home by reason of his employment; and

(d) the amount of any contribution paid, whether under a legal obligation or not, to an occupational pension scheme within the meaning of the Social Security Pensions Act 1975(**e**) or to a personal pension scheme within the meaning of the Social Security Act 1986.

8. There shall be a deduction in respect of contributions payable by the person concerned (whether by deduction or otherwise) under the Social Security Acts 1975 to 1988, of the amount estimated to be so payable in the 12 months following the application for a certificate.

9.—(1) In the case of a householder, there shall be a deduction in respect of rent of the main or only dwelling of the amount of the net rent payable, or such part thereof as is reasonable in the circumstances, and the assessment officer shall decide which is the main dwelling where the person concerned resides in more than one dwelling in which he has an interest.

(2) For the purposes of this paragraph, "rent" includes—

(a) the annual rent payable; and

(b) a sum in respect of yearly outgoings borne by the householder including, in particular, any domestic rates and water and sewerage charges, a reasonable allowance towards any necessary expenditure on repairs and insurance and any annual instalment (whether of interest or of capital) payable in respect of a mortgage debt or heritable security charged on the house in which the householder resides or has an interest;

and, in calculating the amount of rent payable, any housing benefit paid under the Social Security Act 1986 shall be deducted from the amount of rent payable.

(3) In this paragraph, the expression "net rent" means the rent less any proceeds of sub-letting any part of the premises in respect of which the said rent is paid or the outgoings are incurred except that, where any person or persons other than the person concerned, his or her spouse or any dependant of his or hers is accommodated, otherwise than as a sub-tenant, in the premises for which the rent is paid, the rent may be deemed to be reduced by an amount reasonably attributable to such other person or persons.

Amended by the Civil Legal Aid (Assessment of Resources) (Amendment) Regulations 1990 (S.I. 1990 No. 484).

239

10. If the person concerned is not a householder, there shall be a deduction in respect of the cost of his living accommodation of such amount as is reasonable in the circumstances including any net sum payable by him by way of contribution towards the community charge to which the person with a qualifying interest in such accommodation is subject by virtue of section 5 of the Local Government Finance Act 1988.

Amended by the Civil Legal Aid (Assessment of Resources) (Amendment) Regulations 1990 (S.I. 1990 No. 484) with effect from April 1, 1990.

11.—(1) Subject to paragraph (2), in computing the income of the person concerned there shall be a deduction—

(a) in respect of the maintenance of the spouse of the person concerned, where the spouses are living together;

(b) in respect of the maintenance of any dependent child and of any dependent relative of the person concerned, where such persons are members of his household;

at the following rates—

(i) in the case of a spouse at a rate equivalent to 25 per cent. above the amount specified in column (3) of paragraph 6 of Part IV of Schedule 4 to the Social Security Act 1975 (increase for adult dependant of Category A retirement pension) which applied at the beginning of the computation period;

(ii) in the case of a dependent child or a dependent relative, at a rate equivalent to 25 per cent. above the amount specified in paragraph 2 of Part I of Schedule 2 to the Income Support (General) Regulations 1987 which applied at the beginning of the computation period appropriate to the age of the child or relative.

Amended by the Civil Legal Aid (Assessment of Resources) (Amendment) Regulations 1990 (S.I 1990 No. 484).

(2) The assessment officer may reduce any rate provided by virtue of sub-paragraph (1) by taking into account the income and other resources of the dependent child or other dependant to such extent as appears to the officer to be just and equitable.

(3) In ascertaining whether a child is a dependent child or whether a person is a dependent relative for the purposes of this paragraph, regard shall be had to their income and other resources.

12. Where the person concerned is making and, throughout such period as the assessment officer may consider to be adequate, has regularly made *bona fide* payments for the maintenance of—

(a) a spouse who is living apart;

(b) a former spouse;

(c) a child; or

(d) a relative;

who is not a member of the household of the person concerned, there shall be a deduction at the rate of such payments or at such rate (not exceeding the rate of such payments) as in all the circumstances is reasonable.

13. Where the person concerned is required to, or may reasonably provide for any other matter, the assessment officer may make an allowance of such amount as he considers to be reasonable in the circumstances of the case.

14. In computing the income from any source, there shall be disregarded such amount, if any, as the assessment officer considers to be reasonable having regard to the nature of the income or to any other circumstances of the case.

SCHEDULE 3

COMPUTATION OF CAPITAL

1.—(1) Subject to paragraph (2) and to the provisions of these Regulations, in computing the capital of the person concerned, there shall be included the amount or value of every resource of a capital nature belonging to him on the date the legal aid application is made.

(2) Where it comes to the attention of the assessment officer that, between the date the legal aid application is made and the assessment, there has been a substantial fluctuation in the value of a resource or there has been a substantial variation in the nature of a resource affecting the basis of computation of its value, or any resource has ceased to exist or a new resource has come into the possession of the person concerned, the officer shall compute the capital resources of that person in the light of such facts and the resources as so computed shall be taken into account in the assessment.

2. In so far as any resource of a capital nature does not consist of money, its amount or value shall be taken to be—

(a) the amount which that resource would realise if sold in the open market or, if there is only a restricted market for that resource, the amount which it would realise in that market, or

(b) the amount or value assessed in such manner as appears to the assessment officer to be just and equitable.

3. Where money is due to the person concerned, whether it is payable immediately or otherwise and whether payment is secured or not, its value shall be taken to be its present value.

4. Where the person concerned stands in relation to a company in a position analogous to that of a sole owner or partner in the business of that company, the assessment officer may, in lieu of ascertaining the value of his stocks, shares, bonds or debentures in that company, treat that person as if he were a sole owner or partner and compute the amount of his capital in respect of that resource in accordance with paragraph 5 below.

5. Where the person concerned is or is to be treated as sole owner of, or a partner in, any business, the value of such business to him or his share shall be taken to be either—

(a) such sum, or his share of such sum, as the case may be, as could be withdrawn from the assets of such business without substantially impairing the profits of such business or this normal development; or

(b) such sum as that person could borrow on the security of his interest in such business without injuring the commercial credit of that business;

whichever is the greater.

6. The value of any interest in reversion or remainder on the termination of a prior estate, whether legal or equitable, in any real or personal property or in a trust or other fund, whether the person concerned has the sole interest or an interest jointly or in common with other persons or whether his interest is vested or contingent, shall be computed in such manner as is both equitable and practicable.

7. Where the person concerned or his spouse is in receipt of income support paid under the Social Security Act 1986, the person concerned shall, for the period during which income support is received, be deemed to have disposable capital not exceeding the figure for the time being specified in regulation 4(4)(b).

Amended by the Civil Legal Aid (Assessment of Resources) (Amendment) 1990 (S.I. 1990 No. 484).

8. In computing the amount of capital of the person concerned, there shall be wholly disregarded any payment which is made out of the social fund under section 32 of the Social Security Act 1986.

9. Save in exceptional circumstances, no sum shall be included in the amount of the capital of the person concerned in respect of—

(a) the household furniture and effects of the dwelling house occupied by him;

(b) articles of personal clothing; and

(c) the tools and equipment of his trade, unless they form part of the plant or equipment of a business to which the provisions of paragraph 5 of this Schedule apply.

10.—(1) In computing the amount of capital of the person concerned, the value of any interest in the main or only dwelling in which he resides shall be wholly disregarded.

(2) Where the person concerned resides in more than one dwelling in which he has an interest, the assessment officer shall decide which is the main dwelling and shall take into account in respect of the value to him of any interest in a dwelling which is not the main dwelling any sum which might be obtained by borrowing money on the security thereof.

11. Where the person concerned has received or is entitled to receive from a body of which he is a member a sum of money by way of financial assistance towards the cost of the proceedings in respect of which the legal aid application is made, such sum shall be disregarded.

12. The value to the person concerned of any life assurance or endowment policy shall be taken to be the amount which the person concerned could readily borrow on the security thereof.

13. Where under any statute, bond, covenant, guarantee or other instrument, the person concerned is under a contingent liability to pay any sum or is liable to pay a sum not yet ascertained, an allowance shall be made of such an amount as is reasonably likely to become payable within the 12 months immediately following the date of the application for a certificate.

14. Where the person concerned produces evidence which satisfies the assessment officer that the debt or part of the debt will be discharged within the twelve months immediately following the date of the legal aid application, an allowance may be made in respect of any debt owing by the person concerned (other than a debt secured on the dwelling or dwellings in which he resides) to the extent to which the assessment officer considers reasonable.

14A.—(1) Where the person concerned is of pensionable age and his annual disposable income (excluding any net income derived from capital) is less than the figure for the time being prescribed in regulation 4(4)(a) there shall be disregarded the amount of capital as specified in the following table:—

annual disposable income (excluding net income derived from capital)	amount of capital disregard
up to £400	£25,000
£401–900	£20,000
£901–1,400	£15,000
£1,401–1,900	£10,000
£1,901 and above	£ 5,000

(2) in this Schedule "pensionable age" means—

(a) in the case of a man, the age of 65; and

(b) in the case of a woman, the age of 60.

14B. In computing the amount of capital of the person concerned there shall be wholly disregarded any capital payment received from any source which is made in relation to the incident giving rise to the dispute in respect of which the legal aid application has been made.

Amended by the Civil Legal Aid (Assessment of Resources) (Amendment) Regulations 1990 (S.I. 1990 No. 484).

15. In computing the capital of the person concerned, there may also be disregarded such an amount of capital (if any) as the assessment officer may, in his discretion, decide having regard to all the circumstances of the case.

EXPLANATORY NOTE

(This note is not part of the Regulations)

These Regulations replace, with amendments, the Legal Aid (Assessment of Resources) Regulations 1980 (as subsequently amended). These Regulations, together with the Civil Legal Aid (General) Regulations 1989, govern the provision of representation under Part IV of the Legal Aid Act 1988 (legal aid in civil proceedings).

These Regulations make provision for the assessment of the financial resources of the person concerned in order to determine eligibility to receive legal aid and to assess the maximum contribution payable towards the cost of providing representation in the proceedings in respect of which the legal aid application is made.

The main changes made are as follows:

(a) the income and capital eligibility limits (which determine whether a person is eligible to receive legal aid and provide the financial limits above which a contribution is to be payable) are set out in the Regulations and not in the Act (*regulation 4*);

(b) the resources of persons living together as husband and wife are to be treated as if those persons were married (*regulation 7(3)*).

Legal Aid In Criminal and Care Proceedings (General) Regulations 1989*

Coming into force April 1, 1989

ARRANGEMENT OF REGULATIONS

Part I

General

Part II

Applicants for Legal Aid

* As amended by the Legal Aid in Criminal and Care Proceedings (General) (Amendment) Regulations 1990 (S.I. 1990 No. 489) with effect from April 1, 1990 unless otherwise stated.

PART III

STATEMENT OF MEANS AND PAYMENT OF CONTRIBUTIONS

PART IV

LEGAL AID ORDERS

SCHEDULES
1. Regulations revoked
2. Forms
3. Determination of disposable income and disposable capital
4. Contributions

The Lord Chancellor, in exercise of the powers conferred by sections 2(5) and (7), 6, 20(8), 21, 23 to 25, 27, 28, 31, 32, 34, 43 of and paragraph 11 of Schedule 1 to the Legal Aid Act 1988 after consulting the Crown Court Rule Committee and the Magistrates' Courts Rule Committee and with the consent of the Treasury, hereby makes the following Regulations:—

PART I

GENERAL

Citation, commencement and application

1.—(1) These Regulations may be cited as the Legal Aid in Criminal and Care Proceedings (General) Regulations 1989 and shall come into force on 1st April 1989.

(2) Parts I to VI of these Regulations apply to criminal proceedings and Part VII applies to care proceedings.

Revocations

2. The Regulations specified in Schedule 1 are hereby revoked.

Interpretation

3.—(1) In these Regulations, unless the context otherwise requires—

"the Act" means the Legal Act 1988;

"applicant" means, in relation to an application for legal aid made on behalf of a person who has not attained the age of 17 by his parent or guardian, that person and, in the case of any other application for legal aid, the person making the application;

"appropriate authority" means an officer or body authorised to determine costs under the Legal Aid in Criminal and Care Proceedings (Costs) Regulations 1989(**a**);

"appropriate contributor," in relation to a person who has not attained the age of 16, means—

  (a) his father (or any person who has been adjudged to be his father) or his mother; or

  (b) his guardian;

"appropriate officer" means, in the case of the Crown Court, the Chief Clerk or an officer designated by him to act on his behalf;

"appropriate area committee" means the area committee in whose area is situated the court to which an application for or concerning a legal aid order has been made;

"area committee" and "Area Director" have the meanings assigned to them by regulation 4 of the Civil Legal Aid (General) Regulations 1989(**b**) "Area Director" includes any person duly authorised to act on his behalf;

"contribution" means the contribution payable under section 23(1) of the Act in respect of the costs of representation;

"contribution period" means the period of 6 months commencing with the date on which the legal aid order was made;

"Court of Appeal" means the criminal division of the Court of Appeal or the Courts-Martial Appeal Court as the case may be;

"disposable capital" and "disposable income" mean the amounts of capital and income which are available for the making of a contribution after capital and income have been computed in accordance with Schedule 3;

"family credit" means family credit under the Social Security Act 1986(**c**);

"guardian" has the meaning assigned by section 87 of the Child Care Act 1980;

"income support" means income support under the Social Security Act 1986;

"judge of the court" means—

(a) in the case of the Court of Appeal, a single judge of that Court or a judge of the High Court;

(b) in the case of the Crown Court, a judge of the High Court, a Circuit judge, a recorder, or an assistant recorder.

"justices' clerk" includes a person duly authorised by the justices' clerk of a magistrates' court to act on his behalf to the extent that he is so authorised;

"legal aid" means representation under Part V of the Act or representation in care proceedings, as the case may be, and

"legal aid order" means an order granting such representation;

"person concerned" means the person whose disposable income and disposable capital are to be determined or the person whose resources are to be treated as the resources of any other person under these Regulations;

"proper officer" means—

(a) in respect of proceedings in the House of Lords, the Clerk of the Parliaments;

(b) in respect of proceedings in the Court of Appeal, the registrar;

(c) in respect of proceedings in the Crown Court, the appropriate officer;

(d) in respect of proceedings in a magistrates' court, the justices' clerk.

"registrar" means the registrar of criminal appeals or the registrar of the Courts-Martial Appeal Court, as the case may be, and includes any person duly authorised to act on his behalf to the extent that he is so authorised;

"statement of means" means a statement of means submitted in accordance with regulation 23;

(2) Unless the context otherwise requires, any reference in these Regulations to a regulation, Part or Schedule by number means the regulation, Part or Schedule so numbered in these Regulations and a form referred to by number means the form so numbered in Schedule 2.

Forms
4.—(1) The form in Part I of Schedule 2 shall be used where applicable with such variations as the circumstances of the particular case require.

(2) The forms in Part II of Schedule 2, or forms to the like effect, may be used with such variations as the circumstances may require.

Applicants reaching the age of 16
5. An applicant who attains the age of 16 after the date on which an application for legal aid is made but before the making of a legal aid order shall be treated for the purposes of these Regulations as not having attained that age.

Exclusion of solicitors and counsel
6.—(1) The proper officer of each court shall keep a list of solicitors and counsel, notified to him by the Lord Chancellor, who are for the time being excluded from legal aid work under section 47(2) of the Solicitors Act 1974(**a**) or section 42 of the Administration of Justice Act 1985(**b**).

(2) Any reference in these Regulations to solicitors or counsel shall be construed as not including any solicitor or counsel who is so excluded.

Determination in private and in absence of legally assisted person, etc.
7. Where it is provided by these Regulations that any matter may be determined otherwise than by a court, it may be determined in private and in the absence of the applicant, the appropriate contributor, the person concerned or the legally assisted person as the case may be.

Legal aid records
8. The proper officer shall keep such records as the Lord Chancellor may from time to time direct of all cases in which a legal aid order was made by the court or an application for legal aid was made to it, and shall send to the Lord Chancellor such information from those records as the Lord Chancellor shall request.

Area committees and powers of Area Directors
9.—(1) Area Committees and Area Directors appointed by the Board pursuant to regulation 4 of the Civil Legal Aid (General) Regulations 1989 shall exercise functions respectively delegated to them by the Board or conferred on them by these Regulations and, where an area committee is required or entitled to perform any function under these Regulations, that function may, subject to paragraph (3), be performed on behalf of the committee by the Area Director.

(2) An Area Director so appointed shall act as the secretary to the area committee for his area.

(3) Paragraph (1) shall not empower an Area Director to refuse—

(a) an application for review under regulation 17(1);

(b) an application under regulation 52; or

(c) an application referred to the committee under regulation 54.

General power to grant legal aid
10. Subject to the provisions of section 21(2), (3) and (5) of the Act to regulation 23, nothing in Part II or in regulation 36 shall affect the power of a

court, a judge of the court or of the registrar to make a legal aid order, whether an application has been made for legal aid or not, or the right of an applicant whose application has been refused or whose legal aid order has been revoked under section 24(2) to apply to the court at the trial or in other proceedings.

Part II

Applications for Legal Aid

Proceedings in magistrates' courts

11.—(1) An application for a legal aid order in respect of proceedings in a magistrates' court shall be made:

(a) to the justices' clerk in Form 1, or

(b) orally to the court,

and the justices' clerk or the court may grant or refuse the application.

(2) Where an application for a legal aid order is made under paragraph (1)(b), the court may refer it to the justices' clerk for determination.

(3) Except where the applicant is not required to furnish a statement of means under regulation 23(4), a legal aid order shall not be made on an application under paragraph (1) until the court or the justices' clerk has considered the applicant's statement of means.

Notification of refusal of legal aid by a magistrates' court

12.—(1) Where an application for a legal aid order is refused by a magistrates' court or a justices' clerk, the court or the justices' clerk shall notify the applicant on Form 2 that the application has been refused on one or both of the following grounds, namely, that—

(a) it does not appear to the court or the justices' clerk desirable to make an order in the interests of justices; or

(b) it appears to the court or the justices' clerk that the applicant's disposable income and disposable capital are such that, in accordance with regulation 26(1), he is ineligible for legal aid,

and shall inform him of the circumstances in which he may renew his application or apply to an area committee for the decision to be reviewed.

(2) A copy of Form 2, and, where an application for review under regulation 15 may be made, of the completed Form 1 shall be sent to the applicant and to his solicitor, if any.

Determination of contribution where legal aid is refused by a magistrates' court

13. Where a magistrates' court or a justices' clerk has refused to make a legal aid order, the court or the justices' clerk shall determine—

(a) the applicant's disposable income and disposable capital, and

(b) the amount of any contribution which would have been payable and the manner in which it would be payable by the applicant or an appropriate contributor had a legal aid order been made,

and shall notify the applicant of the amounts so determined.

Renewal of application

14.—(1) Without prejudice to the provisions of regulation 15, an applicant whose application under regulation 11 has been refused may renew his application either orally to the court or to the justices' clerk.

(2) Where an application is renewed under paragraph (1), the applicant shall return the notice of refusal which he received under regulation 12 or any such notice received under regulation 17(4).

(3) Where an application is renewed to the justices' clerk, he may either grant the application or refer it to the court or to a justice of the peace.

(4) Where an application is renewed to the court may grant or refuse the application or refer it to the justices' clerk.

(5) The court or a justice of the peace to whom an application is referred under paragraph (3) or (6), may grant or refuse the application.

(6) A justices' clerk to whom an application is referred under paragraph (4), may grant the application or refer it either back to the court or to a justice of the peace.

(7) Except where the applicant is not required to furnish a statement of means under regulation 23(4), a legal aid order shall not be made where an application is renewed under paragraph (1) until the court, a justice of the peace or the justices' clerk has considered the applicant's statement of means.

(8) Regulation 12 shall apply where an application is refused under this regulation with the modification that references to a magistrates' court shall be construed as including references to a justice of the peace.

(9) In this regulation, "a justice of the peace" means a justice of the peace who is entitled to sit as a member of the magistrates' court.

Application for review

15.—(1) Where an application for a legal aid order has been refused after having been considered for the first time by a magistrates' court or a justices' clerk, the applicant may, subject to paragraph (2), apply for review to the appropriate area committee.

(2) An application for review shall only lie to an area committee where—

(a) the applicant is charged with an indictable offence or an offence which is triable either way or/appears or is brought before a magistrates' court to be dealt with in respect of a sentence imposed or an order made in connection with such an offence; and

(b) the application for a legal aid order has been refused on the ground specified in regulation 12(1)(a): and

(c) the application for a legal aid order was made no later than 21 days before the date fixed for the trial of an information or the inquiry into an offence as examining justices, where such a date had been fixed at the time that the application was made.

Procedure on application for review

16.—(1) An application for review shall be made by giving notice in Form 3 to the appropriate area committee within 14 days of the date of notification of the refusal to make a legal aid order and the applicant shall send a copy of Form 3 to the justices' clerk of the magistrates' court to which the first application for legal aid was made.

(2) An application under paragraph (1) shall be accompanied by the following documents—

    (a) a copy of the completed Form 1 returned by the court under regulation 12(2); and

    (b) a copy of the notice of refusal received under regulation 12.

(3) The time limit within which the application for review is to be made may, for good reason, be waived or extended by the area committee.

(4) The justices' clerk and the applicant shall supply such further particulars, information and documents as the area committee may require in relation to an application under paragraph (1).

Determination of review

17.—(1) On a review, the area committee shall consider the application for legal aid and either—

    (a) refuse the application; or

    (b) make a legal aid order.

(2) Where the area committee makes a legal aid order, it shall make a contribution order in accordance with any determination made under regulation 13.

(3) Where a magistrates' court or a justices' clerk has determined under regulation 13 that any legal aid order which is made shall not take effect until a contribution from disposable capital is paid, the area committee shall send the legal aid order to the appropriate justices' clerk.

(4) The area committee shall give notice of its decision and the reasons for it in Form 4 to—

    (a) the applicant and his solicitor, if any, and

    (b) the justices' clerk of the magistrates' court to which the application for legal aid was made.

Proceedings in the Crown Court

18.—(1) An application for a legal aid order in respect of proceeding in the Crown Court shall be made either to the appropriate officer of the Crown Court in Form 1 or

    (a) orally to the Crown Court or to a magistrates' court at the conclusion of any proceedings in that magistrates' court; or

    (b) where a magistrates' court has been given a notice of transfer under section 4 of the Criminal Justice Act 1987(**a**) (serious fraud cases), to the justices' clerk of that magistrates' court in form 1; or

    (c) in the case of an appeal to the Crown Court from a magistrates' court, to the justices' clerk of that magistrates' court in Form 1; or

   (d) where the applicant was granted legal aid for proceedings in the magistrates' court and was committed for trial in the Crown Court under section 6(2) of the Magistrates' Courts Act 1980(**b**), to the justices' clerk of the magistrates' court ordering the committal in such form as may be required; or

   (e) in the case of a retrial ordered under section 7 of the Criminal Appeal Act 1968(**c**), orally to the court ordering the retrial,

and the appropriate officer, the court or the justices' clerk may grant or refuse the application.

(2) Where an application for a legal aid order is made orally to the court, the court may refer it to the proper officer of the court for determination.

(3) Except where the applicant is not required to furnish a statement of means under regulation 23(4), a legal aid order shall not be made on an application under paragraph (1) until the appropriate officer, the court or the justices' clerk has considered the applicant's statement of means.

Notification of refusal of legal aid

19.—(1) Where an application for a legal aid order is refused by the appropriate officer of the Crown Court, the court or a justices' clerk, the appropriate officer, the court or the justices' clerk shall notify the applicant on Form 2 that the application has been refused on one or both of the following grounds, namely, that—

   (a) it does not appear to the officer, the court or the justices' clerk desirable to make an order in the interests of justice; or

   (b) it appears to the officer, the court or the justices' clerk that the applicant's disposable income and disposable capital are such that, in accordance with regulation 26(1), he is ineligible for legal aid,

and shall inform him of the circumstances in which he may renew his application.

(2) A copy of Form 2 shall be sent to the applicant and to his solicitor, if any.

Determination of contribution where legal aid is refused

20. Where the appropriate officer of the Crown Court, the court or a justices' clerk has refused to make a legal aid order, the officer, the court or the justices' clerk shall determine—

   (a) the applicant's disposable income and disposable capital, and

   (b) the amount of any contribution which would have been payable and the manner in which it would be payable by the applicant or an appropriate contributor had a legal aid order been made,

and shall notify the applicant of the amounts so determined.

Renewal of application

21.—(1) An applicant whose application under regulation 18 has been refused may renew his application either orally to the court or to the appropriate officer of the Crown Court.

(2) Where an application is renewed under paragraph (1), the applicant shall return the notice of refusal which he received under regulation 19.

(3) Where an application is renewed to the appropriate officer, he may either grant the application or refer it to a judge of the court.

(4) Where an application is renewed to the court, the court may grant or refuse the application or refer it to the appropriate officer.

(5) A judge of the court to whom an application is referred under paragraph (3) or (6), may grant or refuse the application.

(6) An appropriate officer to whom an application is referred under paragraph (4), may grant the application or refer it to a judge of the court.

(7) Except where the applicant is not required to furnish a statement of means under regulation 23(4), a legal aid order shall not be made where an application is renewed under paragraph (1) until the court or the appropriate officer has considered the applicant's statement of means.

(8) Regulation 19 shall apply where an application is refused under this regulation as if references to a justices' clerk were omitted.

Proceedings in the Court of Appeal or the House of Lords

22.—(1) An application for a legal aid order in respect of proceedings in the Court of Appeal or the House of Lords may be made—

(a) orally to the Court of Appeal, to a judge of the court or the registrar, or

(b) by giving written notice of the application to the registrar in such form as he may direct.

(2) Where an application for a legal aid order is made orally to the Court of Appeal, the court may refer it to a judge of the court or the registrar for determination; and, where such an application is made orally to a judge of the court, he may refer it to the registrar for determination.

(3) Where a judge of the court refuses to make a legal aid order, the applicant may renew his application to the Court of Appeal.

(4) The registrar considering an application for a legal aid order shall—

(a) make an order; or

(b) refer the application to the Court of Appeal or to a judge of the court.

(5) A legal aid order shall not be made until—

(a) a notice of appeal or application for leave to appeal to the Court of Appeal or the House of Lords, as the case may be, has been given, and

(b) except where the applicant is not required under regulation 23(4) to furnish a statement of means, the Court of Appeal, a judge of the court or the registrar has considered the applicant's statement of means.

(6) In making a legal aid order in respect of proceedings in the Court of Appeal, the court, a judge of the court or the registrar may specify the stage of the proceedings at which legal aid shall commence.

(7) Subject to the provisions of this regulation, the powers of the Court of Appeal to determine an application for a legal aid order may be exercised by a judge of the court or the registrar.

(8) The powers of the Court of Appeal to revoke a legal aid order may be exercised by a judge of the court or, where the legally assisted person applies for the order to be revoked, by the registrar.

PART III

STATEMENT OF MEANS AND PAYMENT OF CONTRIBUTIONS

Statement of means
23.—(1) A statement of means submitted by an applicant or an appropriate contributor shall be in Form 5.

(2) Subject to paragraphs (3) and (4), where an applicant does not submit a statement of means when he applies for legal aid, the proper officer to whom, or to whose court he is making the application, shall require him so to do.

(3) Where an applicant is under 16, the proper officer may require either the applicant or an appropriate contributor, or both, to submit a statement of means in accordance with this regulation.

(4) A statement of means shall be required unless—

(a) it appears to the court or the proper officer that, by reason of his physical or mental condition, the applicant is for the time being incapable of furnishing such a statement; or

(b) the applicant has already submitted such a statement in connection with a previous application in respect of the same case and his financial circumstances have not changed.

(5) Nothing in paragraph (4)(a) shall prevent the court or the proper officer from requiring an applicant to furnish a statement of means after a legal aid order has been made where it appears that he is no longer incapable of furnishing such a statement.

Provision of information
24.—(1) At any time after the submission of a statement of means, the court or the proper officer may require the applicant, the legally assisted person or the appropriate contributor to provide evidence of any information given in a statement of means or of any change in his financial circumstances together with such additional information as the court or the proper officer may require.

(2) Where the applicant, the legally assisted person or the appropriate contributor fails to provide any evidence or information required under paragraph (1)—

(a) his disposable income and disposable capital shall be deemed to exceed the limits below which no contribution is payable by virtue of Schedule 4; and

(b) the contribution payable by him shall be such an amount as the court or the proper officer of the court may determine or redetermine.

Determination of contributions
25.—(1) The court or the proper officer shall, when making a legal aid order, determine the amount of any contribution payable by the applicant, the legally assisted person or the appropriate contributor in accordance with regulation 26.

(2) Where the applicant or the legally assisted person has paid or is liable to pay a contribution under section 9(6) of the Act in respect of advice and assistance given in relation to the same proceedings, any contribution which he or an appropriate contributor is liable to make under section 23(1) of the Act in respect of the costs of representation shall be reduced by the total amount of any contribution paid or liable to be paid under section 9(6).

Assessment of resources and method of determining contributions

26.—(1) Representation shall not be granted to a person for any purpose unless it appears that his financial resources are such that he requires assist-ance in meeting the costs which he may incur for that purpose.

(2) The court or the proper officer shall—

    (a) consider the statement of means submitted by the applicant or the appropriate contributor and any other relevant information; and

    (b) subject to paragraph (3), determine his disposable income and dis-posable capital in accordance with Schedule 3.

(3) The court or the proper officer shall not make a determination under paragraph (2)(*b*) where—

    (a) the applicant,

    (b) the appropriate contributor, or

    (c) the spouse of the applicant or appropriate contributor, is in receipt of income support or family credit and this paragraph shall apply to a man and a woman who are living with each other in the same household as husband and wife as it applies to the parties to a marriage.

(4) Subject to paragraph (3), the applicant or the appropriate contributor shall pay a contribution in accordance with the provisions of Schedule 4.

Contribution orders

27.—(1) The court or the proper officer of the court shall make a contribution order, in Form 6, in respect of any contribution determined under regulation 26 above and shall endorse the legal aid order accordingly.

(2) A copy of the contribution order shall be sent to the person ordered to make the contribution, to the legally assisted person's solicitor or counsel (where counsel only is assigned) and to the collecting court.

Earlier contribution orders

28. On making a legal aid order in respect of proceedings in the Crown Court, the Court of Appeal, the Courts-Martial Appeal Court or the House of Lords, the court or the proper officer of the court shall not—

    (a) determine disposable income or disposable capital; or

    (b) make a contribution order,

where a contribution order has previously been made in connection with a legal aid order giving legal aid to the person in question in respect of proceed-ings in the same case in a lower court.

Payment of contributions

29.—(1) Any contribution which is to be paid out of disposable income shall be payable by weekly (or, at the discretion of the court or the proper officer of the court, by fortnightly or monthly instalments) within a period not exceeding the contribution period, and the first such instalment shall fall due 7 days from the making of the legal aid order or of the contribution order, whichever is the later.

(2) Any contribution which is to be paid out of disposable capital shall be paid immediately if the sum is readily available or, if it is not, at such time as the court or the proper officer of the court considers to be reasonable in all the circumstances.

(3) Where a contribution out of disposable capital is to be paid immediately, the legal aid order shall not take effect until such payment is made and the court or the proper officer of the court shall give notice of this fact in Form 7 to—

    (a) the applicant and the appropriate contributor, and

    (b) the solicitor assigned or, where counsel only is assigned, counsel.

Method of payment of contributions

30.—(1) Subject to paragraph (2), payment of contributions shall be made to the proper officer of the collecting court.

(2) Where a legal aid order is not to take effect until a contribution out of disposable capital is paid, such payment shall be made to the proper officer of the court making the legal aid order unless that court otherwise directs.

Change in financial circumstances

31. The legally assisted person or the appropriate contributor shall inform the court or the proper officer of the court of any change in his financial circumstances which has occurred since the submission of his statement of means and which he has reason to believe—

    (a) might make him liable to pay a contribution where such a contribution is not already payable; or

    (b) might affect the terms of any contribution order made in connection with a legal aid order.

Determination where no contribution previously payable

32.—(1) The court or the proper officer of the court shall determine the amount of any contribution payable by a legally assisted person or an appropriate contributor who is not already liable to make such a contribution where—

    (a) further information has become available as to the amount of disposable income and disposable capital available at the time when the legal aid order was made; or

    (b) the circumstances upon which the disposable income or disposable capital were determined at the time the legal aid order was made have altered within the contribution period;

and it appears likely that, were such a determination to be made, the legally assisted person or the appropriate contributor would be liable to make a contribution.

(2) Regulation 26 shall apply where a contribution is determined under paragraph (1) as it applies where a contribution is determined on the making of a legal aid order.

Redetermination of contribution

33. Except where it appears unlikely that any significant change in liability to make a contribution would result, the court or the proper officer of the court shall redetermine the amount of any contribution payable by a legally assisted person or an appropriate contributor under a legal aid order where—

(a) further information has become available as to the amounts of disposable income and disposable capital available at the time when the contribution order was made; or

(b) he circumstances upon which the disposable income or disposable capital were determined at the time when the contribution order was made have altered within the contribution period so that—

    (i) his disposable income may have increased by an amount greater than £750 a year or decreased by an amount greater than £300 a year; or

    (ii) his disposable capital may have increased by an amount greater than £750 a year;

and shall vary or revoke the contribution order accordingly.

Effect of error or mistake

34. Where it appears to the court or the proper officer that there has been some error or mistake in the determination of the legally assisted person's or the appropriate contributor's disposable income, disposable capital or contribution and that it would be just and equitable to correct the error or mistake, the court or the proper officer may vary the contribution order accordingly, may revoke it or may make a contribution order.

Variation and revocation of contribution orders

35.—(1) At the conclusion of the relevant proceedings the court in which those proceedings are concluded may, if it thinks fit—

(a) remit any sum due under a contribution order which falls to be paid after the conclusion of those proceedings; or

(b) remit or order the repayment of any sum due or paid under a contribution order where the legally assisted person has been acquitted,

and, in this regulation, "relevant proceedings" means the proceedings for the purposes of which legal aid was granted under the legal aid order in connection with which the contribution order was made or, where those proceedings are proceedings before a magistrates' court which result in the legally assisted person being committed to the Crown Court for trial or sentence or in his case being remitted to a juvenile court, the relevant proceedings include the proceedings before the Crown Court or that juvenile court.

(2) Where the legal aid order in connection with which a contribution order was made is revoked, paragraph (1) shall apply as if the relevant proceedings had been concluded.

(3) Where a legally assisted person—

(a) successfully appeals against his conviction; or

(b) is respondent to an appeal which is unsuccessful,

the court hearing the appeal may remit or order the repayment of any sum due or paid under a contribution order.

(4) Where a contribution order is revoked, or varied to an amount which is less than that which has already been paid, the court or the proper officer of the court shall order the repayment of any sum paid or overpaid as the case may be.

(5) Where—

(a) a contribution order is varied to an amount greater than that which was previously payable; or

(b) a contribution order is made after a determination under regulation 32;

and any payment is to be made out of disposable income, the court or the proper officer may, for the purpose of such payment, extend the period provided in regulation 29 within which such payment is to be made.

(6) An order varying or revoking a contribution order shall be in Form 8 and a copy of it shall be sent to the person ordered to make the contribution, to the legally assisted person's solicitor (or, where counsel only is assigned, to counsel) and to the proper officer of the collecting court.

Refusal to pay contribution

36.—(1) Where any sums which are due under a contribution order before the conclusion of the proceedings have not been paid by the legally assisted person, the court or the proper officer of that court may—

(a) serve notice on the legally assisted person requiring him to comply with the contribution order and pay any sums due under it within 7 days of receiving such notice; and

(b) if he does not do so, serve notice on him inviting him to make representations as to why he cannot comply with the contribution order.

(2) A notice given under paragraph (1)(a) shall be in Form 9 and a notice given under paragraph (1)(b) in Form 10 and copies of any notices so given shall be sent to the legally assisted person and to his solicitor or, where counsel only is assigned, to counsel.

(3) The court shall consider any representations made under paragraph (1)(b) and, if satisfied that the legally assisted person—

(a) was able to pay the relevant contribution when it was due; and

(b) is able to pay the whole or part of it but has failed or refused to do so,

may revoke the grant of representation.

(4) The revocation of the grant of representation under paragraph (3) shall not affect the right of any legal representative previously assigned to the legally assisted person to remuneration for work done before the date of the revocation.

Termination of contribution period

37.—(1) Where the contribution period has not ended and—

(a) the legally assisted person, the appropriate contributor or the spouse of the legally assisted person or appropriate contributor begins to receive income support or family credit (in this regulation referred to as "income-related benefits"); or

(b) the court remits any sum due under a contribution order which falls to be paid after the conclusion of the relevant proceedings; or

(c) the legally assisted person is sentenced in the proceedings to which the legal aid order relates to an immediate term of imprisonment or a sentence of detention in a young offender institution,

the contribution period shall be deemed to have ended on the date receipt of income-related benefits commenced or on the date of that remission or sentence, as the case may be.

(2) The court making any such remission or passing any such sentence shall inform the collecting court that the contribution period is to be deemed to have ended on the date of the remission or sentence.

(3) Without prejudice to regulation 31, the legally assisted person or the appropriate contributor shall inform the collecting court of the date on which receipt of income-related benefits commenced.

(4) Paragraph (1)(a) shall apply to a man and a woman who are living with each other in the same household as husband and wife as it applies to the parties to a marriage.

Disposal of sums received from legally assisted persons after conviction
38.—(1) Where a legally assisted person or an appropriate contributor to whom this regulation applies has been ordered to make a contribution, any amounts falling due under the contribution order after the conclusion of the relevant proceedings shall, unless remitted or specifically appropriated by the person paying the money to payment of the contribution, be applied (when paid) first, in accordance with the provisions of section 139 of the Magistrates' Court Act 1980 and any sum paid in addition to the sums referred to in paragraph (2) below shall be paid to the Lord Chancellor in accordance with paragraph 4(2) of Schedule 3 to the Act.

(2) This regulation applies to a legally assisted person who is ordered to pay any sum adjudged to be paid on conviction and to an appropriate contributor who is ordered to pay a fine, compensation or costs under the provisions of section 55 of the Children and Young Persons Act 1933 or section 3 of the Children and Young Person Act 1969.

Repayment of contributions
39. On receiving notification of the amount of the costs of representation determined by the appropriate authority under the Legal Aid in Criminal and Care Proceedings (Costs) Regulations 1989(**d**), the collecting court or the proper officer of that court shall, in accordance with section 23(7) of the Act, repay to the legally assisted person or the appropriate contributor, as the case may be, the amount, if any, by which any contribution paid exceeds those costs.

PART IV

LEGAL AID ORDERS

Legal aid orders
40.—(1) A magistrates' court inquiring into an offence as examining justices may make a legal aid order which applies, or amend an order so that it applies,

both to proceedings before the court and, in the event of the defendant being committed for trial, to his trial before the Crown Court and, where such an order is made,—

(a) Form 11 shall be used; and

(b) copies of the order shall be sent in accordance with paragraph (2) below or with regulation 50(3), as the case may be.

(2) A legal aid order for the purposes of proceedings in a magistrates' court, the Crown Court or the Court of Appeal shall be in Form 11, 12 or 13 as the case may be and, subject to regulations 17(3) and 29(3), the court or the proper officer shall send—

(a) one copy to the legally assisted person; and

(b) one copy to the solicitor assigned or to counsel (where counsel only is assigned); and

where the legal aid order is made for the purposes of proceeding before a magistrates' court, a further copy (endorsed "Board copy") shall be sent under sub-paragraph (b) above.

(3) Where a legal aid order is made by an area committee for the purposes of proceedings in a magistrates' court, one copy shall be sent to the proper officer of the court to which the application for legal aid was made.

(4) Where a legal aid order is amended under regulation 50, copies of the amended order shall be sent in accordance with paragraph (3) of that regulation.

(5) Where the solicitor assigned instructs counsel, the instructions which are delivered to counsel shall include a copy of the legal aid order and the solicitor shall inform counsel of any amendments made to the legal aid order.

Withdrawal and revocations legal aid orders

41.—(1) A legal aid order may be withdrawn—

(a) where the legally assisted person declines to accept the terms on which a grant of representation may be made;

(b) at the request of the legally assisted person;

(c) in accordance with the provisions of regulation 50.

(2) Where two legal aid orders and made in respect of the same proceedings, the second order so made shall be deemed to be of no effect and shall be withdrawn as if the legally assisted person had made a request under paragraph (1)(b) above.

(3) An order withdrawing a legal aid order shall be in Form 14 and a copy of it shall be sent to—

(a) the legally assisted person, or

(b) the solicitor assigned or to counsel (where counsel only is assigned); and

(c) where the legal aid order is withdrawn by the area committee, to the proper officer of the court to which the application for withdrawal was made.

(4) Where a legal aid order is withdrawn—

(a) the counsel assigned shall send all papers and other items in his possession relating to the proceedings to the solicitor assigned or (where no solicitor was assigned) to the legally assisted person; and

(b) the solicitor assigned shall send all papers and other items in his possession relating to the proceedings to the legally assisted person.

(5) Where a legal aid order is revoked under regulation 36(3), the foregoing paragraphs of this regulation shall apply, with any necessary modifications, as if the order had been withdrawn.

Notes of evidence and depositions
42. Where a legal aid order is made in respect of an appeal to the Crown Court, the justices clerk shall supply, on the application of the solicitor assigned to the appellant or respondent on whose application such an order was made, copies of any notes of evidence or depositions taken in the proceedings in the magistrates' court.

Transfer of documents
43. Where a person is committed by a lower court to a higher court or appeals or applies for leave to appeal from a lower court to a higher court, the proper officer of the lower court shall send to the proper officer of the higher court the following documents—

(a) a copy of any legal aid order previously made in respect of the same proceeding;

(b) a copy of any contribution order made;

(c) a copy of any legal aid application which has been refused;

(d) any statement of means already submitted.

PART V

LEGAL REPRESENTATION

Nature of representation
44.—(1) Subject to the following paragraphs of this regulation, a grant of representation shall provide for the services of a solicitor and counsel.

(2) A legal aid order granting representation for the purpose of such part of any proceedings before a magistrates' court as relates to the giving of bail shall not include representation by counsel.

(3) A legal aid order granting representation for the purposes of proceedings before a magistrates' court shall not include representation by counsel except—

(a) in the case of any indictable offence, where the court is of the opinion that, because of circumstances which make the case unusually grave or difficult, representation by both solicitor and counsel would be desirable; and

(b) in the case of proceedings under section 1 of the Children and Young Persons Act 1969, where it is alleged that the condition set out in subsection (2)(f) of that section is satisfied in consequence of an indictable offence and the court is of such opinion as is mentioned in sub-paragraph (a) above.

(4) Where a court grants representation for the purposes of an appeal to the Court of Appeal, the court may order that representation shall be by counsel only.

(5) Where the Crown Court grants representation for the purposes of—

(a) an appeal to that court;

(b) proceedings in which a person is committed to or appears before that court for trial or sentence or appears or is brought before the Crown Court to be dealt with;

the court may, in cases of urgency where it appears to the court that there is no time to instruct a solicitor, order that representation shall be by counsel only.

(6) Where the Crown Court or a magistrates' court grants representation for the purposes specified in paragraph (5), the court may, if the proceedings are proceedings in which solicitors have a right of audience, order that representation shall be by a solicitor only.

(7) Where in proceedings in a magistrates' court representation or advice is given before a legal aid order is made, that representation or advice shall be deemed to be representation or advice given under the order if—

(a) the interests of justice required that the representation or advice be provided as a matter of urgency;

(b) there was no undue delay in making an application for legal aid; and

(c) the representation or advice was given by the solicitor who was subsequently assigned under the legal aid order.

Assignment of solicitor and selection of counsel

45.—(1) Subject to regulations 46 and 49, any person who is granted representation entitling him to the services of a solicitor, may select any solicitor who is willing to act and such solicitor shall be assigned to him.

(2) Subject to regulations 46 and 49, where a legal aid order is made providing for the services of solicitor and counsel, the solicitor may instruct any counsel who is willing to act.

Assignment of solicitor or counsel for the Court of Appeal or the House of Lords

46.—(1) In the case of proceedings in the Court of Appeal or the House of Lords, counsel may be assigned by the court, a judge of the court or the proper officer making or amending the legal aid order.

(2) In assigning Counsel or a solicitor to a legally assisted person in respect of an appeal to the Court of Appeal or the Hose of Lords, the court, a judge of the court or the proper officer shall have regard, as far as is reasonably practicable, to the wishes of the legally assisted person, the identity of the solicitor or counsel, if any, who represented him in any earlier proceedings and the nature of the appeal.

Assignment of counsel only

47.—(1) Where a legal aid order granting representation for the purposes of proceedings in the Crown Court is made or amended so as to provide for representation by counsel only, counsel shall be assigned by the court or proper officer making or amending the legal aid order.

(2) Where a legal aid order granting representation for the purposes of proceedings in the Court of Appeal or the Courts-Martial Appeal Court is made or amended so as to provide for representation by counsel only, counsel shall be assigned by the court, a judge of the court or the proper officer.

Assignment of Queen's Counsel and two counsel

48.—(1) A legal aid order may provide for the services of more than one counsel only in the cases specified and in the manner prescribed by the following paragraphs of this regulation.

(2) The cases specified for the purposes of this regulation are trials in the Crown Court or proceedings in the Court of Appeal or the House of Lords—

(a) on a charge of murder, or

(b) where it appears to the court or the person making the legal aid order that the case is one of exceptional difficulty, gravity or complexity and that the interests of justice require that the legally assisted person shall have the services of two counsel.

(3) Subject to paragraphs (4) and (5), a High Court judge or a circuit judge, in the case of proceedings in the Crown Court, or a judge of the Court of Appeal or the Registrar, in the case of proceedings in the Court of Appeal, may make a legal aid order to provide for the services of two counsel in the following terms—

(a) a Queen's Counsel with a junior counsel;

(b) a Queen's Counsel with a noting junior counsel;

(c) two junior counsel; or

(d) a junior counsel with a noting junior counsel,

but in considering which order to make may have regard to the choice by the legally assisted person of any one particular counsel.

(4) A magistrates' court shall not make an order in the manner prescribed by paragraph (3)(b), (c) or (d) and may make an order in the manner prescribed by paragraph (3)(a) on a charge of murder.

(5) Before making an order under paragraph (3), the judge or the Registrar shall consider whether the services of a Queen's Counsel alone should be provided and, if so, shall so order.

(6) In a case specified in paragraph (2), a legal aid order which provides—

(a) for the services of one counsel, may be amended to provide for the services of two counsel in any manner prescribed by paragraph (3);

(b) for the services of two counsel, may be amended to provide for the services of the same number of counsel but in another manner prescribed by paragraph (3).

Assignment of one solicitor or counsel to more than one legally assisted person

49. A solicitor or counsel may be assigned to two or more legally assisted persons whose cases are to be heard together, unless the interests of justice require that such persons be separately represented.

Amendment of legal aid orders

50.—(1) A court having power to make a legal aid order may, on application, amend any such order by substituting for any legal representative or representatives previously assigned under the order any legal representative or representatives whom the court could have assigned if it had then been making the legal aid order.

(2) A court having power to make a legal aid order may withdraw any such order if the only legal representative or all the legal representatives for the time being assigned under the order withdraws or withdraw from the case and it appears to the court that, because of the legally assisted person's conduct, it is not desirable to amend the order under paragraph (1) above.

(3) An order amending a legal aid order shall be in Form 15 and a copy of it shall be sent to—

(a) the legally assisted person;

(b) the solicitor assigned by the legal aid order or to counsel (where counsel only is assigned) and to any solicitor and counsel assigned by the amended legal aid order; and

(c) where the legal aid order is amended by an area committee, to the proper officer of the court to which the application for amendment was made.

(4) Where a new solicitor or counsel (where counsel only was assigned) is assigned by an order amending a legal aid order, the solicitor or counsel originally assigned shall send all papers and other items in his possession relating to the proceedings to the new solicitor or counsel.

Applications for amendment of legal aid orders, etc.

51.—(1) An application for—

(a) representation by counsel in any proceedings of a kind specified in regulation 44(3); or

(b) the amendment or withdrawal of a legal aid order under regulation 50(1) or (2),

shall be made to the proper officer stating the grounds on which the application is made and the proper officer may grant or refuse the application.

(2) Where an appliction under paragraph (1) is refused, the applicant may renew his application both to the court and (except where paragraph (6) applies) to an area committee, and the proper officer shall notify the applicant of the circumstances in which an application may be renewed.

(3) Where an application is renewed to the court, the court may grant or refuse the application or refer it to the proper officer.

(4) The proper officer to whom an application is referred under paragraph (3), may—

(a) grant the application; or

(b) where the proper officer is a justices' clerk, refer it either back to the court or to a justice of the peace; or

(c) where the proper officer is not a justices' clerk, refer it to a judge of the court.

(5) The court, a judge of the court or a justice of the peace to whom an application is referred under paragraph (4) may grant or refuse the application.

(6) An application may be renewed under paragraph (2) to an area committee except where—

    (a) an application under the same sub-paragraph of paragraph (1) in the same proceedings has previously been refused by an area committee or by the court; or

    (b) the application was made—

        (i) in the case of proceedings in the Crown Court, more than 14 days after the committal for trial or sentence or the date of giving of notice of appeal; or

        (ii) in the case of proceedings in a magistrates' court, less than 14 days before the date fixed for the trial of an information or the inquiry into an offence as examining justices, where such a date had been fixed at the time the application was made; or

    (c) the application is an application in respect of proceedings in the Court of Appeal, the Courts-Martial Appeal Court or the House of Lords.

Renewal to area committee of application for amendment of legal aid order, etc.

52.—(1) Where an application under regulation 51 is renewed to an area committee, the legally assisted person shall send to the Area Director the following documents—

    (a) a copy of the legal aid order and of the notice of refusal;

    (b) any papers presented to the proper officer by the legally assisted person or his solicitor in support of the application; and

    (c) any other relevant documents or information.

(2) The proper officer and the legally assisted person or his solicitor shall supply such further particulars, information and documents as the area committee may require.

Consideration by area committee

53.—(1) The area committee shall consider the application and any further particulars, information or documents submitted to it under regulation 52 and any other relevant information and shall grant or refuse the application and, where necessary, amend or revoke the legal aid order accordingly.

(2) The area committee shall notify the proper officer of the court and the legally assisted person and his solicitor of its decision.

PART VI

AUTHORITY TO INCUR COSTS AND RESTRICTIONS ON PAYMENT OF LEGAL REPRESENTATIVES

Powers of area committee to authorise expenditure

54.—(1) Where it appears to a legally assisted person's solicitor necessary for the proper conduct of proceedings in a magistrates' court or in the Crown

Court for costs to be incurred under the legal aid order by taking any of the following steps—

    (a) obtaining a written report or opinion of one or more experts;

    (b) employing a person to provide a written report or opinion (otherwise than as an expert);

    (c) bespeaking transcripts of shorthand notes or of tape recordings of any proceedings, including police questioning of suspects;

    (d) where a legal aid order provides for the services of solicitor and counsel, instructing a Queen's Counsel alone without junior counsel; or

    (e) performing an act which is either unusual in its nature or involves unusually large expenditure;

he may apply to the appropriate area committee for prior authority so to do.

(2) Where an area committee authorises the taking of any step specified in paragraph (1)(a), (b), (c) or (e), it shall also authorise the maximum fee to be paid for any such report, opinion, transcript or act.

Restriction on payment

55. Where a legal aid order has been made, the legally assisted person's solicitor or counsel shall not receive or be a party to the making of any payment for work done in connection with the proceedings in respect of which the legal aid order was made except such payments as may be made—

    (a) out of the legal aid fund or by the Lord Chancellor, or

    (b) in respect of any expenses or fees incurred in—

        (i) preparing, obtaining or considering any report, opinion or further evidence, whether provided by an expert witness or otherwise; or

        (ii) bespeaking transcripts of shorthand notes or tape recordings of any proceedings, including police questioning of suspects;

    where an application under regulation 54 for authority to incur such expenses or fees has been refused by the area committee.

PART VII

CARE PROCEEDINGS

Application of Parts I to VI

56. Subject to the following provision of this Part, Parts I to VI shall apply, with any necessary modifications, to the grant of representation in care proceedings as they apply to the grant of representation in criminal proceedings.

Scope of care proceedings

57. In section 27(1)(f) of the Act there shall be inserted, after the words "(access orders)," the words "except appeals from decisions of juvenile courts to the High Court."

269

Interpretation

58. The definition of "applicant" in regulation 3(1) shall include a guardian *ad litem* but nothing in this Part shall have the effect of making a guardian *ad litem* an appropriate contributor for the purposes of these Regulations;

Statement of means and contributions

59.—(1) Regulation 23(4) shall not apply where representation is granted under this Part.

(2) Where a person has been made a party to care proceedings because he has a contrary interest in those proceedings, regulation 25 shall not have the effect of requiring him to pay a contribution in respect of the costs of representing the child who is the subject of the care proceedings in addition to the costs of his own representation.

Applications for emergency orders

60.—(1) An application for a legal aid order in respect of proceedings before a justice of the peace under section 12E of the Child Care Act 1980(a) may be made orally to a justice of the peace.

(2) A legal aid order shall not be made until the justice of the peace had considered the applicant's statement of means and, in respect of the proceedings referred to in paragraph (1), such statements may be provided orally or in writing.

(3) In this regulation, "justice of the peace" means a justice of the peace who is entitled to sit as a member of a juvenile court.

Proceedings before a juvenile court

61.—(1) An application for a legal aid order in respect of care proceedings before a juvenile court shall be made—

(a) to the justices' clerk in Form 16, or

(b) orally to the court,

and, subject to the following paragraphs of this regulation, regulations 11 to 14 shall apply as if the application was an application for a legal aid order in respect of proceedings in a magistrates' court.

(2) The powers of the court to determine an application under paragraph (1) may be exercised by a justice of the peace and, in this regulation, "justice of the peace" has the meaning given by regulation 60(3) above.

(3) Regulations 15 to 17 shall not apply to applications under paragraph (1).

Proceedings in the Crown Court

62.—(1) An application for a legal aid order in respect of an appeal to the Crown Court from a decision of a juvenile court in care proceedings shall be made—

(a) orally to the Crown Court or to the juvenile court at the conclusion of any proceedings in that juvenile court; or
appropriate officer of the Crown Court in Form 16; or

(b) appropriate officer of the Crown Court in Form 16; or

(c) to the justices' clerk in Form 16.

and, subject to the following paragraphs of this regulation, regulations 18 to 21 shall apply as if the application was an application for a legal aid order in respect of proceedings in the Crown Court.

(2) The powers of a juvenile court to determine an application under paragraph (1) may be exercised by a justice of the peace or the justices' clerk and, in this regulation—

(a) "juvenile court" means the juvenile court from which the appeal is brought;

(b) "justice of the peace" has the meaning given by regulation 60(3) above; and

(c) "justices' clerk" means the justices' clerk to the juvenile court.

SCHEDULES

SCHEDULE 1

REGULATIONS REVOKED

Title	Reference
The Legal Aid in Criminal Proceedings (General) Regulations 1968	S.I. 1968/1231
The Courts-Martial Appeal Legal Aid (General) Regulations 1969	S.I. 1969/177
The Legal Aid in Criminal Proceedings (General) (Amendment) Regulations 1970	S.I. 1970/1980
The Legal Aid in Criminal Proceedings (General) (Amendment) Regulations 1976	S.I. 1976/790
The Legal Aid in Criminal Proceedings (General) (Amendment) Regulations 1980	S.I. 1980/661
The Legal Aid in Criminal Proceedings (General) (Amendment No. 2) Regulations 1980	S.I. 1980/1651
The Legal Aid in Criminal Proceedings (General) (Amendment) Regulations 1983	S.I. 1983/1863
The Legal Aid in Criminal Proceedings (General) (Amendment) Regulations 1984	S.I. 1984/1716
The Legal Aid in Criminal Proceedings (General) (Amendment) Regulations 1985	S.I. 1985/1632
The Legal Aid in Criminal Proceedings (General) (Amendment) Regulations 1986	S.I. 1986/274
The Legal Aid in Criminal Proceedings (General) (Amendment) Regulations 1987	S.I. 1987/422
The Legal Aid in Criminal Proceedings (General) (Amendment) Regulations 1988	S.I. 1988/468
The Legal Aid in Criminal Proceedings (General) (Amendment) (No. 2) Regulations 1988	S.I. 1988/2303

SCHEDULE 2

FORMS

PART 1

Form 1

PART 2

Forms 2 to 16

Application for Legal Aid in Criminal Proceedings Magistrates' or Crown Court

Form 1.

Regs 11 & 18

I apply for Legal Aid—

* Cross out whichever does not apply

For the purposes of proceedings before | the | Crown/Magistrates'/Juvenile Court*

1. Personal Details: (Please use BLOCK letters and BLACK ink)

1. Surname

5. Date of birth

2. Forenames

3. Permanant address

4. Present address
   (if different from above)

2. Case Details:

1. Describe briefly what it is
   you are accused of doing,
   e.g. "stealing £50 from my
   employer", "kicking a door
   causing £50 damage."

2. The following other person(s)
   is/are charged in this case

3. Give reasons why you and the
   other persons charged in this
   case, if any, should not be
   represented by the same
   solicitor.

3. Court Proceedings: *(Complete section 1 or 2 whichever applies)*

* Cross out whichever does not apply

1. I am due to appear before..... | the | Magistrates/Juvenile Court*
   | On | 19 at am/pm*

272

or

2. I appeared before . . . . | the | Magistrates/Juvenile Court* |
On | 19 at am/pm* |

| and | ☐ | I was Committed for trial to the Crown Court |

| | ☐ | I was convicted and committed for sentence to the Crown Court |

(tick whichever applies) | ☐ | I was convicted and/or sentenced and I wish to appeal against | conviction and/or sentence* |

4. Outstanding Matters:

1. If there are any other outstanding criminal charges or cases against you give details including the court where you are due to appear (only those cases that are not yet concluded)

5. Your Financial Position *(Tick the box which applies)*

1. ☐ I attach a statement of my means in these proceedings *(details of your income and expenditure)*

2. ☐ I have already given a statement of my means to the | Magistrates' Court |
and there has been no change in my financial position *(A new statement is required if there has been any change)*

3. ☐ I am under 16 and attach a statement of my parents' means. If you are unable to provide a statement of their means give their name and address

6. Legal Representation:

Note: 1. If you do not give the name of a solicitor the court will select a solicitor for you.
2. You must tell the solicitor that you have named him, unless he has helped you complete this form.
3. If you have been charged together with another person or persons, the court may assign a solicitor other than the solicitor of your choice.

1. The Solicitor I wish to act for me is

2. Give the firm's name and address (if known)

7. Signature:

I understand that the court may order me to make a contribution to the costs of legal aid, or to pay the whole costs if it considers that I can afford to do so and if I am under 16, may make a similar order with respect to my parents.

Signed | **Dated:** |

8. Reasons for wanting legal aid
● To avoid the possibility of your application being delayed or legal aid being refused because the court does not have enough information about the case, you must complete the rest of this form.

● When deciding whether to grant you legal aid, the court will need to know the reasons why it is in the interests of justice for you to be represented.

● If you need help completing the form, and especially if you have previous convictions, you should see a solicitor. He may be able to advise you free of charge or at a reduced fee.

Please complete pages 3 & 4

Reasons for wanting Legal Aid

Note: If you plead NOT GUILTY neither the information in this form nor in your statement of means will be made available to the members of the court trying your case unless you are convicted or you otherwise consent. If you are acquitted, only the financial information you have given in your statement of means will be given to the court.

Tick any boxes which apply and give brief details or reasons in the space provided.

		For Court use only
1. I am in real danger of a custodial sentence for the following reasons *(You should consider seeing a solicitor before answering this question)* ☐		
2. I am subject to a: suspended or partly suspended prison sentence ☐ conditional discharge .... ☐ supervision order .... ☐ probation order .... ☐ deferment of sentence .... ☐ community service order .... ☐ care order .... ☐ *Give details as far as you are able including the nature of offence and when the order was made*		
3. I am in real danger of losing my job because: ☐		
4. I am in real danger of suffering serious damage to my reputation because: ☐		
5. I have been advised by a solicitor that a substantial question of law is involved *(You will need the help of a solicitor to answer this question)* ☐		
6. Witnesses have to be traced and interviewed on my behalf *(State circumstances)* ☐		

3.

274

Reasons (Contd) *Tick any boxes which apply and give brrief details or reasons in the space provided.*

			For court use only
7. I shall be unable to follow the court proceedings because: a) My understanding of English is inadequate ☐ b) I suffer from a disability ☐ *(give full details)*			
8. The case involves expert cross examination of a prosecution witness ☐ *(Give brief details)*			
9. The case is a very complex one, for example, mistaken identity ☐ *(You may need the help of a solicitor to answer this question)*			
10. Any other reasons: ☐ *(give full particulars)*			

Reasons for Refusal

This section must be completed by the Justices' Clerk if the application is refused because:
(a) It does not appear desirable in the interests of justice, and
(b) The applicant is entitled to apply for legal aid to the area committee.
State briefly the reasons for that decision.

Signed . . . . Justices' Clerk

Date . . . .

For court use only

Notification of Refusal to grant Legal Aid and determination of Contribution

Form 2.

Regs. 12, 13, 19 and 20

To

Your application for legal aid has been refused by the court/a judge of the court/a justice of the peace/a proper officer of the court on the following grounds:

* (a) it does not appear desirable to make an order in the interests of justice; and/or

* (b) it does not appear that your means are such that you require assistance in meeting the costs you may incur.

If legal aid had been granted you would have been ordered to pay a contribution of £   per week from income and £   from capital [payable on   ] towards the costs of your case/legal aid would have been conditional on immediate payment of £

You are entitled:
* (i) to apply for legal aid to an area committee (in some cases where your application has been refused under paragraph (a) above). If you wish to do this you should complete Form 3 overleaf. You must apply within 14 days of the date of this notification.
  (ii) to renew your application to the court [to the Crown Court] at any time. If you wish to do so you should complete the bottom section of this form and return the whole form to the Court at the address stated.
  (iii) In any event to apply for legal aid to the court of trial on the day of the trial.

* Delete as necessary

Signed:
Justices' Clerk/An officer of the Crown Court

Date:

I wish to renew my application for legal aid to the court.

I have/have not* made an application to an area committee.

Signed:

Date:

NOTE: (i) You should enclose any additional or new information you think is relevant to your application.
(ii) if there has been any change in your financial circumstances you must complete and enclose a new statement of means form.
(iii) If you have made an application to an area committee you should enclose a copy of the notification of decision.

* Delete as appropriate

Form 3.

Court Code

Offence Code

Solicitor's acc. no.

Application for Review of Refusal to grant Legal Aid   Reg. 16

To the Area Director, Area Committee for Area No.....................................
(Address)

I wish to

apply for a review by the area committee of the refusal by the court on the .... 19 ....

to grant me legal aid in connection with a charge of

My case is due to be heard on*

* (Delete if date has yet to be fixed)

I have/have not* renewed my application for legal aid to the court.

Signed

Dated

NOTE: (i) This application must be made within 14 days of the date of the notice of the refusal to make a legal aid order.

(ii) You should send the enclosed copy of your original application, and any additional or new information you think is relevant to your application.

(iii) A copy of this completed form must be forwarded to the Clerk to the Justices of the Court which refused legal aid.

Notification for decision of the Area Committee on Review of Refusal to grant Legal Aid

Form 4.
Reg. 17

To:

Your application for legal aid has been granted/refused because it appears/does not appear desirable to make an Order in the interests of justice on any of the following grounds:-

(1) You are in real danger of a custodial sentence.

(2) You are in real danger of losing your livelihood or suffering serious damage to your reputation.

(3) The determination of the case may involve consideration of a substantial question of law.

(4) You are unable to understand the proceedings or state your own case because:-
    (a) Your knowledge of English is inadequate
    (b) You suffer from a disability, namely ....

(5) Your case involves tracing and interviewing witnesses or expert cross-examination of a prosecution witness.

(6) It is in the interests of another that you be represented.

(7) Any other reasons.

* Delete as appropriate.

The Committee reached this decision because:-

Date: Secretary to the Area Committee

Statement of Means   **Form 5.**
by Applicant or Appropriate Contributor   **Reg. 23**
for Legal Aid purposes

To apply for criminal legal aid you must complete this form. If you are not yet sixteen, then your mother or father may also be asked to complete one. If you have applied for legal aid for your child, and your child is sixteen years old or over, then you do not need to fill in this form. Your child should complete it, giving details of his or her own income.

This information is needed before legal aid can be granted, so to avoid any delay in your application being considered, please complete this form as fully and as carefully as possible.

1 Personal details (please use BLOCK letters)

1.   Surname   Mr ☐   Mrs ☐   Miss ☐   Ms ☐

2.   Forenames

3.   Date of birth

4.   Home address

5.   Marital status
(please tick one box)   Single ☐   Single and living together ☐   Widow(er) ☐

        Married ☐   Married but separated ☐   Divorced ☐

6.   Are you claiming legal aid for a dependent child who is not yet sixteen: YES ☐

If YES, give the following details about the child: NO ☐   (go to Section 2)

Surname

Forenames

Date of birth

Home address
(if different
from yours)

Your relationship to him or her (e.g. father)

2 Whether you are entitled to free legal aid

1.   Do you receive Income Support or Family Credit?
(You may also answer YES if your spouse or partner are, providing that you are living together).

YES ☐   Give (a) The address of the Social Security office dealing with the benefit:

(b) The Income Support reference number:

Now sign the Declaration at Section 6. You do not need to answer any more questions.

NO ☐   Please go to Section 3, even if you are receiving other state benefits.

278

3 Financial details—Part A: Income

In this section you are asked to give details of the money you receive. If you are living together then you must provide details of the income of your spouse or partner as well. The details will be used to work out whether you have to pay a contribution towards legal aid. If you do, it will be collected on a weekly basis, so your answers must show the amount you get *each week* (if you receive it every two or four weeks divide the amounts by the number of weeks to give a weekly figure).

If any of the sections do not apply, write NONE in the space.

Amount received

Work	Employer's name and address	Your income	Income of spouse or partner	Official use
Enter take-home pay *per week* (after tax and insurance), including overtime, commission or bonuses. Attach wage slips for the last three months. If your pay changes each week show amounts for the last 13 weeks, or as many as you can, and attach slips.		£		
If you are self employed write SELF EMPLOYED. Show your take home pay and attach the most recent accounts showing gross income.			£	
Part time work. Enter take-home pay *per week* (after tax and insurance), from any part time job not included above.		£	£	
State Benefits Enter weekly amounts e.g. from unemployment benefit, child benefit etc. Say which benefit(s) you get in the space provided.	Types of benefit	£ £ £	£ £ £	
Money from property Enter weekly amounts (before any deductions), of money from sub-letting a house or rooms.		£	£	
Any other income Please give details and weekly amounts		£	£	

Important: If the information you have given above is going to change soon, please give details of the changes in Section 5 of this form.

Financial details—Part B: Capital and Savings

Please give details of all your capital and savings. If you
are living together you must also give details of the
capital and savings of your spouse or partner.

Amount

Property	You		Spouse or Partner		Official use
Do you own a house or property other than your main or only dwelling?	YES ☐	NO ☐	YES ☐	NO ☐	
If YES, state the value (approximate selling price) and	£		£		
amount of any outstanding mortgage	£		£		

		You	Spouse or Partner
Savings Give details of where your savings are, and the amounts. Include money in any bank, building society, National Savings Certificates, cash, stocks and shares or any other investments.		£	£
Articles of value Give details of any article of value that you own (e.g. jewellery, furs, paintings) with their approximate value.		£	£

4 Allowances and Deductions

N.B. Dependants are the people you and your spouse or partner look after financially.

1. Enter the NUMBER of dependants who are living with you. If you are claiming legal aid for a child, please include that child.

Spouse or Partner ☐	Children 18 and over ☐	Children 16 and 17 ☐	Children 11 to 15 ☐	Children under 11 ☐

Others (please say who) ☐

2. If you pay maintenance to any dependant who does NOT live with you, please give details of the amount you pay:

Age(s) of dependant(s) ☐	Your relationship to him or her ☐	Amount per week £ ☐

3. Give the following details of housing expenses of you and your spouse/partner. If you own more than one house only give details for the house in which you live. If you are paying the expenses of a dependant who is not living with you, enter the details in the spaces on the right.

Rent	£	/week	Amount for dependant(s)	£ /week
Mortgage payment	£	/week		£ /week
Ground rent	£	/week		£ /week
Service charge	£	/week		£ /week
Rates	£	/week		£ /week
Board and lodging	£	/week		£ /week
Bed and breakfast	£	/week		£ /week

Allowances and Deductions (continued)

		You	Spouse or Partner
4.	How much does it cost you and your spouse or partner *each week* to travel to and from work?	£	£
5.	Give details of any other expenses which you think the court should know about. You may include any payments on court orders, and contributions to approved pension schemes, but not: hire purchase payments or money for food, clothing or heating.	£	£
6.	If a solicitor has already given you advice in this case, under the "Green Form" scheme, and you have paid or been asked to pay towards this, give the name and address of the solicitor and the amount.		£

5 Further information

This part of the form is for you to give any financial information that you think the court should have when deciding upon your application for legal aid. You may also use this part of the form to tell the court of any future changes in circumstances that might alter your position.

6 Declaration

If you knowingly make a statement which is false, or knowingly withhold information, you may be prosecuted. If convicted, you may be sent to prison for up to three months, or be fined, or both.

After your application has been considered by the court, you may be asked to give further information or to clarify information that you have already given. In particular you may be required to provide proof of the information that you have given (e.g. wage slips, rent books etc.).

If you stop receiving income support or family credit, or if your financial position changes in any way after you have submitted this form, you must tell the court.

This is a requirement of the Legal Aid Regulations.

I declare that to the best of my knowledge and belief, I have given a complete and correct statement of my income, savings and capital (and that of my spouse or partner)* (and that of my child)**

Signed

Date

* Delete if you are single or if you are not living with your spouse or partner.
** Delete if legal aid is not sought for your child.

Legal Aid Contribution Order

To

In accordance with the provisions of section 23(1) of the Legal Aid Act 1988 the Court/area committee (a) orders you to pay a contribution of £   towards the cost of representation to be provided for you under a legal aid order:-

This contribution is:-

* payable in one lump sum of £ . . . . . . on or before

* payable at the rate of £   per week/per month the first instalment to be paid on or before and subsequent instalments to be paid weekly/monthly. The final instalment is due on

  *NB. In fixing the date from which weekly instalments are payable you have been credited with £   in respect of the green form contribution to which you are liable. The first payment is therefore due on the date shown and the number of weekly instalments is reduced from 26 to

* Delete as necessary.

This money should be paid to the Clerk to the Justices . . . . Magistrates' Court.

Signed

(Secretary to the area committee)(a)

Date

(a) Delete as necessary.

NOTES

The figures overleaf show how the contribution was calculated. If you are not satisfied with the calculations used, you may apply to this court for your means to be redetermined. If your means change, you must inform the court which is hearing your case IMMEDIATELY so that your contribution can be reassessed and changed if necessary. If you do not want legal aid on these terms, you MUST inform the court IMMEDIATELY by tearing off and returning the slip overleaf. If your legal aid order is revoked, you may still have to pay some money towards any costs already incurred.

If you should prefer to pay monthly, you should inform the Clerk to the Justices who will decide whether you should pay weekly or monthly.

Legal Aid Contribution Order—calculations used

Part One—	Figures used				
(1)	Average weekly net INCOME			£	(A)
(2)	Allowances against income	—dependants		£	
		—housing		£	
		—travel		£	
		—others		£	
		Total allowances		£	(B)
				£	
(3)	Total CAPITAL				
Part Two—	Calculation of contribution from INCOME				
(1)	Disposable income is (A) − (B) =			£	(C)
(2)	Contribution is (C)–£50, divided by 4 =			£	

Note: Contributions are rounded to the nearest whole pound. The minimum weekly contribution is £1.

Part Three—   Summary

Your contribution from INCOME is £

Your contribution from CAPITAL is £

Please turn to the front sheet for details of how and when to pay.

Tear off along here ....

I   of (address)

have been granted legal aid by the   Court at

I hereby apply for my legal aid order to be withdrawn. I understand that I may be required to pay towards any costs already incurred.

Return this form IMMEDIATELY to:

                  Signed

                  Date

Notice of Withholding of Legal Aid Order

Form 7.
Reg. 29

To

The   Court has made an order granting you legal aid in respect of the proceedings before it/the Court. It has also made an order, a copy of which is attached, requiring you to make a contribution out of capital towards the cost of your case.

In accordance with regulation 29(3) of the Legal Aid in Criminal and Care Proceedings (General) Regulations 1989 the court requires you to make immediate payment of that capital contribution to the Clerk to the Justices.

Note: You will NOT receive the legal aid order until you have made this payment and your solicitor and counsel will not be covered by the order until it has been received.

A copy of this notice has been sent to your solicitor/counsel.

                  Signed

                  Date

Variation or Revocation of Contribution Order

Form 8.
Reg. 35

To

In accordance with the provisions of regulation 33 or 34 of the Legal Aid in Criminal and Care Proceedings (General) Regulations 1989, your means have been reassessed and the court now varies the contribution order made on .... as follows. The total amount that you are now required to pay is £
You have already paid £

* Therefore you are no longer required to pay any more instalments of your contribution. Should your means change again, you MUST inform this court, which will then determine whether you should start to pay instalments again.

* The court hereby revokes the contribution order made on

* The sum of £   overpaid by you will be returned to you by the Clerk to the Justices at

* The balance remaining is now £   This sum should be paid to the Clerk to the Jutices at
  * on or before
  * at the rate of £   per week/month. The first instalment to be paid on or before the and subsequent instalments to be paid weekly/monthly.

    NOTE: If your instalmetns have now increased, and you do not want legal aid on these terms, you must inform the Court IMMEDIATELY.

* Delete as appropriate

                  Signed

                  Date

Notification of Arrears of Payment of Contribution Order

Form 9.

Reg. 36(1)(a)

To

You have fallen into arrears in the payment of instalments in respect of your legal aid contribution order. You have missed   instalments of £   and are now £   in arrears.

You must pay this sum to the Clerk to the Justices at   WITHIN SEVEN DAYS OF RECEIPT OF THIS NOTICE. If you fail to do so, this court will consider revoking legal aid.

A copy of this form has been sent to your solicitor(s)/counsel.

Signed

Date

Warning of Revocation of Legal Aid Order for Non-payment of Contribution

Form 10.

Reg. 36(1)(b)

To

You were recently sent a warning of arrears in respect of your legal aid contribution order. The arrears now stand at £   . The court is now considering revoking your legal aid. You are entitled to explain to the court why you have fallen into arrears, and to invite the court not to revoke your legal aid.

If you wish to do this, YOU MUST RETURN THIS FORM TO THIS COURT WITHIN SEVEN DAYS OF RECEIPT otherwise your legal aid might be revoked.

A copy of this form has been sent to your solicitors.

Signed

Date

I have fallen into arrears because:-

Signed

Date

Legal Aid Order (Magistrates' Court and Crown Court)

Form 11.

Reg. 40

In accordance with the Legal Aid Act 1988 the Court now grants legal aid, to   for the following purpose.

Delete (1) to (5) as necessary.

(1)   Proceedings before a magistrates' court in connection with

(2)   Appealing to the Crown Court against a decision of the Magistrates' Court on

(3)   Resisting an appeal to the Crown Court against a decision of the Magistrates' Court.

(4)   Proceedings before (both a magistrates' court and*) the Crown Court in connection with

including, in the event of his being convicted or sentenced in those proceedings, advice and assistance in regard to the making of an appeal to the criminal division of the Court of Appeal.

(5)   A retrial by the Crown Court ordered by the Court of Appeal or the House of Lords.

* Delete as necessary

The legal aid granted shall consist of the following representation:—

Magistrates' court proceedings—   Solicitor/solicitor and counsel

Crown Court Proceedings—   Solicitor/solicitor and counsel/solicitor and 2 counsel/counsel only

including advice on the preparation of the case for the proceedings.

The solicitor/Counsel assigned is

of

The legally assisted person has been committed to
prison/released on bail and may be communicated with at

Dated this   day of   19

(Signed)

A contribution order of £   was made in respect of this order.

Legal Aid Order (Area Committee)

Form 12.
Reg. 40

The area committee now grants legal aid to

for proceedings before a magistrates' court in connection with

The legal aid granted shall consist of representation by a solicitor [and Counsel].

The solicitor assigned is

of

A contribution order of £   was made in respect of this order.

Signed

Secretary to the area committee

Date

Legal Aid Order (Court of Appeal/Courts—Martial Appeal Court)

Form 13.
Reg. 38

APPELLANT Forenames	Surname (block letters)

WHERE DETAINED	Number	Address if not detained

CROWN COURT/ Date(s)	before whom tried
COURT MARTIAL	or sentenced

The   , in accordance with Part V of the Legal Aid Act 1988 now grants legal aid to the appellant for the following purposes:-

The legal aid granted consists of representation by

Solicitors   Counsel
Two Counsel

Who are assigned as follows:-

	Name	Addres
Solicitor		
Counsel		
Counsel		

A contribution order of £   was made in respect of this order.

Date:

Signed: Registrar of Criminal Appeals/Courts-Martial Appeal Court of Royal Courts of Justice, London, WC2.

285

Order Withdrawing Legal Aid

The   Court/area committee now withdraws, from this date, the order granting
legal aid to

of

For the purpose of

because:

      (i) he/she has applied for legal aid to be withdrawn.
     (ii) his/her legal representative(s) has/have withdrawn and it is not in the interests of justice to assign
         new representatives.
    (iii) he/she has failed to pay sums due under legal aid contribution order.

    (Delete as necessary)

Signed

Date

NOTE TO LEGALLY ASSISTED PERSON

You are no longer entitled to legal aid. You may be required to pay towards any costs already incurred. Your
solicitor and Counsel (if any) will cease to act further for you unless you yourself re-employ them, and if you do
so, you will be responsible for their costs from the above date.

Order Amending Legal Aid Order

   To

The order granting legal aid to

of
is hereby amended, by substituting for the solicitor named in the order another solicitor, namely
of

and by authorising the instruction of counsel (in place of counsel already instructed)*

Signed
(Secretary to the area committee)*

Date

* Delete as necessary.

Application for Legal Aid in care proceedings in the Juvenile Court or Crown Court

(Please use BLOCK letters and BLACK ink)

1. The Child:

             1. Surname

             2. Forenames

             3. Home
               address

             4. Date of birth

2. The Applicant:

Are you the child applying on your own behalf? *(tick a box)*   Yes ☐   No ☐

If you have ticked box "No" please complete the next boxes 1–4:

1. Surname
2. Forenames
3. Address

4. Please complete either (a) OR (b)

(a) If you are a parent, grandparent or guardian made party to the proceedings under section 32A or 32C of the Children and Young Persons Act 1969 tick a box to show your relationship to the child.

Parent ☐

Grandparent ☐

Guardian ☐

(b) If you are applying on behalf of the child state your relationship to or involvement with the child in this box

3. Your Financial Position   *(Tick the box which applies)*

☐   I attach a statement of my means. *(details of your income and expenditure in form 5)*

☐   A statement of my means has already been sent to the Court and there has been no change in my financial position. (A new statement is required if there has been any change.)

4. Case Details:

Legal Aid is required for the purpose of:

*Cross out whichever does not apply

1. proceedings before the: | Juvenile Court

the case is due to be heard on: | at   am/pm*

2. an appeal to the: | Crown Court

against the decision of the: | Juvenile Court

the case is due to be heard on: | at   am/pm*

3. the proceedings before the court are: (give brief details of the case)

5. Legal Representation: *Tick the appropriate box from either 1 or 2.*

1. ☐ I wish to have assigned to me

   ☐ The child wishes to have assigned to him/her

   a solicitor from the Law Society's panel of solicitors for the child care cases.

   ☐ I wish to have assigned to the child

   or

2. ☐ The solicitor I wish to act for me is

   ☐ The solicitor the child wishes to act for him/her is —————

   Enter the solicitor's name:

   ☐ The solicitor I wish to act for the child is

   Give the name and address of his/her firm:

3. The reason I am entitled to make such a nomination is:

   (Complete only if you are making this application on behalf of the child)

6. Signature:

Signed

Child/Guardian/Parent/Grandparent/Guardian-ad-litem*

Date

* *Cross out whichever does not apply*

SCHEDULE 3

DETERMINATION OF DISPOSABLE INCOME AND DISPOSABLE CAPITAL

General

1.—(1) In computing the disposable income and disposable capital of the person concerned, the financial resources of any spouse of his shall be treated as his resources except where—

   (a) the person concerned and his spouse are living separate and apart; or

   (b) the spouse has a contrary interest in the proceedings in respect of which an application for legal aid has been made; or

   (c) in all the circumstances of the case, it would be inequitable so to do.

(2) Where a spouse fails to provide information as to his financial resources in response to the request of the proper officer, the proper officer may make an estimate of the likely resources of the spouse on the basis of any information which is available.

2. Paragraph 1(1) and (2) above and the provisions of this Schedule shall apply to a man and a woman who are living with each other in the same household a husband and wife as they apply to the parties to a marriage.

3. Where it appears to the proper officer that the person concerned has with intent to reduce the amount of his disposable income or disposable capital, whether for the purpose of reducing his liability to pay a contribution towards legal aid or otherwise—

(a) directly or indirectly deprived himself of any resources; or

(b) converted any part of his resources into resources which under these Regulations are to be wholly or partly disregarded, or in respect of which nothing is to be included in determining the resources of that person;

the resources of which he has so deprived himself or which he has so converted shall be treated as part of his resources or as not so converted as the case may be.

Amended by the Legal Aid in Criminal and Care Proceedings (General) (Amendment) Regulations 1990 (S.I. 1990 No. 489).

Disposable income

4.—(1) The income which the person concerned receives during the contribution period shall be taken to be his income for the purposes of this Schedule.

(2) The income received during the contribution period may be estimated on the basis of the income received by the person concerned during the three months prior to the commencement of the contribution period.

5.—(1) Where the person concerned receives the profits from any trade, business or gainful occupation other than employment at a wage or salary, the profit which accrues during the contribution period shall be taken to be his income for the purposes of this Schedule.

(2) The income received during the contribution period may be estimated on the basis of the profits made during the last accounting period for which accounts have been prepared.

6. In computing disposable income, there shall be disregarded—

(a) attendance allowance paid under the Social Security Acts 1975–1988;

(b) mobility allowance paid under the Social Security Acts 1975–1988;

(c) constant attendance allowance paid as an increase to a disablement pension under section 61 of the Social Security Act 1975;

(d) housing benefit paid under the Social Security Act 1986; and

(e) payments made out of the social fund under section 32 of the Social Security Act 1986.

7. In computing disposable income there shall be deducted—

(a) the total amount of any tax payable on that income;

(b) the total amount of any contributions payable under the Social Security Acts 1975–1988;

(c) reasonable expenses of travelling to and from the place of employment;

(d) the amount of any contribution paid, whether under a legal obligation or not, to an occupational pension scheme within the meaning of the Social Security Pensions Act 1975(**a**) or to a personal pension scheme within the meaning of the Social Security Act 1986; and

(e) reasonable expenses in respect of the making of reasonable provision for the care of any dependent child living with the person concerned because of that person's absence from home by reason of employment.

7A. In computing disposable income there shall be deducted any sums payable (net of community charge benefit) by the person concerned in respect of the personal community charge to which he is subject by virtue of section 2 of the Local Government Finance Act 1988.

Amended by the Legal Aid in Criminal and Care Proceedings (General) (Amendment) Regulations 1990 (S.I. 1990 No. 489) with effect from April 1, 1990.

8.—(1) In computing disposable income there shall be a deduction in respect of the main or only dwelling in the case of a householder of the amount of the net rent payable, or such part thereof as is reasonable in the circumstances.

(2) For the purposes of this paragraph, "rent" includes—

    (a) the annual rent payable; and

    (b) a sum in respect of yearly outgoings borne by the householder including, in particular, any domestic rates and water and sewerage charges, a reasonable allowance towards any necessary expenditure on repairs and insurance and any annual instalment (whether of interest or of capital) payable in respect of a mortgage debt or heritable security charged on the house in which the householder resides or has an interest and,

in calculating the amount of rent payable, any housing benefit paid under the Social Security Act 1986 shall be deducted from amount of rent payable.

(3) In this paragraph, the expression "net rent" means the rent less any proceeds of sub-letting any part of the premises in respect of which the said rent is paid or the outgoings are incurred except that, where any person or persons other than the person concerned, his or her spouse or any dependant of his or hers is accommodated, otherwise than as a sub-tenant, in the premises for which the rent is paid, the rent may be deemed to be reduced by an amount reasonably attributable to such other person or persons.

Amended by the Legal Aid in Criminal and Care Proceedings (General) (Amendment) Regulations 1990 (S.I. 1990 No. 489) with effect from April 1, 1990.

9. Where the person concerned is not a householder, there shall be a deduction in respect of the costs of his living accommodation of such an amount as is reasonable in the circumstances including any net sum payable by him by way of contribution towards the collective community charge to which the person with a qualifying interest in such accommodation is subject by virtue of section 5 of the Local Government Finance Act 1988.

Amended by the Legal Aid in Criminal and Care Proceedings (General) (Amendment) Regulations 1990 (S.I. 1990 No. 489) with effect from April 1, 1990.

10.—(1) Subject to sub-paragraph (2) below, in computing disposable income, there shall be a deduction—

    (a) in respect of the maintenance of the spouse of the person concerned, where the spouses are living together;

    (b) in respect of the maintenance of any dependent child and of any dependent relative of the person concerned where such persons are members of his household;

at the following rates—

    (i) in the case of a spouse at the rate equivalent to 25 per cent. above the amount specified for the time being in column (3) of paragraph 6 of Part IV of Schedule 4 to the Social Security Act 1975 (increase for adult dependant of Category A retirement pension);

(ii) in the case of a dependent child or a dependent relative, at the rate equivalent to 25 per cent. above the amount specified for the time being in paragraph 2 of Part I of Schedule 2 to the Income Support (General) Regulations 1987(c) appropriate to the age of the child or relative.

(2) The proper officer may reduce any rate provided by virtue of sub-paragraph (1) by taking into account the income and other resources of the dependent child or other dependant to such extent as appears to the officer to be just and equitable.

(3) In ascertaining whether a child is a dependent child or whether a person is a dependent relative for the purposes of this paragraph, regard shall be had to their income and other resources.

11. Where the person concerned is making and, throughout such period as the proper officer may consider to be adequate, has regularly made bona fide payments for the maintenance of

(a) a spouse who is living apart;

(b) a former spouse;

(c) a child; or

(d) a relative;

who is not a member of the household of the person concerned, there shall be a deduction at the rate of such payments or at such rate (not exceeding the rate of such payments) as in all the circumstances is reasonable.

12. In computing disposable income, there shall be a deduction in respect of any sum or sums payable by the person concerned under an order made by, or arising from any conviction before, the High Court, the Crown Court, a county court, or a magistrates' court in any proceedings other than those in respect of which the legal aid order was made.

13. Where the person concerned is required to, or may reasonably, provide for any other matter, the proper officer may make an allowance of such amount as he considers to be reasonable in the circumstances of the case.

14. In computing the income from any source, there shall be disregarded such amount, if any, as the proper officer considers to be reasonable having regard to the nature of the income or to any other circumstances of the case.

Disposable capital
15.—(1) In computing the capital of the person concerned, there shall be included the amount or value of every resource of a capital nature belonging to him on the date of the assessment.

(2) In so far as any resource of a capital nature does not consist of money, its amount or value shall be taken to be—

(a) the amount which that resource would realise if sold in the open market, or if there is only a restricted market for the resource, the amount which it would realise in that market, after deduction of any expenses incurred in the sale, or

(b) if such an amount cannot be ascertained, an amount which appears to the proper officer to be reasonable.

16. In computing the capital of the person concerned, there shall be disregarded—

(a) any savings of mobility allowance paid under the Social Security Act 1975 which the person concerned intends to use in connection with mobility;

(b) for a period not exceeding 12 months from the date of receipt, any arrears of—

(i) attendance or mobility allowance paid under the Social Security Act 1975–1988;
(ii) income support or family credit; and

(c) any payments made out of the social fund under section 32 of the Social Security Act 1986.

17. Except where it is reasonable in the circumstances so to do, no sum shall be included in the amount of the capital of the person concerned in respect of the value of the assets of any business owned in whole or in part by him.

18. Save in exceptional circumstances, no sum shall be included in the amount of the capital of the person concerned in respect of—

(a) household furniture and effects of the main or only residence occupied by him;

(b) articles of personal clothing; and

(c) tools and equipment of his trade.

19. In computing the amount of the capital of the person concerned, the value of any interest in the main or only residence in which he resides shall be wholly disregarded.

20. In computing the capital of the person concerned, there may also be disregarded such an amount of capital (if any) as the proper officer decides to disregard taking into account the nature of the capital or any other circumstances of the case.

SCHEDULE 4

CONTRIBUTIONS

Contributions from disposable income

The weekly instalment of contribution payable by the applicant or the appropriate contributor where his disposable income falls within a range specified in the first column of the following table, is the amount specified in relation to that range in the second column.

Average Weekly Disposable Income	Weekly Contribution
Exceeding £55 but not exceeding £61	£1
Exceeding £61 but not exceeding £65	£2
Exceeding £65 but not exceeding £69	£3
Exceeding £69 but not exceeding £73	£4
Exceeding £70 but not exceeding £77	£5
Exceeding £74 but not exceeding £81	£6
Exceeding £78 but not exceeding £85	£7

The weekly instalment of contribution shall be increased by £1 for each £4 or part of £4 by which average weekly disposable income exceeds £85.

Amended by the Legal Aid in Criminal and Care Proceedings (General) (Amendment) Regulations 1990 (S.I. 1990 No. 489).

Contributions from disposable capital

The contribution from capital payable by the applicant or the appropriate contributor shall be such an amount as is equal to the amount by which his disposable capital exceeds £3,000.

EXPLANATORY NOTE

(This note is not part of the Regulations)

These Regulations replace, with amendments, the Legal Aid in Criminal Proceedings (General) Regulations 1968 (as subsequently amended). These Regulations govern the provision of representation under Part V and Sections 27 and 28 of the Legal Aid Act 1988 (legal aid in criminal and care proceedings).

These Regulations make provision for the assessment of the financial resources of the applicant or the appropriate contributor in order to determine eligibility to receive legal aid and to determine the contribution payable towards the cost of providing representation in the proceedings in respect of which the application for a legal aid order is made.

The main changes made are as follows:

(a) a single form of application for a legal aid order is prescribed, the use of which is mandatory (regulation 4 and Schedule 2 Part I);

(b) court clerks are given power to refuse an application for a legal aid order subject to a right to renew the application (regulations 11, 14, 18, and 21);

(c) the resources of persons living together as husband and wife are to be treated as if those persons were married (regulations 26, 37 and Schedule 3, paragraph 2);

(d) a solicitor assigned under a legal aid order who instructs counsel is to provide counsel with a copy of the legal aid order (regulation 40);

(e) Parts I to VI of the Regulations are applied, subject to a number of modifications, to the grant of representation in care proceedings and, in exercise of the power conferred by section 27(2), section 27(1)(f) of the Act is varied to exclude from the categories of care proceedings for the purposes of which representation is available under sections 27 and 28 of the Act appeals from decisions of juvenile courts to the High Court (regulations 56 and 57).

Legal Aid in Criminal and Care Proceedings (Costs) Regulations 1989*

Coming into force April 1, 1989

ARRANGEMENT OF REGULATIONS

---

* As amended by the Legal Aid in Criminal and Care Proceedings (Costs) (Amendment) Regulations (S.I. 1990 No. 488).

The Lord Chancellor, in exercise of the powers conferred on him by sections 2(5), (7), 25(2), 34 and 43 of the Legal Aid Act 1988, having had regard to the matters specified in section 34(9) and consulted the General Council of the Bar and the Law Society, and with the consent of the Treasury, hereby makes the following Regulations:—

Citation, commencement, revocations and transitional provisions

1.—(1) These Regulations may be cited as the Legal Aid in Criminal and Care Proceedings (Costs) Regulations 1989 and shall come into force on 1st April 1989.

(2) Subject to paragraph (3), the Legal Aid in Criminal Proceedings (Costs) Regulations 1988 and the Legal Aid in Criminal Proceedings (Costs) (Amendment) Regulations 1988 shall be revoked.

(3) These Regulations shall apply for the determination of costs which are payable in respect of work done on or after 1st April 1989 and costs payable in respect of work done before that date shall be determined as if these Regulations had not been made.

(4) Where a review under regulation 12 relates to a claim made before 1st June 1989, regulation 13(1) and (2) shall not apply and the solicitor may appeal in writing within 21 days of receipt of notification of the decision on the review to a committee appointed by the Board.

Interpretation

2.—(1) In these Regulations, unless the context otherwise requires—

"the Act" means the Legal Aid Act 1988;

"appropriate authority" has the meaning assigned by regulation 3;

"area committee" has the meaning assigned to it by regulation 4 of the Civil Legal Aid (General) Regulations 1989;

"area committee" has the meaning assigned to it by regulation 4 of the Civil Legal Aid (General) Regulations 1989;

"appropriate area committee" means the area committee in whose area is situated the magistrates' court at which a legal aid order was made;

"costs" means, in the case of a solicitor, the fees and disbursements payable under section 25 of the Act and, in the case of counsel, the fees payable under that section;

"counsel" means counsel assigned under the legal aid order;

"Court of Appeal" means the criminal division of the Court of Appeal or the Courts-Martial Appeal Court as the case may be;

"determining officer" means an officer appointed under regulation 3(2);

"disbursements" means travelling and witness expenses and other out of pocket expenses incurred by a fee-earner in giving legal aid;

"fee-earner" means a solicitor, a legal executive or any clerk who regularly does work for which it is appropriate to make a direct charge to a client;

"legal aid" and "legal aid order" have the meanings respectively assigned by the General Regulations;

"legal aid area" has the meaning assigned by paragraph 1(2) of Schedule 1 Part I;

"legal executive" means a fellow of the Institute of Legal Executives;

"registrar" means the registrar of criminal appeals or the registrar of the Courts-Martial Appeal Court, as the case may be;

"the General Regulations" means the Legal Aid in Criminal and Care Proceedings (General) Regulations 1989;

"solicitor" means a solicitor assigned under the legal aid order;

"trial judge" means the judge who presided at the hearing at which the defendant was substantively dealt with and in respect of which the costs are payable;

"taxing master" means a taxing master of the Supreme Court.

(2) Unless the context otherwise requires, any reference in these Regulations to a Regulation or Schedule by number means the Regulation or Schedule so numbered to these Regulations and any reference to a Part of a Schedule by number means the Part so numbered in that Schedule.

The appropriate authority

3.—(1) Subject to paragraphs (2), (3) and (4) the appropriate authority shall be—

    (a) the registrar in the case of proceedings in the Court of Appeal;

    (b) an officer appointed by the Lord Chancellor in the case of criminal proceedings in the Crown Court;

    (c) the Board in the case of criminal proceedings in a magistrates' court;

    (d) the Board in the case of care proceedings.

(2) The appropriate authority may appoint or authorise the appointment of determining officers to act on its behalf under these Regulations in accordance with directions given by it or on its behalf.

(3) For costs claimed in respect of advice or assistance as to an appeal from the Crown Court to the Court of Appeal, the appropriate authority shall be:—

    (a) (except in the case of an appeal under section 9(11) of the Criminal Justice Act 1987(**a**)) the register where, on the advice of counsel or the solicitor assigned, notice of appeal is given, or application for leave to appeal is made, whether or not such appeal is later abandoned;

    (b) an officer appointed by the Lord Chancellor under paragraph (1)(b) in all other cases.

(4) For costs claimed in respect of advice or assistance as to an appeal from a magistrates' court to the Crown Court, the appropriate authority shall be the Board.

General

4.—(1) Costs in respect of work done under a legal aid order shall be determined by the appropriate authority in accordance with these Regulations.

(2) In determining costs, the appropriate authority shall, subject to and in accordance with these Regulations—

(a) take into account all the relevant circumstances of the case including the nature, importance, complexity or difficulty of the work and the time involved, and

(b) allow a reasonable amount in respect of all work reasonably done.

Claims for costs by solicitors

5.—(1) Subject to regulation 17, no claim by a solicitor for costs in respect of work done under a legal aid order shall be entertained unless the solicitor submits it within three months of the conclusion of the proceedings to which the legal aid order relates.

(2) Subject to paragraph (3), a claim for costs shall be submitted to the appropriate authority in such form and manner as it may direct and shall be accompanied by the legal aid order and any receipts or other documents in support of any disbursements claimed.

(3) A claim shall—

(a) summarise the items of work done by a fee-earner in respect of which fees are claimed according to the classes specified in regulation 6(1) or in paragraph 4(2) of Schedule 1 Part II;

(b) state, where appropriate, the dates on which the items of work were done, the time taken, the sums claimed and whether the work was done for more than one assisted person;

(c) in the case of proceedings in the Crown Court or Court of Appeal, specify, where appropriate, the fee-earner who undertook each of the items of work claimed;

(d) give particulars of any work done in relation to more than one indictment or a retrial;

(e) specify any disbursements claimed, the circumstances in which they were incurred and the amounts claimed in respect of them.

(4) Where the solicitor claims that—

(a) regulation 44(7) of the General Regulations, or

(b) paragraph 3 of Schedule 1 Part I, should be applied in relation to an item of work, he shall give full particulars in support of his claim.

(5) Where there are any special circumstances which should be drawn to the attention of the appropriate authority, the solicitor shall specify them.

(6) The solicitor shall supply such further particulars, information and documents as the appropriate authority may require.

Determination of solicitors' fees

6.—(1) Subject to paragraph (5), the appropriate authority may allow work done by fee-earners in the following classes—

(a) preparation, including taking instructions, interviewing witnesses, ascertaining the prosecution case, advising on plea and mode of trial, preparing and perusing documents, dealing with letters and

299

telephone calls which are not routine, preparing for advocacy, instructing counsel and expert witnesses, conferences, consultations, views and work done in connection with advice on appeal or case stated;

(b) advocacy, including applications for bail and other applications to the court;

(c) attendance at court where counsel is assigned, including conferences with counsel at court;

(d) travelling and waiting;

(e) dealing with routine letters written and routine telephone calls.

(2) The appropriate authority shall consider the claim, any further particulars, information or documents submitted by the solicitor under regulation 5 and any other relevant information and shall allow—

(a) such work as appears to it to have been reasonably done under the legal aid order (including any representation or advice which is deemed to be work done under that order) by a fee-earner, classifying such work according to the classes specified in paragraph (1) as it considers appropriate; and

(b) such time in respect of each class of work allowed by it (other than dealing with routine letters written and routine telephone calls) as it considers reasonable

and, in any proceedings which are specified in paragraph 1(2) of Schedule 1 Part II, the appropriate authority shall proceed in accordance with the provisions of paragraph 3 of that Part of that Schedule.

(3) Subject to paragraphs (2), (4) and (5), the appropriate authority shall allow fees for work allowed by it under this regulation in accordance with Schedule 1 Part I; provided that, where any work allowed was done after 30th June 1991, it may allow such fees as appear to it to be reasonable for such work having regard to the rates specified in that Part of Schedule 1.

(4) In the case of criminal proceedings in the Crown Court and the Court of Appeal, the fees allowed in accordance with Part I of Schedule 1 shall be those appropriate to such of the following grades of fee-earner as the appropriate authority considers reasonable—

(a) senior solicitor,

(b) solicitor, legal executive or fee-earner of equivalent experience,

(c) articled clerk or fee-earner of equivalent experience.

(5) In the case of care proceedings in the Crown Court, the appropriate authority shall allow such fees in respect of such work as it considers reasonable in such amounts as appear to it to be reasonable remuneration for such work.

(6) This regulation applies to work in respect of which standard fees are payable under Part II of Schedule 1 only to the extent that that Part specifically so provides.

Amended by the Legal Aid Criminal and Care Proceedings (Costs) (Amendment) Regulations 1990 (S.I. 1990 No. 488).

Determination of solicitors' disbursements

7.—(1) Subject to the provisions of this regulation, the appropriate authority shall allow such disbursements claimed under regulation 5 as appear to it to have been reasonably incurred; provided that:

(a) if they are abnormally large by reason of the distance of the court or the assisted person's residence or both from the solicitor's place of business, reimbursement of the expenses may be limited to what would otherwise, having regard to all the circumstances, be a reasonable amount; and

(b) in the case of an appeal to the Court of Appeal, the cost of a transcript, or any part thereof, of the proceedings in the court from which the appeal lies obtained otherwise than through the registrar shall not be allowed except where the appropriate authority considers that it is reasonable in all the circumstances for such disbursement to be allowed.

(2) Subject to paragraph (3), a solicitor may claim a disbursement in respect of fees of counsel instructed by him in proceedings in a magistrates' court where counsel has not been assigned under the legal aid order.

(3) The appropriate authority shall determine the amount of any disbursement payable under paragraph (2) by estimating the sum which it would have allowed the solicitor under these Regulations by way of costs had he undertaken the case without counsel and shall allow counsel and the solicitor such reasonable costs as do not together exceed that sum.

(4) No question as to the propriety of any step or act in relation to which prior authority has been obtained under regulation 54 of the General Regulations shall be raised on any determination of costs, unless the solicitor knew or ought reasonably to have known that the purpose for which the authority was given had failed or become irrelevant or unnecessary before the costs were incurred.

(5) Where costs are reasonably incurred in accordance with and subject to the limit imposed by a prior authority given under regulation 54 of the General Regulations, no question shall be raised on any determination of costs as to the amount of the payment to be allowed for the step or act in relation to which the authority was given.

(6) Where costs are incurred in taking any step or doing any act for which authority may be given under regulation 54 of the General Regulations, without authority to do so having been given or in excess of any fee authorised under regulation 54 of the General Regulations, payment in respect of those costs may nevertheless be allowed on a determination of costs.

Claims for fees by counsel

8.—(1) Subject to regulation 17, no claim by counsel for fees for work done under a legal aid order shall be entertained unless counsel submits it within three months of the conclusion of the proceedings to which the legal aid order relates.

(2) Subject to paragraph (3), a claim for fees shall be submitted to the appropriate authority in such form and manner as it may direct.
A claim shall—

(a) summarise the items of work in respect of which fees are claimed according to the classes specified in regulation 9(4);

(b) state the dates on which the items of work were done, the time taken where appropriate, the sums claimed and whether the work was done for more than one assisted person;

(c) give particulars of any work done in relation to more than one indictment or a retrial.

(4) Where counsel claims that—

(a) it would be inappropriate to allow a standard fee under regulation 9(2); or

(b) regulation 9(5)(b) should be applied in relation to an item of work, he shall give full particulars in support of his claim.

(5) Where there are any special circumstances which should be drawn to the attention of the appropriate authority, counsel shall specify them.

(6) Counsel shall supply such further particulars, information and documents as the appropriate authority may require.

Determination of counsel's fees

9.—(1) The appropriate authority shall consider the claim, any further particulars, information or documents submitted by counsel under regulation 8 and any other relevant information and shall allow such work as appears to it to have been reasonably done.

(2) Where the work allowed has been done by junior counsel in the Crown Court, the appropriate authority shall, subject to paragraph (3), allow such of the standard fees specified in Part I of Schedule 2 as may be applicable to that work, unless it appears to the appropriate authority that the standard fee would be inappropriate taking into account all the relevant circumstances of the case, in which case it shall allow fees in accordance with paragraphs (4) and (5).

(3) The appropriate authority may not allow a standard fee in respect of—

(a) committals for trial in which the indictment includes counts in respect of an offence which is classified as a class 1 or 2 offence in accordance with directions given by the Lord Chief Justice under section 75 of the Supreme Court Act 1981(a);

(b) proceedings in any other case—

(i) which lasted more than three days or which at the time of listing were reasonably expected to last more than three days;

(ii) in which the indictment is disposed of by a plea of guilty but which if contested would reasonably have been expected to last more than three days,

unless counsel requests that a standard fee be allowed.

(4) The appropriate authority may, except in relation to work for which a standard fee is allowed under paragraph (2), allow any of the following classes of fee to counsel in respect of work allowed by it under this regulation—

(a) a basic fee for preparation including preparation for a pre-trial review and, where appropriate, the first day's hearing including, where they took place on that day, short conferences, consultations, applications and appearances (including bail applications), views and any other preparation;

(b) a refresher fee for any day or part of a day during which a hearing continued, including, where they took place on that day, short conferences, consultations, applications and appearances (including bail applications), views and any other preparation;

(c) subsidiary fees for—

    (i) attendance at conferences, consultations and views not covered by sub-paragraph (a) or (b);

    (ii) written advice on evidence, plea, appeal, case stated or other written work;

    (iii) attendance at pre-trial reviews, applications and appearances (including bail applications and adjournments for sentence) not covered by sub-paragraph (a) or (b).

(5) In the case of proceedings in the Crown Court or a magistrates' court, the appropriate authority shall, except in relation to work for which a standard fee is allowed under paragraph (2), allow such fees in respect of such work as it considers reasonable in such amounts as it may determine in accordance with Part II of Schedule 2; provided that:

(a) where any work allowed was done after 30th June 1991, the appropriate authority may allow such fees in such amounts as appear to it to be reasonable remuneration for such work having regard to the amounts specified in Part II of Schedule 2; or

(b) where it appears to the appropriate authority, taking into account all the relevant circumstances of the case, that owing to the exceptional circumstances of the case the amount payable by way of fees in accordance with Part II of Schedule 2 would not provide reasonable remuneration for some or all of the work it has allowed, it may allow such amount as appears to it to be reasonable remuneration for the relevant work.

(6) In the case of proceedings in the Court of Appeal, the appropriate authority shall allow such fees in respect of such work as it considers reasonable in such amounts as appear to it to be reasonable remuneration for such work.

(7) Where prior authority has been obtained to instruct a Queen's Counsel alone under regulation 54 of the General Regulations, no question as to the propriety of that act shall be raised on any determination of counsel's fees, unless the solicitor knew or ought reasonably to have known that the purpose for which the authority was given had failed or become irrelevant or unnecessary before the fees were incurred.

Amended by the Legal Aid in Criminal and Care Proceedings (Costs) (Amendment) Regulations (S.I. 1990 No. 488).

Payment of costs

10.—(1) Having determined the costs payable to a solicitor or counsel in accordance with these Regulations, the appropriate authority shall notify the solicitor or counsel of the costs payable and authorise payment accordingly.

(2) Where the costs payable under paragraph (1) are varied as a result of any review, redetermination or appeal made or brought pursuant to these Regulations, then—

(a) where the costs are increased, the appropriate authority shall authorise payment of the increase;

(b) where the costs are decreased, the solicitor or counsel shall repay the amount of such decrease; and

(c) where the payment of any costs of the solicitor or counsel is ordered under regulation 15(14) or 16(8) or under paragraph 8(4) of Schedule 1 Part II, the appropriate authority shall authorise such payment.

(3) Any payment in respect of counsel which is determined under regulation 7(3) shall be paid to counsel direct.

Notification of collecting court

11.—Having determined the costs payable to a solicitor or counsel in accordance with these Regulations, the appropriate authority shall notify the collecting court of the amount determined in each case in which a contribution order under section 23(1) of the Act has been made.

Review of determinations by the Board

12.—(1) If, in a case in which the Board is the appropriate authority, a solicitor or counsel is dissatisfied with a determination made under these Regulations, the solicitor or counsel may within 21 days of receipt of notification of the costs payable under regulation 10(1) apply to the appropriate area committee to review that determination.

(2) On an application under paragraph (1), the appropriate area committee shall review the determination whether by confirming, increasing or decreasing the amount of it.

Appeals to committee appointed by the Board

13.—(1) A solicitor or counsel who is dissatisfied with the decision of an area committee on a review under regulation 12 may within 21 days of receipt of notification of the decision apply to that committee to certify a point of principle of general importance.

(2) Where an area committee certifies a point of principle of general importance, the solicitor or counsel may within 21 days of receipt of notification of that certification appeal in writing to a committee of the Board against the decision of the area committee under regulation 12.

(3) On an appeal under this regulation the committee appointed by the Board may reverse, affirm or amend the decision of the area committee under regulation 12.

Redetermination of costs by appropriate authority other than the Board

14.—(1) Where—

(a) a solicitor or counsel is dissatisfied with the costs (other than standard fees allowed under Schedule 1 Part II or under regulation 9(2)) determined under these Regulations by an appropriate authority for proceedings other than criminal proceedings before a magistrates' court or care proceedings; or

(b) counsel is dissatisfied with the decision to allow standard fees,

he may apply to the appropriate authority to redetermine those costs or to review that decision as the case may be.

(2) Subject to regulation 17, the application shall be made, within 21 days of the receipt of notification of the costs payable under regulation 10(1), by giving notice in writing to the appropriate authority specifying the matters in respect of which the application is made and the grounds of objection and shall be made in such form and manner as the appropriate authority may direct.

(3) The notice of application shall be accompanied by—

(a) in the case of a solicitor, the particulars, information and documents supplied under regulation 5; and

(b) in the case of counsel, the particulars, information and documents supplied under regulation 8.

(4) The notice of application shall state whether the applicant wishes to appear or to be represented and, if the applicant so wishes, the appropriate authority shall notify the applicant of the time at which it is prepared to hear him or his representative.

(5) The solicitor or counsel shall supply such further particulars, information and documents as the appropriate authority may require.

(6) The appropriate authority shall—

(a) redetermine the costs, whether by way of increase, decrease or in the amounts previously determined; or

(b) review the decision to allow standard fees under regulation 9(2) and confirm it or allow fees in accordance with regulation 9(4) and (5),

in the light of the objections made by the applicant or on his behalf and shall notify the applicant of its decision.

(7) The applicant may request the appropriate authority to give reasons in writing for its decision and, if so requested, the appropriate authority shall comply with the request.

(8) Subject to regulation 17, any request under paragraph (7) shall be made within 21 days of receiving notification of the decision.

Appeals to a taxing master

15.—(1) Where the appropriate authority has given its reasons for its decision under regulation 14, a solicitor or counsel who is dissatisfied with that decision may appeal to a taxing master.

(2) Subject to regulation 17, an appeal shall be instituted, within 21 days of the receipt of the appropriate authority's reasons, by giving notice in writing to the Chief Taxing Master.

(3) The appellant shall send a copy of any notice given under paragraph (2) to the appropriate authority.

(4) The notice of appeal shall be accompanied by—

(a) a copy of the written representations given under regulation 14(2);

(b) the appropriate authority's reasons for its decision given under regulation 14(7); and

(c) the particulars, information and documents supplied to the appropriate authority under regulation 14.

(5) The notice of appeal shall—

    (a) be in such form as the Chief Taxing Master may direct,

    (b) specify separately each item appealed against, showing (where appropriate) the amount claimed for the item, the amount determined and the grounds of objection to the determination, and

    (c) state whether the appellant wishes to appear or to be represented or whether he will accept a decision given in his absence.

(6) The Chief Taxing Master may, and if so directed by the Lord Chancellor either generally or in a particular case shall, send to the Lord Chancellor a copy of the notice of appeal together with copies of such other documents as the Lord Chancellor may require.

(7) With a view to ensuring that the public interest is taken into account, the Lord Chancellor may arrange for written or oral representations to be made on his behalf and, if he intends to do so, he shall inform the Chief Taxing Master and the appellant.

(8) Any written representations made on behalf of the Lord Chancellor under paragraph (7) shall be sent to the Chief Taxing Master and the appellant and, in the case of oral representations, the Chief Taxing Master and the appellant shall be informed of the grounds on which such representations will be made.

(9) The appellant shall be permitted a reasonable opportunity to make representations in reply.

(10) The taxing master shall inform the appellant (or his representative) and the Lord Chancellor, where representations have been or are to be made on his behalf, of the date of any hearing and, subject to the provisions of this regulation, may give directions as to the conduct of the appeal.

(11) The taxing master may consult the trial judge, the appropriate authority or the determining officer and may require the appellant to provide any further information which he requires for the purpose of the appeal and, unless the taxing master otherwise directs, no further evidence shall be received on the hearing of the appeal and no ground of objection shall be valid which was not raised under regulation 14.

(12) The taxing master shall have the same powers as the appropriate authority under these Regulations and, in the exercise of such powers, may—

    (a) alter the redetermination of the appropriate authority in respect of any sum allowed, whether by increase or decrease as he thinks fit;

    (b) confirm the decision to allow standard fees under regulation 9(2) or allow fees in accordance with regulation 9(4) and (5).

(13) The taxing master shall communicate his decision and the reasons for it in writing to the appellant, the Lord Chancellor and the appropriate authority.

(14) Except where he confirms or decreases the sums redetermined under regulation 14 or confirms a decision to allow standard fees, the taxing master may allow the appellant a sum in respect of part or all of any reasonable costs (including any fee payable in respect of an appeal) incurred by him in connection with the appeal.

Appeals to the High Court

16.—(1) A solicitor or counsel who is dissatisfied with the decision of a taxing master on an appeal under regulation 15 may apply to a taxing master to certify a point of principle of general importance.

(2) Subject to regulation 17, an application under paragraph (1) shall be made within 21 days of notification of a taxing master's decision under regulation 15(13).

(3) Where a taxing master certifies a point of principle of general importance, the solicitor or counsel may appeal to the High Court against the decision of a taxing master on an appeal under regulation 15, and the Lord Chancellor shall be a respondent to such an appeal.

(4) Subject to regulation 17, an appeal under paragraph (3) shall be instituted within 21 days of receiving a taxing master's certificate under paragraph (1).

(5) Where the Lord Chancellor is dissatisfied with the decision of a taxing master on an appeal under regulation 15, he may, if no appeal has been made by the solicitor or counsel under paragraph (3), appeal to the High Court against that decision, and the solicitor or counsel shall be a respondent to the appeal.

(6) Subject to regulation 17, an appeal under paragraph (5) shall be instituted within 21 days of receiving notification of the taxing master's decision under regulation 15(13).

(7) An appeal under paragraphs (3) and (5) shall be instituted by originating summons in the Queen's Bench Division and shall be heard and determined by a single judge whose decision shall be final.

(8) The judge shall have the same powers as the appropriate authority and a taxing master under these Regulations and may reverse, affirm or amend the decision appealed against or make such other order as he thinks fit.

Time limits

17.—(1) Subject to paragraph (2), the period of time within which any act is required or authorised to be done under these Regulations by a solicitor or counsel may, for good reason, be extended by the appropriate authority; provided that where any such act is required or authorised to be done under regulation 15 or 16, the period of time thereby allowed may be extended, for good reason, only by a taxing master or the High Court as the case may be.

(2) Where a solicitor or counsel without good reason has failed (or, if an extension were not granted, would fail) to comply with a time limit, the appropriate authority, the Chief Taxing Master or the High Court, as the case may be, may, in exceptional circumstances, extend the time limit and shall consider whether it is reasonable in the circumstances to reduce the costs; provided that costs shall not be reduced unless the solicitor or counsel has been allowed a reasonable opportunity to show cause orally or in writing why the costs should not be reduced.

(3) A solicitor or counsel may appeal to the Chief Taxing Master against a decision made under this regulation by an appropriate authority in respect of proceedings other than proceedings before a magistrates' court and such an appeal shall be instituted within 21 days of the decision being given by giving notice in writing to the Chief Taxing Master specifying the grounds of appeal.

House of Lords

18.—(1) In the case of proceedings in the House of Lords, the costs payable to a solicitor or counsel under section 25 of the Act shall be determined by such officer as may be prescribed by order of the House of Lords.

(2) Subject to paragraph (1), these Regulations shall not apply to proceedings in the House of Lords.

SCHEDULES

SCHEDULE 1

SOLICITORS' FEES

PART I

FEES DETERMINED UNDER REGULATION 6

1.—(1) Subject to paragraphs 2 and 3, the appropriate authority shall allow fees for work allowed by it under regulation 6 at the following basic rates:

(a) Magistrates' court criminal proceedings

Class of work	Rate
Preparation	£39.25 per hour—(£41.75 per hour for a fee-earner whose office is situated within legal aid area 1, 13 or 14)
Advocacy	£49.50 per hour
Attendance at court where counsel assigned	£26.25 per hour
Travelling and waiting	£22 per hour
Routine letters written and routine telephone calls	£3.05 per item—(£3.15 per item for a fee-earner whose office is situated within legal aid area 1, 13 or 14)

(b) Magistrates' court care proceedings

Class of work	Rate
Preparation	£47.25 per hour—(£50.50 per hour for a fee-earner whose office is situated within legal aid area 1, 13 or 14)
Advocacy	£57 per hour
Attendance at court where counsel assigned	£30 per hour
Travelling and waiting	£26.50 per hour
Routine letters written and routine telephone calls	£3.40 per item

(c) Crown court criminal and Court of Appeal proceedings

Class of work	Grade of fee-earner	Rate
Preparation	Senior solicitor	£46 per hour—(£48.50 per hour for a fee-earner whose office is situated within legal aid area 1, 13 or 14)
	Solicitor, legal executive or fee-earner of equivalent experience	£39.50 per hour—(£41.75 per hour for a fee-earner whose office is situated within legal aid area 1, 13 or 14)
	Article clerk or fee-earner of equivalent experience	£26.00 per hour—(£30 per hour for a fee-earner whose office is situated within legal aid area 1, 13 or 14)
Advocacy	Senior solicitor	£57.00 per hour

	Solicitor	£49.50 per hour
Attendance at court where counsel assigned	Senior solicitor	£37.50 per hour
	Solicitor, legal executive or fee-earner of equivalent experience	£29.50 per hour
	Article clerk or fee-earner of equivalent experience	£18.25 per hour
Travelling and waiting	Senior solicitor	£22.00 per hour
	Solicitor, legal executive or fee-earner of equivalent experience	£22.00 per hour
	Article clerk or fee-earner of equivalent experience	£11.00 per hour
Routine lettes written and routine telephone calls		£3.05 per item—(£3.15 per item for a fee-earner whose office is situated within legal aid area 1, 13 or 14)"

(2) In paragraph (1), "legal aid area" means an area specified by the Board under regulation 4(1) of the Civil Legal Aid (General) Regulations 1989(a) and legal aid area 1, 13 or 14 means the area so numbered by the Board.

Amended by the Legal Aid in Criminal and Care Proceedings (Costs) Regulations 1990 (S.I. 1990 No. 488).

2. In respect of any item of work, the appropriate authority may allow fees at less than the relevant basic rate specified in paragraph 1 where it appears to the appropriate authority reasonable to do so having regard to the competence and dispatch with which the work was done.

3. In respect of any item of work, the appropriate authority may allow fees at more than the relevant basic rate specified in paragraph 1 where it appears to the appropriate authority that, taking into account all the relevant circumstances of the case, the amount of fees payable at such specified rate would not reasonably reflect—

(a) the exceptional competence and dispatch with which the work was done, or

(b) the exceptional circumstances of the case.

PART II

STANDARD FEES

Application

1.—(1) Subject to sub-paragraphs (3) and (4), this Part of this Schedule applies to the fees for work done by a fee-earner regardless of his grade in relation to the proceedings in the Crown Court specified in sub-paragraph (2).

(2) The following proceedings are specified for the purposes of sub-paragraph (1)—

(a) committals for trial in which the indictment consisted of counts in respect of an offence which is classified as a class 3 or 4 offence in accordance with directions given by the Lord Chief Justice under section 75 of the Supreme Court Act 1981 and

    (i) where the trial (including any case prepared for trial in which no jury was sworn) lasted two days or less and at the time of listing was reasonably expected to last two days or less; or

    (ii) where the case was listed and disposed of as a plea of guilty;

(b) appeals against conviction;

(c) appeals against sentence, and

(d) committals for sentence (including proceedings which arose out of a breach of

309

an order of the Crown Court, proceedings in which sentence was deferred and other similar matters).

(3) Where in any proceedings specified in sub-paragraph (2), the trial judge—

(a) is dissatisfied with the solicitor's conduct of the case; or

(b) considers that, for exceptional reasons, the fees should be determined under regulation 6,

he may direct that the fees should be determined under regulation 6 and in that event this Part of this Schedule shall not apply.

(4) If a solicitor so elects, he may claim standard fees under this Part of this Schedule in respect of work done by him notwithstanding that the proceedings in relation to which the work was done are not specified in sub-paragraph (2), and the provisions of this Part of this Schedule shall apply to such a claim with the necessary modifications, save that, where a solicitor elects to claim the principal standard fee for preparation in respect of a trial which lasted more than two days, he shall be paid that fee (together with the appropriate standard fees for the other classes of work specified in paragraph 4(2)) and paragraph 2 shall not apply.

(5) For the purposes of this Part of this Schedule, the standard fees which are payable and the classes of work for which such fees may be paid are specified in paragraph 4 and the "lower fee limit" and the "upper fee limit" have the meanings given by paragraph 4(3).

Allowance of standard fees

2.—(1) The appropriate authority shall allow the standard fee for preparation which has been claimed by a solicitor (together with the appropriate standard fees for the other classes of work specified in paragraph 4(2)) unless, where the principal standard fee for preparation has been claimed, such a fee is considered to be excessive in which case the lower standard fee shall be allowed.

(2) A solicitor who has been allowed the lower standard fee instead of the principal fee claimed may—

(a) accept that lower fee;

(b) request the appropriate authority in writing to review its decision, or

(c) provide the appropriate authority with a detailed claim in the form directed by the appropriate authority requesting in writing that the fees for preparation be determined under regulation 6.

(3) Where the appropriate authority is requested to review its decision under sub-paragraph (2)(b), the authority shall either—

(a) allow the principal fee; or

(b) request the solicitor to provide a detailed claim in the form directed by the appropriate authority.

(4) Where a solicitor fails to make a request under sub-paragraph (2)(b) or to supply a detailed claim for the purposes of sub-paragraph (2)(c) or (3)(b) within six weeks of the decision to allow the lower fee or the request to supply a detailed claim, whichever is the later, the decision to allow the lower standard fee shall be deemed to be confirmed.

3.—(1) Where a solicitor—

(a) submits a claim for determination under regulation 6 in a case to which paragraph 1(2) applies; or

(b) disputes the allowance of the lower standard fee and provides a detailed claim under paragraph 2(2)(c) or (3)(b),

the appropriate authority shall first determine the fees for preparation work within the meaning of paragraph 4(2)(a) of this Part of this Schedule.

(2) If the fees so determined are—

(a) less than the lower fee limit, the appropriate authority shall allow and pay the lower standard fee together with the standard fees for all other classes of work specified in paragraph 4(2);

(b) not less than the lower fee limit and not more than the upper fee limit, the appropriate authority shall allow and pay the principal standard fee together with the standard fees for all other classes of work specified in paragraph 4(2);

(c) more than the upper fee limit, no standard fees shall be payable and all fees shall be determined in accordance with regulation 6.

Standard fees

4.—(1) The classes of work for which standard fees shall be payable are those specified in sub-paragraph (2) and the fees for classes of work which are not so specified shall be determined in accordance with regulation 6.

(2) The classes of work specified for the purposes of sub-paragraph (1) are—

(a) preparation within the meaning of regulation 6(1)(a) but including routine letters written and routine telephone calls, within the meaning of regulation 6(1)(e);

(b) advocacy in respect of applications for bail;

(c) attendance at court (including waiting) where counsel is assigned;

(d) travelling except—

(i) to undertake work for which standard fees are not payable, or
(ii) where sub-paragraph (2)(b) applies,

and, for the purpose of this paragraph, "travelling" shall be deemed to include waiting in connection with preparation work, within the meaning of sub-paragraph (2)(a) above.

(3) The standard fees payable under this Part of this Schedule are the fees specified in the Table below and in this Part of this Schedule the "lower fee limit" and the "upper fee limit" mean the lower and upper fee limits specified in the Table.

Type of proceedings		Lower standard fee	Lower fee limit	Principal standard fee	Upper fee limit
Jury trials (including any case prepared for trial in which no jury was sworn)		£114	£157	£220	£274
	London rate	£121	£163	£229	£287
Guilty pleas		£72	£96	£154	£198
	London rate	£76	£100	£160	£207
Appeals against conviction		£45	£60	£135	£204
	London rate	£47	£62	£140	£214
Appeals against sentence		£32	£46	£82	£115
	London rate	£34	£48	£86	£119
Committals for sentence		£37	£45	£86	£124
	London rate	£39	£47	£90	£128
Advocacy in respect of bail applications		£23			
	London rate	£25			
Attendance at court (including waiting) where counsel assigned		£19 per hour			
Travelling		£16.25 per hour			

(4) A solicitor shall be entitled to the "London rate" of the standard fees specified in the Table where his office is situated within legal aid area 1, 13 or 14 within the meaning of paragraph 1(2) of Schedule 1, Part I.

(5) The hourly rate specified in the Table for attendance at court shall, subject to sub-paragraph (6), be paid in respect of the period of time beginning 30 minutes before the case was listed and ending

(a) where the client was present at court, 15 minutes after the hearing ended on that day, or

(b) where the client was not present at court, when the hearing ended on that day,

and, save in exceptional circumstances, shall not be payable during the luncheon adjournment.

(6) Where a fee-earner attends a court centre for the purposes of more than one case, the solicitor may claim the attendance fee in respect of the second or subsequent case only for the time actually spent in attendance in addition to the time for which payment is made under sub-paragraph (5).

(7) The hourly rate specified in the Table shall be paid for time spent travelling (within the meaning of sub-paragraph (2)(d)) and, where a fee-earner travels to appear as an advocate in respect of a bail application, the rate payable shall be the rate appropriate to the grade of fee-earner for travelling and waiting under paragraph 1(1)(c) of Schedule 1, Part I.

(8) Where a solicitor acts for more than one defendant, the appropriate authority shall—

(a) allow whichever of the appropriate standard preparation fees is the greater and increase that fee by 20 per cent. for each additional defendant;

(b) increase the standard advocacy fee by 20 per cent. for each additional defendant who is represented on a bail application,

but no percentage increase shall be made to the standard fees for attendance at court or for travelling.

(9) Where a solicitor acts for a defendant in respect of more than one—

(a) indictment,

(b) appeal against conviction,

(c) appeal against sentence, or

(d) committal for sentence

or in respect of any combination of (a) to (d) above, the appropriate authority shall allow whichever of the appropriate standard preparation fees is the greater and increase that fee by 20 per cent. for each additional indictment, appeal or committal for sentence as the case may be.

(10) Where a solicitor prepares a case with a view to counsel appearing at the substantive hearing without the solicitor or his representative attending court, the standard preparation fee payable after application of any increase required by paragraphs (8)(a) or (9) shall be further increased by £26.25 (or by £28 for a solicitor whose office is situated within legal aid area 1, 13, or 14).

(11) Where a fee-earner listens to a tape recording of an interview conducted under a code issued by the Secretary of State under section 60 of the Police and Criminal Evidence Act 1984(**a**), the standard preparation fee payable after application of any increase required by paragraph 8(a) or 9 shall be further increased by £9.40 for every 10 minutes of the total running time of all tapes or parts of tapes listened to and by the same amount for any remaining period.

(12) Where the standard fee payable is increased by virtue of sub-paragraph (8)(a), (9), (10) or (11), then for the purposes of paragraphs 3, 6 and 8—

(a) the upper fee limit shall be increased by the same amount by which the principal standard fee has been increased, and

312

(b) the lower fee limit shall be increased by the same amount by which the lower standard fee has been increased.

Amended by the Legal Aid in Criminal and Care Proceedings (Costs) (Amendment) Regulations 1990 (S.I. 1990 No. 488).

Disbursements
5. Nothing in this Part of this Schedule applies to disbursements which shall be determined in accordance with regulation 7.

Re-determinations and appeals
6.—(1) A solicitor who is dissatisfied with a decision on a determination under paragraph 3 may apply for the costs to be re-determined and, subject to sub-paragraph (2), the provisions of regulation 14(2) to (8) shall apply with the necessary modifications to an application under this paragraph as they apply to an application under regulation 14.

(2) On a re-determination under this paragraph, the appropriate authority shall determine the fees for preparation work within the meaning of paragraph 4(2)(a) and if the fees so determined are—

(a) less than the lower fee limit, the lower standard fee shall be allowed together with the standard fees for all other classes of work specified in paragraph 4(2);

(b) not less than the lower fee limit and not more than the upper fee limit, the principal standard fee shall be allowed together with the standard fees for all other classes of work specified in paragraph 4(2);

(c) more than the upper fee limit, the fees for all classes of work shall be determined in accordance with regulation 6.

7. Irrespective of any dispute under paragraph 2 as to whether the principal standard fee should have been allowed instead of the lower standard fee, where a solicitor is satisfied with a decision to allow a standard fee but contends that—

(a) a standard fee which is not apt for the type of work done has been allowed; or

(b) the provisions of paragraph 4(4) to (12) have been incorrectly applied,

he may, within six weeks of receipt of notification of the decision, make a written request setting out his reasons why the decision should be reviewed and, if the appropriate authority confirms its decision, written reasons shall be given.

8.—(1) A solicitor may appeal to a taxing master where he is dissatisfied with—

(a) a decision on a re-determination under paragraph 6, or

(b) a decision on a review under paragraph 7.

(2) Where a solicitor appeals to a taxing master in respect of a decision under paragraph 6, the taxing master shall determine the fees for preparation within the meaning of paragraph 4(2)(a) and if the fees so determined are—

(a) less than the lower fee limit, the lower standard fee shall be allowed by the taxing master together with the standard fees for all other classes of work specified in paragraph 4(2);

(b) not less than the lower fee limit and not more than the upper fee limit, the principal standard fee shall be allowed by the taxing master together with the standard fees for all other classes of work specified in paragraph 4(2);

(c) more than the upper fee limit, the fees for all classes of work shall be determined by the taxing master in accordance with regulation 6.

(3) Where a solicitor appeals to a taxing master in respect of a decision made on a review under paragraph 7, the taxing master shall allow whichever standard fee he considers to be apt for the type of work done or, as the case may be, re-apply the provisions of paragraph 4(4) to (12).

(4) Where a taxing master allows an appeal in whole or in part, he may allow the solicitor a sum in respect of part or all of any reasonable costs (including any fee payable in respect of the appeal) incurred by him in connection with the appeal.

(5) This paragraph only applies to appeals in proceedings for which standard fees are payable and the provisions of regulation 15 shall apply to appeals in proceedings for which standard fees are not payable.

(6) Subject to the foregoing provisions of this paragraph, the provisions of regulations 15 to 17 relating to appeals by solicitors shall apply with the necessary modifications to appeals in proceedings for which standard fees are payable under this Part of this Schedule as they apply to appeals in proceedings for which standard fees are not payable.

SCHEDULE 2

COUNSEL'S FEES

PART I

STANDARD FEES

1. The appropriate authority shall allow the fees specified in the Table and

    (a) a standard basic fee shall cover preparation and the first day's hearing including, where they took place on that day, short conferences, applications and appearances (including bail applications), views and any other preparation;

    (b) a standard refresher fee shall cover any day during which a hearing continued, including, where they took place on that day, short conferences, applications and appearances (including bail applications), views and any other preparation;

    (c) a standard written work fee shall cover written advice on evidence, plea, appeal, case stated and other written work;

    (d) a standard appearance fee shall cover attendance at applications and appearances (including bail applications and adjournments for sentence) together with, where they took place on that day, short conferences where attendance is not covered by (a) or (b) but shall not cover attendance at a pre-trial review.

2. For the purpose of determining which of the standard refresher fees specified in the Table should be allowed—

    (a) a half day refresher fee shall be allowed where

      (i) a hearing begins and ends before the luncheon adjournment, or
      (ii) a hearing begins after the luncheon adjournment and ends before 5.30 pm; and

    (b) a full day refresher fee shall be allowed where

      (i) a hearing begins before and ends after the luncheon adjournment but before 5.30 pm, or
      (ii) a hearing begins after the luncheon adjournment and ends after 5.30 pm; and

    (c) a more than a full day refresher fee shall be allowed where a hearing begins before the luncheon adjournment and ends after 5.30 pm.

3. The standard basic fee specified for "committals for sentence" shall be allowed to junior counsel in respect of proceedings arising out of a breach of an order of the Crown Court or other similar matters.

4. Where a case listed for jury trial does not proceed on the day for which it is listed the appropriate authority shall allow a sum equal to half of the standard basic fee for a jury trial.

5. Where counsel attends in respect of—

    (a) a case listed for plea which is adjourned for trial; or

    (b) a case to which neither paragraph 4 nor paragraph 6 applies, which is listed for hearing but not opened due to the failure of the defendant or a witness to attend or the non-availability of a social enquiry report or for some good reason,

the appropriate authority shall allow the standard appearance fee.

Amended by the Legal Aid in Criminal and Care Proceedings (Costs) (Amendment) Regulations 1990 (S.I. 1990 No. 488).

6. Where counsel attends in respect of a case which is listed for plea and on which a guilty plea is taken, and which is adjourned part-heard, the appropriate authority shall allow—

    (a) the standard basic fee for first hearing; and

    (b) the standard appearance fee for the hearing at which the case is disposed of.

Amended by the Legal Aid in Criminal and Care Proceedings (Costs) (Amendment) Regulations 1990 (S.I. 1990 No. 488).

7. Where counsel represents more than one defendant the appropriate authority shall

    (a) increase the standard basic fee by 20 per cent. for each additional defendant who is substantively dealt with at the hearing in respect of which that standard basic fee is to be paid; or

    (b) where paragraph 4, 5 or 6 applies, increase the sum payable by 20 per cent. for each additional defendant.

8. Where counsel appears on behalf of a defendant on the same day in respect of more than one

    (a) indictment,

    (b) appeal against conviction,

    (c) appeal against sentence, or

    (d) committal for sentence,

or in respect of any combination of (a) to (d) above, the appropriate authority shall allow whichever of the standard basic fees is the greater and shall increase it by 20 per cent. for each additional indictment, appeal or committal for sentence, as the case may be.

9. Where counsel appears at the substantive hearing of a case without his instructing solicitor or representative attending court, the standard basic fee payable after application of any increase required by paragraph 7(a) or 8 shall be further increased by £17.

Amended by the Legal Aid in Criminal and Care Proceedings (Costs) (Amendment) Regulations 1990 (S.I. 1990 No. 488).

10. Where counsel listens to a tape recording of an interview conducted under a code issued by the Secretary of State under section 60 of the Police and Criminal Evidence Act 1984, the standard basic fee payable after application of any increase required by paragraph 7(a) or 8 shall be further increased by £9.40 for every 10 minutes of the total running time of all tapes or parts of tapes listened to and by the same amount for any remaining period.

Amended by the Legal Aid in Criminal and Care Proceedings (Costs) (Amendment) Regulations 1990 (S.I. 1990 No. 488).

11. Where counsel is instructed to appear in a court which is not within 25 miles of his chambers, the appropriate authority may allow an amount in respect of counsel's attendance at that court to cover any travelling and hotel expenses reasonably incurred and necessarily and exclusively attributable to counsel's attendance at that court, provided that the amount allowed shall not be greater than the amount, if any, which would be payable to counsel practising from the nearest local Bar unless counsel can justify his attendance having regard to all the relevant circumstances of the case.

Type of proceedings	*Standard basic fee*
Jury trials (including any case prepared for trial in which no jury is sworn)	£193
Guilty pleas	£102
Appeals against conviction	£102
Appeals against sentence	£64
Committals for sentence	£64
Standard appearance fee	£40
Standard refresher fee	
(1) Half day	£71
(2) Full day	£136
(3) More than a full day	£207
Standard written work fee	£26

Amended by the Legal Aid in Criminal and Care Proceedings (Costs) (Amendment) Regulations 1990 (S.I. 1990 No. 488).

PART II

DETERMINATION OF OTHER FEES

1. The appropriate authority shall allow such fee in respect of an item of work allowed under regulation 9(5), not exceeding the maximum amount specified in respect of that item of work, as appears to it to provide reasonable remuneration.

2. Where an hourly rate is specified in a Table in this Part of this Schedule in respect of an item of work allowed under regulation 9(5), the appropriate authority shall determine any fee for such work in accordance with that hourly rate; provided that the fee determined shall not be less than the minimum amount specified.

3. Where a refresher fee is claimed in respect of less than a full day, the appropriate authority shall allow such fee as appears to it reasonable having regard to the fee which would be allowable for a full day.

4. The fees allowed to junior counsel for proceedings in the Crown Court arising out of a breach of an order of the Crown Court or other similar matters shall not exceed the maximum amounts specified for "committals for sentence."

5. Paragraph 11 of Part I of this Schedule shall apply where counsel's fees are determined in accordance with this Part of the Schedule as it applies where standard fees are allowed in accordance with Part I of the Schedule.

The following tables are amended by the Legal Aid in Criminal and Care Proceedings (Costs) (Amendment) Regulations 1990 (S.I. 1990 No. 488).

TABLE 1: JUNIOR COUNSEL

Court	Type of proceedings	Basic fee	Full day refresher fee	Subsidiary fees		
				Attendance at consultations, conferences & views	*Written work*	*Attendance at pre-trial reviews, applications and other appearances*
Magistrates' Court	All cases	Maximum amount: £448	Maximum amount: £155	£26 per hour Minimum amount: £13	Maximum amount: £49	Maximum amount: £90
Crown Court	Jury trials	Maximum amount: £522				
	Cases prepared for trial in which no jury is sworn	Maximum amount: £304				
	Guilty pleas	Maximum amount: £184	Maximum amount: £171	£30 per hour Minimum amount: £15	Maximum amount: £56	Maximum amount: £95
	Appeals against conviction	Maximum amount: £201				
	Appeals against sentence	Maximum amount: £103				
	Committals for sentence	Maximum amount: £103				

TABLE 2: QUEEN'S COUNSEL

Court	Type of proceedings	Basic fee	Full day refresher fee	Subsidiary fees		
				Attendance at consultations, conferences & views	*Written work*	*Attendance at pre-trial reviews, applications and other appearances*
Magistrates' Court	All cases	Maximum amount: £4,317	Maximum amount: £289	£50 per hour Minimum amount: £25	Maximum amount: £102	Maximum amount: £199
Crown Court	All cases	Maximum amount: £5,243	Maximum amount: £321	£57 per hour Minimum amount: £29	Maximum amount: £116	Maximum amount: £250

EXPLANATORY NOTE
(This note is not part of the Regulations)

These Regulations consolidate the Legal Aid in Criminal Proceedings (Costs) Regulations 1988, as amended, (which are revoked subject to the provisions of regulation 1(3)) and provide for the determination of the costs which may be paid to the legal representatives of a person given legal aid under Parts I and VI of the Legal Aid Act 1988 (legal aid in criminal proceedings and care proceedings).

Regulations 5 and 6 provide for the determination of solicitors' fees, and hourly rates (including separate rates for work in care proceedings) are prescribed together with (in Schedule 1 Part II) a system of standard fees. Regulations 8 and 9 provide for the determination of counsel's fees and scales of payment are prescribed together with a system of standard fees for certain items of work done by junior counsel in the Crown Court. Regulations 12 to 16 and paragraphs 6 to 8 of Schedule 1 Part II provide for the redetermination of fees and for appeals.

These Regulations increase the rates of remuneration previously payable under the 1988 Regulations with an overall increase of six per cent.

Legal Advice and Assistance (Duty Solicitor) (Remuneration) Regulations 1989

Coming into force April 1, 1989

The Lord Chancellor, in exercise of the powers conferred on him by sections 34 and 43 of the Legal Aid Act 1988, with the concurrence of the Treasury, hereby makes the following Regulations:—

Title, commencement, revocations and transitional provisions

1.—(1) These Regulations may be cited as the Legal Advice and Assistance (Duty Solicitor) (Remuneration) Regulations 1989 and shall come into force on April 1, 1989.

(2) The Regulations specified in the schedule are hereby revoked.

(3) Where a review under regulation 8 relates to a claim made before June 1, 1989, regulation 9(1) and (2) shall not apply and the solicitor may appeal in writing within 21 days of receipt of notification of the decision on the review to a committee appointed by the Board.

Interpretation

2. In these Regulations, unless the context otherwise requires:—

"the 1988 Act" means the Legal Aid Act 1988;

"appropriate area committee" means the area committee in whose area is situated the magistrates' court at which a solicitor has given advice or assistance in accordance with arrangements made by the Board under regulation 7 or 8 of the Legal Advice and Assistance Regulations 1989;

"area committee" has the meaning assigned to it by regulation 4 of the Civil Legal Aid (General) Regulations 1989;

"bank holiday" means a bank holiday in England and Wales under the Banking and Financial Dealings Act 1971;

"duty day" means a day during which a duty solicitor is present at a magistrates' court in accordance with a scheme;

"duty solicitor" means a solicitor who is present at a magistrates' court in accordance with a scheme;

"duty solicitor scheme" means any arrangements made by the Board under regulation 31 or 33 of the Legal Advice and Assistance Regulations 1989;

"the 1989 regulations" means the Legal Aid in Criminal and Care Proceedings (Costs) Regulations 1989.

General

3.—(1) Remuneration shall be determined by the Board in accordance with these Regulations.

(2) The Board shall appoint or authorise the appointment of determining officers to act on its behalf under these Regulations in accordance with directions given by it or on its behalf.

Claims for remuneration

4.—(1) A claim for remuneration by a duty solicitor shall be submitted to the determining officer in such form and manner as the Board may direct and any such claim shall be submitted within three months of the duty day in respect of which the claim is made.

(2) The duty solicitor shall supply such further particulars, information and documents as the determining officer may require.

(3) The time limit within which the claim for remuneration must be submitted may, for good reason, be extended by the determining officer.

Determination of remuneration

5.—(1) The determining officer shall consider the claim, any further particulars, information or documents submitted by the duty solicitor and any other relevant information and allow:—

(a) such time as he considers reasonable in respect of work done, including attendance and waiting, at a magistrates' court which he considers has been actually and reasonably done in accordance with a scheme; and

(b) such time as he considers was reasonably taken by a duty solicitor in travelling from his place of work (or, on a bank holiday, a Saturday or a Sunday from his place of residence) to a magistrates' court; and in returning therefrom, where that solicitor is called out to (or, on a bank holiday, a Saturday or a Sunday, attends at) the Court to act as a duty solicitor.

(2) Subject to paragraph (3), the determining officer shall allow remuneration:—

(a) in respect of (1)(a) above at such rate as is the average of the two separate basic rates provided for advocacy and for travelling and waiting respectively in paragraph 1(1)(a) of Part I of Schedule 1 to the 1989 Regulations; and

(b) in respect of (1)(b) above at the same rate as the basic rate provided for travelling and waiting in paragraph 1(1)(a) of Part I of Schedule 1 to the 1989 Regulations;

provided that the basic rates shall be those which would apply to work done under the 1989 Regulations on the same day as the duty day in respect of which the claim is made.

(3) Remuneration allowed in accordance with paragraph (2)(a) shall be increased by 25 per cent. in respect of work done on a bank holiday, a Saturday or a Sunday.

Travelling expenses

6. Where the determining officer allows travelling time under Regulation 5(1)(b) above, he may also allow such travelling expenses as he considers have been actually and reasonably incurred.

320

Payment of remuneration

7.—(1) The determining officer shall authorise payment to the duty solicitor in the amounts determined (whether by him or on review or appeal) in accordance with these Regulations.

(2) Where the costs payable under paragraph (1) are varied as a result of any review or appeal in accordance with these Regulations, then—

(a) where the costs are increased, the determining officer shall authorise payment of the increase;

(b) where the costs are decreased the solicitor shall repay the amount of such decrease.

Review of determination

8.—(1) If a solicitor is dissatisfied with the decision of a determining officer under these Regulations, the solicitor may within 21 days of receipt of notification of the costs payable under regulation 7(1) apply to the appropriate area committee to review that decision.

(2) On an application under paragraph (1), the appropriate area committee shall review the determination of the determining officer whether by confirming, increasing or decreasing the amount of the determination.

Appeals to Committee Appointed by the Board

9.—(1) A solicitor who is dissatisfied with the decision of an area committee on a review under regulation 8 may within 21 days of receipt of notification of the decision apply to that committee to certify a point of principle of general importance.

(2) Where an area committee certifies a point of principle of general importance, the solicitor may within 21 days of receipt of notification of that certification appeal in writing against the decision of the area committee to a committee appointed by the Board.

(3) On an appeal under this regulation the committee appointed by the Board may reverse, affirm or amend the decision of the area committee.

SCHEDULE

REVOCATIONS

Regulations revoked	*References*
The Legal Advice and Representation (Duty Solicitor) (Remuneration) Regulations 1987.	S.I. 1987/443.
The Legal Advice and Representation (Duty Solicitor) (Remuneration) (Amendment) Regulations 1988.	S.I. 1988/447

EXPLANATORY NOTE
(This note is not part of the Regulations)

These Regulations replace with amendments the Legal Advice and Representation (Duty Solicitor) (Remuneration) Regulations 1987. They provide for

321

determination and review by the Legal Aid Board of the remuneration payable to duty solicitors providing advice and assistance by way of representation at magistrates' court under regulations 7 and 8 of the Legal Advice and Assistance Regulations 1989. The main changes are:—

(a) to reflect the taking over of responsibility for the administration of legal aid by the Legal Aid Board; and

(b) to increase by 25 per cent. remuneration for work done at a magistrates' court on a bank holiday, a Saturday or a Sunday (regulation 5).

The rates of remuneration are fixed by reference to the rates provided for advocacy and for travelling and waiting (currently £46 and £20.50 per hour respectively) in paragraph 1(1)(a) of Part I of Schedule 1 to the Legal Aid in Criminal and Care Proceedings (Costs) Regulations 1989. (*Now £49.50 and £22.00*).

Legal Advice and Assistance at Police Stations (Remuneration) Regulations 1989*

Coming into force April 1, 1989

The Lord Chancellor, in exercise of the powers conferred on him by sections 34 and 43 of the Legal Aid Act 1988, and with the concurrence of the Treasury, hereby makes the following Regulations:—

Citation, commencement, revocations and transitional provisions

1.—(1) These Regulations may be cited as the Legal Advice and Assistance at Police Stations (Remuneration) Regulations 1989 and shall come into force on April 1, 1989.

(2) The Legal Advice and Assistance at Police Stations (Remuneration) Regulations 1988 are hereby revoked except in relation to work done before April 1, 1989.

(3) Where a review under regulation 7 relates to a claim made before June 1, 1989, regulation 8(1) and (2) shall not apply and the solicitor may appeal in writing within 21 days of receipt of notification of the decision on the review to a committee appointed by the Board.

Interpretation

2.—(1) In these Regulations, unless the context otherwise requires—

"the 1988 Act" means the Legal Aid Act 1988;

"advice" and "assistance" mean respectively advice and assistance under the 1988 Act;

"appropriate area committee" means the area committee in whose area is situated the police station or other premises at which a solicitor has given advice or assistance in accordance with arrangements made by the Board under regulation 6 of the Legal Advice and Assistance Regulations 1989;

"area committee" has the meaning assigned to it by regulation 4 of the Civil Legal Aid (General) Regulations 1989;

"duty period" means any period of 24 hours during which a duty solicitor holds himself available to give advice and assistance in accordance with a duty solicitor scheme;

"duty solicitor" means any solicitor, and any representative of a solicitor, who provides advice and assistance in accordance with a duty solicitor scheme;

"duty solicitor scheme" means any arrangements made by the Board under regulation 6 of the Legal Advice and Assistance Regulations 1989;

"own solicitor" means a solicitor who gives advice and assistance to a person arrested and held in custody or to a volunteer otherwise than as a

---

* As amended by the Legal Advice and Assistance at Police Stations (Remuneration) (Amendment) Regulations 1990 (S.I. 1990 No. 487) with effect from April 1, 1990.

duty solicitor;

"serious service offence" means an offence under any of the Army Act 1955, the Air Force Act 1955 or the Naval Discipline Act 1957 which cannot be dealt with summarily or which appears to an interviewing service policeman to be serious;

"unsocial hours" means between the hours of 5.30 pm and 9.30 am on any weekday and any time on a Saturday, Sunday or bank holiday;

"volunteer" means a person who, for the purpose of assisting with an investigation, attends voluntarily at a police station or at any other place where a constable is present or accompanies a constable to a police station or any such other place without having been arrested.

General

3.—(1) Remuneration shall be determined by the Board in accordance with these Regulations.

(2) The Board shall appoint or authorise the appointment of determining officers to act on its behalf under these Regulations in accordance with directions given by it or on its behalf.

Claims for remuneration

4.—(1) A claim for remuneration by a duty solicitor or an own solicitor shall be submitted to the determining officer in such form and manner as the Board may direct and any such claim shall be submitted within three months of the duty period or of the day on which the advice and assistance was given.

(2) The solicitor shall supply such further particulars, information and documents as the determining officer may require.

(3) The time limit within which the claim must be submitted may, for good reason, be extended by the determining officer.

Determination of remuneration

5.—(1) The determining officer may allow work done in the following classes:

    (a) availability during duty period;

    (b) advice and assistance given to a person arrested and held in custody or being interviewed in connection with a serious service offence or to a volunteer;

    (c) travelling and waiting;

    (d) advising and assisting over the telephone;

    (e) routine telephone calls.

(2) The determining officer shall consider the claim, any further particulars, information or documents submitted by the solicitor under regulation 4 and any other relevant information, and allow:

    (a) such work as appears to him to have been actually and reasonably done by a duty solicitor or an own solicitor, classifying it according to the classes specified in paragraph (1); and

    (b) such time in respect of each class of work allowed by him (other than advising over the telephone and dealing with routine telephone calls) as he considers reasonable.

(3) Subject to paragraph (5), the determining officer shall allow fees for the work allowed by him under this regulation in accordance with the Schedule.

(4) Subject to paragraph (5), the determining officer may allow a reasonable sum in respect of:

(a) hotel expenses actually and reasonably incurred by a duty solicitor where attendance in accordance with a rota is allowed under paragraph (1)(a);

(b) travelling expenses actually and reasonably incurred by a duty solicitor or an own solicitor where travelling and waiting is allowed under paragraph (1)(c);

(c) any disbursement actually and reasonably incurred by a duty solicitor or an own solicitor.

(5) Subject to paragraph (6) the fees allowed under the Schedule, except any fee allowed in respect of work done under paragraph (1)(a), together with any expenses allowed under paragraph (4)(b) and (c), shall not exceed the limit prescribed by regulation 4(1)(a) of the Legal Advice and Assistance Regulations 1989.

(6) Paragraph (5) shall not apply to fees for advice or assistance which the determining officer is satisfied was required in the interests of justice be given as a matter of urgency.

Payment of remuneration

6.—(1) The determining officer shall authorise payment to the duty solicitor or an own solicitor in the amounts determined (whether by him or on review or appeal) in accordance with these Regulations.

(2) Where the costs payable under paragraph (1) are varied as a result of any review or appeal in accordance with these Regulations, then—

(a) where the costs are increased, the determining officer shall authorise payment of the increase;

(b) where the costs are decreased the solicitor shall repay the amount of such decrease.

Review of determination

7.—(1) If a solicitor is dissatisfied with the determination of a determining officer under these Regulations, the solicitor may within 21 days of receipt of notification of the costs payable under regulation 6(1) apply to the appropriate area committee to review that determination.

(2) On an application under paragraph (1), the appropriate area committee shall review the determination of the determining officer whether by confirming, increasing or decreasing the amount of his determination.

Appeal to committee appointed by the Board

8.—(1) A solicitor who is dissatisfied with the decision of an area committee on a review under regulation 7 may within 21 days of receipt of notification of the decision apply to that committee to certify a point of principle of general importance.

(2) Where an area committee certifies a point of principle of general importance, the solicitor may within 21 days of receipt of notification of that

certification appeal in writing against the decision of the area committee to a committee appointed by the Board.

(3) On an appeal under this regulation the committee appointed by the Board may reverse, affirm or amend the decision of the area committee.

SCHEDULE

1.—(1) The Board shall, subject to paragraph 2 in the case of item (a), allow fees for work allowed by it under regulation 5 at the following rates:

Class of work	*Rate*
(a) availability during duty period	£3.15 per hour served, to a maximum of £75.60 (£3.20 per hour served to a maximum of £76.80 in respect of a solicitor whose office is situated within legal aid area 1, 13 or 14)
(b) advice and assistance to a person arrested and held in custody, or being interviewed in connection with a serious service offence or to a volunteer, given	
(i) by a duty solicitor in unsocial hours	£52.25 per hour
(ii) by a duty solicitor in all other hours	£39.25 per hour (£41.75 per hour in respect of a solicitor whose office is situated within legal aid area 1, 13 or 14)
(iii) by an own solicitor	£39.25 per hour (£41.75 per hour in respect of a solicitor whose office is situated within legal aid area 1, 13 or 14)
(c) travelling and waiting	
(i) by a duty solicitor in unsocial hours	£52.25 per hour
(ii) by a duty solicitor in all other hours	£39.25 per hour (£41.75 per hour in respect of a solicitor whose office is situated within legal aid area 1, 13 or 14)
(iii) by an own solicitor	£22 per hour
(d) advising and assisting over the telephone	£17.75 per item £18.25 per item in respect of a solicitor whose office is situated within legal aid area 1, 13 or 14)
(e) routine telephone calls	£1.90 per item (£2 per item in respect of a solicitor whose office is situated within legal aid area 1, 13 or 14)

Amended by the Legal Advice and Assistance at Police Stations (Remuneration) (Amendment) Regulations 1990 (S.I. 1990 No. 487).

(2) In paragraph 1(1), "legal aid area 1, 13 or 14" means the area so numbered by the Board under regulation 4(1) of the Civil Legal Aid (General) Regulations 1989.

2. The fee allowed under paragraph 1(1)(a) shall be reduced by the amount of any other fees allowed under that paragraph for work done as a duty solicitor during that duty period to a maximum of one half of the fee allowed under paragraph 1(1)(a).

EXPLANATORY NOTE

(This note is not part of the Regulations)

These Regulations replace with amendments the Legal Advice and Assistance at Police Stations (Remuneration) Regulations 1988 (which are revoked except in relation to work done before April 1, 1989).

The Regulations provide for determination and review by the Legal Aid Board of the remuneration of solicitors (including duty solicitors acting in accordance with arrangements made under regulation 6 of the Legal Advice and Assistance Regulations 1989) who give advice and assistance to suspects at police stations, and prescribe rates of payment for that remuneration. The main changes are:—

(a) to reflect the taking over of responsibility for administration of legal aid by the Legal Aid Board;

(b) to remove the lower limit on fees hitherto applied to certain work (regulation 5(1));

(c) to increase the rates previously payable under the 1988 Regulations by six per cent. overall (Schedule).

Legal Aid Board Duty Solicitor Arrangements 1989

The following arrangements have been approved by the Board and will come into effect on April 1, 1989. These arrangements replace the Legal Aid (Duty Solicitor) Scheme 1988.

PART I—GENERAL

1. A committee member appointed or reappointed under the Legal Aid (Duty Solicitor) Scheme 1988 shall be deemed to have been appointed or reappointed under these Arrangements for the remainder of the period for which he was so appointed or reappointed and any decision validly made under the Legal Aid (Duty Solicitor) Scheme 1988 or any previous Scheme shall be deemed to continue to have been validly made.

Interpretation

2. In these Arrangements, unless the context otherwise requires:—
"advice" means "advice and assistance" under Part III of the 1988 Act;

"appropriate area committee" means the area committee in the area of which are situated the magistrates' courts at which advice and representation is provided or police stations at which advice is provided;

"appropriate regional duty solicitor committee" means the regional duty solicitor committee appointed by the Duty Solicitor Committee in the region of which are situated the magistrates' courts at which advice and representation is provided and police stations at which advice is provided;

"appropriate local duty solicitor committee" means the local duty solicitor committee appointed by the appropriate regional duty solicitor committee for the purpose of making arrangements whereby advice and representation is provided by duty solicitors at one or more specified magistrates' courts and advice is provided by duty solicitors to persons at police stations;

"appropriate local law society" means the society or societies in the district or districts of which are situated the magistrates' courts at which it is proposed to provide advice and representation or police stations at which it is proposed to provide advice;

"area committee" means the area committee appointed by the Board in respect of each legal aid area;

"area director" means an area director appointed by the Board in accordance with Regulation 4 of the Civil Legal Aid (General) Regulations 1989 and includes any person duly authorised to act on his behalf;

"Board" means the Legal Aid Board appointed under the 1988 Act;

"clerk of the court" means a justices' clerk or a member of the staff of a justices' clerk acting as a clerk in a magistrates' court;

"duty solicitor" means a solicitor who in accordance with arrangements made by the appropriate local duty solicitor committee is in attendance at a magistrates' court for the purpose of providing advice and representation or giving advice at a police station or both and, in each case, has been selected in accordance with these Arrangements;

"Duty Solicitor Committee" means the committee appointed by the Legal Aid Board;

"duty solicitor's representative" means any person selected in accordance with paragraph 47;

"local duty solicitor committee" means the committee appointed by the appropriate regional duty solicitor committee for the purpose of making arrangements whereby advice and representation is provided by duty solicitors at one or more magistrates' courts and advice is provided at police stations;

"local law society" means a society or group of societies which is for the time being recognised as a local law society by the Law Society and, in London, includes the London Criminal Courts Solicitors' Association;

"panel" means an arrangement whereby the regional telephone service telephones the duty solicitors in the order upon which they appear on the panel until finding one willing to give advice and assistance at a police station. The regional telephone service will then start with the next duty solicitor on the panel in respect of the next suspect requiring advice and assistance at a police station;

"police station" means a police station, or any other place where a constable is present or, except where expressly excluded by these Arrangements, any place where Service personnel are assisting with an investigation under paragraph 56(2);

"region" means one of the regions referred to in paragraph 3;

"regional duty solicitor committee" means the committee appointed by the Duty Solicitor Committee for each region for the purpose of making arrangements whereby duty solicitors shall be in attendance at magistrates' courts and police stations within that region;

"regional telephone service" means the telephone service established by the Duty Solicitor Committee to receive initial requests for advice from suspects at police stations;

"regulations" means the Legal Advice and Assistance Regulations 1989, the Legal Advice and Assistance (Scope) Regulations 1989; the Legal Advice and Assistance (Duty Solicitor) (Remuneration) Regulations 1989 and the Legal Advice and Assistance at Police Stations (Remuneration) Regulations 1989;

"representation" means "assistance by way of representation" under Part III of the 1988 Act:

"rota" means a rota of duty solicitors to give advice and representation at magistrates' courts and advice at police stations;

"Services Discipline Acts" mean the Army Act 1955, the Air Force Act 1955 and the Navy Discipline Act 1957;

"Services police" means members of the Royal Naval Special Investigations Branch, members of the Corps of Royal Military Police or Women's Royal Army Corps Provost, Royal Air Force Provost Officers or members of the Royal Air Force Police;

"Services person" means a person assisting with an investigation by the Services police;

"suspect" means a person who for the purposes of assisting with an investigation attend voluntarily at a police station or who accompanies a constable to a police station without having been arrested or who has been arrested and is being held in custody in a police station or other premises or a Services person assisting with an investigation by Services police under para. 56(3).

Regions
3. For the purposes of this Scheme, England and Wales shall be divided into the regions which are set out in Schedule I.

PART II—THE DUTY SOLICITOR COMMITTEE

Appointment of Duty Solicitor Committee

4. The Duty Solicitor Committee is appointed by the Board and shall perform its duties and exercise its powers in accordance with any guidance and directions issued by the Board.

Powers and Duties

5. (1) The Duty Solicitor Committee shall:

(*a*) appoint the members of each regional duty solicitor committee;

(*b*) determine appeals from a regional duty solicitor committee under paragraph 17 and from a local duty solicitor committee under paragraph 31. The Duty Solicitor Committee shall give the appellant reasons for its decision when the appeal has been determined;

(*c*) give such directions and guidance to regional duty solicitor committees as it considers necessary;

(*d*) maintain records and call for such reports from the regional and local duty solicitor committees as are necessary for the committee to fulfil its responsibilities properly; and

(*e*) make reports and recommendations to the Board in respect of the provisions and operations of these Arrangements.

(2) The Duty Solicitor Committee may:

(*a*) modify any provision in these Arrangements except in relation to paragraphs 61 and 62, in connection with the provision of advice and representation at particular courts or advice at particular police stations;

(*b*) remove from office for due cause any member of a regional duty solicitor committee or local duty solicitor committee;

(*c*) where arrangements have not been approved under paragraph 15(2), or where any such arrangements are no longer in force, consider and if appropriate make a recommendation to the Board to enter into a contract for the provision of advice in accordance with a procedure approved by the Duty Solicitor Committee or where any arrangements which have been approved under paragraph 15(2) have ceased to operate to its satisfaction, direct that those arrangements should cease to have effect and consider, and if appropriate, make the same recommendation;

(*d*) at the request of the appropriate regional duty solicitor committee appoint a representative of a police force of lesser rank than Chief Superintendent to be a member of a regional duty solicitor committee.

PART III—REGIONAL DUTY SOLICITOR COMMITTEES

Size of membership

6. The members of a regional duty solicitor committee shall be such as the Duty Solicitor Committee shall from time to time appoint but shall not be fewer than 10 nor more than 35.

Categories of membership

7. The members of each regional duty solicitor committee shall be the following:—

(1)   at least one member of each local duty solicitor committee in the region following the appointment of a committee or committees under paragraph 14(1)(a), such member to be a solicitor with considerable current experience of advocacy in criminal cases in magistrates' courts to be appointed after consultation with the appropriate local duty solicitor committee;

(2)   one member of the appropriate area committee, such member to be a solicitor advocate experienced in criminal law and nominated by the appropriate area committee;

(3)   one or more Justices of the Peace, nominated by the Magistrates' Association;

(4)   one or more Justices' Clerks, nominated by the Justices' Clerk Society;

(5)   two persons neither practising as barristers or solicitors nor coming within any of the categories specified in paragraphs 7(3), (4), (6), (7), (10) and (11);

(6)   one or more representatives of the police force or forces in the region of no less rank than chief superintendant nominated by the chief officer(s) of police;

and may also include:

(7)   one or more representatives of the probation service or services in the region nominated by that service or those services;

(8)   one or more other persons not practising as barristers or as solicitors;

(9)   subject to paragraph 6 and to consultation with the appropriate local law society, any number of practising solicitors with considerable current experience of advocacy in criminal cases in magistrates' courts to represent those parts of the region not represented under paragraph 7(1);

(10)   one representative of the Crown Prosecution Service nominated by the Director of Public Prosecutions;

(11)   in London, a stipendiary magistrate nominated by the Chief Metropolitan Stipendiary Magistrate.

Solicitor members

8. A solicitor appointed under paragraph 7(9) to represent a particular part of the region shall, upon the appointment of a solicitor under paragraph 7(1) to represent that part of the region, cease to be a member of the regional duty solicitor committee.

Majority of members

9. The majority of members of a regional duty solicitor committee shall be solicitors appointed under paragraphs 7(1), (2) and (9).

Adjudication on appeals and exclusions

10. (1) Only solicitors appointed under paragraphs 7(1), (2) and (9) shall be entitled to hear and determine appeals under paragraph 16(7) or to exclude or suspend solicitors under paragraph 16(5) unless the appellant requests that those members appointed under paragraphs 7(5) and (8) should participate in the hearing and determination of the appeal or in the decision to exclude or suspend.

(2) A solicitor who is a member of the local duty solicitor committee which has made the decision from which the appeal is being made shall not participate in the hearing and determination of such appeal.

Period of Service

11. Every member of a regional duty solicitor committee shall be appointed for a period not exceeding three years and may be reappointed by the Duty Solicitor Committee, subject to such consultation or nomination as is required by paragraph 7, for successive periods not exceeding three years until he has either attained 65 years of age or completed 15 years of consecutive service as a member of a regional duty solicitor committee whichever is the earlier.

Eligibility for further term

12. A member of a regional duty solicitor committee who has served for 15 consecutive years and is therefore not eligible for reappointment in accordance with paragraph 11

shall nevertheless at the expiration of a further three years become so eligible provided that he has not then attained 65 years of age.

Vacancies

13. Any vacancy on a regional duty solicitor committee caused by the retirement or otherwise of members appointed under paragraphs 7(1) to (6) (inclusive) shall be filled by the Duty Solicitor Committee and, in respect of vacancies under paragraphs 7(7) to (11), may be filled by the Duty Solicitor Committee, subject in each case to such consultation or nomination, if any, as is required under those paragraphs.

Powers and duties—magistrates' courts

14. In accordance with the provisions of Regulations 6 and 7 of the Legal Advice and Assistance Regulations 1989 and subject to any directions and guidance given to it by the Duty Solicitor Committee and in consultation with the appropriate local law society every regional duty solicitor committee shall:

(1) in consultation with the appropriate magistrates' courts:

(*a*) decide in which magistrates' courts in the region it would be appropriate, in accordance with guidance laid down by the Duty Solicitor Committee, for duty solicitors to be in attendance whether or not any defendant wishes to consult a duty solicitor, and for each such court or courts shall establish and appoint the members of a local duty solicitor committee, and shall supervise such committee;

(*b*) in relation to those magistrates' courts in the region which do not come within the provisions of paragraph 14(1)(a), make such arrangements as it thinks fit for the provision of advice and representation in accordance with guidance laid down by the Duty Solicitor Committee;

(2) consider and, if satisfied, approve applications under paragraph 27(4);

Powers and duties—police stations

15. In accordance with the provisions of Regulation 6 of the Advice and Assistance Regulations 1989 and subject to any directions and guidance given to it by the Duty Solicitor Committee and in consultation with the appropriate local law society every regional duty solicitor committee:—

(1) in consultation with the appropriate police force or forces, shall consider what arrangements are required for the provision of advice by duty solicitors at police stations in the region, and establish and appoint the member of local duty solicitor committees for the purpose of making such arrangements and shall supervise such committees. Such local duty solicitor committees may be either the committees appointed under paragraph 14(1)(a), or committees appointed solely for the purposes of this sub-paragraph:

(2) shall consider and, if satisfied, approve arrangements prepared by the appropriate local duty solicitor committees in accordance with guidance laid down by by Duty Solicitor Committee for the provision of advice by duty solicitors at police stations;

(3) may approve the use of duty solicitors' representatives in connection with the provision of advice at police stations covered by a particular local duty solicitor committee.

Powers and duties—general

16. In accordance with the provisions of Regulations 6 and 7 of the Advice and Assistance Regulations 1989 and subject to any directions and guidance given to it by the Duty Solicitor Committee and in consultation with the appropriate local law

society every regional duty solicitor committee shall administer these Arrangements within its region and in particular, and without prejudice to the generality of the foregoing:—

(1)   may if it thinks fit, consent to a proposal by a local duty solicitor committee, or direct a local duty solicitor committee, to exclude solicitors from providing advice and representation at magistrates' courts unless such solicitors are willing to provide advice at police stations as duty solicitors subject to the right of appeal against any such direction set out in paragraph 31;

(2)   shall monitor the arrangements by appropriate local duty solicitor committees for advice and representation at magistrates' courts and advice at police stations;

(3)   shall require a local duty solicitor committee to take any steps specified by the regional duty solicitor committee to facilitate the provision of advice and representation by duty solicitors and ensure that arrangements exist for dealing with emergencies;

(4)   shall if not satisfied with the arrangements made by the appropriate local duty solicitor committee for the provision of advice and representation at any magistrates' court or advice at any police station, give notice to the appropriate local duty solicitor committee requiring it to provide adequate arrangements within the period specified in the notice which shall not be less than three calendar months. If at the end of that period the appropriate regional duty solicitor committee is still not satisfied with the arrangements it may, with the consent of the Duty Solicitor Committee, disband the appropriate local duty solicitor committee forthwith and appoint a new committee in its place;

(5)   may if it thinks fit, exclude, or suspend for a period of up to six months, a duty solicitor from providing either advice and representation at magistrates' courts or advice at police stations or both in the event of his failure to carry out his duties or for some other good cause provided that the solicitor has been notified of any complaint against him and that he may make written representations or given notice of his intention to make oral representations within 21 days of the committee having notified him of the complaint. If the committee decides to exclude or suspend the duty solicitor it shall provide him with a written statement of the reasons for its decision;

(6)   may if it thinks fit, recommend to the Duty Solicitor Committee that any provision in these Arrangements except in relation to paragraphs 61 and 62 be modified in connection with the provision of advice and representation at a specified magistrates' court or advice at specified police stations;

(7)   shall determine appeals under paragraphs 30, 39, and 49 and in connection with such appeals:

(a)   each appeal shall be by way of a rehearing;

(b)   the appellant shall submit written representations when giving notice of appeal and shall send a copy of such representations to the appropriate local duty solicitor committee;

(c)   the appropriate local duty solicitor committee may submit written representations about the appeal to the appropriate regional duty solicitor committee and if it does so shall send a copy of such representations to the appellant;

(d)   the appellant shall have the right to make oral representations to the appropriate regional duty solicitor committee in support of the appeal;

(e)   the appellant shall be given written reasons for the appeal decision;

(f)   where the regional duty solicitor committee is of the opinion that the local duty solicitor committee has not complied with the procedure laid down in paragraphs 37 and 38 or with any directions and guidance given by the Duty Solicitor Committee under paragraph 5(1) it may refer the matter back to the appropriate local duty solicitor committee for reconsideration;

(8)   shall investigate complaints about the provision of advice and representation at magistrates' courts and advice at police stations by duty solicitors;

(9) shall report to the Duty Solicitor Committee any circumstances where duty solicitors have inadequate access to defendants in custody or suspects at police stations or inadequate facilities to enable them to carry out their functions;

(10) may if it thinks fit, approve rules made by a local duty solicitor committee under paragraph 29(7);

(11) shall make an annual report to the Duty Solicitor Committee on the operation of these Arrangements and make copies available to appropriate local duty solicitor committees and other interested persons;

(12) shall supply to the Duty Solicitor Committee such reports statistics estimates and other information as the Duty Solicitor Committee may from time to time require;

(13) shall keep the police, courts and other relevant organisations in the region informed about the existence and responsibilities of the regional duty solicitor committee;

(14) may revoke any consent, direction or approval it has given under paragraphs 15(2), 15(3), 16(1), 27(4), 27(6) and 29(7).

Appeals to Duty Solicitor Committee
17. Where a solicitor

(a) is excluded or suspended from providing either advice and representation at magistrates' courts or advice at police stations or both under paragraph 16(5), or

(b) is dissatisfied with the determination of an appeal under paragraph 16(7),

he may appeal in writing to the Duty Solicitor Committee within 28 days of such exclusion, suspension or determination being notified to him by the appropriate regional duty solicitor committee subject to the Duty Solicitor Committee having discretion to accept an appeal outside the period of 28 days for good reason.

PART IV—LOCAL DUTY SOLICITOR COMMITTEES

Size of membership
18. The members of a local duty solicitor committee shall be such as the appropriate regional duty solicitor committee shall from time to time appoint but shall not be fewer than four nor more than 15.

Categories of membership
19. The members of each local duty solicitor committee shall be the following:

(1) at least three solicitors with considerable current experience of advocacy in criminal cases in magistrates' courts but excluding solicitors employed on a full-time basis by a Prosecuting Solicitor's Department or the Crown Prosecution Service;

(2) after such consultation as the appropriate regional duty solicitor committee deems appropriate, one person neither practising as a barrister or solicitor nor coming within any of the categories specified in paragraphs 19(3), (4), (6) or (7);

and may also include:

(3) one or more Justices of the Peace;

(4) one or more Justices' Clerks;

(5) a solicitor with considerable current experience of advocacy in criminal cases in magistrates' courts employed on a full-time basis by a Prosecuting Solicitor's Department or the Crown Prosecution Service;

(6) one or more representatives of the Probation Service or services nominated by that service or those services;

(7) one or more representatives of the police force or forces nominated by the chief officer(s) of police; and

(8) after such consultation as the appropriate regional duty solicitor committee deems appropriate, not more than two additional persons not practising as barristers or solicitors.

Solicitor members
20. Solicitor members appointed under paragraph 19(1) shall be appointed after consultation with the appropriate local law society.

Majority of members
21. The majority of members of a local duty solicitor committee shall be solicitors appointed under paragraph 19(1).

Adjudication on selection or exclusion
22. Only solicitors appointed under paragraph 19(1) above may deal with the selection or reselection of a duty solicitor under paragraph 37 or 40 or the exclusion or suspension of a duty solicitor from providing advice and representation at magistrates' courts or advice at police stations or both under paragraph 29(3) unless the applicant or duty solicitor agrees that those members appointed under paragraphs 19(2) and (8) should participate in such selection, reselection, exclusion, or suspension.

Period of service
23. Every member of a local duty solicitor committee shall be appointed for a period not exceeding three years and may be reappointed by the appropriate regional duty solicitor committee, subject to such consultation as is required under paragraph 25(2), for successive periods not exceeding three years until he has either attained 65 years of age or completed 15 years of consecutive service as a member of a local duty solicitor committee whichever is the earlier.

Eligibility for further term
24. A member of a local duty solicitor committee who has served for 15 consecutive years and is not eligible for reappointment in accordance with paragraph 23 shall nevertheless at the expiration of a further three years become so eligible provided that he has not attained 65 years of age.

Vacancies
25. Any vacancy on a local duty solicitor committee caused by retirement or otherwise may be filled by the appropriate regional duty solicitor committee:
(1) in the case of a solicitor appointed under paragraph 19(1) after consultation with the appropriate local law society;
(2) in the case of a member appointed under paragraph 19(2)–(5) after such consultation as the appropriate regional duty solicitor committee deems appropriate.

Duties
26. The appropriate local duty solicitor committee shall subject to any directions given to it by the appropriate regional duty solicitor committee make arrangements for advice and representation to be provided by duty solicitors at the court or courts and advice at police stations in connection with which the committee is appointed under paragraph 14(1)(a) or 15(1) respectively.

Detailed arrangements—magistrates' courts
27. In connection with providing advice and representation under Part VII the appropriate local duty solicitor committee:

(1) shall ensure that arrangements exist to inform all defendants who are eligible for advice or representation in accordance with the provisions of paragraph 52 of the availability of the duty solicitor;

(2) shall ensure that arrangements exist for a duty solicitor to be present at court, or available to the court, as the regional duty solicitor committee may specify so as to provide advice and representation as specified in paragraph 52 to defendants who are eligible to receive such advice and representation;

(3) shall ensure that arrangements exist for defendants who wish to receive advice and representation by a duty solicitor as specified in paragraph 52 to receive such advice and representation;

(4) shall apply to the appropriate regional duty solicitor committee for approval where it is proposed that more than one duty solicitor is regularly to be on duty at the same court at the same time;

(5) shall ensure where practicable that arrangements are made to provide advice and representation where sittings in addition to ordinary sittings of courts are involved;

(6) may, with the consent of the appropriate regional duty solicitor committee, specify the maximum number of courts before which a solicitor may appear as duty solicitor;

(7) may require a duty solicitor, whilst acting as duty solicitor, not to undertake any cases in connection with which he has previously received instructions;

(8) may make appropriate arrangements for duty solicitors to be assisted by representatives of voluntary organisations to make initial contact with defendants and provide advice to defendants and their families;

(9) shall use its best endeavours to ensure compliance with Part VII;

(10) may, with the consent of the appropriate regional duty solicitor committee, exclude solicitors from providing advice and representation at magistrates' courts unless such solicitors are willing to provide advice at police stations as duty solicitors.

Detailed arrangements—police stations

28. In connection with the provision of advice at police stations the appropriate local duty solicitor committee either by itself or in conjunction with other local duty solicitor committees:

(1) shall ensure that arrangements exist for suspects to receive advice at police stations in accordance with paragraph 56–58;

(2) shall, with the approval of the appropriate regional duty solicitor committee under paragraph 15(2), ensure that arrangements exist for duty solicitors to be available at all times of the day and night to give advice at police stations by means of a rota or a panel arrangement or by a combination of both;

(3) may require a duty solicitor to be available to go to a police station with the least possible delay;

(4) may, with the consent of the appropriate regional duty solicitor committee, permit the provision by duty solicitors' representatives of advice at police stations;

(5) may, where the appropriate regional duty solicitor committee consent to the use of duty solicitors' representatives, decide to select only solicitors as duty solicitors' representatives;

(6) shall prepare and distribute to police stations a list of all solicitors who are willing to act for suspects provided that the solicitors' offices are, in the opinion of the local duty solicitor committee, within a reasonable distance of the police stations for which the list is prepared, such list to include the office and out of office telephone numbers of all such solicitors and to indicate which solicitors on the list are duty solicitors.

Detailed arrangements—general

29. In connection with the provision of advice and representation at magistrates' courts and advice at police stations the appropriate local duty solicitor committee:

(1) shall satisfy itself that duty solicitors are not improperly or unnecessarily prevented from providing advice and representation to defendants and advice to suspects and, if the committee is not so satisfied, it shall report the matter to the appropriate regional duty solicitor committee;

(2) shall be responsible for the selection of duty solicitors in accordance with the procedure specified in Part V;

(3) may exclude a duty solicitor, or suspend him for a period of up to six months, from providing advice and representation at magistrates' courts or advice at police stations or both if satisfied that he has failed to carry out his duties or to meet any of the criteria set out in Part V, or is in breach of any rule made under paragraph 29(7), or that there is some other good cause provided that the solicitor has been notified of the complaint against him and that he may make written representations or give notice of his intention to make oral representations within 21 days of the committee having notified him of the complaint. If the committee decides to exclude or suspend the duty solicitor it shall provide him with a written statement of the reason for its decision. Where a solicitor is under investigation or has been charged in connection with a criminal offence or is the subject of an investigation by the Solicitors' Complaints Bureau the Chairman with the concurrence of two other members of the local duty solicitor committee may suspend a duty solicitor for a period of up to six weeks without his having been notified of the complaint against him or having the opportunity to be heard. The period of suspension may be extended for good reason on one occasion for a further period of six weeks by the Chairman with the concurrence of two members of the local duty solicitor committee. On suspension the duty solicitor must be given a statement of the reason or reasons for his suspension;

(4) shall, where a rota is required, by itself or in conjunction with other local duty solicitor committees arrange rotas of individual duty solicitors for periods not exceeding six months which may include more than one duty solicitor from the same firm, and send copies of the rota as appropriate to the court, the regional telephone service, each solicitor on the rota, the appropriate regional duty solicitor committee and such other organisations as the committee may determine;

(5) may appoint one or more administrators to prepare and issue the rota or rotas of duty solicitors, to receive applications from solicitors who wish to become duty solicitors, to convene meetings of the committee and generally to deal with the day to day matters including liaison with the courts and police;

(6) may apply to the appropriate regional duty solicitor committee to exercise its power of recommendation under paragraph 16(6) where the committee considers that modification of these Arrangements are required;

(7) may, with the approval of the appropriate regional duty solicitor committee,

    (a) make rules relating to the procedure to be adopted by duty solicitors to comply with Parts VII and VIII and

    (b) issue notes for guidance and publicity;

(8) shall, if so required, submit an annual report to the appropriate regional duty solicitor committee about the operation of the arrangements in the courts or police stations for which it is responsible;

(9) shall supply to the appropriate regional duty solicitor committee such reports, statistics, estimates and other information as that committee may from time to time require;

(10) may exclude a duty solicitor's representative, or suspended him for up to six months, from providing advice if satisfied that he has failed to satisfy any of the criteria set out in paragraph 47(1) or that there is some other good cause provided that the duty solicitor employing the representative has been notified of the complaint against him and that the appropriate duty solicitor may make written representations or give notice of his intention to make oral representations within 21 days of the committee having notified him of the complainant. If the committee decides to exclude or suspend the representative it shall provide the appropriate duty solicitor with a written statement of the reasons for its decision. Where a duty solicitor's representative is

under investigation or has been charged in connection with a criminal offence, the Chairman with the concurrence of two other members of the local duty solicitor committee may suspend a duty solicitor's representative for a period of up to six weeks without his having been notified of the complaint against him or having the opportunity to be heard. The period of suspension may be extended for good reason on one occasion for a further period of six weeks by the Chairman with the concurrence of two members of the local duty solicitor employing the duty solicitor committee. On suspension the duty solicitor's representative must be given a statement of the reason or reasons for his suspension; and

(11) shall comply with any revocation by the appropriate regional duty solicitor committee under paragraph 16(14) subject to an appeal to the Duty Solicitor Committee under paragraph 31(1).

Appeal to Regional Duty Solicitor Committee
30. (1) Where a duty solicitor has been excluded or suspended from providing advice and representation at magistrates' courts or advice at police stations or both under paragraph 29(3) or not reselected under paragraph 40 he may appeal to the appropriate regional duty solicitor committee within 28 days of the decision being notified to him, subject to that committee having discretion to accept an appeal outside the period of 28 days for good reason.

(2) Where a duty solicitor's representative has been excluded or suspended from providing advice under paragraph 29(10), the duty solicitor employing the representative may appeal in writing to the appropriate regional duty solicitor committee within 28 days of the decision being notified to him, subject to that committee having discretion to accept an appeal outside the period of 28 days for good reason.

Appeal to Duty Solicitor Committee
31. Where a local duty solicitor committee objects to being required by the appropriate regional duty solicitor committee to exclude solicitors from providing advice and representation at magistrates' courts under paragraph 16(1) or to a revocation by the appropriate regional duty solicitor committee under paragraph 16(14), the local duty solicitor committee may appeal in writing to the Duty Solicitor Committee within 28 days of the decision being notified to the local duty solicitor committee by the relevant regional duty solicitor committee, subject to that Committee having the power to accept an appeal outside the period of 28 days for good reason.

Payment of administrators
32. The administrators appointed under paragraph 29(5) above may be paid for any reasonable expenses actually incurred by them.

PART V—SELECTION OF DUTY SOLICITORS

Application
33. The appropriate local duty solicitor committee shall require solicitors who wish to become duty solicitors to complete an application form in the form set out in Schedule II.

Selection criteria—magistrates' courts
34. (1) The criteria for the selection of a duty solicitor to provide advice and representation at a magistrates' court shall be as follows:—

   (a) the solicitor's office shall, in connection with a magistrates' court at which a duty solicitor is required to be in attendance under paragraph 14(1)(a), be reasonably accessible to the appropriate magistrates' court for the convenience of any defendant who wishes to instruct the duty solicitor to continue to act for him;

(b) the solicitor shall, in connection with a magistrates' court at which a duty solicitor is required to be in attendance under paragraph 14(1)(a), normally be in attendance at the office referred to in paragraph 34(1)(a) and that office shall be open during the majority of normal business hours;

(c) the solicitor's office shall, in connection with a magistrates' court or courts not falling within paragraph 14(1)(a), be reasonably accessible to the court or courts taking into account relevant local considerations;

(d) the solicitor shall hold a current practising certificate;

(e) the solicitor shall be willing to act personally as duty solicitor;

(f) the solicitor shall regularly practise in criminal defence work, other than as a duty solicitor, and shall have comprehensive experience of criminal defence work including advocacy in magistrates' courts throughout the previous 18 months unless the solicitor has been in recent full-time employment as a prosecuting solicitor for at least 18 months in which case he must have had the experience of criminal defence work referred to throughout the period of six months immediately prior to the application or unless the solicitor has throughout the previous 12 months comprehensive experience of criminal defence work including advocacy in magistrates' courts in which case he must attend an interview under paragraph 36(1) and may not withhold his agreement under paragraph 22 to the participation of members who are not solicitors in his selection. The experience of criminal defence work need not have been gained in the magistrates' court or courts in connection with which the local duty solicitor committee is appointed. In computing whether a solicitor has the requisite period of experience any interval of up to six months during which the solicitor was incapable of work because of sickness or injury or absent from work because of pregnancy or confinement may be disregarded if the six month interval occurred during or at the end of the requisite period of experience;

(g) subject to the approval or direction of the appropriate regional duty solicitor committee under paragraph 16(1), the solicitor shall provide or be willing to provide advice at police stations as a duty solicitor and, where that sub-paragraph is in effect, the local duty solicitor committee shall exclude a duty solicitor from providing advice and representation at magistrates' courts if he is not willing to provide advice at police stations;

(h) any other criteria as approved by the appropriate regional duty solicitor committee and the Duty Solicitor Committee.

(2)   In assessing an application the local duty solicitor committee shall have regard to the nature, frequency and quality of the solicitor's advocacy including

(a) an ability to provide advice and representation to a number of defendants in a limited time without the opportunity to prepare the cases before arriving at court;

(b) an adequate knowledge of the procedure in magistrates' courts; and

(c) an adequate knowledge of the law relating to the more common offences coming before the court.

Selection criteria—police stations

35. The criteria for the selection of a duty solicitor to provide advice at a police station shall be as follows:

(1)   the criteria set out in paragraphs 34(1)(d) to (h) and 34(2);

(2)   the solicitor's office shall be reasonably near to the relevant police station or stations and the solicitor shall be prepared, while on duty during out-of-office hours, to

make arrangements to be reasonably accessible to the relevant police station or stations; and

(3) adequate experience of providing advice to persons arrested and held in custody at police stations.

Interview

36. (1) The appropriate local duty solicitor committee shall interview an applicant except where that committee decides that such an interview is not necessary because the applicant has, during the period of 18 months immediately preceding the application, practised regularly in a court or courts or regularly attended a police station or police stations within that committee's district.

(2) An interview may be conducted by a sub-committee of the appropriate local duty solicitor committee.

Approval of applications

37. If the applicant meets the criteria set in paragraph 34 or 35 (whichever is appropriate) the appropriate local duty solicitor committee shall, within 90 days of the submission of the application, approve the application and give notice of such approval to the applicant.

Rejection of applications

38. If the appropriate local duty solicitor committee is not satisfied that the criteria in paragraph 34 or 35 as appropriate have been met it shall give notice of its intention to reject the application to the applicant and invite him to make written and/or oral representations to it. Any such written representations and notice of the intention to make any such oral representations must be submitted within 21 days of the committee having given notice of its intention not to allow the application. If the committee decides not to allow the application it shall provide the applicant with a statement of the reasons for its decision.

Appeal to regional duty solicitor committee

39. (1) Where an application has been rejected under paragraph 38 the applicant may appeal to the appropriate regional duty solicitor committee within 28 days of the decision being notified to him subject to the appropriate regional duty solicitor committee having discretion to accept an appeal outside the period of 28 days for good reason.

(2) Where an appeal is referred back to the appropriate local duty solicitor committee under paragraph 16(7)(f), the local duty solicitor committee must approve or reject the application within 90 days.

(3) If the appropriate local duty solicitor committee has not approved the application within a period of 90 days from the date of its submission or where an appeal is referred back to the appropriate local duty solicitor committee under paragraph 16(7)(f) the application shall be deemed to have been rejected and the applicant may within 28 days of the expiration of such period appeal to the appropriate regional duty solicitor committee subject to that committee having discretion to accept an appeal outside the period of 28 days for good reason.

Reselection

40. A duty solicitor shall be subject to reselection by the appropriate local duty solicitor committee every three years. If the committee is satisfied that the duty solicitor meets the criteria set out in paragraphs 41 or 42—whichever is appropriate—it shall reselect him and give him notice of such reselection. If it is not satisfied that he meets such criteria, the committee shall give him notice of its intention not to reselect him and a statement of any representations received under paragraph 43 and shall invite him to

make written and/or oral representations to it. Any such written representations and notice of a solicitor's intention to make any such oral representations must be submitted within 21 days of the committee having given notice of its intention not to reselect the duty solicitor. If the committee decides not to reselect the duty solicitor it shall provide him with a statement of the reasons for its decision.

Reselection criteria—magistrates' courts
41. The criteria for the reselection of duty solicitors providing advice and representation at magistrates' courts shall be:
    (1)   a continued ability to satisfy the criteria in paragraph 34;
    (2)   regularity of personal attendance at court as duty solicitor; and
    (3)   compliance with these Arrangements and any rules made under paragraph 29(7)(a).

Reselection criteria—police stations
42. The criteria for the reselection of duty solicitors providing advice at police stations shall be:
    (1)   a continued ability to satisfy the criteria in paragraph 35;
    (2)   the availability of the duty solicitor to receive telephone calls concerning requests for advice from suspects at police stations;
    (3)   the attendance of the duty solicitor at police stations when appropriate to do so; and
    (4)   the appropriate use of duty solicitors' representatives at police stations.

Representations about performance
43. The appropriate local duty solicitor committee may when considering reselection take into account any representations received as to the performance of the duty solicitor or duty solicitor's representative, provided that where any such representations are received the duty solicitor or appropriate duty solicitor where a representative is involved shall be provided with a written statement of them and shall have an opportunity in any representations he may make under paragraphs 40 or 50 to respond.

Changes in circumstances—duty to report
44. A duty solicitor shall notify forthwith the appropriate local duty solicitor committee if he changes his practising address or is unable to continue to comply with the criteria set out in paragraphs 34, 35, 41 or 42.

Changes in rota
45. A duty solicitor may arrange for another duty solicitor to take his place on a rota provided that the appropriate local duty solicitor committee or its administrator and the regional telephone service, in connection with the provision of advice at police stations, and the court, in connection with the provision of advice and representation, are notified of any such arrangement.

PART VI—DUTY SOLICITORS' REPRESENTATIVES

Application
46. When the appropriate regional duty solicitor committee gives its consent to the use of duty solicitors' representatives under paragraph 15(3), an application in the form set out in Schedule III shall be submitted to the appropriate local duty solicitor committee by the appropriate duty solicitor.

Selection criteria
47. (1) When an application is received in respect of a duty solicitor's representative the local duty solicitor committee must be satisfied that the person referred to in the application:

(*a*) is in the full or part-time employment of or a partner in the same firm as the duty solicitor whose name appears on the application form referred to in paragraph 46, and who is not in the employment of any other solicitor; and

(*b*) has had experience of providing advice at a police station on behalf of the duty solicitor (having gained such experience as the result of having worked in a solicitor's office); and

(*c*)

(i) if a solicitor, has had at least four months' experience of criminal cases as a solicitor or articled clerk; or

(ii) if a solicitor's clerk, has had at least three years' experience of criminal defence work; or

(iii) if an articled clerk, has had at least six months' experience of which four months are of criminal cases;

(*d*) and is competent to act as a duty solicitor's representative.

(2) If the person in respect of whom an application has been submitted meets these criteria the local duty solicitor committee shall approve the application, and give notice of such approval to the applicant and the appropriate duty solicitor. If the committee is not satisfied that the person in respect of whom an application has been submitted meets these criteria, it shall give the appropriate duty solicitor notice of its intention not to approve the application and invite him to make written and/or oral representations to it. Any such written representations and notice of the intention to make any such oral representations must be submitted within 21 days of the committee having given notice of its intention not to approve the application. The committee shall decide whether or not to allow the application in the light of any representations received and if it decides not to allow the application shall provide the applicant with a statement of the reasons for its decision.

Interview
48. The appropriate local duty solicitor committee or a sub-committee of it shall require any person who is the subject of an application made under paragraph 46 to attend for an interview; however where that person has been approved by any other local duty solicitor committee the appropriate local duty solicitor committee is under no duty to interview him but may in its discretion do so.

Appeal to regional duty solicitor committee
49. (1) Where an application has been refused under paragraph 47(2), an appeal may be made by the duty solicitor making the application to the appropriate regional duty solicitor committee within 28 days of the decision being notified to him subject to that committee having discretion to accept an appeal outside the period of 28 days for good reason.

(2) If the appropriate local duty solicitor committee has not approved the application within a period of 90 days from the date of its submission, the application shall be deemed to have been rejected and the applicant may, within 28 days of the expiration of such period, appeal to the appropriate regional duty solicitor committee subject to that committee having a discretion to accept an appeal outside the period of 28 days for good reason.

(3) Where a duty solicitor's representative has not been reselected under paragraph 50 the appropriate duty solicitor may appeal to the appropriate regional duty solicitor committee within 28 days of the decision being notified to the duty solicitor subject to that committee having a discretion to accept an appeal outside the period of 28 days for good reason.

Reselection criteria
50. A duty solicitor's representative shall be subject to reselection by the appropriate local duty solicitor committee every three years. If the committee is satisfied that the

duty solicitor's representative meets the criteria set out in paragraph 47(1) it shall reselect him and give notice of such reselection to the duty solicitor. If it is not satisfied that he meets such criteria, the committee shall give the appropriate duty solicitor notice of its intention not to reselect the representative and a statement of any representations received under paragraph 43 and shall invite the appropriate solicitor to make written and/or oral representations to it. Any such written representations and notice of the intention to make any such oral representations must be submitted within 21 days of the committee having given notice of its intention not to reselect the representative. The committee shall decide whether or not the duty solicitor's representative shall be reselected in the light of any representations made and if it decides not to reselect the representative shall provide the appropriate duty solicitor with a statement of the reasons for its decision.

PART VII—SCOPE OF SERVICE—MAGISTRATES' COURT

Defendant's right to instruct other solicitor

51. (1) A duty solicitor at a magistrates' court shall inform every defendant to whom he offers advice or representation that the defendant is entitled to instruct any solicitor; the duty solicitor shall then ask the defendant if he has a solicitor whom he wishes to represent him and if the defendant has such a solicitor the duty solicitor shall not act for the defendant save in the circumstances mentioned in sub-paragraph (2) below.

(2) If the defendant wishes to be represented by a named solicitor or firm but that solicitor or member of the firm is not available, then provided the defendant so wishes, the duty solicitor may give advice and representation to him on that occasion but shall not thereafter act for the defendant in that matter unless the defendant specifically asks him to do so in writing.

Services to be provided

52. (1) A duty solicitor at a magistrates' court shall provide the following services to any defendant who wishes to receive advice and representation from the duty solicitor:—

  (*a*) advice to a defendant who is in custody;

  (*b*) the making of a bail application unless the defendant has received such assistance on a previous occasion.

 (2) The duty solicitor shall subject to paragraph 53(1) also provide:—

  (*a*) representation of a defendant who is in custody on a plea of guilty where the defendant wishes the case to be concluded at that appearance in court, unless the duty solicitor considers that the case should be adjourned in the interests of justice or of the defendant or the defendant has previously received such assistance on the same charge or charges;

  (*b*) where necessary, advice and representation to a defendant who is before the court as a result of failure to pay a fine or other sums ordered on conviction or to obey an order of the court, and such failure may lead to the defendant being at risk of imprisonment;

  (*c*) advice and, where appropriate, representation of any other defendant who is not in custody where, in the opinion of the duty solicitor, such defendant requires advice or representation;

  (*d*) help to a defendant to make an application for a legal aid order in respect of any subsequent appearance of the defendant before the court. Where such an application is made the duty solicitor shall enquire whether the defendant wishes to instruct another solicitor to act for him. If the defendant does so wish, the duty solicitor shall insert the name of that solicitor in the application form.

Prohibition of certain services

53. (1) A duty solicitor shall not under paragraph 52 provide representation in committal proceedings or on a not guilty plea, nor save in circumstances which the duty solicitor considers exceptional, advice or representation to a defendant in connection with a non-imprisonable offence.

(2) On any adjourned hearing, a duty solicitor shall not, as duty solicitor, represent a defendant to whom he or any other duty solicitor has provided advice or representation in the same case except in connection with defendants coming within paragraph 52(2)(b).

(3) A duty solicitor shall not advise or represent any defendant at a sitting when that duty solicitor or any member of his firm is representing the Crown Prosecution Service in the same courthouse.

Duty to remain at court

54. A duty solicitor shall remain at the court until it has become clear to him after consulting the clerk of the court where practicable that advice and representation is not required by any defendant under paragraph 52.

PART VIII—SCOPE OF SERVICE—POLICE STATIONS

Initial advice

55. (1) A duty solicitor on a rota shall accept a case referred to him by the regional telephone service unless he is already engaged in connection with another suspect at a police station or at a hearing of an application for a warrant of further detention or an extension of such a warrant.

(2) The duty solicitor shall provide such advice under these Arrangements as he considers necessary in the interests of the suspect.

(3) The duty solicitor on a panel who accepts a case from the regional telephone service and a duty solicitor on a rota shall initially consider each case personally and may only arrange for a duty solicitor's representative to give advice under paragraph 59 after such personal consideration has been given.

Cases in which attendance at a police station may be required

56. Where the suspect:

(1) has been arrested and held in custody in connection with an offence which is defined as an arrestable offence under section 24 Police and Criminal Evidence Act 1984, or

(2) is a Services person at a Services establishment or elsewhere assisting with an investigation by the Services police and suspected of offences contrary to the Services Discipline Acts where:

   (a) the investigation involves any offences which cannot be dealt with summarily, or

   (b) the offence appears to the interviewing Services police to be serious

the duty solicitor shall attend personally upon the suspect where he considers that such attendance is necessary for the protection of the suspect's interests.

Circumstances in which attendance may not be necessary

57. In assessing whether his attendance is necessary under paragraph 56 for the protection of the suspect's interests, the duty solicitor shall have regard to:

(1) whether he can speak directly to the suspect on the telephone, and is satisfied that the matter can be adequately dealt with through that medium and in particular that the suspect is not inhibited from the fear of being overheard or the instructions given by

the suspect to the duty solicitor do not deal with sensitive matters requiring a greater guarantee of confidentiality than is afforded by that medium;

(2) where the suspect has already been charged, and no further police interview is proposed;

(3) whether the suspect is under the influence of drink or drugs (in which case attendance may be necessary later); or

(4) whether the suspect wishes to instruct his own solicitor whom the duty solicitor is able to contact.

Suspects in connection with other offences

58. The duty solicitor may attend personally upon any suspect not referred to in paragraph 56.

Advice by duty solicitor's representative

59. The duty solicitor may, where it is appropriate to do so, arrange for a duty solicitor's representative approved under paragraph 47 to give advice to the suspect at a police station provided that the police are prepared to allow the clerk the same rights of access as the solicitor. The suspect must be informed before advice is given in such circumstances of the status of the representative giving such advice and assistance. A duty solicitor's representative may not give advice to a Services person unless this representative is himself a solicitor.

Continued instructions

60. The duty solicitor may, when he has given advice to the suspect at the police station, indicate to the suspect that he may be instructed by the suspect to continue to act for him, except in cases under paragraph 56(2) which are dealt with under summary Service procedures, subject to:

(1) advising the suspect that the suspect is entitled to instruct any solicitor; the duty solicitor should then ask the suspect if he has a solicitor whom he wishes to instruct and if the suspect has such a solicitor the duty solicitor shall not act for the suspect save in the circumstances mentioned in sub-paragraph (2) below;

(2) if the suspect wished to receive advice from a named solicitor or firm but that solicitor or a member of the firm was not available, the duty solicitor shall not thereafter act for the suspect in that matter unless the suspect specifically asks him to do so in writing and such written instructions are filed within seven days with the local duty solicitor committee or the administrator thereof.

PART IX—REMUNERATION

Report form and payment

61. The Duty Solicitor Committee shall approve appropriate forms which shall be fully completed by the duty solicitor and lodged with the appropriate area director. The duty solicitor's firm will be paid in accordance with the regulations.

Appeals to the area committee

62. Any duty solicitor aggrieved at any sum allowed under the regulations may make written representations to the area committee within 21 days of receiving an assessment from the appropriate area director and the area committee may, subject to the provisions of the regulations, make such alteration, if any, as appears to it proper in any sum which has been allowed on that assessment.

PART X—REGIONAL AND LOCAL DUTY SOLICITOR COMMITTEES— GENERAL PROVISIONS

Election of chairman and vice-chairman

63. A committee shall, at the first meeting after its appointment and thereafter annually, elect a chairman and, in the case of a regional duty solicitor committee, a vice-chairman to hold office for such period not exceeding one year as the committee may determine. A chairman or vice-chairman shall be eligible for re-election at the expiration of such period, provided that no chairman or vice-chairman shall hold office for more than three years.

Quorum

64. A quorum shall consist of not less than one-third of the members of the committee or sub-committee or, where a committee is considering a matter where not all members of the committee are entitled to participate, one-third of such members who are entitled to participate in either case with a minimum of two members.

Minutes

65. A committee or a sub-committee shall keep minutes of its proceedings with the names of the members present at each meeting, and such minutes shall be signed by the chairman of the appropriate meeting.

Procedure

66. The ruling of the chairman of a committee or sub-committee on any matter of procedure arising at that meeting of such committee or sub-committee shall be final and conclusive.

Resignation

67. A member of a committee may resign by giving notice in writing to the area director whereupon his office shall become vacant.

Disqualification

68. (1) The office of a member of a committee shall be vacated by disqualification if a receiving order in bankruptcy is made against him, or if he becomes of unsound mind, or if he abstains without leave of the committee from attending meetings of the committee for one year, or if he ceases to be a nominee of the body or organisation he was appointed to represent.

(2) A resolution of the appropriate regional duty solicitor committee declaring a member of a regional duty solicitor committee or a local duty solicitor committee disqualified as aforesaid shall be conclusive as to the fact and ground of disqualification stated in the resolution.

Travelling and other expenses

69. (1) Travelling and other proper expenses and subsistence allowances on such scale as the Board shall from time to time direct shall be paid to members attending meetings of regional duty solicitor committees or sub-committees thereof and to chairmen and vice-chairmen or regional duty solicitor committees attending any meeting convened by the Duty Solicitor Committee.

(2) Travelling expenses shall be paid to members of regional duty solicitor committees appointed under paragraphs 7(5), (7) and (8) and to members of local duty solicitor committees appointed under paragraphs 19(2) and (8) when visiting appropriate magistrates' courts and police stations for the purpose of inspecting arrangements for the provision of advice and representation and advice and assistance by duty solicitors.

SCHEDULE 1

DUTY SOLICITOR REGIONS

Legal Aid Area	Duty Solicitor Regions covered	Legal Aid Area	Duty Solicitor Regions covered
1. (London South)	No. 1 The London Boroughs of: Bexley Bromley Croydon Ealing Greenwich Hounslow Kingston Lambeth Lewisham Merton Richmond Southwark Sutton Wandsworth	4. (South Western) *continued*	No. 4B districts of Somerset: Weston Super Mare Long Ashton Radstock Wiltshire
2. (South Eastern)	No. 2 East Sussex Kent Surrey West Sussex	5. (South Wales)	No. 5 Dyfed South Glamorgan Mid Glamorgan West Glamorgan Gwent The following Districts of Powys: Brecknock Radnor
3. (Southern)	No. 3A Berkshire Buckinghamshire Oxfordshire	6. (West Midlands)	No. 6A Hereford & Worcester Warwickshire West Midlands (Metropolitan Boroughs of Solihull and Coventry)
	No. 3B Dorset Hampshire Isle of Wight		No. 6B The following districts in Staffordshire: Cannock Chase Lichfield South Staffordshrie Tamworth West Midlands (Metropolitan Boroughs of Birmingham, Sandwell, Dudley, Walsall and Wolverhampton)
4. (South Western)	No. 4A Cornwall Devon The following districts of Somerset: Sedgemoor Yeovil Taunton Deane		
	No. 4B Avon Gloucestershire The following		

350

DUTY SOLICITOR REGIONS

Legal Aid Area	Duty Solicitor Regions covered	Legal Aid Area	Duty Solicitor Regions covered
7. (North Western)	No. 7A Greater Manchester	9. (North Eastern) *continued*	No. 9A York West Yorkshire
	No. 7B The following districts of Cumbria: Barrow-in-Furness South Lakeland The following districts of Lancashire: Blackburn Burnley Chorley Hyndburn Lancaster Pendle Ribble Valley Rossendale		No. 9B The following districts of Humberside: Beverley Boothferry Holderness Kingston-upon-Hull North Wolds South Yorkshire
		10. (East Midlands)	No. 10A Derbyshire The following districts of Humberside: Cleethorpes Glanford Grimsby Scunthorpe Lincolnshire Nottinghamshire
8. (Northern)	No. 8A The following districts of Cumbria: Allerdale Carlisle Copeland Eden Northumberland Tyne and Wear		No. 10B Leicestershire Northamptonshire
	No. 8B Cleveland Durham The following districts of North Yorkshire: Hambledon Richmondshire Ryedale Scarborough	11. (Eastern)	No. 11A Cambridgeshire Norfolk Suffolk Bedfordshire
			No. 11B Hertfordshire Essex
9. (North Eastern)	No. 9A The following districts of North Yorkshire: Craven Harrogate Selby	12. (Chester and North Wales)	No. 12A Clwyd Gwynedd The following district of Powys: Montgomery

351

DUTY SOLICITOR REGIONS

Legal Aid Area	Duty Solicitor Regions covered	Legal Aid Area	Duty Solicitor Regions covered
12. (Chester and North Wales) *continued*		14. (London West)	No. 14 The London Boroughs of:
	No. 12B Cheshire Shropshire The following districts of Staffordshire: East Staffordshire Newcastle-under-Lyme Stafford Staffordshire Moors Stoke-on-Trent		Barnet Brent Enfield Hammersmith Haringey Harrow Hillingdon Kensington & Chelsea Westminster
		15. (Merseyside)	No. 15 Merseyside The following districts of Lancashire:
13. (London East)	No. 13 The City of London The London Boroughs of: Barking Camden Hackney Havering Islington Newham Redbridge Tower Hamlets Waltham Forest		Blackpool Fylde Preston South Ribble Wyre West Lancashire

LEGAL AID BOARD

SCHEDULE II

DUTY SOLICITOR ARRANGEMENTS 1989
DUTY SOLICITOR APPLICATION FORM

Solicitor's name ....

Firm's name ....

Address ....

....

Office telephone no.   (STD) ....

Out of office telephone no.   (STD) ....

1   Name of Court(s) and/or police station(s) at which you wish to become duty
     solicitor...

2 Date of Admission . . . .

3 Do you hold a current practising certificate?   YES/NO

4 Is the above address the address at which you will normally see clients?
                                                                   YES/NO

   If not, please give the address at which you will see clients:-

   . . . .

   . . . .

5 To which other duty solicitor schemes do you belong? . . . .

   . . . .

6(a) Have you been refused membership of or been suspended or excluded from any
     scheme?   YES/NO

  (b) If "yes", identify scheme(s) from which you have been excluded:

   . . . .

7 Are you willing to act personally as duty solicitor in accordance with the Duty
   Solicitor Arrangements 1989?   YES/NO

8(a) Have you acted as an advocate in criminal cases in magistrates' courts including
     the representation of defendants at contested trials
     at least once a week on average? [   ] during the last 12 months? [   ]
     less than once a week on average? [   ] during the last 18 months? [   ]

  (b) Do you satisfy the appropriate criteria in paragraphs 34 and 35 of the Duty
      Solicitor Arrangements 1989?   YES/NO

  (c) Please list the courts in which you have appeared:-

   . . . .

   . . . .

9 Please give details of cases undertaken in the previous 6 months if you have acted
   as an advocate less than once a week.

Signature of solicitor . . . . Date: . . . .

Names of magistrates' courts	Date of case	Charge(s) involved

LEGAL AID BOARD

SCHEDULE III

DUTY SOLICITOR ARRANGEMENTS 1989
DUTY SOLICITORS' REPRESENTATIVE APPLICATION FORM

Name of duty solicitor making application ....

Proposed Representative's name ....

Address ....

....

....

Office telephone no.   (STD) ....

Out of hours telephone no.   (STD) ....

1   In connection with which police stations does the proposed representative wish to act as a duty solicitor's representative:-

2   Has an application by you to any other local duty solicitor committee in respect of the proposed representative been refused?   YES/NO

3(a) Is the proposed representative in your employment, or a partner of yours, and not in the employment of any other solicitor?   YES/NO

  (b) Has the proposed representative had experience of providing advice at police stations having gained such experience as the result of having been employed in a solicitor's office   YES/NO
      and

  (c)   (i) if the proposed representative is a solicitor, does he have at least four months experience of criminal cases as a solicitor or articled clerk?   YES/NO
         or

      (ii) if the proposed representative is a solicitor's clerk, does he have at least three years experience of criminal defence work?   YES/NO
         or

     (iii) if the proposed representative is an articled clerk, does he have at least six months experience of which four months are of criminal cases?   YES/NO

4   Names of police stations the proposed representative has attended to advise clients:

....

5   Please set out the experience of the proposed representative of criminal cases including an indication of the number of times he has advised clients at police stations and the types of offences involved:

Signature of duty solicitor ....

Signature of proposed representative ....

Date ....

Certificate by duty solicitor

Name of duty solicitor ....

I certify that:

(a) I am currently a 24 hour duty solicitor in connection with the police stations referred to in question 1 above;

(b) I consider the proposed representative to be competent to act as a duty solicitor's representative;

(c) I wish the proposed representative to be approved as my representative in accordance with the provisions of the Duty Solicitor Arrangements, 1989;

(d) I will decide in connection with each individual case where a suspect asks for a duty solicitor whether it is appropriate to ask the proposed representative to act as my representative;

(e) I understand that any complaint as to the ability or conduct of my proposed representative or the inappropriate use of my proposed representative could result in my exclusion as duty solicitor.

Signature of duty solicitor ....

Date ....

Members of Legal Aid Board

Addresses of Legal Aid Offices

The Legal Aid Offices are grouped by area. You should telephone or write rather than attend in person. Offices are:

London/Brighton Group

London (Area No. 1)
29-37 Red Lion Street
London WC1R 4PP
Tel: 071-405 6991
DX 170

Brighton (Area No. 2)
9-12 Middle Street
Brighton BN1 1AS
Tel: 0273 27003
DX 2752

North East Group

Newcastle (Area No. 8)
Eagle Star House
Fenkle Street
Newcastle upon Tyne
NE1 5RU
Tel: 091-232 3461
DX 61005

Leeds (Area No. 9)
City House
New Station Street
Leeds LS1 4JS
Tel: 0532 442851
DX 12068

North West Group

Manchester (Area No. 7)
2nd Floor
Elisabeth House
16, St. Peter's Square
Manchester M2 3DA
Tel: 061-228 1200
DX 14343

Chester (Area No. 12)
Pepper House
Pepper Row
Chester CH1 1DW
Tel: 0244 315455
DX 19981

Liverpool (Area No. 15)
Cavern Walks
8 Matthew Street
Liverpool L2 6RE
Tel: 051-236 8371
DX 14208

Midlands Group

Birmingham (Area No. 6)
Podium Centre
City House
(Smallbrook Queensway)
5 Hill Street
Birmingham B5 4UD
Tel: 021-632 6541
DX 13041

Nottingham (Area No. 10)
5 Friar Lane
Nottingham NG1 6BW
Tel: 0602 482424
DX 10035

Cambridge (Area No. 11)
Kett House
Station Road
Cambridge CB1 2JT
Tel: 0223 66511
DX 5803

Wales and the West Group

Bristol (Area No. 4)
Whitefriars
Middlegate
Lewins Mead
Bristol BS1 2LR
Tel: 0272 214801
DX 7852

Cardiff (Area No. 5)
Marland House
Central Square
Cardiff CF1 1PF
Tel: 0222 388971
DX 33006

Reading (Area No. 3)
80 Kings Road
Reading RG1 4LT
Tel: 0734 589696
DX 4016

HEAD OFFICE: Legal Aid Board
5th Floor
Newspaper House
8–16 Great New Street
London EC4 3BN
Tel: 071-353 7411
DX 450

FINANCIAL CONTROLLER
Legal Aid Accounts Department
12 Roger Street
London WC1N 2JL
Tel: 071 405 4333
DX 328

Index